For C

Hap

Love from,

Daniel

MAN, MUSIC AND COSMOS

ANNY VON LANGE

ANNY VON LANGE

MAN, MUSIC AND COSMOS

A Goethean Study of Music

Volume I

RUDOLF STEINER PRESS

Translated by Florence Hough

Revised by Nancy Hummel
with Editorial Assistance from Joan M. Thompson

This publication was made possible through
the generous bequest of Florence Hough

ISBN : 1 85584 160 6

Cover illustration
Detail from *Christ Glorified in the Court of Heaven*
by Fra Angelico
Reproduced by courtesy of the Trustees
The National Gallery, London

Typeset by Imprint, Crawley Down
Printed and Bound in Great Britain by
Billing & Sons Limited, Worcester

This work is dedicated
to a future art of music
which knows it is founded in the being of man
as image of cosmic harmonies.
It arose from an ever-present living remembrance
of what we owe to
GOETHE
and
RUDOLF STEINER

In all the world
Man's being weaves.
Within man's kernel
The world's reflection reigns.
The I connects them both
And so creates
True meaning of existence.

Rudolf Steiner

CONTENTS

PART FOUR
The Nature and Activity of the Keys

FOREWORD (1956)

The venture of publishing suggestions for a Goethean study of music is only justifiable if it tackles the phenomena of music in such a way that they become transparent for the spirit working in them. This book is the result of nearly thirty years' striving for these 'revealed mysteries' and was written at the request of many who took part in courses and lectures given by the author.

Nothing that is given can be regarded as a finished product but only as a seed for the future. This will not be a scientific book in the ordinary sense, but rather a practical guide inviting the reader to prove its content and to continue working on it. Teaching in the Goethean sense must have as its goal the establishing, through individual experience, of the relationship between microcosm and macrocosm, between I and the World. Universal laws correspond ultimately with those in man, and the purpose of this book is to try and experience through hearing the unity of man, music and cosmos. This means that hearing must be directed from quantity to quality, complementing the one with the other, in a lucid and methodical way. This work only became possible because Rudolf Steiner gave in Anthroposophy a picture of the world and of man that illumined a forgotten cosmic background in a contemporary way. He showed how artistic objectivity can be achieved through an intensification of inner forces, rather than by excluding the self from external influences as in technical and scientific studies. In the realm of music one can unreservedly follow Goethe's directions concerning the effect of individual phenomena, in order to develop an 'inner tonal sense' through the senses, as described in his study of musical sound. In this attentive listening to the qualitative rather than to the quantitative nature of the basic musical elements lies the central motive of this work. The spirituality of man, as creator of musical sound, will be recognized as the stage on which musical entities work. In this inner activity the living forces of the sound itself can be consciously experienced. The pure phenomenon becomes manifest in the listening soul, in so far as it is selfless, and the stress must lie on self-*less*. At the same time it will be found that in hundreds of cases, among listeners of various nationalities, of all ages and stages of development within western cultural circles, certain basic musical elements are experienced in the same kind of way, so that in time an objective picture emerges of the nature of each phenomenon, as in a continuously repeated scientific experiment. One complements the other and gradually a totality arises, whose conformity to law not only throws light on the past, but also reveals indications for the future in the present.

In this way, musical experience acquires an objective basis without losing its relationship to the creative human being. This in itself is the wisdom of the Goethean spiritual method; the human being himself, depending on the degree of his enhanced soul forces, is the bearer of each piece of objective world-knowledge. He reaches through his senses to the ethical. An inner acoustic awakens, which can become an organ for the moral world-order lying at the basis of artistic creation.

A method such as this brings a renewal of musical experience to professional and music-lover alike. Many will mock this book and lay it aside as unscientific; and all the more so as it deals with the development of a musical domain which many people claim has already been superseded. The diatonic system of seven notes, heptaphony, with which this first * volume is mainly concerned, is in danger of being brushed aside by atonality, dodecaphony, and mechanical electronic contrivances of the present time. Many of our contemporaries are in danger of losing the faculty for experiencing the diatonic system altogether.

We do not in any way gainsay the value of contemporary efforts, yet it seems necessary to experience in a new way the many as yet unknown and therefore not fully exploited artistic possibilities of earlier forms of expression. The system of tonality known as the diatonic major/minor system, which gave mankind so much that had never been heard of before, should be regarded as 'uncontemporary' and 'out-moded' only when all its dimensions have been revealed, both to the listener and to the composer. This is still far from being the case. Its magnificent, objective, cosmic spiritual background is for the most part unknown today. It is waiting to be revealed, waiting for human beings ready and inwardly capable of revealing it. The seven- and twelve-note structures are built organically into the being of man,

* Note: The second volume was never completed and so far has not been translated.

and in whatever continually changing forms and subtle differentiations the tonal systems may be clothed in the course of the centuries, there will always be a sevenfoldness — possibly in a new form, but still with a voice to be heard.

The totality of the cosmos is presented in the twelvefold zodiac. It is important to acquire a living experience of these forces and their musical reflections. It is hoped that the geometrical diagrams in the text and the plates may imprint themselves as deeply as possible on the reader, as they represent clearly the changing relationships. The more they are meditatively contemplated, the more will they become 'sounding pictures', the beauty of which can be felt and enhanced by inner effort.

The unity of man, music and cosmos experienced in this way will then no longer be disputed. It bestows life, disclosing not only to the musician and those who are 'gifted' but more especially to the layman, something of the very nature of man. In the midst of increasing music festivals, music courses, virtuoso performances, money-seeking and competition — Goethe and Rudolf Steiner, if they are rightly understood and if their indications are worked upon in the realm of music, lead back to the health-giving stillness and cosmic expanse of man's true being.

In conclusion, I should like to give especial thanks to Dr. Peter von Siemens for having made this publication possible after many years of friendly co-operation.

Anny von Lange
(1887 — 1959)

PART ONE

THE NATURE OF MUSIC

Chapter One

THE SPIRITUAL BACKGROUND OF MUSIC

In wishing to be clear about the nature of music, it is good to start where the deep spiritual setting of this art can be read through the light of divine, cosmic figures in mythology. The ancient Greeks regarded Apollo as the god of the sun and of music. 'The Sun resounds in ancient ways...'. Where does the musical nature of the sun, the light of Apollo, lie?

In early times people spoke of a twofold, sometimes a threefold, aspect of the sun. They experienced it as a comprehensive spirit-being working down on to the earth. This spiritual, invisible power of light was recognized as that which could awaken in the soul of earthly man his higher being. Leaders of humanity in distant times were aware of this and of its lofty, divine nature. It was proclaimed in the mysteries up to the time of Ancient Greece, where it was recognized as the creative word, the Logos. But the shining, earthward-streaming power of the sun was always recognized and it was said that Helios drove in his chariot of gold across the starry heavens, defining day and night and the seasons of the year. It was the journey of the sun that was seen as a life-regulating force and honoured in Helios. Apollo, however, was worshipped not only as the outer, shining light, but rather as the activity of the sun in the elements surrounding the earth, in the earth itself, and even in the human soul. This was a transforming, illuminating activity, rousing and harmonizing life.

Can it be said that these forces peculiar to the sun also flow through music? No doubt, even today, music — given a good performance — has the power to awaken the soul of earthly man to his higher nature. For example, in listening to a Bruckner symphony, or to beautiful chamber music, one seems to rise out of the everyday self into a higher world, and this remains a vivid memory, warming the soul and freeing it from the things of everyday life. A light from beyond the earth streams through the music and awakens moral impulses in the heart. These may only rarely be fulfilled, but they live on in the inner being as irrefutable evidence of some cosmic being awaiting revival.

A heritage has been handed down from Ancient Greece to the West, showing the great significance of this art. There was a deep ethical content in the musical culture of that time. Music was recognized as more important than anything else in influencing character, that is to say, in the development of the individual towards the divine and the good. Plato writes in his *Republic*:

> Education through music is of paramount importance, because rhythm and harmony penetrate powerfully into the innermost part of the soul and lay hands upon it, bearing grace with them, so making graceful him who is rightly trained, and him who is not, the reverse.

When the artist works on the human being, he reveals it as it should be, not as it is, and mediates the powers of the spiritual world which stream from the lofty being of the sun, the Logos.

This Logos was always described as the harmonious unity of that which sounded forth from individual world beings in their creative activity. With this it is possible to understand the connection of music with Helios. It is of a similar nature to the harmony of the spheres, whose constellations the sun passes through as it runs its course. At the beginning, Goethe's words 'The Sun resounds' were quoted. In the world at large it is 'The stars resound'. What does this mean? A being becomes audible and in doing so reveals activity. But Helios — one can refer to him as the foreshadowing of the Logos — included in his course the totality of the music of the spheres. All musical systems of the ancient world stemmed from a deep knowledge of this connection, this combination of cosmic and earthly laws.

But it is only Apollo who can personify for man the actual inner nature of music. And why? Because — and this is of great moment — a moral element fills his whole being. The most significant impression this deity made on the Greeks was that of his struggle with, and overcoming of, the dragon-serpent, Python. Inseparable as the Archangel Michael and his fallen monster are Apollo and Python; a Michaelic element is seen in him and this flows into all music that is not succoured by the instincts. Such music gives forces which stand over and against the dragon — the deep and dark regions of the soul — against uprising evil. Shakespeare says in *The Merchant of Venice*:

The man that hath no music in himself,
Nor is not mov'd with concord of sweet sounds,
Is fit for treasons, stratagems and spoils;
The motions of his spirit are dull as night,
And his affections dark as Erebus:
Let no such man be trusted.

The dragon-possibilities of 'treasons, stratagems and spoils' lie within everyone. They are constant spurs towards the making of free, moral decisions in life. But to what extent is it possible for music, purely of its own nature, to overcome these tendencies? One may test this by several phenomena, not of that earlier time, but of the immediate present.

It has been described above that man is awakened to his higher being through the activity of the spirit-power of the sun. On the other hand, the tendency towards the dragon dormant in him endeavours at all times to keep him away from his higher being. In this century humanity is swayed by a materialistic and scientific mentality, that sees man merely as a higher animal. The spiritual world is more and more shut off and replaced by ever-intensifying earthly control. This tendency is so powerful that man betrays himself and his divine origin. Yet speech and music can directly express a creative event, a spiritual revelation possible only to man among all living beings. For instance, even the simplest song proves the reality of his spiritual origin. It may be only a cradle song which a mother sings to her child. It is no betrayal, but acknowledgement of a higher self which is called up in the soul. (Here it must be said that this book is concerned only with music produced by man himself, not with sounds produced mechanically or electronically.)

When we speak of murder, we have to think of a striking characteristic of modern social life. Does not the struggle for existence, which determines almost every life, bring about the almost inevitable endeavour to deprive one's fellow men of as much living space and air as possible for one's own sake? Death does not happen only to the physical body. There is murder, and pleasure in it, within the realm of the soul, and this governs human intercourse much more than is admitted. How often attack, wounding, calumny and even 'murder' take place through the spoken word, not to mention the ever-intensifying scientific efforts aiming at the destruction of the earth and humanity.

Everything is so permeated by the dragon that one hardly notices it any more. Here again, music of its own nature brings powers of healing to the human soul. Harmony implies giving room to sounds, to themes for their mutual development; they sustain one another, yield to one another, and weave around each other so that they can come to full expression, singly and in combination, in all beauty as of necessity in the wisdom of their interrelationships. Where music is an important factor in life, not necessarily professionally, a new and positive social feeling can develop.

It might be objected here that this harmonious result does not always occur. Nearly everything new meets with opposition. For instance, in 1856 a correspondent of the *New York Times* reported of *Lohengrin* that the music from beginning to end contained barely a dozen measures which could be termed truly melodic, while another said that the music was a moaning body of sound, frigid, freezing in equal measure the senses and the spirit.

In facts such as these it is possible to see how further refinements of the organ of hearing develop from century to century. Sensations which seem at one time inharmonious and unmusical may later flow as life-giving forces.

The fact that malice — and that means insincerity — is accepted as a matter of course is closely connected with what has been stated above. The feeling that an utterance must accord with the facts has, in general, been lost. An utterance is made in such a way as to bring personal gain. Words veil rather than reveal. Even at the beginning of this century, a malicious, not entirely truthful person, was not considered to have integrity. But nowadays he who tries to adhere to the truth is eccentric and unpractical. Here again, music can act as a corrective, even if it works through the unconscious. A melody, however simple, cannot be a pretence, but is there in all reality, and nothing can be produced musically without identifying oneself with it. Even in a more superficial sense, a C is a C, sounds as a C, is given and heard as such. Healing forces can stream in, warding off dangers — a world of light appears. If experienced in connection with Michael's sword or Apollo's arrows of light, the whole moral and healing influence of music can be understood. In reality, its deepest appeal is to allow ever again the bond with the spirit —

love and light-filled orderliness — to be roused in the soul through its creations, be they ever so modest. Apollo, as god of the sun and of music, in keeping with his being creates clarity and warmth and gives the possibility of development. It is not saying too much to state that responsible leaders of humanity have always known that music is the art through which, in every single one of its elements, man can most readily be guided towards perfection.

If the divine form of Apollo is seen with inner vision connected with the dragon Python in the depths of the earth, he should also of necessity be seen in the heavenly Parnassus, in the sphere of the nine Muses. Here it is also revealing to hark back to the world of Greek mythology. The Muses were born in nine nights as the offspring of the love between Zeus and Mnemosyne, the goddess of memory, also recorded as being ruler of the land of freedom, Eleutheria.

Zeus, overcoming the creative chaos of his father Chronos, set the cosmic forces in order, making the cosmos manifest and able to reveal cosmic wisdom. As the principle of the eternal masculine ruling in reason, he gave to his daughters the power to inspire the human soul in accordance with cosmic thought. What is the essential activity of music in this connection? For the Greeks, the term 'music' included the art of verse, as well as the all-embracing art of music. But this was of a thought-filled nature, and thereby humanity was taught to think through the experience of music. It was the time when human consciousness had to accomplish the transition from the mythological to the conceptual. One can understand the great transforming deed of Pythagoras, who established this conceptual element by identifying the relationship of musical intervals with number, in order to strengthen the development of logical thought by way of musical feeling. When the singer tuned his lyre in accordance with certain measurements, scales and intervals, these conformed to the laws of pure mathematics. By this means all musical inspiration united the soul with the sphere of archetypal thought and filled it with forms of word and music, and the laws of cosmic intelligence, of the harmony of the spheres, became audible in the earthly realm.

Mnemosyne also gave to her daughters the power to inspire singers and poets with the gift of prophecy. Through them shone great visions of cosmic origin, divine destinies, drawn from the picture world of myths, or from legends depicting the initiation of heroes. Hesiod describes the journey of the Argonauts in a magnificent song of Orpheus in contest with Chiron:

> But I myself took after him the sounding lute and poured forth from my throat the melodious antiphony. First the song of mystery, as primeval chaos was lost in nature, and the boundaries of heaven enclosed it; then the birth of the outspread earth and the depths of the ocean; also the most sublime, wise and self-perfecting Eros, as he gave being to all, and separated each from each; also the destructive Chronos, and how to the thunderer, Zeus, came the kingly power of the immortal holy gods. Then sang I of the birth and separation of the younger gods; of Brimos and the Giants, and the horrible deeds of Bacchus; then also my lips extolled the scattered tribes of powerless humanity; and the sound flew forth to the summit of the mountain and the thickly-wooded valleys of Pelion; through the ice pinnacles of the heights themselves, resounded the song. And the uprooted oaks pressed forward in their course towards the forecourt; here also the rocks crashed, and the ravening wild animals, enticed to the cave by the harmony, remained still, timid in their sojourn; also the birds of prey circled round Chiron's oxen stables with pinions poised, and forgot their own nests. Such things saw the centaur, and was struck with amazement, clapping his hands with delight as he stamped on the ground with his hooves.

Inspiring and guiding the dance of the Muses, Apollo apprehends and pictures the threefoldness of the human soul, its thinking, feeling and will. And when a primeval singer like Orpheus, his son and priest, still sang out of an inspired unity with the cosmic spheres, he forcefully influenced the life of the earth's being. He shattered the rocks so that they cracked open. Plants and animals affected in their growth and in their wild nature, hastened to him with joy and gratitude. They felt they were understood and exalted. Out of this power the servant of Apollo was able to call all things by their true, divinely-willed name. Through this omnipotent power of the word he helped all creation to reach the fullness of its own being. These are deeds which were impressed upon the earth's existence, and raised man to a state in which he took part in the creative activity of nature.

Modern thought often finds such descriptions far-fetched and incredible — fairy tales for children, full of magic and fantasy, only estranging man from practical life on earth. But attention has been drawn to them again by recent experiments in the healing powers of music, especially those of the Swedish doctor, Eric Pontvic, in his hospital in Stockholm. Similarly, experiments have shown the influence of sound on the growth of plants and also on the life-processes of animals. American statistics show an increase in the milk yield of cows, and egg-laying among hens, owing to the influence of music. Perhaps a reappraisal of these fairy tales is due. We shall come back to them later.

It was the nine Muses who embraced the whole being of man, not only his soul but also his body and spirit. To each was assigned one particular field of inspiration. In connection with the physical, Terpsichore ruled over rhythm; Melpomene inspired dance; and Calliope, mother of Orpheus, gave beauty to the voice. Breath and heart, movement of the limbs, the organs of speech and song, were penetrated with sound by this first trinity. The second group, Clio, Erato and Euterpe were concerned with qualities of soul. Through them, the melodic principle in straightforward song could be developed into elegy or comedy. The loftiest musical creations, hymns — choral and religious — and expressions of divine spiritual life were due to the grace of Polyhymnia, Thalia and Urania. A simple diagram of three triangles in three expanding circles shows this cosmic play of forces united in Apollo.

Physical sphere = inner
Soul sphere = middle
Spirit sphere = outer

Three times three — who does not think here of the spiritual hierarchies who, by their outpourings, help man and universe on in their development.

A third element in relation to Apollo must still be considered. Orpheus, archetype of the great, creative singer, was known as the son of Apollo and the muse Calliope. Another legend describes him as son of the King of Thrace. In every aspect he was seen as a leader of humanity, an initiate, far surpassing his fellow men. He was seen as a demigod. In the mythological sense Thrace indicates a heavenly, higher world of light. His hereditary descent was from the sun, from ether and from song. His tragedy was that he could not bring this to full expression on the earth. He stood at a turning point in time, where man began to lose his direct connection with the divine world. Clairvoyance was giving way to earthly, logical thinking. For that reason his soul, the nymph Eurydice, was overcast by the shadow of Hades. She was bitten by a snake, and had to descend into the dark realm of night, the unconscious. She was bound to the earth, and to the kingdom of death. Orpheus had the power, through music, to lead the soul back to the upper world. Yet only under one condition: that he should keep her pure, archetypal image before his eyes, and not look back at her. The myth said that if he were to do this, if he tried to see her in the shadow of death, he would lose her forever.

The tragic destiny of Orpheus indicates a change of consciousness and the dangers developing in the relationship between man and his music. In the evolution of Western man towards the era of science and materialism, the soul was ever more and more ensnared in the earthly world, held captive in it, regarded with increasing intensity in its death-destined being, backwards to the Fall. But this means that it is no longer grasped in the reality of its super-natural being and ethereal beauty. And so, by degrees, Apollonian sounds are no longer heard and even the singer, turning towards the earthly, loses the redeeming power of music. These are the spiritual facts mirrored in the myth of Orpheus and Eurydice, in which the tragedy of present-day music plays its part. Destiny draws close to the individual and throws over humanity the gloomy shadow of Hades.

Something has still to be added to complete the picture of the archetypal singer and to understand him as standing at a turning point in time. As the son of Apollo he was naturally his priest. Yet he was at the same time a priest of Dionysus, and this dual function was of supreme importance. Apollo, encircled by the Muses, revealed the light of the gods, the Logos. His music was the music of the stars. In the strings of his lyre or zither lived the shining reality of the divine universe, set in motion and borne by the winds of heaven. But Dionysus ruled in the depths of the human soul. In the Orphic initiation the mysteries which served him, especially the oldest at Samothrace, stood over against the Delphic oracle in apparent contrast but as a necessary complement. The goat-footed fauns and the raving maenads surrounding Dionysus, represent those unpurified natural impulses, the inscrutable world of the passions, linked with dream and the blood, that inner region of the soul bound to the lower gods in the depths of the earth. All this could change if Apollo's message of light — the rays of the Sun-Logos — were accepted. But the transformation had to be an act of free will in those who strove to penetrate the mysteries. Music as revelation of the cosmic word, proclaimed from above, could touch each individual through the understanding of his heart.

Nevertheless, for man's response, for his purification, his own will for action had to be the impelling force. Only in this way could the ground be prepared for a higher harmony between light and will-enfilled warmth of soul, between the highest spirit-word and man's instinctive nature — pole and counter-pole. In Dionysian circles the instrument was the flute. Borne by the breath and the individual's vital rhythm, the way of purification of the soul could be expressed by the flutes of Pan or the other wind instruments of the aulos type which were used in the different Mystery centres.

The legend tells us that Orpheus was dismembered by the maenads of Dionysus while he was sacrificing to Apollo. Here we see the tragedy of his destiny. He had not been able to rescue his soul of light, Eurydice, from the bonds of the underworld. He stood between two worlds, bound by obligation to both, filled by the forces of both, drawn by two opposite ways of life. The picture of his death shows the vehement convulsive reality not only of his own soul-situation, but of the greater part of humanity of those earlier times and even of today. It is never said of Orpheus that he played the flute. The lyre and his own voice were his creative and appointed instruments. Nevertheless it was his destiny that he had to surrender his leadership to Dionysus for a period of time. Dionysus was regarded as old and ugly, surrounded by beings from a sub-human sphere, yet, as god of the mysteries of the awakening ego-force, he was young and beautiful, a guide to the future of mankind.

It must be stressed that Orpheus, as son of Apollo and Calliope, or as son of the mythical King of Thrace, could not give full play on earth to the higher possibilities that were his by descent. But he could lead humanity to these higher powers. By the creative power of his music he could stimulate thinking. He could also, as inaugurator of the Dionysian Mysteries, purify and regulate from the beginning the soul-life of the individual. In this way, the beginning of human music, as an independent art, could come by degrees to echo the light-filled and divine cosmic music of Apollo. Orpheus must suffer and come to ruin through the discordant circumstances of his destiny, but could the Logos not make, through him, a first, inner encounter with the human soul?

This touches on the innermost sanctuary of music, its essential task for mankind. Even today, thought lights up in the harmonious, clear austerity of the canons of music. The directness of its creative power of expression regulates and warms the heart, enabling it to experience its higher self. And in accordance with this ultimate truth of the nature of music, the early Christians painted in the catacombs the Logos, the lofty Sun-Being, Who in Christ united Himself with the earth, as the new Orpheus. 'Orpheus as the true Christ' says an inscription of that time. Those people perceived a holy symbol filled with the power of the divine cosmic word in the son of Apollo. The sight of his lyre must have inspired them ever again to make music. Their souls were uplifted through these sounds to the wonder of a newly-arising community of mankind.

Against the background of such magnificent pictures it is understandable that music should be given a special place among the arts, for in it — that is in those gifted with music — lies the capacity, as Schopenhauer declared, to reveal directly the pulse-beat of the divine will, of the cosmic will itself. From the viewpoint of the gods, there arises a visible world-structure out of every 'And He spoke...' It is a resounding expression of self-creating world destiny. Of the human reflection that is also true. Here there is a creative will for self-expression imprinting itself on the earth as a deed, resounding — with all its consequences — through the course of human evolution.

Chapter Two

THE WONDER OF MUSICAL SOUND

It is difficult for our contemporaries to acquire any idea of the creative singing of a bygone age. It is equally difficult for them to understand how humanity at that time heard a musical sound and reacted to it. A good approach is through present-day musical experience. From this we may hope to obtain a deeper insight into the mysteries of musical sound and the nature of music.

Above all we must never lose sight of the fact that the relationship to music of those living in the twentieth century is completely different from, and even radically opposite to that around 2000 BC. As described in Chapter One, the human being was then surrounded and supported by universal music in a comprehensive way. Just as a modern child is embedded in his environment from the beginning of his life until certain inner capacities awaken, and is unable to detach himself from it, so also childlike man of earlier times was pliable, open, and easily moulded by the influences coming in from the outer world. All his senses, including his hearing, were open to the outer world with a degree of receptivity hardly conceivable by 'civilized' man. This outer world was experienced clairvoyantly as the work of spiritual beings, both lofty and lowly, who peopled the elements, the stars and the realms of nature. They also influenced the weal and woe of man. The outer world of family, kinsfolk, race, neighbouring peoples, was also influenced in this way, but above all it was the leading personalities — kings, priests and singers — who directed the social structure according to higher insight. In all reality earthly existence was experienced as universally musical. The same wisdom-filled powers shaped the harmony of the heavens — sun, moon and earth — into a resounding cosmos, in which every plant, every animal and mineral, indeed every living being sounded its cosmic note. They worked as cosmic forces, gradually evolving man's consciousness from dream-like seclusion to vigilant independence. As *musica mundana* they awakened in him the laws of his being in the form of *musica humana*. And when the singer of earlier times filled his surroundings with the sound of his voice, then *musica mundana* worked through him without let or hindrance. In this way he expressed all things around him in song and speech, teaching understanding of the environment and creating it anew.

Here and there, remnants and traditions of those olden times can still be found. Walter Eidlitz in his book, *The Mantle of the Great Mother*, describing his acquaintanceship with a Swede who had lived for many years among the Lapps, says:

> Karl Tirén is the best authority on the secret customs of the Lapps, their habits and magic arts, and above all their mysterious music. The Laplanders have preserved many thousands of musical motifs which have remained unaltered through time. They always recite to this music, in the same rhythm, different words with different content. They have motifs for the flowing of a brook, for a mountain, rounded or sharply peaked. A mocking theme, a theme of awkward heavy stamping for a horse — an animal they despise — and an endearing motif — trip, trip — for the reindeer, the steps of the reindeer in the snow. They have a theme for the Tornetrask Sea when it swells with high waves, another for a different sea when the waves are gentle. A great, mighty motif for a bear, another for the wolf, the marmot, and the mosquitoes...
>
> When foreign peoples — Finns, Swedes, and Norwegians — met with the Lapps for the first time, they were perceived by the nomads not only externally, but also as a musical experience. Karl Tirén wrote down the folk themes, the themes of the Finnish, Norwegian and Swedish peoples, the theme of the holy mountain, which shone in the picture on the wall, the bird theme, which was remarkably like the theme of the bird in Wagner's opera *Siegfried* — though he certainly knew nothing of Lapp music, for Tirén was the first to investigate it.

We may also think of the drum messages of the Negro peoples, and the earlier, not the modern, yodelling of mountain dwellers as a last, faint memory of this kind of music.

Modern man no longer experiences this. Nevertheless, he can always find a way to cosmic wisdom and cosmic love, to the Logos, through his moral and thought-endowed creative ego. The question arises: Does a single note taken purely as a sound phenomenon reveal his ego-being? And, if it does, how does it do so?

This is a question we normally do not ask, but in this context it is justified, even necessary. In the first place it is a purely physical acoustic fact that a musical note in its fullness is defined by a series of tones sounding sympathetically in it, the so-called overtones or partial series. The single note expands to a resounding sphere, to a world of musical sound, governed by certain fixed mathematical rules. This single, straightforward note, which is used in musical compositions as a clearly defined building-stone, is revealed as an organism of living members. We know that it was Pythagoras, approximately 600 years before Christ, who ventured to make the transition in music from a mythological to a conceptual consciousness. This is an indication of how sound no longer mediates for man — no longer clairaudient or clairvoyant — an instreaming world of the harmonizing cosmic working of the gods. Earthly definition, giving contours, begins to lay hold of supersensible movements and images. Cosmic rhythm becomes measure, cosmic melody becomes number, cosmic harmony becomes weight, as a matter of experience. We must realize that the symbols 1, 2, 3, etc., grown so abstract today, released in the soul of Pythagoras a deep experience of the music of the spheres. 'One' spoke plainly to him of the Divine Origin, 'two' of the separating-off of the world of appearance, and so on. When he grasped the relationships of the different sounds as intervals according to this numerical process, they were qualitative values that he experienced. In accordance with the changing consciousness of humanity, he showed how the music of the spheres could be united in an inward way with the individual. How could this occur more radically than through emphasis on the unity of music and thought? Thought appeared in the garment of number, understood by contemplating the order of the heavens, and was still the mediator of divine good. A traditional Pythagorean saying, quoted by H. Abert, (*Illustriertes Musiklexicon*, 1927) runs:

> 'The human soul is in constant movement and, like the constellations of the heavens, is arranged according to fixed numerical values. Therein lies the origin of the powerful moral force of music.'

It is from considerations such as these that the series of overtones with its intervals, fixed numerically, acquires its proper universal background. We are justified in assuming that essential knowledge may be obtained from this series, whose laws can only be revealed when heard, quite objectively from interval to interval, by listening qualitatively to the way they work in the soul. 'Objectively' here means with the exclusion of all personal opinion, memory, knowledge, transient moods and so on. In the greatest possible stillness and selflessness, as if heard for the first time, at source and origin, the listener opens himself to what is given. This is a preliminary requirement if one wishes to acquire new access to music. It is of equal significance for the more difficult transformation of hearing, which will be dealt with in the second part of this book, with suggestions for certain exercises.

In the notes unfurled from the low cello C (two octaves below middle C), the following overtones can be heard: four octaves, with the fivefold repetition of the note C. (Let it be noted yet once again that all these statements refer to the audible musical note to which we are accustomed, and not to mechanical electronic tones, with which other vibrations with other numerical proportions can be placed at will). It is clear, even to ordinary observation, that the number of overtones in each octave doubles that is, from 1 to 2 to 4 to 8.

The law of division emerges as determining this sounding expression of man. All living, organic growth is controlled by division. And when this principle of the 2 is referred to as the number of the Son — that is, as the power of divine self-revelation — it is evident that the power of the Word — in fact of every creative human utterance — must stand under the banner of the Logos. The note C, in accordance with this law, doubles the number of intervals from octave to octave, that is, one step from the fundamental note to the next C, two steps to the next C, four to the third and eight to the last high C, and it is the same with all the tones. G stands in third place in the series and in its progress to the next octave must double this number. It appears in the sixth place, then in the twelfth, and so on. For E as the fifth, B flat as the seventh, and D as the ninth, the same relationship holds good.

In studying objectively the range of this sequence of sounds, one asks: Why just these four octaves? A simple exercise will give the answer. While standing, listen attentively to the whole tonal system, from the lowest notes to the highest. You will then experience clearly that the entire range of the audible, from the extremes of high to low, cannot be experienced entirely within man. We hear, as it were, up above the head, or down below the feet. The human form as such is not the boundary of audibility. But a distinction is perceptible; these extreme pitches are felt to be outside, not so intimately connected with the life-functions and the world of feeling. The low C in the bass and the upper C four octaves higher are thresholds where the sounds enter and leave the human frame. Present-day humanity has, so to say, an intimate, bodily relationship to the four octaves heard in the overtones. In normal circumstances this is the span of sound within the vocal range, from bass to soprano. If one would wish by conscious means to extend the whole range of our tonal system with equal expression of will and equal composure, it would require a significant intensification of soul and spirit forces. When, for example, voices have a wider range than the usual three octaves, they are considered to be exceptional. They do not correspond to what is normal.

This comparatively narrow vocal range is part of the shrinking related to the whole hardening, intellectualizing process of past centuries, and is by no means at an end. It can well be imagined that the further one goes back into the past, the more freely and unrestrictedly did the range of voice encompass all four octaves, and more. These natural voices were still bound up with the ethereal streams of sound in the world. So man still sang 'as the bird sings', in blissful unselfconsciousness, the song of songs unchecked and uncurtailed.

It may be assumed that the sympathetic sounding of the overtones was not only felt more strongly, but also went beyond four octaves. With scientific apparatus 40 overtones can now be determined. According to the law of division mentioned above, this would mean an extension to five-and-a-half octaves, that is, to somewhere around the E in the sixth octave. In these new regions of pitch, the intermediate tones are divided into fourths and eighths of a whole tone. The fact that it is possible for human hearing to perceive even more subtle differentiations is demonstrated in the different tonal systems of peoples and races other than the European. These still have a vocal flexibility lost to Europeans, that is, to peoples of our leading cultures. However, both the compass of the voice and the capacity to hear and express subtle differences in the note can be regained by correct management of the voice and a new schooling of hearing.

So far we have been concerned with the more external impression of the world of sound within the single note. But the question at issue is whether a single note can reveal the nature of the ego, of the I, and if so in what way. This can only be answered by a qualitative study of the intervals in the series of overtones.

Everyone regards his physical body, its shape and form, as his own. It is to him, as a matter of course, the expression of his ego, his I, and is recognized as such by others. The specific characteristics of race, family and nation are peculiar to it and, in so far as it embraces the life of his physical functions, it gives to the soul and spirit part of his being the possibility to be active, to reveal itself in its earthly environment as a being bound to the earth. The sounding of the low C in the bass gives a feeling of firm support. It is like the ground under our feet, upon which we can stand securely and rise to an upright posture. It gives a feeling of security and repose. This note gives the basic experience of keynote, musically speaking. The human being knows himself to be a denizen of the earth and at the same time he finds an earthly standpoint within his physical being, to which he can refer each event. Also, in this single note, he sees the possibilities of his life, of his vocation, of his earthly tasks.

While still listening to the basic keynote the first tone sounding with it can be heard in the octave. The original note was sufficient unto itself, as though resting in the lap of divine archetypes, but now a new sphere of life begins to sound. The octave, this interval of division, sounding in purity in the vibrational relationship 1:2, the expression of a higher spiritual ego in man, brings to the original keynote as lower ego, fulfilment and perfection. Experience of the octave always points to the self as dwelling in heaven in the light of the spirit. It brings the goal and attainment of true human existence by laying hold of the divine principle in man. This interval is at one and the same time an end and a new beginning, the true answer of humanity to the divine Alpha and Omega revealed in the Son-principle, the Logos. Man as bearer of the Cosmic Word — this is the proclamation of the first tone vibrating sympathetically in each single note.

The unfolding of the second octave produces something new — a fifth. The I of man, the human ego, is found to be a self-enclosed spirit-individuality. This is always the case in the interval of the fifth; in the polarity of the divine origins of lower and higher worlds the ego is seen as a unique individual spirit-form, seeking and finding its destination when the inner being turns towards the spiritual. As in a straightforward scale each fifth opens the door to the octave, so does the interval here allow an inner principle of light to come to life. The ego as individual light-bearer, belonging to the world, yet experienced archetypally as cosmic.

The step towards the earth sounds in the following interval of a fourth, from G to the third C. Again, a completely new sphere of experience is reached. The human being grasps his earthly ego in conscious affirmation. The individual becomes a person. In the fifth, the first apprehension of the ego sounded like an echo of a light-filled entity, and here, in crystal clearness, the human being is revealed as the destined bearer of karma, as an earthly personality.

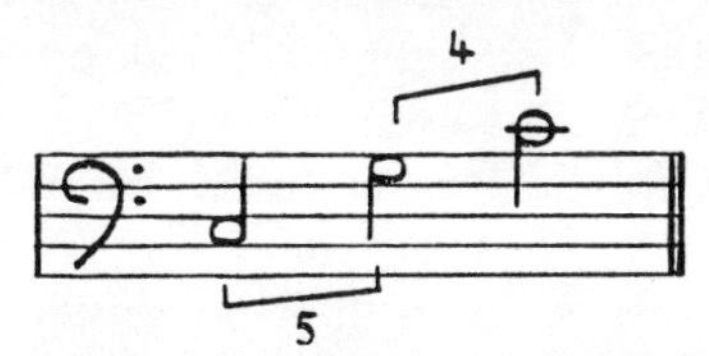

This interval of the fourth is often used as upbeat in folk song. It is as if the listener were summoned to take note of what is coming. A strong experience of awakening touches upon the soul. *Per-sonare* — that means to sound through: a clear, independent note rings out, playing its part in the great symphony of earth existence.

The third C (middle C), appears in the middle of the series of overtones. It has a kind of key position which will become clearer as we proceed. Meanwhile it has the value of a threshold. In contrast to the absolutely objective character of the octave, fifth and fourth, which are defined as perfect consonances, a variable, subjective element now arises in the succession of thirds. It should be noted that the B flat as a natural sound lies somewhat lower than on the keyboard. It inclines towards A, and gives to this third a more intimate sound.

The last interval approaching the higher C is like a very small fourth third. In this sphere of the third octave, what inner experience is aroused in the listening soul? The human personality has awakened to its earthly task. Now it must develop its own soul-forces to deal with its earthly concerns and fulfil its destiny. It must experience the inner world of feeling in all abundance and in its mysterious depths and spontaneous reactions. The I sees itself placed between an outer and an inner world, and the life-giving factor lies in the breathing interchange between them both. In the sounding first of the major third from C to E, rounded off as it is, complete in itself, can be heard something like a memory of the surrounding world, which makes sure of itself in the following minor third, from E to G, as if on a threshold, and turns inwards. The third, from G to B flat, awakens questions in the soul in matters concerning the relationship of the surrounding world to the inner nature of man.

Proceeding to the fourth third, diminished in the sense already described, its quality can best be grasped by listening to A and B flat together with C. It is like sinking into the vibrating fullness of the entire gamut of human feeling. The essence of this consists mostly in the fact that it is not always clearly comprehensible. Its changing subjective nature is determined for the most part by the subconscious.

The fourth octave reveals the actual earthly task of the ego-being. After crossing the threshold in the fourth C, an octave above middle C, there is a succession of tones and semitones. The second is the eternally indeterminate, questioning interval on the one hand, the element creating connections on the other, the bearer of metamorphosis from stage to stage. Does man's spiritual mission not lie in this? By means of his thinking he recognizes and combines the things of earthly existence, fully understanding their interconnections. He reveals the wisdom hidden in the flux of life, experiencing in change the powers and laws of transformation. These overtones climb from question to solution and again to question, until the 'scale' reaches fulfilment in the uppermost C.

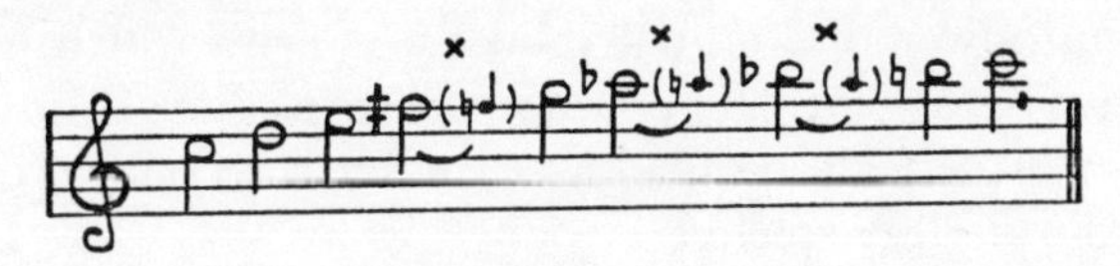

There are three steps here which fall out of the normal course of tempered sounds: in addition to the B flat, already mentioned in connection with the sequence of thirds as being slightly lower, inclining towards A, there are two more intervals which tend to be either slightly lower — F sharp inclining towards F, or slightly higher — A flat inclining towards A. What is the spiritual significance of such phenomena? Should we not expect something of special significance here?

This is, in fact, the case. These sounds not heard in their normal form are the only two of the seven basic notes — C D E F G A B — missing in the system of overtones: F and A. The intervals of the perfect fourth and the major sixth cannot arise out of the keynote C. They sound only in other positions, from G to C and from D to G; and from G to E and D to B (the minims in the following example, sixths bracketed above and fourths below).

It is all the more surprising because, in the case of the fourth, G to C in the second octave, the awakening to earthly existence, the grasping of oneself as a personality was characterized as an all-important experience of man in relation to himself. But swinging out of the G into C as exponent of the physical, this 'becoming a personality', is experienced much more strongly than it would have been if the fourth had unfolded from the earthly note, C to F. Something similar occurs in the distinction between the major sixths G to E and C to A. In the first case, in spite of the wide interval, a quite intimate grasping of the inner life can be felt. E opens up the succession of subjective thirds. C to A, however, proceeding from the keynote C, is felt as swinging out into space beyond the earthly. It is amazing how the faint foreshadowing of these F and A spheres gives the feeling that the two are standing, barely audible, spiritually in the background, just as in the unfolding power of spiritual thinking — with which we are concerned here — the deepest impulses such as inspirations and intuitions are not always readily accessible but come as gifts of grace from another sphere.

In both these mysteriously sounding stages of the raised F and the lowered A — that is F sharp and A flat — the whole sphere of chromaticism opens up as colouring or as tendency towards movement. It is as if this new, subtle inner differentiation of the original major second, C to D, would find in these deviations the clear semitonal relationship ultimately in the interval B to C. On reaching the chromatic, we make an interesting observation: the pitch of the note and the feeling no longer coincide. An F sharp will always be regarded by every musically experienced person as lying higher than a G flat. In pitch it does not correspond to this spontaneous feeling but reveals exactly the opposite. The physical aspect is the opposite of the soul aspect. The latter contains an inner, living dynamic corresponding to the forces working in the music, reaching towards light, or inclining towards heaviness.

These naturally given moments indicate a direction up or down, in the course of which resolution follows tension as a kind of goal. The pitch, however, tends towards the sphere of the note proper to it: F sharp tends towards F, G flat towards G. According to the musical feeling the note F sharp in the fourth octave would be more like G flat with its inclination towards F, just as A flat with its nearness in sound to A seems like a G sharp, and here there already sounds, as if in germ, a new law — the enharmonic. This germ goes on to develop as the quarter tone in the fifth octave.

What has all this to do with the I, the ego, or with the interval of the second in this fourth octave? We spoke of the creative element creating connections, of understanding through thinking, and the binding together of things in earthly existence in their wisdom-filled interrelationships. We also spoke of the second as bearer and revealer of the laws of metamorphosis. In all this striving for knowledge, manifesting musically here as the vocation of the ego, it is a question of bringing about a living interpenetration of the great polarities of the earthly — spirit and matter — of penetrating matter with spirit, and of disclosing the spirit in matter. In other words, it is the living, combining vision of two aspects, as was stated above, in contrasting the feeling with the acoustically defined position of pitch. The vigilant human being is summoned through listening to the recognition, even the necessity, of the two spheres of life, each in contrast to the other and yet of equal importance, the combining of which is the significance of this final octave.

The title given to this chapter is 'The Wonder of Musical Sound'. The revelation of the laws of the ego in the overtones should have made this wonder clear. The four octaves reveal man to the astonished listener, according to the fundamental laws of his nature, in his true earthly calling. And even if we were to stop here at the end of this series, it would still give a basic picture of man's own being to the unprejudiced and attentive listener. By following attentively the musical events of the last few decades, we perceive quite clearly two different things — the predominance of the semitone, either chromatically, or standing alone within the twelve-note principle — and the tendency towards a quarter-tone system. This means that Western man must apply himself to mastering the laws of the fifth octave of overtones. For the sake of the picture of the ego unfolded here, we must glance at this fifth octave, from the C two octaves above middle C to the octave beyond it.

A rise into the uppermost regions of pitch is always experienced as a spiritualizing force. The vibrating of these tones above the head, as already mentioned, gives the listener the sensation of coming into a glistening, scintillating world of stars and constellations. And it is a reality corresponding to this sensation that the semitone, determinative today, seeks in some way or other the bridge to cosmic zodiacal pictures and their activity. Without at this stage entering further into this matter it is possible, with the help of such an obvious contemporary phenomenon, to indicate that a completely new conception of the world of music and, connected with it, an essentially different kind of experience will emerge. This fifth octave of overtones is the transition to the experience of cosmic space. This means that each single one of the twelve semitones contains within itself a spatial principle. 'Time becomes space' are the words of Gurnemanz to Parsifal in the ascent to the Castle of the Grail. Everything experienced as living movement in one direction or another, pursued in its inner dynamic in the course of time, is now combined into a complete whole and seen from the harmonic viewpoint as being either opposite or conjoined. In following the paths of the stars in cosmic space, as they move in their forward or backward direction, one sees how at each moment they create definite constellations in space and, as such, have their effect. From this point on, similar rules start to sound within the note. The quarter tones, in their proximity to one another, reveal not so much a temporal, melodic element, but rather the harmony in the note, the enharmonic. Stratifications arise, contrary movements, reflections, and so on, which enter at each moment into a constellation with the given note as in the following example, with G.

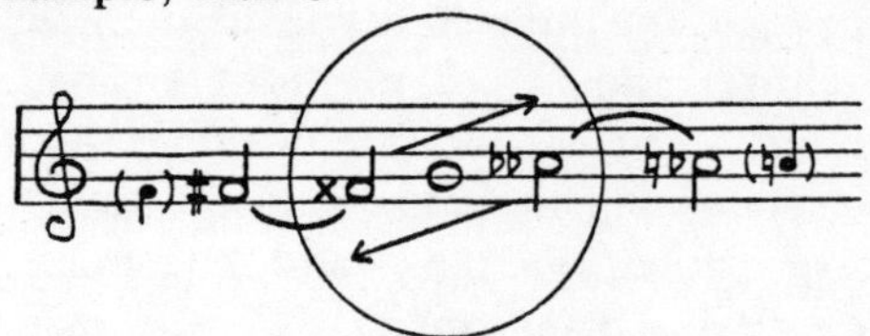

Musical movement, however, inasmuch as it not only runs in two directions, towards light or heaviness, requires a completely new impetus within this enharmonic space of each of the twelve semitones. It is a turning point, which is always connected with a kind of 'leap through the universe', as if one leapt out of the path of one star into another moving in the opposite direction. This moment of absolute freedom, when one path is abandoned in order to take another, is the true enharmonic event. The very fact that only an infinitesimal variation of pitch occurs, scarcely audible to many listeners, demands a still stronger activation, moulding the soul and spirit powers of expression for its musical form.

Here musical sound reveals the ego's capacity to realize through inner spiritual flexibility an occurrence almost inaudible in itself, and to control it in complete freedom. This transition from one direction to another in the sphere of enharmonic processes, always in some measure mysterious, reveals unequivocally that we are beginning to move towards the threshold of the transcendental. The door is opened to the supersensible in so far as the externally audible sense-element vanishes to give place to a freedom of movement which activates the moral pole of the human being. With this one enters the centre of the ego-being: that is, freedom and self-surrender in creative action.

When the sixth octave is reached, the development of the ego-being is complete. The boundary of the earthly, which appears in the region of the sixth octave, lies in the fact that further divisions, such as eighths of a tone or still smaller divisions, can be heard only by the soul which experiences music in full withdrawal, in an existence beyond the earthly. For the European this condition would be either pathologically atavistic or the result of a conscious schooling for the purpose of intensifying soul and spirit forces through initiation. Such a condition will be indispensable for the future if musical evolution is to take a healthy, positive course, adapted to the great tasks pending for humanity.

An attempt has been made within the framework of this work to answer the question: Does a single note reveal the ego-nature of man and, if so, how? That this is revealed magnificently and unequivocally can be seen with ever-growing amazement if one listens qualitatively and objectively to the laws inherent in the series of overtones. There is nothing which may more aptly be described as an archetypal phenomenon than the single note. Scarcely anything more fully justifies Goethe's remarks, which Eckermann reports:

> Then we spoke of the deep significance of the archetypal phenomena, behind which one believes oneself to be directly aware of the Godhead. 'I do not question,' said Goethe, 'whether this highest Being has understanding and reason, but I feel that it is understanding, is reason. All creation is permeated by it, and man has as much of it as enables him to recognize parts of the Highest.'

This study of the Wonder of Musical Sound is not yet quite finished. In view of such an amazing, striking and far-reaching revelation of the nature of the ego a further question is justified.

Human beings live from century to century, determining the development of culture. Through their will and work history arises. As the life of an individual causes a melody to sound in the great progress of the cosmos, so the historic ebb and flow of peoples and cultures is the great melody of mankind. It is not without significance that Clio, the musical inspirer of song, is also the muse of history. Is then the course of the history of music mirrored in musical sound? As the discovery of the numerical relationships in music, equivalent to a conceptual outline of individual values, dates from Pythagoras, this question may be examined in connection with the southern stream of musical evolution stemming from Greece.

The great new contribution made by the Western peoples was polyphony. Apart from the fact that recent research has found something of the kind in northern countries also, it may be permissible here to glance at the more familiar southern stream of development.

In Greek music, the combining of many voices was, in practice, a singing in octaves, both above and below. The Greek choir sang in unison, but within the whole range of sound. The interval of the octave at the beginning of the series of overtones, as the all-fulfilling consonance, controlled music as it was performed by a number of artists. But it was an intuitive octave experience, which did not, as in the content of the second and third octaves, give expression to a higher principle of being, but which gave cosmic union in deeper or higher levels of sound, that is within various spheres of the octave. It is said that Pythagoras truly experienced the music of the spheres. In any case, at that time cosmic music was still by tradition fully alive. By listening, people learned the laws of music according to the cosmic relationships of the stars. They also sought to have them mirrored in their whole social structure. They tried to find out how they worked even into the forces of nature. Singing in octaves, brought an experience in imitation of this universal world of music. 'Harmoniai' meant they knew themselves to be enclosed in the sounding-together of all spheres. Today the octave indicates the attaining of the higher ego, because this ego is fully united with the human being. At that time, the individual human being was not yet so consolidated within himself. His ego was still borne cosmically by the gods. In singing in octaves he felt himself to be permeated by the ringing forces of the creative world-being, and to be vibrating in sympathy with them.

With the development of Christian culture during the first century after the Mystery of Golgotha, a completely new element gradually penetrated into the Greek tonal system. The intervals of fifth and fourth were introduced into concerted music. In observing these intervals from the second octave of overtones it was stated that the ego of man is comprehended as an enclosed individuality. Man could now grasp his earthly I. In the series of overtones a law has already been revealed which defines the course of musical evolution: each new octave brings a new interval, experienced qualitatively as a new consonance. Much discussion and misunderstanding has arisen out of this emergence of feeling for fifth and fourth. An age with a pronounced feeling for the major and minor experience — an experience purely of soul nature — could bring little understanding to meet it. However, listening qualitatively to these intervals gives rise to a completely neutral, that is, objective feeling. These intervals are an expression of the spirit and not so much of a heartfelt subjective soul experience. Man's feeling at that time was directed, within the framework of the church, to the vision of the spiritual mysteries of the Christian faith. Music was experienced as a deepening of the wonder of God in man, rather than as an expression of the sensations of the secular world. So it is quite understandable that these intervals, as the first expression of such an ego-feeling, were felt to be like the opening of a door to the other side, as well as being a pleasing combination of sounds. Our contemporaries, who once again strive to attain an impersonal objective cosmic orientation, have long since overcome the former prohibition of consecutive fourths and fifths. For example, no one today will fail to experience the magic of Debussy's progressions of sound, because they bear so suprapersonal, so cosmic a character.

The third octave of overtones, with its succession of thirds, opens up a new feeling for consonance. Today it is hard to imagine that in this southern Roman stream the interval of the third was regarded as a discord until the Middle Ages. It was the incursion of the musical element from the north, flowing over from Britain to the continent, as well as the somewhat earlier Arab stream with its centre in Paris, that brought with it the change to the experience of the third. The door was opened to the great flowering of the classical period. This age of the major and minor system with its threefold cadence structure finds in the succession of thirds within the note its prophecy and its fulfilment. Music becomes expression of the personal experience of destiny.

Today we stand before a new consonance, the interval of the second. The whole tone has, in general, lost all the shock of discord, of irresolution and unrest, and we can fully understand how that has come about and what it signifies. In melody the major second has a questioning, onward-leading character. It brings about connections and is representative of a musical and organic logic. In harmony it gives the impression as of iridescent colours on water, of gently rippling waves, moving hither and thither. In both cases it expresses an element of motion. But what is it that more and more rules musical life today? It is the striving of each individual to have his own system based on logic, a coming to terms with form, corresponding to an experience of music thoroughly constructional and taking its bearings from thought; and there is a quite definite talent for the technical element and for the element of movement. All this is inspired by a striving for logic, for objectivity, for conformity to rule. It is a striving for the becoming audible of a frame of mind trying to free itself of all romanticism. Emphasis on the simultaneous presence of opposite elements, pointed out in regard to the interval of a second, is clearly evident in modern music. These trends show up plainly in everything that has come to light since the turn of the century, in multiple rhythms, polytonality, harmony, stratifications and oppositions, also in the gradual appearance of the enharmonic element, which prepares the way for development into the next octave and the coming of the quarter-tone system.

It must be conceded that the course of history is mirrored in the single note, and it would be a wonderful and exceedingly rewarding task for every musical investigator to research these things in detail. Changing consciousness, already manifest from octave to octave in the series of overtones, in that in each octave a new interval becomes consonant, could clarify many a controversial question in a truly objective way; that is, entirely out of the nature of the object which is musical sound itself.

At the beginning it was stated that, in comparison with earlier times, man now gains access to world-wisdom and world-love, to the Logos, only through his moral and thought-endowed ego-being. But faced with the marvellous depth of musical sound which so fully reveals this ego-being, one could substitute for the word 'only' a joyous 'surely still', for this higher centre in the being of man is of one substance with the Logos. And when an individual human being has consciously learnt to form his relationship with Him, with the Christ-Being, then such a spiritual frame of mind will indicate a way to that cosmic music which was present in the natural world surrounding an earlier humanity. How this may be experienced will be illustrated in the following chapters. The revealing of the mysteries of musical sound gives the possibility of regaining inner access to earlier kinds of experience.

Chapter Three

THE COMPLEMENTARY SERIES

All that has so far been revealed in the single note could be found only through qualitative hearing. This is different from a purely quantitative way of listening to variations in pitch, intensity of volume, changes in tempo, and so on. In all these spheres we are still only in the antechamber of music. The difference between qualitative and quantitative listening lies in the endeavour to find a way through these audible sounds to the power working in them. The effect of the musical element on the listener enables him to find within himself the qualitative nature of the musical sound. He is taken over by it, and comes inwardly under the influence of certain movements, feelings of lightness and heaviness, stability and buoyancy. It is evident that feelings may be enkindled which not only move the soul with desire or aversion, sorrow, sobriety or joy, but also take hold of it with deep emotion. Such experiences do not arise from a temporary subjective mood, but are a direct transmission of the creative force of the phenomenon. As such they have a universal objective character. From each one of them spiritual laws can be read against the background of their very nature. True artistic experience begins here, true musical knowledge. And this knowledge is especially relevant for contemporary man. The search for objectivity brings about the rejection of all romanticism, of all that is too subjective in the soul. From this stems the present dangerous tendency of becoming entangled in intellectualism, in construction based on a quantitative experience, because we believe it is an objective foundation. Only by entering into the qualitative sphere does the way to an infallible, truly objective experience open up.

We might think that this also is subjective. But we find that various people of every age, every stage of culture, every nationality, come in the end to the same characterization of an individual element. No one will experience a major triad as minor, no one will hear in a unison the swinging, light-filled nature of a sixth, although the kind of experience of the unison can be different in each case. The problem is to find the transition from quantitative listening which, with Goethe, we can call the 'external sense for musical sound', to the first stage of an 'inner sense'. This comprehensive kind of hearing, better spoken of as a living archetype-building force, begins to open up into the inner experience of an entirely new spiritual world. The previous chapter showed how deeply new connections, as yet unthought of, are experienced and not invented. One thing grows out of another and, with quiet surprise, tentatively feeling the way, the first steps are made from the forecourt into the inner sanctum of music.

Here we are no longer so much in the sphere of the senses. If this must, as a matter of course, be the starting point, it soon drops away — it is no longer of such great interest. The pitch of the note, the volume of the sound, the timbre of the instrument — these are no longer essentials; the question now is: What effect does it have? How does it move and take on shape in the sphere of soul and spirit? What kind of forces are they in reality that exist in living, moving sound? The understanding of these forces does not come through the outer faculties of sense given by nature, but in a moral and ethical way. To listen is to make oneself selfless, in order to be adequate for the transition that has to be made. It is a question of an inner resonance, that is of a sounding, vibrating together, of a receptivity, which seemingly corresponds to the activity of listening. Within the realm of qualitative hearing, this receptivity, unconscious in the ordinary way, is borne by the selfless, ethical will. Its basic attitude is by no means given automatically, but must be acquired through practice, and established anew again and again. It is the force of a higher ego, the free impact of a moral will which is called forth and now begins to unfold 'self-creatively' in so far as, through it, new powers burgeon in the soul. The growing knowledge of the very being of music, which awakens in this way, invigorates the human being and enables him to comprehend and transform himself. The consciousness of self which he experiences in these still and modest strivings towards a new inner tonal sense, is the language of the capacity for love in the soul. In the *re*-sonance he trains himself to become a listening being, open to the inner life of another. Hearing in this way means constant readiness for self-sacrifice, for becoming empty with regard to every movement relating to oneself. Goethe speaks of the ear as a 'mute sense'. In keeping with this attitude of true hearing one learns nothing of one's own opinion, wish and will, but only of the course of life, the laws of life, inherent in what takes hold of the listener so that he unites with its true being. He sinks into the life welling up from the world, and finds it again in his I. It was Fichte who pointed out this self-creative nature of man, confirming it in philosophy. In a lecture, *Fichte Among Us*, Rudolf Steiner spoke of this experience:

> That is the I itself, that I which in every moment creates itself anew; that I at the basis of which lies, not a completed being, but an inner activity. That I therefore, which cannot be robbed of its existence, because its existence is in its creation, in its own self-creation. And into this self-creation flows all that which has true being.

In such words the universal sickness of our time is brought to consciousness: this inner inflexibility regarding the qualitative nature of things, the fact that man no longer hears consciously, can no longer be rid of himself if he wishes to experience the inwardness of other things, gives to this true, freely-developed *re*-sonance in the listening soul a deep social meaning. It also throws light on the fact that what is presented today as a challenge to the I was neither possible or necessary for a childlike, pre-Christian humanity. For the mental attitude of that time was so permeable and open that the human being was to a certain degree lifted out of his body through music. Only in Greek times did this gradually cease. Until then, the ruling harmonious, macrocosmic, creative forces swung through and rang through his being, those same spiritual forces of life that man is now trying to approach microcosmically. A simple geometrical figure represents these cosmic truths.

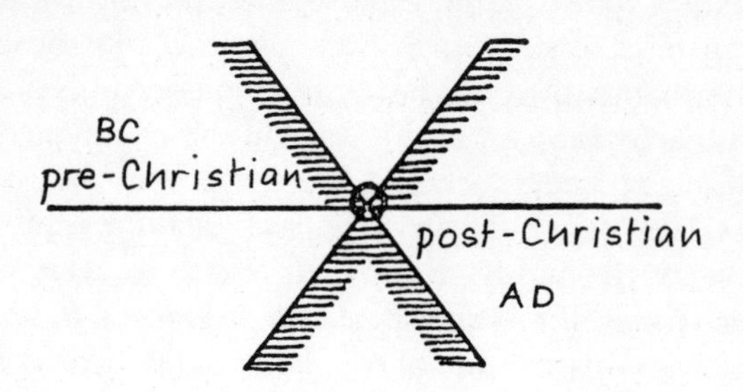

A reversal has taken place in the relationship of man to music, an interchange of outer and inner, of receptivity and being filled with self. A macrocosmic consciousness has been transformed into a microcosmic one. This is no longer given automatically through music, but must be acquired step by step through free ego-forces in the inmost being of the soul. Only conscious attention to these laws of life can guarantee a healthy human evolution, can bring the great human symphony which Clio recorded as history to the anxiously seeking human soul.

Through considering such processes of resonance and reversal an understanding can arise, and something similar in the process of hearing can be observed. This will be examined more fully in the second part of this book. The degree to which man attains complete selflessness in music will gradually show how a counter-force comes to life within him. If, for example, we strike a low note over and over again, and surrender completely to the depths, there comes a moment when we can bear it no longer. We are drawn down into the bass regions. Where is the star to which we can hold? Something like an inner demand is felt as a challenge leading to an opposite balancing force. For example, if the low C is struck in the bass a high note is inwardly required to balance it out. A continuous inaudible counter-event, enkindled by the externally audible event, is gradually experienced in the soul. And this synchronization in the polarity of the externally audible and the inner spiritual counter-event constitutes the fullness of experience. So subtle are these inaudible inner counter-effects that, in the beginning, they seem to be concealed by the audible sound. But every attentive person has access to them.

This clears the way for an understanding of the phenomenon of a counter-series. It is the inaudible counterpart to the overtones and, for contemporary man, corresponds to the inner creative counter-thrust over against them. The counter-series is a phenomenon that has been known since ancient times. But, in contrast to earlier times, it is not regarded as of equal importance today and does not win the same recognition as the series of overtones. This is because the counter-series is not audible. In a materialistically-orientated time like the present, which regards as reasonable only what can be grasped by the senses, it is considered to be of no special importance and not worthy of attention. Yet it is simply a fact that while these tones may not be heard within the actual sound, none the less they exist in surrounding space. And no observation concerning sound may be judged complete without reference to what space means. It is, in every sphere — be it in the human surrounding or inwardly as bodily resonance or space of soul — the precondition for the unfolding of sound in its entirety. A sounding note brings bodies around it capable of sounding into sympathetic vibration. But only those objects vibrate in sympathy whose own sounds lie lower than the main note and are in the same interval-relationship to each other as in the series of overtones. Here again an important polarity is revealed on the basis of which all life can unfold. If, so far, in relation to resonance a counter-thrust has been mentioned, then this is created in the sounding of space through the correspondence between outer and inner. The phenomenon of the counter-series shows that something corresponding to the inner soul processes also exists physically.

Nevertheless, it is regrettable that in contemporary scientific thought the reality of such a phenomenon is never acknowledged or incorporated into any commentary. We read in Paul Hindemith's *Treatise on Composition*:

> I consider it absurd to admit the existence of a force capable of producing a mirrored arrangement of the partial series. Such a force would suspend the efficacy of the force of gravity which expresses itself in the series of overtones. No evidence can be found for the activity of such a force.

And yet the author has to admit:

> In electronic acoustics there is indeed the common appearance of a series of undertones, which may be mistaken for such a structure.

Nevertheless, he can impute no significance to this phenomenon:

> This series of undertones has no influence on the colouration of the note and also lacks the advantages in other respects of

of the note and also lacks the advantages in other respects of the series of overtones, which in truth always come unsought and without any artificial assistance. No evidence is found in nature for an apparent mirroring of the series of overtones.

If we understand this much-disputed phenomenon as not being similar to the naturally given series of overtones but as their polar opposite, then all difficulties drop away. As minus corresponds to plus, as the world of spirit to the world of matter, as the inaudible to the audible, so the reality of this series cannot be regarded as a structure artificially conceived, but must be acknowledged in its own sphere in full consciousness and then its own laws of life will be revealed.

After the exercise with the low C in the bass, in answer to which the inner counter-claim of the 'star' working in a higher octave appeared, and starting now from this 'star', two octaves above middle C, the tones sounding sympathetically in space as the series of undertones unfold from interval to interval. Words of Novalis, from his *Fragments*, state:

> The observation of the world begins in the infinite absolute treble, in the centre, and comes down the scale; the observation of our self begins in the infinite absolute bass, the periphery, and goes up the scale. Absolute unification of bass and treble. This is the systole and diastole of divine life.

The structure of the counter series follows that of the partial series: four octaves with five times C and the other tones lying in between.

What do these state in the way of experience? Are they also to be found in man?

In considering the fifth octave of overtones it was pointed out that every rise in pitch is felt to be a process of spiritualization which frees man from the feeling of being firmly anchored in the physical. He goes beyond himself in that he feels himself expanding outside his physical body. In the same kind of way, but in the opposite direction, from outside inwards, he descends in feeling into himself, 'in-carnates' in the counter series. In repeating anew the question concerning the revelation of the I, we can say its purely spiritual nature is audible from the very first high note. It is embedded in a region of weightless light. The more one expands out into it, the more the impression disappears that this high note is fixed. A boundless world of light weaving in infinitude seems to encircle the soul, and its pleasing expanse shines through every bodily feeling, raising it aloft. A new feeling for keynote arises, established in the spirit, to which there is no limit. The I is part of the World-I.

As in the first octave of overtones a development began which brought the unfolding of possibilities of life out of a germinal note, so also here with the counter-series a downward impulse becomes audible. This downward octave is like a gentle foreboding of a grasping of self. Not that one steps out of the sphere of spiritual light completely. One is still in harmony with it, but the will is awakened to descend. How strong the force of light is in truth, how much it is able to hold back the dark foreboding, can clearly be felt by the inclination of the lower C of this octave to swing back into the light.

The next step brings to experience in full clarity the severance from the world of light. The sounding of the downward fifth gives expression to an individualizing principle.

If it was possible to speak in the series of overtones of C to G as the hearing of a spirit form, of a *re*-sonance of cosmic man, then in this case it is the arising of an individual sphere tending towards the earth. Each fifth, if listened to again and again, each in its own direction, reveals a kind of rounding off — like something completed — on the one hand from inside outwards, creating a periphery towards the light through expansion (a), on the other hand the creation of form out of space, from outside inwards (b).

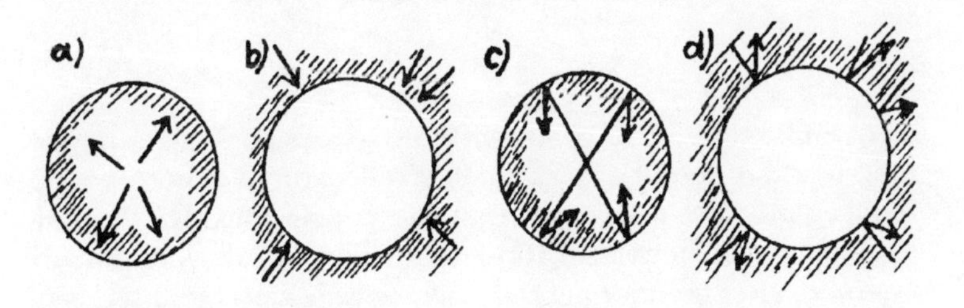

These two aspects of sound-space and spirit-space show their complementary nature still more strongly in the experience of the fourth which follows. In the direction upwards, this interval brought with it the moment when the listener grasped his personality as a clearly defined bearer of destiny, in almost crystalline form. The periphery works back inwards from the light (c). Now, out of space, one hears in the descending fourth, F to C, something like a yearning to turn back into the light.

The middle C, reached now from both directions, has something of the nature of a threshold, a kind of key position. It is the note in which both series meet and intersect. The geometrical figure showing the reversal in the relation between man and music from earlier epochs to the present day should be recalled here. In the two series something similar takes place; the picture is applicable in both instances. Within the realm of the note the sequence of thirds upwards signalled the awakening of the human personality to the earthly plane. Now this human personality must develop its own forces of soul and must learn to master the demands of earthly life. It stands between itself and the surrounding world, to which it surrenders in feeling, knowledge and will in complete devotion. From spirit-space, in the descending thirds, the turning and awakening to self begins. A mystical, inner attitude takes over, penetrating the very depths of soul. The I emerges as standing between two worlds, directing its life outwards or inwards: the major triad of the partial series is answered by the minor triad of the counter-series.

Against such a background it is no longer possible to regard the world of minor as a calculated reflection of major. It is no longer possible to acquiesce in the conclusions of a leading personality such as Paul Hindemith who, in the work already quoted, after mentioning the 'theoretically calculated series of undertones' continues:

> But what in reality is the minor triad? I consider it, following a theory not quite new, to be a darkening of the major triad. As it is not even possible to differentiate between major and minor thirds objectively, I do not believe in a polar contrast between the two chords. They are the high and the low, the strong and the weak, the light and the dark, the penetrating and the dull version of one and the same chord.

Regarding this 'theory not quite new', Goethe in his time contradicted Zelter in the most emphatic way:

> A theorist of Nordic nations, who set out from the minor sounds, might just as well say that the major third is put in the place of the minor one.

And further:

> My hypothetical Nordic theorist would be justified in saying the major third is a raised minor.

The derivation of the minor as a diminution of the major is a point of view that could only arise as a result of the one-sided aspect of regarding the generating note of the partial series as the basis of music. Everything would be grasped in firmly fixed proportions in accordance with the major principle instead of being felt as a breathing alternation between two polar principles. It is truly always arises. It is not in the least necessary. In past times the intervals of the partial series were related to the dividing of a string — $1:{}^1/_2:{}^1/_3$, etc., while downwards, as the minor series, they were determined by the length of the string — 1:2:3, etc. From ancient times it was known that music rested on the nature of breathing, the principle of polarity in life, on the complementary factor.

The extent to which these two phenomena unite to make a whole, and only as such present a satisfactory explanation, can be heard by listening to this third octave with its thirds in both series. The notes in each case combine to form a dominant chord of which the tonic lies in the opposite series.

C – E – G – B flat – C upwards leads into the F minor of the lower series, while C – A flat – F – D – C downwards goes back to C major. The harmony sounding in the note has a dominant relationship to the harmony corresponding to it in space, and the opposite. Neither is satisfactory in itself nor truly the bearer of life, any more than in-breathing or out-breathing can stand alone.

It has already been pointed out that in the fourth octave with its succession of seconds the discrepancy between feeling and pitch arises with the arrival of chromaticism. This was the case with the partial series and it is the same in the case of the counter-series. The G flat in fourth place feels as if it were leaning towards F, but its exact pitch inclines towards G. In comparing the two series something like the reciprocal relationship between dominant and tonic, that was so pronounced in the third octave, is indicated again.

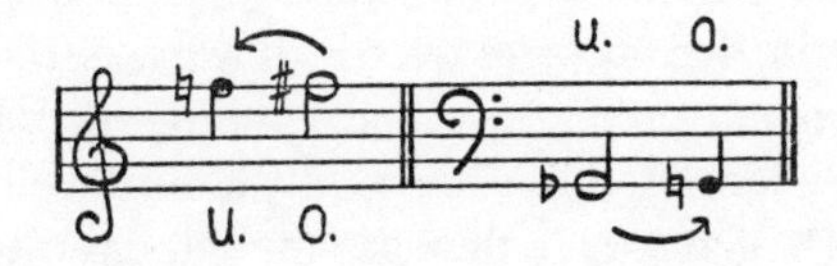

The F sharp in the series of overtones approximates towards F in pitch, as if it would point to the fifth sounding in space in the counter-series. On the other hand the lower G flat with its higher pitch casts something like a bridge over into the fifth in the series of overtones. In the second volume of this work, the subtle differentiations in each phenomenon will be investigated more thoroughly. Attention is drawn here to this phenomenon to indicate how a quiet, qualitative study may reveal connections, however ethereally fine and fluctuating they may be.

In the sphere of the overtones a fifth and sixth octave led out into an experience of cosmic space, to the enharmonic and to quarter-tones, and it may be assumed that in the realm of the counter-series the opposite is the case. There was mention of stratification, of constellations, that were created in the semitone by the crossing over of various movements between lightness and heaviness. Time became space. The experience of C, for instance, can be felt in different ways. The continually repeated characterization 'upright' leads in reality to three clearly differentiated currents of sound. One stretches upwards, the head encompassing the light-world of the firmament, but at the same time one feels the support of the depths, which link up with the central point of the earth, and a third thing is given emanating from a central force, a clear feeling of inwardly holding these polarities together. There is a constellation of three forces. Corresponding to this reality is the enharmonic differentiation B sharp — D double flat — C.

The course of development in the lower reaches of the counter-series calls up a completely different feeling. Many people cannot distinguish the semitone in the lower octaves, far less any finer differences. To them these depths are like a foundering, like being drawn into an impenetrable mass of sound. The steadiness of the keynote experienced with certainty in the low C in the bass, melts away into a soft pulpy flowing of one thing into another in which it is difficult to find a footing. Something wonderful happens here: the holding power, which the I can no longer find aurally in this matting-up of the depths, goes over, as it were, into the heart, into the centre of man. But 'centre' means finding the balance, means resting in the polarities. Space, from which the development of the counter-series began, grasps time as 'simultaneity' through an ever deeper penetration into the creative nature of the I.

Just how much the achieving of this stance of the centre is needed by our age is proven by the difficulty so many people have in listening to modern music. They meet with sounds which are often tense and laden with contrarieties and are, for the most part, not immediately transparent to the hearing. Justice can only be done when the inner state of balance, the power of resting in polarities, is schooled so that extremes are gradually balanced out and become harmony. The two series are given below again in notation, the partial series sounding within the note and the counter-series in space:

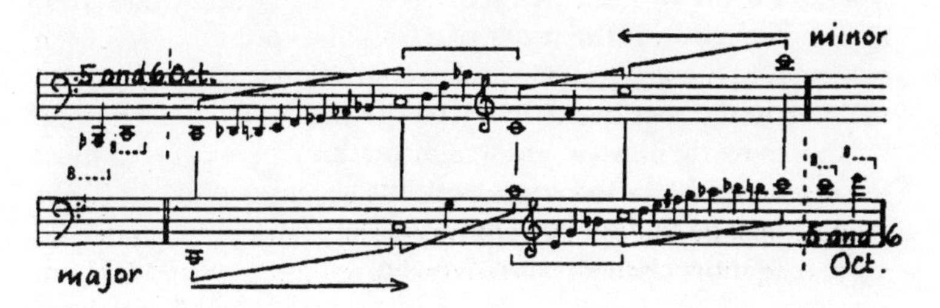

Continual practice in listening should bring all that has been stated, with its background of spirit and soul, ever more and more to consciousness.

Finally let us look back again to prehistoric times, for instance to Wäinemoinen, the Finnish singer in the *Kalevala*, or to the influence of Orpheus in the South. Perhaps we shall now be able to understand what the relationship of man to music was in those days; it was the opposite of what it is today. Man did not so much experience the physical, audible sound but was possessed by it and made to sound, to vibrate with it: he experienced music as cosmic force in surrounding space, and a process of incarnation was unconsciously wrought by it, an increasing awakening to self, as the above comments on the counter-series sought to make clear. A great 'moulding of man', consciously directed by the initiates, was brought about by means of music and was experienced as such with profound emotion and joy. It was the rule of the gods that resounded and, for the most part, it was this ruling that was the verbal content of their singing. The magnificent description of the voyage of the Argonauts quoted in the first chapter was an example. The Finnish *Kalevala* describes something similar. Wäinemoinen descends to the ruler of the depths, Vipunen, so as to learn from him three words that were lacking for the building of a new boat. He

> sang what came of all creation,
> magic words in every order,
> how erstwhile with God's permission,
> in agreement with th' Almighty,
> earthly air itself was active,
> from the air the water parted
> and the ground itself grew solid,
> on the rocks were many plants.
> Sang then of the moon's formation,
> sang also of the sun's position
> and the bounds of shafts of air
> and the signs of starry heaven.
>
> Sang the songs through lengths of days,
> sang through nights one after other:
> Sun itself stood still to listen,
> and the golden moon was watchful.
> Waves were ebbing in the distance,
> breakers surging in the bays,
> eddies deep refrained from raging,
> Rutia's fall refrained from foaming;
> Vuksen's cataract stood still,
> even Jordan stemmed its flowing.

It is understandable that right into the Middle Ages, until the stronger awakening of the ego-consciousness, the tonal systems in their basic forms went from above downwards, as with the minor system. Music was received from heaven. The soul, in union with the gods, was open to the extra-terrestrial. And so it can be understood that for the ancient Chinese around 3000 BC the low notes were the highest and the high ones the lowest. It is the awareness that humanity has to acquire again today from phenomena such as the complementary law which is illustrated by the harmonic series and its counterpart, but this time there must be full consciousness of self. How did the people of old hear? This question can be answered by saying: they heard qualitatively, rather than quantitatively. They heard *re*-sonance;

they heard in the sense of the complementary series, in sympathy, laid hold on by what they heard, and their whole organization was moulded by this, right into the very nature of the physical, which means they were formed musically.

There is a physical experiment which most people know from their school days, but without attaching any significance to it — that of the Chladni sound figures. A thin glass plate, held in one corner, is strewn with fine sand. A violin bow is drawn across some place on the edge of the plate and the sand begins to jump, to move, and to settle in regular patterns, often of wondrous beauty. Each tiny difference of sound brings about new forms. However such things may be accounted for 'naturally', the immediate and arresting impression is that the sound not only sets the earthly material in motion, but brings about regular forms and figures. It is surely no accident, but profound wisdom on the part of the spirit of language if it uses the same word for the immaterial sound and the material it forms. (In the German language the word 'Ton' means both 'sound' and 'clay'.)

Out of that very same mystery of the creative word there springs an old Chinese saying of Lü Po We in *Spring and Autumn*:

> Morals and music reflect the feelings of Heaven and Earth. They bring about union with the living forces of the heavenly gods. They call the upper gods down and the lower gods up and allow the fine and the coarse to assume shape and form.

Chapter Four

THE INSTRUMENTS OF MUSIC

In surveying briefly man's relationship with his musical instruments throughout the ages we must seek to clarify the attitude of an earlier humanity to the world of music. The starting-point has always to be this earlier state of consciousness. It has been stated that people of olden times heard qualitatively, not quantitatively. They heard resonance, reverberation. They heard in the sense of the descending series, vibrating and sounding in sympathy, and their entire organism was given shape and form by what they heard. They could hear in this way because they were carried away by the sounds, as if enchanted.

In such a state of consciousness the experience was not of the self within, but rather of the spiritual forces beyond the earth with which man became one. Everything that came to meet him out of the realm of nature was filled with good and evil spirits, a part of the macrocosmic environment into whose power he was committed. A faint indication of this condition can be gleaned today from the child. It is only by hearing that he learns to speak and sing. What joy he finds in every noise he makes! He often needs to shout at the top of his voice, to shriek, bawl, shout with joy or yell! The imitative instinct is coupled with the need for self-assertion and a feeling for security, given by his own strength, his own growth and development. A young person's musical experience is like a vital breathing process: a strong will to go out into the world alternating with a real feeling of self. The further one goes back to ancient times — even to Plato's description of Atlantis, referred to in all mythology as the time of the Great Flood — the more one goes back to the musical experience of races other than the European and the traditions of instrumental practice, the more does the feeling for self recede and the pre-Christian attitude prevail. The intervals of fifth and fourth in the counter-series also played their part.

It is understandable that for the human being of earlier times all musical activity was magical, that this was for him essential. He came to know himself in ecstasy as part of the divine order of the world. He experienced the effect it had on him as working out of the whole earthly environment. When he began to grasp the forms and substances of the spirit-filled creative beings in nature around him, when he found the possibility of expressing himself through them, then he was fully aware that the essential beings of nature were enchanted in his often primitive instruments of music. For his part, he learnt to pursue and judge the course of his music and the effect it had in the divinely-ordered world around him in imaginative pictures, quite objectively. He stood on the threshold between himself and the world, and in his singing and instrumental music tried to make these two spheres sound together. In ancient times singing was more an imitation of the noises and voices of the external world, in as far as it was not connected with the word as recitative. Only gradually did instrument and voice separate from one another.

In his book *Singing Stones* (*Singende Steine*, Kassel 1955) Markus Schneider gives the following interesting quotations from the *Upanishads*:

> As sound represents the primordial substance common to all things and beings and its unfolding into song is the singing power that moves the cosmos, so is song the only means of entering into a direct and substantial interrelationship with the furthermost powers. Singing or rhythmical speech is in the deepest sense a direct participation in the primordial substance of the universe. It is an active summons to be creative and active within the basic acoustical stratum of the world. It is an imitation of the resounding command which once called the world into being and thereby built a bridge between heaven and earth on the basis of the sounding substance both worlds have in common. Because of this the gods, who are pure song, are literally nourished by hymns of praise.

The primordial singing language was divided and three quarters of it given to animals.

> So animal voices constitute an indispensable component of religious singing. When the priests tried to reconstitute this primordial language for their rituals they had of necessity to

incorporate the sounds of animals. They probably created the text with the quarter that belonged to them and tried to sing it with the power of sound vested in the animals, by imitating the animal sounds.
Rigveda-prâtishâkhya XIII, 10 and 17, enumerates three times of day and three *stanas* (registers or tones of voice) which the priests had to bear in mind during their ritual singing. In the morning they were to imitate the roaring of the lion with their chest-voice, in the afternoon the goose with their throat-voice and in the evening the peacock with their head-voice. Rigveda VII, 103 and IX 97, 57 contain hymns to be produced with the voice of frog and vulture, while other formulae are to sound like the bellowing of an ox or the humming of a bee. Even in the Hellenic-Egypto Mithras liturgy of the third century AD, whistling, snorting, roaring — according to T. Reizenstein — played a great part when the mystics met their gods in their seven stages of consecration. In the course of time the freely intoned singing and imitation of animal voices gradually gave way to a rational system with fixed pitch. The ancient tradition remained only in a certain colouring of sound and the names of animals with which one named the various degrees of the musical tonal system.

The present age has inherited from the ancient Chinese, the Egyptian, Greek and Nordic cultures advanced and highly-developed products of a long musical evolution.

The beginnings in particular were, for this primordial humanity, an enchantment of good or evil spirits into their world of music and its forms. The trunk of a tree, as a great cleft drum, still bore within it the power of the spirit of the tree. With festoons of rattles, bells, stones, tubes of wood, clay or metal, with cymbals and with drums — with everything — they invoked the spirits of light or darkness ruling in these realms of nature. There was always conversation with them, whether externally in the realm of the elemental forces of nature, or internally as motions of the soul or incipient speech. Professor Curt Sachs reports in his book on instruments that pan-pipes, made of bamboo or other reeds of differing length fitted together, qualify as the oldest instrument for scales. But they were excluded from public life and from ritual. Their tone, linked to nature and yet so full of longing, was appropriate for expressing purely human sentiments of love. Also the earliest stringed instruments, allotted only to women, brought with their more subtle, intimate tone, the first beginnings of melody. There was a strict difference between instruments allotted to men and those allotted to women. Death was the penalty for wrong use. Men represented the solar, women more the lunar principle. Festivals and traditions connected with puberty, the maturing of youths and maidens were accompanied by special instrumental music. The magic of love, sexual stimulus and the mysteries of fructification were also accompanied by music.

Musical performance, from its most primitive to its most sophisticated forms, served mainly ritualistic purposes. A relationship was sought, and established, not only to the surrounding spirits of nature but also to the whole world of stars. Some examples can be taken from the work by Professor Curt Sachs mentioned above. He reports the use of a nasal flute on the island of Bali, through which a 'magical relationship to the world' was established in the following way:

East

right *South* *North* left

The player stands facing eastwards. Inhalation is through the right nostril, exhalation through the left. He acquires — looking eastwards — a connection with the southerly forces through inhaling with the right nostril, with the northerly forces through exhaling from the left.

The nostrils play a significant part in a musical and cosmic connection. They are the gates through which the divine breath enters man. Everything that sounds is borne by the medium of air and the inhaling of this moving air bestows life on the living and on the dead. Hermann Pfrogner, in his book *Music*, (*Musik*, München 1954) tells of the following inscription from an Egyptian tomb, concerning the handing over of sistra and necklaces to the *Ka* of the deceased:

> Thou hast received them to hold to thy nostrils. Thou hast found favour with Ammon, thy lord, through being close to him for innumerable years. He determined thou shouldst live in his retinue. He has renewed the air in thy nostrils. Thou art eternal as the heavens, thy life is eternal. Thou wilt become young again, like the fresh water.

A kind of meditative formula is reported in connection with the nasal flute: 'AUM AM', the active red sensation on the right, and 'AUM UM', the dark, black sensation on the left. The interrelationship between the more southerly and the more northerly forces of the world can be felt.

All similar Egyptian inscriptions show female forms swinging the sistrum. This instrument, in keeping with feminine nature, points in the cult to the invocation of the lunar forces and is brought into close connection with the goddess Hathor, daughter of the Sun-god, Re. As the heart of this goddess usually burns with rage, she is always appeased by the playing of the sistra. 'Play to the golden one to make her gracious', runs an inscription, and she is referred to as 'the lady of the sistra'. One of her replies, to a Pharaoh who offered her these instruments, runs:

> Welcome in peace! My heart is glad for that which thou hast done and my wrath is assuaged because thou makest music for me.

One of the many forms of this instrument is like the symbol of life that is put into the hands of gods and pharaohs.

Curt Sachs explains that the handle above is taken from the world-embracing circuit of the moon, the crossbar from the elements, and that the shaking movement when playing it, as also with such things as rattles and whirlers, corresponds to 'the mobility of all that is'. Here is an instrument in the hand of woman that fills the soul and rouses it to intercourse with divine beings.

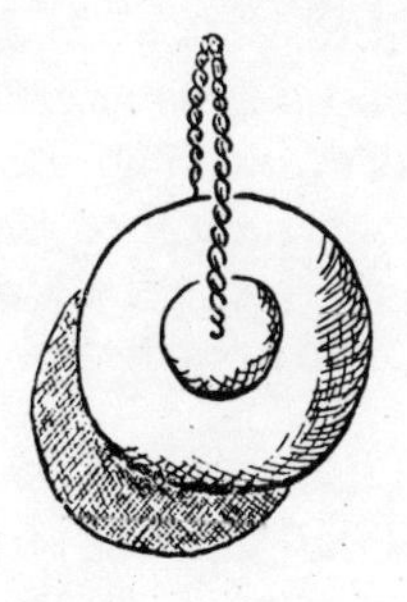

The various cymbals were also played by women. Struck gently in a horizontal position, they served to revere the loftier gods of light. Struck energetically in a vertical position, they summoned the lower gods.

And an example from China: It is said of a kind of zither, a 'classical stringed instrument' of the Far East, that the upper part was 'round like the sky' but the lower part was 'flat like the earth'. Five strings represented five (!) elements, a further seven strings the seven planets. A hole in the centre is connected with the eight (!) winds, another with the four seasons of the year. Thirteen frets are connected with the thirteen (!) months of the Chinese year and a further important number of 366, with the number of days in the year. A classical instrument such as this in all its forms and measures, is a perfect picture of the world, of heaven and earth, of elements and planets, of winds and seasons, of the rhythms of years and days and, even in our time, is still more than a picture.

In this connection part of a wonderfully meaningful legend may be quoted, which throws light on the profound educational and cosmological significance of music in mythological times. It comes from the ancient Chinese *True Book of the Fountainhead*, and is taken from the book by Hermann Pfrogner already cited.

> ...When Gu Ba struck the zither the birds circled above him and the fish leapt out of the water. The music master, Wen

of Dscheng heard it. He left his house and followed Master Siang on his travels. He touched the strings with his finger for three long years without a melody emerging. Master Siang said, 'Go you home again'.

Master Wen laid the zither aside, sighed and said: 'It is not that I know not how to touch the strings, it is not that I produced no melody; what lies within my mind bears no relation to the strings; what I strive for bears no relation to the sounds. As long as I do not attain to it inwardly in my heart I cannot give expression to it on my instrument; for that reason I do not dare to move my hand and touch the strings. Give me a little time and then see what I can do.'

Not long afterwards he approached Master Siang again, who said: 'How is it with thy playing on the zither?' Master Wen said: 'I have achieved it; please test my playing.'

Then during the spring he struck the Schang-string and let the eighth reed accompany it. Suddenly a cool breeze arose and herb and tree bore fruit. When autumn came he struck the Güo-string and let the second reed reply. There came a mild breeze gently flowing and herb and tree unfolded all their splendour. During the summer he struck the Yü-string and let the eleventh reed accompany it. Frost and snow fell mingled together, rivers and lakes became quite rigid. When winter came he struck the Dschi-string and let the fifth reed reply. The glare of the sun was burning hot and the hard ice melted away altogether. Lastly, he let the Gung-string sound and combined it with the four other strings, then gentle breezes rustled, clouds drifted, bearing good fortune, sweet dew fell and springs gushed powerfully.

It is difficult to read a legend such as this without noticing the profound ethical content which at that time determined the relationship of man to music. This chapter originated in the question: How did people of bygone ages hear? We have now reached an important point in historical development in the ancient Chinese culture. Apart from the ecstasy in the primitive stages and the endeavour to establish through music a real relationship with the world of spirits and of demons, with the possibilities and forms of expression available at the time, progress is described in the knowledge that the healing power of music is a matter of self-creative moral forces in every single soul. Musical activity reaches the ego-centre of man. He no longer loses himself in music. Only from this moment on is it possible to speak in any real sense of the beginnings of an individual capacity for music in soul and spirit, a capacity that tries to gain conscious access to universal forces. The legend speaks of the 'music master' and it is clear that he teaches those who are still lithe and supple, not only the control of natural bodily determined forces but also the development of moral values.

From this moment on, instrument and man gradually separated. In a state of ecstasy activity and experience were one, but to the extent that the player awoke he distanced himself from his instrument. There was a mutual emancipation, a new and more objective hearing on the one hand and an inner experience pressing for well-defined expression on the other. Musical sound and word gave rise to melody which, right up to the time of Greek civilization, was followed in unison by the instrument. During these centuries music was born as an independent art. Man with his ego, ripe for conceptual thinking, turned away from divine guidance with Promethean will. He became responsible for himself and conscious of his own destiny. He created, through grasping differences in pitch more clearly, the material for an art in which the laws of his ego could be revealed. From roaring, howling and imitating the noises around him — as mentioned in the book *Singing Stones* — there grew, with increasing self-assurance, the necessity to approximate the sounds of his voice to the divine mathematical measures of the cosmos. It has been shown in the two chapters 'The Wonder of Musical Sound' and 'The Complementary Series' how he created a tonal expression of himself as the 'Image of God' and this, in a sense, culminated at the time of Pythagoras. Subsequent chapters will continue to reveal this unity of music and the human ego.

Newly acquired independence brought to consciousness the difference between the human voice and the instrument. The human voice was still given by nature, but this was no longer the case with the instrument. During the course of evolution they had separated. The instruments were now set apart, and the player had to practise on them, work on them, win them back again as described in the Chinese legend of Master Wen. He also had to acquire technical mastery in the purely external sense. At the end of the Greek age the 'virtuoso' appears and is paid large sums of money for his performance. The present age, in competition with the machine, leads this development to an extreme, and the question may well be asked: Where does the connection lie between the human being and his instrument now that it is external to him? Does this, his work, remain external, or is it none the less — even if unconsciously — connected with him in such a way that it is still possible to speak of an essential unity?

Broadly speaking, it can be said that at present there are three types of instrument: wind, stringed and percussion. There is also a threefold difference in the handling of them, requiring as they do the use of different parts of the physical organism by the performer; they also appeal to different soul-forces.

Wind instruments in every form, whether of wood or of metal, are connected with the breathing and the head of man. Lips, palate, tongue — in other words, the instruments of speech — are activated so as to guide and control the stream of breath coming from the chest, as the bearer of musical sound. The limbs, fingers and hands, are also necessary for the formation of sound by opening and closing the keyholes and stops. It may be said that the whole human being participates in producing the sound. The wind instruments have been regarded through the ages from the viewpoint of speech, and under certain circumstances the player even speaks into them. The significance of nasal breathing has already been mentioned, and also the melodic nature of the pan-pipes. The wind instruments may readily be called the bearers of melody.

The intimate connection of man to the wind instruments is apparent. Musically, the scale, the melodic line with its changing structure, is the bearer of thinking. It moves from note to note and one listens attentively, as if following the words in a sentence. The musical 'idea' that seeks to come to expression is revealed in it. The soul experience bears the character of a clearly visualized train of thought. Head, thought and wind instrument, borne by the stream of the breath, belong to the upper part of man, striving towards the light.

It is certainly not mere fancy when tubas and trombones, used from time immemorial on ritualistic occasions, are put in the hands of angels in Christian paintings. Horns and trumpets, with their more aggressive quality of tone, were used in war to fire the armies and give courage. One can also imagine that the subtle experience and the following through of the path of one's own breath in the air, into which the player sinks his tone, was at the basis of the various forms given to wind instruments — straight, round, curved, or intertwined.

It is quite different with the stringed instruments. They are conceived from quite another aspect — whether they are played with the bow, like the violin, plucked like harp, lyre, lute and zither, or struck like the mandolin or Russian balalaika. It is no longer the character of the word, of proclamation. The dialogue with which we are here concerned is intimate, a coming to terms with oneself, harkened and carried by the heart, by the middle region of man. The Greek spoke of the lyre of Apollo in connection with the 28 strands of the nerves running along the spine. They constitute the finest organ of hearing which has a direct relationship with the 'inner world system' — the solar plexus, through which subtle supersensible faculties may be developed. It seems as if, in softly plucking the strings or drawing the bow, there is something like the reminiscence of a divine hand or a heavenly breath of life shining like a star on the soul.

'The sinews of the morning star are stretched and will bestow life...' says an old Mexican inscription. The ancient singer Wäinemoinen in the *Kalevala* pleads for the golden hairs of a virgin as strings for his kantela. It was known that the hairs, rather like the nervous system, were there to capture the streaming light of the cosmos. Pictures of old harps often show the whole human figure, head and feet are connected with a wooden bow between which the strings are strung. The smaller instruments, but not the cello, are held to the heart. It is harmony, connected with the heart and with human feeling, that corresponds most nearly to the stringed instruments. If we pay attention to the way we listen to stringed instruments and to harmony in music, it is in no way similar to tracing a melody. In dreamlike surrender one is enveloped in a more consonant or more dissonant world of sound. A feeling for major or minor takes hold of the soul; and the heart, not the thinking, responds directly with yes or no, with pleasure or pain.

But it is out of the will, impelled by the fiery forces of the blood, that one grasps the rhythmic element with the instruments of percussion. Hold and let go is the actual life of hands as well as of feet, whether in stroking or striking, in walking or running. Music here is determined by touching and releasing, controlled and contained by alternating long and short notes, by the throb of the pulse, by the free play of the duration of sound and the breathing swing of the air in the beat. Rhythm is the element that actually bears music, releases it and holds it together, just as in the life of the world at large. In this connection it is interesting that all peoples, with the exception of Europeans, regard the drum as sacred. It was the instrument of kings. It had its own hut, tended by people of high rank. Large herds of sacred cattle grazed all round — sacrificial animals, from whose blood a paste was made which was spread on the drumskin. Even today, for important ceremonies, the rhythm of a percussion instrument goes right into the limbs enkindling purely vital forces, as everybody knows. It may well be said that one hears the elements of rhythm and beat with the limbs.

During the transition from medieval times to the present day keyboard instruments have gradually been developed, but we shall not enter into this here. Keyboard instruments all have something of a mechanical character and represent basically a combination of various instrumental principles. The element of air is no longer used directly, but enclosed in organ-pipes and supplied from outside. The strings of the piano, clavichord and harpsichord are not touched by the player's hand, but contacted mechanically. One can certainly say that something akin to the whole human being is represented, but intellectually. Most of them bear the mark of Western civilization and in this way are fully justified. But, on the whole, they are not akin to the other instruments, which have their special value and beauty of tone through their connection with various aspects of the human being. The keyboard instruments take the mutual emancipation of man and instrument a step further. It is something like a first beginning of the total exclusion of the purely human element that is becoming ever clearer today. Mechanical procedures are pushed in between the player and his music, and so-called objectivity is in danger of running into a process of death. The later parts of this work will try to show how this can be counteracted.

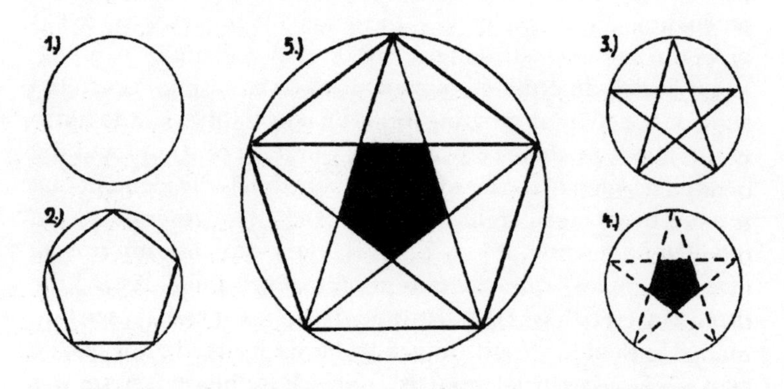

The geometrical diagrams above, seen singly and together, were given by Pythagoras to his pupils for meditation, so that they could learn from them the laws of man's being. Pythagoras spoke of the spirit-organ of the I revealed in the circle (1), of the soul-organs in the pentagon (2), of the life-organs in the pentagram (3), and the sense organs in the inner, smaller pentagon pointing downwards (4). A fourfold human being in the picture of the 5! For each one of these figures he also gave the numerical forces ruling in them: the one in the spirit-organ of the I, the three in the soul-organs of thinking, feeling and will, the seven in the laws of the flowing functions of life and the twelve in the total organization of the senses and the form-creating forces.

It was said of Pythagoras that he could hear the harmony of the spheres. This great initiate experienced universal cosmic laws. He consciously incorporated man as well as music into this cosmos. In his language, which speaks even today, clarifying the background of life in the light of spiritual science, the numbers mentioned point to the interplay between earth and universe. One, the I, that unique immortal part of man, unfolds in connection with the Earth. Three, the number of all the exalted forces active in body, soul and spirit — image of the divine trinity — corresponds to sun, moon and earth. Seven, connected with the functions of life, all processes of growth and the mysteries of reproduction, points to the world of the planets; and twelve to the form-giving forces of the zodiac. The second volume of this work will deal with these connections. These are reflected in music in the single note, in the threefold structure of harmony, in the heptaphony of the scale, and in the dodecaphony of the semitones in the octave.

In connection with instrumental music it may be as well to bring the following to mind. Without doubt, the abundance of percussion instruments links up with the small inner pentagon of the senses. It is determined by the twelve to lead, through beat, to feelings of firmness and solidity. The wind instruments on the other hand live in the realm of the seven scales and intervals. In moving up and down they give rise to the development of living thought as an artistic and structured organism. Stringed instruments bring life to this organism with every shade of feeling. They beautifully reveal the heart of man, and the triad of existence originating in the divine is proclaimed harmonically whether with or against, rejoicing or lamenting, in solo or in concert.

And what of the human voice? One asks: Is it not *the* instrument of all instruments, entrusted to the spirit-organ, the I. This is the wonder of it and its destiny, that it cannot be an instrument made to sound by external means. In accordance with the nature of the I it can only be revealed from within in self-creating activity.

It develops like the child. The child hears and learns from the surrounding world by imitating and trying out its strength. Every child shouts and hums, copies animal voices and the sounds of nature, practising zealously. It has small rattles, clappers, drums, pipes and flutes — the more primitive the better. All children give vent to their joy by shouting and singing together and they fit words and rhymes to their own little tunes. Is it really a wonder that they repeat the stages of an erstwhile childhood of humanity in this way? Millennia pass by again, ever anew, in the development of each one of us.

Until — just as in ancient Greece — the awakening to the I brings, or should bring, a new consciousness: love and enthusiasm, a new ear for beauty, for the demands of music as such. Something akin to a moral feeling of responsibility arises. The I begins to speak softly. Then the influence from outside ceases, even the unconscious effect of world-music. Music gradually starts to become new, morally determined, especially for people of today, who no longer sing and play out of a bubbling and unconscious vitality, but enter with music into a sphere of beauty and love in which a loftier moral determination prevails. Every young person with healthy feelings sets foot on the path of musical education with this wish and knows of these ideals. Those who want to sing are normally filled with a feverish anticipation that they will one day bestow on humanity both their song and their speech.

But so many are shipwrecked by the reefs and dangers of present-day thinking. There was mention of the human voice as the instrument of the I, the spirit-organ. The mentality of our age is attuned to the visible world of the senses, to the physical and material. We cannot enter here into the problems of voice production; that is the province of qualified persons. Thousands of gifted singers give up daily because of inner catastrophe. They founder because it is thought that even voice production must start from the physical. Training consists in the placement of the voice, in breathing exercises, singing into a mask, working on bodily resonances, working with tongue, teeth and lips. Hearing, according to a professional, is disturbing. There is virtually no talk of musical matters. The present day regards it as a kind of ideal to be objective, but in this case it thinks and behaves as unobjectively as is possible. What is 'objective' in the actual meaning of the word? It is allowing oneself to be determined by the nature of the object. The object in this case is the human voice and the formation of tone. Therefore, voice production should be guided by the knowledge of the nature of musical sound.

In dealing with the over- and undertones, it was shown how

a qualitative, objective hearing can lead to the very essentials. Basically speaking, the externally audible note with the series of sympathetically rising overtones goes through a kind of dematerialization in the fourth, fifth and sixth octaves. It dissolves into space, expands into that infinite and unlimited weaving of the world of light, in which it has its actual existence. If taken seriously a phenomenon such as this can, from the very beginning, lead the attention of the singer away from the bodily process in the larynx to what happens and is experienced in space. But that was the very sphere from which the spiritual event of the counter-series started. The note, stemming from those regions, is of its very nature to be sought inwardly, in soul, and grasped inwardly. External and audible phonetics in the larynx and inner hearing in the soul interlink one with the other. They are both carried by spiritual activity rather than by physical processes. Larynx and ear are one organ, simultaneously producing sound and listening to it. They create that polarity on the basis of which a sound really felt and formed can flower and take effect. This is the wholeness of attitude of which we shall speak again and again in succeeding chapters.

But there is one thing more. The singer today is dealing with musical sound as well as with sounds of speech. Both are of a spiritual nature; that means, for those hearing qualitatively, they work as bearers of moral forces conveyed through the senses. They form the soul of man, and not only that. The example of the Chladni sound figures, as well as the Chinese legend mentioned at the end of the third chapter, shows that this power of formation goes deep into the physical. In pursuing a really objective development of the voice it would be a case of hearing and experiencing the phenomena of music and speech in their spiritual being and practising them repeatedly, following up the effect they have, so that the whole organism of the singer is formed by them. It would be a forming — and that is the important difference in method — corresponding to the very nature of the I, the nature of the voice, of music and speech, working from the spiritual into the physical. It is a method that does not start with an injurious bodily training. The sounds of speech, as cosmic forces, mould the speech organs. Musical sounds give the specific colouring, give breadth and mobility.

In keeping with development from the spiritual into the

physical, and not the other way round, the means of expanding the human voice must be that of a conscious, active and creative spiritualization of matter, just as the I itself gradually lays hold on the body out of spiritual spheres so as to reveal its supersensible powers and tasks in life. On this path a voice can never be destroyed. On the contrary, the work makes the whole human being healthy; it changes his countenance and his nature. People who have never sung and think they are unmusical discover to their own amazement that they have a beautiful voice. They discover they are spiritual in this destructive, demonic, perilous and materialistic age. It is one of the most important tasks of our time to restore with spiritual forces this noble and most essential organ, faced as it is with obvious destruction. Truly, it is the question of a new humanity, of a new spiritual direction, that opens up here.

In concluding this part on the nature of music, let us glance at the connection with its sister-arts. We see on the one hand the visual arts — architecture, sculpture and painting — and on the other hand the art of music, poetry and the arts of movement: a plastic principle in space and a musical one in time. What is their relationship to each other? Novalis writes in his *Fragments* some very interesting and illuminating words:

> Whosoever sees everything spatially, with figuration, sculpturally, his soul is musical; forms appear through unconscious vibration. Whoever sees musical sound, movements, etc. within himself, his soul is plastic, for the variety of sounds and movements only arises through figuration.

Going more deeply into these trains of thought, it may be observed that when looking at a building one is especially sensitive to symmetry, harmony and balance. The soaring, supporting pillars, the weight of the sheltering roof, the crossbeams or parallels, the perspectives and divisions of space — they all bring us into powerful movement, in so far as we try to experience them inwardly and consciously. In following the forms and the lines and reacting musically, one discovers that the effect of this architectural work is the opposite of its solid nature. The soul reacts musically in that it dissolves the solid structure, or 'frozen music', as Goethe called it. It becomes one with the musical soul of the artist, moving with it in an imitative way.

Something similar occurs in the realm of music. It has been shown that musical sound with the whole world of its partials, its overtones and their reflection, is a harmonic structure in itself. The intervals and the sympathetic tones are not arbitrary, but follow a definite law. One feels the 'plastic' soul expressed in these formations of sound, and the listener reacts accordingly. The spirit of language expresses it directly by saying, after a musical experience: 'I feel edified, sound'. In the course of music man experiences sculptural, forming forces, which lay hold on him, create him anew and change him. The statements regarding the development of the vocal organism, guided by qualitative hearing, gave expression to this. All the differentiations — the whole streaming diversity of sound — flow ultimately into the calm of an inner, comprehensive, musical and sculptural power of soul, which through its spirituality reveals formation and figuration in the higher sense.

In considering the words of Novalis again, it becomes clear — if one would penetrate knowingly into the course of events — that there is always a polarity of forces. Man is a being predisposed to totality. This totality is his divine heritage. The task that lies ahead of him is to make the 'revealed mysteries' of his microcosm consciously his own. They worked unconsciously in times gone by. The future needs the awakened ego-being of man, that creates knowingly out of its own centre of morality and is able to endow humanity with the true reflection of archetypal purity.

PART TWO

THE TRANSFORMATION OF HEARING

Based on indications given in
Goethe's Theory of Musical Sound

Chapter One

THE NATURE OF HEARING

People often ask whether our contemporaries are musical. Before answering this, we must ask another question: What, or who is musical? Usually it is considered to be anyone who can sing accurately and has a good ear for pitch. If, when a note is sounded, a person can immediately say that it is C, or E, or whatever, he is considered to be musical. O joy and pride if, over and above this, he has the gift of absolute pitch! On the other hand, if children sing out of tune they are immediately branded as unmusical. Usually it is not considered necessary to let them take part in the making of music.

Now there are many false deductions in such judgements, though they seem to be universally made. In fact there are no truly unmusical people, that is, those to whom the world of music is completely closed or disagreeable. It may be that an illness or an apparent malformation of soul due to destiny brings about cramp or mental disturbance. But, in so far as man is a microcosm, he must indeed reflect the proportions and laws of the universe. But these are musical in an all-embracing sense. So, if a person is branded as unmusical and is prevented from taking part in the making of music, he is as if cut off from the resounding origin of his own being. It is not surprising that in almost all such cases inferiority complexes and illnesses arise in the course of development.

Moreover, when children sing incorrectly, something else must be taken into account. What we call absolute pitch today has been based for hundreds of years on the tuning by equal temperament of the Western tonal system. This took over from the so-called true intonation which was in use up to the time of Bach. But what has happened?

Depending on its function as interval from a given keynote, every note changes its pitch slightly according to the interval. The relationship in the interval of the prime is 1:1, in the interval of the second 8:9, in the third 4:5, the fourth 3:4, the fifth 2:3, the sixth 3:5, the seventh 8:15 and in the octave 1:2. When the medieval tonal system developed into the uniformity of the major/minor system, there were seven or more different scales, but then afterwards only two basic forms were recognized and were transposed with modifications of sharps and flats; the notes, also, had to develop a stable relationship with one another, so an average of all the differences was taken and the octave was divided into twelve equal semitones. This was known as 'well-tempering'. In reality, all the intervals except the octave became slightly out of tune. What is today referred to as absolute pitch is incorrect by name. When children, and even adults, have difficulty in singing in tune in the tempered sense, this is due in many cases to a subtle musical sense, which agrees in a free and uninhibited way with an inner absolute pitch. If we meet children, and even grown-ups, who have difficulty in singing in tune in the tempered sense, we often find they are more musical, more free and uninhibited in inner regions of absolute pitch. They mostly have a fluctuating soul-nature and need more time to find their way into arbitrary musical relationships rooted in intellectuality. But, on the other hand, these are people who have a deep, intense, qualitative experience of music. As children they cannot understand why their companions do not appreciate their singing, and through all too harsh rebuffs and prohibitions they often receive a shock which affects the whole of their lives. For in the deepest recesses of their being they are truly musical people. Time and loving guidance enable them to waken unconstrainedly into the tempered sounds.

An equally interesting phenomenon is apparent in those of the opposite kind, who are gifted with absolute hearing in the modern sense. They are generally admired and are favoured with all the advantages of a musical education. When people said that Pythagoras could still hear the music of the spheres, they meant that he still experienced numbers, concepts and sounds with the soul; not as we do now externally and intellectually with the brain. His experiences were of living quality, not mere quantity, as at the present time. 'Musical sound is vibrating number' was the answer, suitable for the time, given by a renowned leading musical personality to the question: 'What is musical sound?'. Only the husk is comprehended in this definition. The kernel is no longer considered essential. And what is called absolute pitch is the innate capacity, inherited through the centuries, of grasping with infallible certainty only the husk. It is increasingly difficult for such people to have a real experience, that is, to hear with the soul. To characterize it with a remark of Goethe's, music remains for them 'suspended in the ear', but it enables them to acquire, as a result of their special training, a definite mastery of above-average musical demands and techniques. Certainly there are also exceptions, and one often hears of deeply gifted natures among them, who suffer just because of this hearing and feel it as a distressing restriction. In this connection we do not refer to exceptions such as Bach and Mozart. Men of genius, because of the mission they have to fulfil, bring with them through destiny an exceptional ear. This is connected with the law of selection which governs genius. Richard Wagner, for example, did not outwardly have such a very good ear. He always needed a piano in order to hear the effects of his music. By destiny, however, his inner, cosmic fire of experience was that much deeper and more refined. The same was said of Brahms. And what about Beethoven, who poured out his last works, filled with spirit, in a state of deafness — that is to say, without any ordinary hearing?

And so the introductory question: 'What, or who is musical?' cannot be unequivocally answered, either in one way or the other. But it can be deduced from these facts, which everyone concerned with musical activity must encounter, that there are two different kinds of hearing, an inner and an outer. It was this which induced Goethe in his *Theory of Musical Sound* to introduce the section which deals with the organic side of hearing in the following way:

> In that the world of musical sound is revealed out of and by man himself, and determines through the senses moral enthusiasm and a cultivation of the inner and outer sense.

This would mean, in a Goethean sense, that a twofold hearing is needed — qualitative and quantitative. The qualitative will need more fostering today, because at present the outer ear is considered the only measure. It is a phenomenon similar to that of the overtones and the complementary series.

In the following studies on the transformation of hearing, we must of necessity probe the very depths and the canons of music if we are to discover musical experience from the qualitative aspect. We must start with the external tonal sense, for it is this which our contemporaries generally bring with them as musicianship. A recent statistical investigation has proved that 95 per cent of all school children are musical. But what will come of this if, through outer ambition and striving and exaggeration of this one aspect, the possibility of true inner experience and the capacity of the soul for knowledge is ruined and dies?

What is the starting point for the cultivation of qualitative hearing? Beginning as far as possible with an unprejudiced attitude towards a basic musical phenomenon — a single note, an interval, a harmony or what one will, it is a question primarily of observing accurately and calmly what is heard, and taking stock of the moral influence of this sense impression on the soul. But our contemporaries cannot take such a living hearing for granted. The first observation to be made is that one stands in one's own way. It is a question of getting rid of oneself, and that means it is a question of the will to will nothing, to bring about an absolute inner emptiness and quietude. And this is difficult. It becomes an almost continuous struggle at a thousand gateways of the soul both manifest and concealed, both great and small, against whims and surprises, against incursions by undesired memories, by demons of doubt, wishes, intolerance and so on. It is these that are mostly present. They appear in the guise of so-called 'goodwill'. Moreover, patience is a power which life does not allow. It is banished from childhood on. 'Hurry! Hurry! Hurry!' 'Time is money!' 'Be finished in time.' These are guiding principles which threaten everyone almost like a whiplash. But the stream of blessing of a purely musical experience in whatever form, whether in modesty or perfection, is a gift by the grace of God. At this point the words of Christian Morgenstern come to mind:

> Patience, thou tremendous word,
> whoever grasps and comprehends thee,
> henceforth he grasps, and comprehends
> what God creates, what Godhead ripens.

Nowadays everyone suffers from the illness which is the death of all true musical values, from the weary business of 'I have no time!'. In general, people are compelled to spend themselves under the utmost stress in activity directed outwards, and all too soon they reach exhaustion. If someone in such an age and under such conditions is required to be quite still and calm, to will nothing at all, to have no opinions, to know and remember nothing, but only to listen, perhaps to one single sound, quite simply as if hearing it for the first time, then it is conceivable that this proves difficult. To begin with, there arises uncomprehending, contemptuous laughter; the listener even becomes nervous. And this state lasts a long time, until the inner relaxation is achieved without which qualitative hearing cannot be attained. And this inner peace and stillness must be maintained as a basic mood of soul. It is not enough to experience it only once and then to believe one knows what is meant. On the contrary, the first truly creative work of man upon himself begins here. This basic attitude is not something which one has, but it must continually be acquired anew by a free effort of will.

In this stillness we make the amazing discovery that previously, in spite of all supposed musicality, we have not been listening correctly. External bustle, continuously spurring on to action, seems to close the inner ear instead of opening it. Two different people move through a landscape. One treats it as a long-distance run. He takes in little or nothing of the beauty and the life of the surrounding world. Blind and deaf, with closed senses, he runs through the countryside. For him the world is a 'tract of land'. But the other goes quietly, with open senses, listening, watching, breathing. To him every blossom, the outline of every hill, every breath of air, speaks of the wonder of life, of the superabundance of a world filled with wisdom. Truth, beauty and goodness will be the gifts with which he is blessed. The world thanks him for his quiet listening. It well may thank him because he listens with his soul. Here it will also be noted that only inner quietness creates the possibility for true hearing. A preliminary warmth-giving stream of deep devotion spreads and is saturated with that awe and wonder which is the beginning of all true knowledge. The soul opens like a chalice.

But we ourselves do not form this chalice. The musical sound begins to give it shape. It gives it contours, stretches it, makes it firm or loosens it, fills it with oppressing weight, or begins to shine through it, to cool or to warm it until we are truly what we hear. And now for the first time, we begin not only to listen to music with the usual feelings, but to be music through the heart-forces of self-dedication. In this sense, then, we may speak of a truly living hearing. For here a musical occurrence, whether modest or all-embracing, is inwardly recreated. Man creates himself anew. It is a self-creative activity in which he lives musically.

At this stage a question arises which the individual can answer only through experience: Has the fruit of such an exercise an objective, universal validity? Seemingly, we are in the midst of absolute subjectivity. But in such measure as one succeeds through these exercises in selfless stillness and dedicated listening in being 'rid of oneself' in the truest sense of the word, does one develop towards cosmic man, become bearer of an objective consciousness beyond the personal — chalice and mouthpiece for the laws of the universe. The musical elements acquired through living hearing become letters, sounds, out of which one learns in all objectivity to decipher and to understand the first germinal words of a macrocosmic relationship. That is why it is so important to start this training from the pure, basic phenomena. They are the only artistic factors by means of which, when selflessly experienced, we can find our way back to the objective spirituality of our material. These elements are withdrawn from the wilfulness of man; they prepare his artistic activity through their straightforward purity. Every attempt to achieve objectivity will have to begin by regaining the material as such, with its own spiritual will. In this way one can be freed from the realm of subjective 'comprehension'. Certainly one's own will-nature is activated to gain inner concentrated stillness; certainly one's feeling-nature is placed without reservation into selfless surrender; certainly one knows oneself to be creative in life springing from the ego. One watches this in order to unite it with the great stream of cosmic events, for the powerful reality of which the art of music has always been the special expression. Everything depends on fitting it out of a renewed consciousness into the great thought-relationships of the world, into the music of the spheres.

Here the work in connection with the third requirement begins to be of the greatest importance; that is to say, the bringing clearly to consciousness of the inner experiences and observations made while listening, so that they form a conceptual image. If this does not happen, the experiences easily sink back again into the impenetrable dream-region of the soul, which is never quite comprehensible, its sensations and feelings surging up and down, its moods, memory-pictures and so on coming and going involuntarily. But the attentive attitude of the ego in qualitative listening demands a clear and active pursuit of what actually happens inwardly. This is not to be confused in any way with the activity of speculative and abstract 'thinking about' the matter. It is simply a characterizing of what is observed, what is heard. The phenomena themselves gradually speak within man's inner being, and his task is related more and more to the understanding of this, their language, to learning by listening to the ideal content of their words. Only in this way does the experience become one's own possession. Only then can it be incorporated, imbued with thinking, into the region of objective and living knowledge.

The soul-life of man falls in a threefold way into will, feeling and thinking. Three times must he lay hold on himself and begin to purify himself. There are three starting points if he wishes to find his place creatively in music in a manner appropriate to the spirit of his time — an awe-filled quietness, a selfless dedication and a knowing awareness. The ego wishing to give utterance is transformed inwardly into the instrument of heavenly man, so that it can offer itself in purity to become mediator of the deepest harmonies, melodies and rhythms sounding as expression of its divine origin.

It is evident from what has been stated that we are concerned with enhancing capacities of soul and that this is not easy. Goethe, too, was clear about the demands he made in his studies of archetypal phenomena. In a conversation with Eckerman, he said:

> To comprehend a simple archetypal phenomenon, to understand it in all its high significance and to work with it, requires a productive spirit, which must be able to cast a penetrating glance over many things; and this ability is an unusual gift, found only among exceptional people. And that is not all. For just as a person of genius who knows all the rules is not yet a painter, but must come to this through constant practice, so it is not enough that the student of painting knows the rules and works in the right spirit, but he must also set himself to work continually with each single, often very mysterious phenomenon with its derivations and combinations. We all know quite well that the colour green originates through a mixing of yellow and blue; but when someone says that he comprehends the green of the rainbow, or the green of foliage, or the green of sea-water, this demands such a many-sided penetration of the realm of colour and, arising out of it, such a depth of insight, that until now hardly anyone has succeeded in attaining it.

In the sphere of music we must pursue these studies continually.

It is not enough to test occasionally, just by the way, one thing or another qualitatively, but training must build a foundation for every musical activity and keep pace with it. It is not a case of giving an airing to some special fancy. The value of this work goes further and is of the greatest importance even beyond the bounds of pure music. The present age, more than a century and a half after Goethe's conversation, has an even more urgent need of the 'productive spirit', which Goethe finds so rarely in his contemporaries, and of the 'depth of insight' into archetypal phenomena. This is worthwhile not only for 'exceptional' people but, in general, for those active in any art. A brief glance at the present time will help towards an understanding of this. For what is the preponderant feature of the spirit of our age, determined as it is by technology?

Because mechanization and automation tend to produce ever more refined machinery for calculating and thinking as a substitute for time-consuming and monotonous mental work, we are becoming detached in increasing numbers from work in the traditional sense. Through this man has at his disposal for personal development the forces which formerly were needed for manual labour, if he knows how to use them. But the tribute which the 'spirit of technology' demands in return for this material relief is the exposure of man to the danger of being drawn, as the 'attendant of the machine', into a mechanization and automation hostile to life. For example, in the sphere of music, which is the matter under consideration here, behind wonderful electro-magnetic constructions and electro-acoustical instruments of different kinds, lurk monstrous dangers to the practical musician, in the form of preservation, convenience, inactivity and insensitivity. The abuse of possibilities not only lays waste individual forces, as experience shows, but also leads only too often, especially in the case of the young, to physiological and psychological injuries.

The consequences of these dangers has not yet been properly assessed for the whole feel of life, for all normal progress and for health. Nevertheless, up to a point an antidote can be offered by the work suggested here. For what is brought about through these new activities from a general human point of view? The awakening, the practical proof and the enhancement of new, profounder and stronger soul forces! The work done with the aid of basic objective phenomena awakens the human archetype. These new powers can see right through the dangers rising out of the earthly, and can counteract them consciously. The continuing appeal, by means of these exercises, to man's moral and creative centre and for the realization of a higher ego, calls forth a new human kingdom whose power everyone can experience if he himself sets out on the path. Were these not the kind of people for whom Goethe longed — creative, productive human beings with deep insight, well above the commonplace?

What about hearing? What is musical? These were the questions with which we began this chapter. Our investigation has shown that the difficulty, or in other words, the one-sidedness of hearing and of musicianship arises as a result of the spirit of the times, from a materialistic, passive, automatic point of view which needs to be remedied. Once again it is Goethe who points out, in the introduction to his *Theory of Musical Sound*, the remedy with a few words on the ear. Because of the spirit-soul-body trinity of man, he demands in the first place a moral enthusiasm for the spirit enkindled by the senses. This does not mean an ardour which soon burns itself out, but the thrusting open of a door to a deep, light-filled layer of being, out of which new inspiration flows into the soul. The formula 'a cultivation of the inner sense of hearing', along with the 'outer sense of hearing', indicates that we are dealing with a method of practice which can also be grasped by the body in its audibly sounding environment.

In the case of Goethe, who constructed his words and sentences with utmost care, it is important not to skim over them lightly, but to pay attention to them. For example, it is a matter of method that he builds up the structure from the spiritual, in order to lead the way down through the soul-world into the earthly. He uses the same principle of training as was suggested for the development of the voice and which must be used in all things musical. In his *Theory of Colour* he puts at the beginning the question of the conditions under which the colours originate against various bodies, and only gradually penetrates to the physiological and, finally, soul relationships between man and colour. In the study of musical sound he begins straight away with man himself and points unmistakably to the necessity of a training, of a transformation, developing a new spiritual sense. In this connection Goethe wrote to Zelter, when he sent him his *Theory of Musical Sound*, which he refers to as 'tables', in October, 1826:

> You see the gravity of the manner in which I have sought to outline this immense realm, at least for the purposes of knowledge. Each chapter, each paragraph points to something weighty; the method of presentation may be allowed to stand. It was chosen by me because I thought it resembled the form of my 'Theory of Colour'. I had planned many another and laid them aside because of the tempo of life.

And we can see from a further letter to Zelter written almost three years later, on May 17th 1829, how he was working continually on this material:

> I enjoy my tabulation as a certainly naked but well-articulated skeleton, which only the genuine artist may clothe with flesh and skin, give to it inner organs and introduce it into life through practice and thinking. By this means I survey in a wonderful way a region which at one time I could not even enjoy, let alone think about with pleasure.

What, then, of hearing, one may finally ask? In the duality of a newly-acquired inner and outer sense it is to be elevated within man, to give back to him a conscious union with the world of his origin, with the harmony of the spheres. A person practising this would be truly musical. Through him, 'musicianship' would reveal the world-uniting, world-transforming element existing between the realm of the spirit and the realm of the senses — the central force, the heart-force of the sun animating all things, ennobling man and all humanity.

Chapter Two

AT THE BEGINNING...

At the beginning of all research it is important to find the right, that is, the objectively applicable starting point. This ensures that it fits into the general course of musical evolution and also forms a positive contribution to present-day spiritual requirements. In the previous chapter it was pointed out that the present musical situation requires a schooling in qualitative hearing starting from the pure, basic phenomenon — it needs to acquire anew the material of music in the appropriate spirit. Out of the abundance of these basic elements it is best to start with what appears to be the simplest. That is the single note. This does not mean that every other musical sphere will not be explored step by step. How far this starting point corresponds to the spirit of the age, which strives so strenuously for objectivity, may be gathered from the fact that every creative personality in the musical life of modern times — Bartók, Hindemith, Stravinsky, Schoenberg, Hauer, Messiaen and others — begins by sorting out his 'material', by arranging it and assembling it methodically so as to create an individual system. This indicates that music has become the language of the individual ego. The question is, by which part of this ego-being — that related to the earthly or that related to the spirit — will the onward path be determined?

In any case, the starting point for the present work is the single note. This was recognized in connection with the Pythagorean pentagon and pentagram within the circle as musically representing the ego.

But we touch here on a sphere that many people find difficult to understand. The first objection made, with apparent justification, is that the nature of music can be grasped only in the relationship between the notes. The interval from one note to another is seen as the primary element. Without wishing to attack the accuracy of this view, the commentary concerning the partials and their complementary series in the first part of this book should have shown that an interval also lives in the single note, as a plant within the seed. Both belong inseparably together, the one depending upon and finding fulfilment in the other. Only since the awakening of the ego in Greek times has man learnt to find and control the relationship of his destiny to the environment. The words 'Man, know thyself' direct his knowledge inwards to the singularity of the self and likewise the single note is of prime importance to music bearing the impress of the ego. Only through listening to the character of its inner life and what pertains to it, that is, to the life within the single note and not being determined by neighbouring notes, will inspiration be found to new paths, new laws, and new challenges. Individual examples and exercises will be given in the second volume of this work. All that needs to be said here is that each phenomenon gives a quite distinct experience. What could be more natural than to make these experiences — which can progress through living hearing into the dramatic element, but carried by the laws of their own nature — the basis of musical composition, whether it is cast in a smaller or larger mould, whether slight or profound? Not out of an arbitrary subjective mood, but music flowing as inspiration out of itself! Some indication has been given that instead of the so-called 'theoretical' basis of music, we shall find new rules and directives — sometimes seemingly revolutionary, but heard out of one's own objective listening to the phenomenon. This matter will be explored later.

And now the question arises: With which note is it best to begin the task of listening? It is important, in the light of experience, not to set to work arbitrarily. The place must be found from which an organic development is ensured. It is good to choose a starting point that is objective and universally valid. This is provided in the keynote of our musical system, in the note C.

The keynote of an epoch is no accident, even if it were to be explained away superficially. An age borne by the mentality of those living in it has a generally approved note which is regarded as its keynote. This points to the fact that special qualities belong to this note, corresponding in general to the existing or evolving state of consciousness in people of that particular age. So the study of phenomena is built up from this note, quite objectively, into the whole soul and spirit configuration of the prevailing cultural period, disregarding personal preference for this or that sphere of sound — a preference which may emerge during the course of study, but which will then rest on the right basis.

Since this keynote C sounds in at least seven different octaves, it is important to decide with which of these to begin, and we find it is best with the C known as middle C.

Regardless of the fact that it is more difficult to hear distinctly in very low or very high regions of pitch, to which many people nowadays cannot find access, we can say that this C is a significant threshold within our tonal system. In this connection we may refer to the details concerning the partials and the complementary series in the second and third chapters of the first part of this book. There it was said of this C when reaching the third octave of overtones: 'The human being grasps his earthly ego in conscious affirmation. The individual becomes a person.' In discussing the descending series it was said of this same C that with it 'the turning and awakening to self begins'. In the relationship between the two series this C is the crossing point, and from here the process of reversal between inner and outer begins. The position of the ego between two worlds and the directing of its life between its own inner being and that of the external world appears in the series of thirds, unfolding first in an upward and then in a downward direction. The dominant harmonies developing out of them find their resolution in both instances in the opposite series. The whole event is as if hinged on this middle C or, better still, as if anchored in it. What, then, would be more appropriate than to musically cast anchor here?

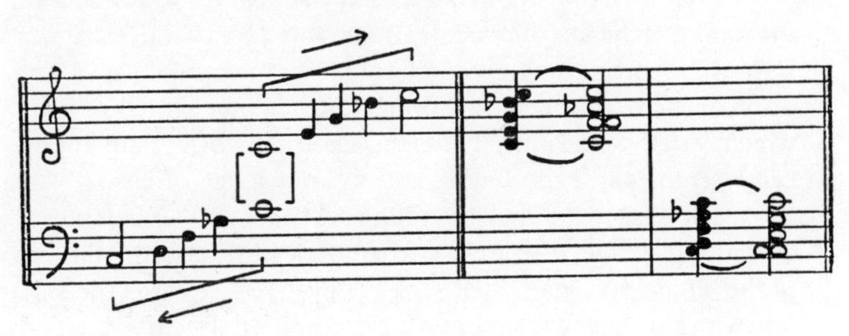

We still have to ask which instrument is the most suitable for the study of hearing. It must be one that is as objective as possible. It goes without saying that the exercises may be carried out on every instrument. However, it should be evident that a percussion instrument, a violin, or a flute are not so suitable, for with these instruments there is always the danger of introducing the personality of the player. The note should be as neutral as possible, detached from the player. The piano renders good service and is nearly always available. Most people are not so very sensitive to differences of touch and expression with this instrument and it is the one most likely to give an impersonal dry tone. It is very important not to influence or manipulate the feelings of the listener in any way. The note should be neither too loud nor too soft. A lyre from the workshop of Lothar Gärtner, (Constance or Quésain, Eckwälden) or possibly a lute may be suitable, but not instruments such as the zither, as their tone is too metallic. The gently struck strings of the lyre give a full and beautiful sound, which rings in space and envelops the listener, and enables him to listen in peace. It is this quiet following up of a sound as it fades away and attention to the feeling it leaves behind which is of special value. It follows that the note should not be struck again too quickly. It is essential that the note really sounds acoustically in space. The study must always begin with what is physically audible. The dutiful observation of all these requirements gives a healthy basis for further studies. With this in mind it is clear that a mere mental exercise would be of no value. These exercises should be carried out with the same love and precision with which Goethe pursued his observations on the archetypal plant in Nature. The looking, or in this case the listening, usually opens up a new sense.

Another question is often asked at the beginning: What about the tuning of the instrument? The main thing is that the instrument should be properly tuned in equal temperament. It is fully justifiable to question in this connection whether a tonal system in which, strictly speaking, all intervals except the octave are impure, can lead to valid experiences and to knowledge of lasting value as was indicated in the beginning of the previous chapter. Is everything deduced from it perhaps not also false? In the case of the single note its partial series is pure. But what is the situation with all the other elements of the tempered system — intervals, harmonies, scales and so on? One should remember that man is made to macrocosmic measure. And so in his feeling he unconsciously corrects, through his ego, everything he hears according to this heavenly norm. Certainly, the extent of this adjustment is restricted and this is perceptible in qualitative listening. We should also state here that as man's consciousness changes the pitch alters. Bach's well-known lower C and C major is associated with this fact. Two or three hundred years ago, the experience of C laid hold on man more deeply, more in the heart. But today, everything slips into the intellect and in this tension draws the pitch up with it. In experiencing the nature of a note, say C, it is certainly the same for everyone in the present cultural period. Its level of pitch, however, can change.

After these preliminaries we can turn to the first note to be considered, the middle C, taken purely from the acoustical aspect. What remains after taking away all the outer trappings, such as the sound of the instrument, the strength of the tone, tempo, expression and so on? In purely acoustic, quantitative form the sound as such remains, together with a faint sounding of the octave and the fifth. We meet an indication of the overtones which, however, at this level of pitch cannot unfold comprehensively and distinctly for the human ear. None the less they can be traced. This represents the physical body of the sound, an organism built according to rule, with a wonderful structure that can be pondered on ever anew.

Pythagoras made use only of intervals resulting from the relationships of the first three numbers: 1,2 and 3. To him they signified the rule of the Divine Trinity, designated in Christianity as the principles of Father, Son and Holy Spirit. He established musical sound within the being of the Godhead. The number 4, which falls on middle C, was the number of man and bore for him a great mystery. It was at the same time the number of the earthly, of the square and the cross. As such, it pointed directly to the Mystery of Golgotha. Arising out of the number of the Logos, the 2, it indicated man, and within the whole world of numbers was the only one which by addition and multiplication brought the same result: 2 + 2 is the same as 2 x 2, that is, 4.

Not until the Middle Ages, when humanity had acquired the inner maturity of soul for experiencing the consonance of the third, could the next number in the partial series, the 5, be introduced. It indicates that every expansion of the tonal system basically implies the further refinement of man's consciousness. Leibnitz, in connection with his much quoted remark concerning music as an 'unconscious counting exercise of the soul', points out:

> It is not out of the question that elsewhere living beings exist which possess higher musical sensations than we do, and find joy in musical proportions which do not say so much to us. We do not count above five in music.

But:

> Were a more comprehensive organism bestowed upon us, we could advance to the number seven. And I am of the opinion that there are indeed some such organisms.

That we have drawn near to this time is shown by the fact that the minor seventh, as well as the major second, has now been declared a consonance. But before the various aspects of this are discussed the question arises: What is the deeper significance of the number 5, the number of the interval of a third? What great experience was made manifest in this number? It was the secret of unending division.

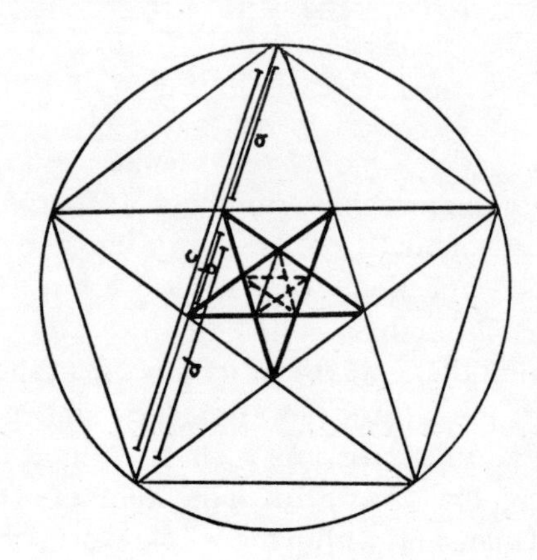

It was the certainty that 'to divide' need not mean 'to destroy', but that in small as well as in great divisions, the law of the whole is revealed. The well-known A:B as C:D in the above diagram is relevant here. The pentagon reappears with its pentagram, continuing into the infinite inwards as well as outwards. The quotation from Leibnitz speaks profoundly out of the mentality of that time of all that the new experience of the third indicates — the determining of the major/minor experience. That is to say, the individual soul becomes the content of music. The triad is a sound-picture of man in his trinity of body, soul and spirit, in which the soul, alternating between inner and outer, microcosm and macrocosm, could express in musical sound the relationship between the small and the large, the part and the whole, as the profoundest law of man's own being. For the image of man still bore the imprint of the divine. This true nature of the triad should not be seen as a difference in size calculated from a keynote, as it was thought to be later. Until the sixteenth century it was said that thirds were different only according to their position.

It is the same principle as that in the relationship between the overtones and the descending series. The secret of the golden section in music is also connected with this divine proportion, which in the approximate values of the major sixths — G:E is as 3:5, E:C is as 5:8, and C:A is as 8:13 — seems to go along with this. This is mentioned to show another essential part of the background of the century-old predominance of the experience of the third.

The next prime numbers — 7, 11 and 13 — belong to the group for which Leibnitz demanded a 'more comprehensive organism', and with which, in the Goethean sense, we cannot come to a 'decisive experiment'. They give unusual fractions. It is of value to quote part of a letter from Goethe to Zelter written in the year 1808. It not only throws light on his deep relationship to music, but points to facts which obstruct penetration into spiritual connections. He writes:

> Man in himself, in so far as he makes use of his senses, is the greatest and most accurate physical apparatus that exists. The greatest evil of more recent physics is that experiments have been separated, as it were, from man, and that a knowledge of nature is acquired only through man-made instruments; even what can be achieved is restricted and proven through them. It is the same with calculation. Much is true that we cannot account for, just as there is much that does not admit of being brought to a decisive experiment.

Should this not perhaps warn us to be especially attentive? Are these intervals or their approximate forms special moments, those upon which the future depends? Where earthly calculation does not tally the spirit sounds through. And so it must be admitted that these intervals with the numbers 7, 11 and 13 are especially important today. The eleventh tone lays hold of the notorious tritones, C to F sharp in the overtones and C to G flat in the descending series. This polarity of sound, charged with tension, is the harmony which corresponds to the soul-situation of present-day man. It is therefore not surprising that it plays a leading role. It will probably not be very long before it is proclaimed a consonance. And through the thirteenth tone, A flat, in its relationship to the C above middle C, 8:13 — an interval approximating to the golden section — completely new constellations of sound may be disclosed in the not too distant future. Surely Leibnitz's progress to 'higher musical sensations' may then be fulfilled. And in view of the whole course of evolution is one not entitled to assume such a fact? Is the younger generation in particular not already on the way?

Let us ask, before closing this chapter, what we hear when a single note is played, detached completely from every other phenomenon. What, in a purely acoustical sense, does one hear as the essential nature of the note? The answer of the musical celebrity already mentioned runs: Its vibrational number, its relationship in pitch to other notes, whether these are played with it or not. The neutral, central position of the middle C, as it is neither high nor low, leaves the soul in a state of equilibrium. It lays no stress upon the feelings, the will or the thinking, but creates an expectant feeling of being as yet nothing. And it is correct to say that this note is only a building stone, receiving its true meaning and value only through the context into which it is inserted. In itself it is as good as nothing.

Nevertheless, it is the expression of a fixed numerical value. And if, without sinking into nebulous mysticism, one succeeds in freeing this basically essential world of number from dead abstraction through musical sound, then it can acquire a certain transparency. It can point towards a qualitative background of a purely musical kind. One draws near to that 'arithmetical exercise of the unconsciously counting spirit' which is music according to Leibnitz, and also according to the Pythagorean experience. The first tiny opening into an inner world is seen, for:

> Even if the soul counts imperceptibly it becomes aware of the effect of the imperceptible counting, either in feelings of comfort through consonance, or discomfort through dissonance.

But it comes as a matter of course, that such feelings lead over to the realization of what a musical sound, whether experienced instrumentally or vocally, in fact is. It is the direct revelation of the creative power in man, the power of the word in the living sphere of music, which is his and his alone, and arises from his own spiritual faculties. It proclaims ever anew the origin of all existence.

Chapter Three

THE NEXT STEP

As this work is based on Goethe's method of observation it is essential to refer to his indications and to render these accessible to the needs of the present day. It is important to recall that through the spiritual insight of Rudolf Steiner, Goethe's indications have not only found support and confirmation, but also show the way for further investigation.

In his observations on the ear Goethe distinguishes five stages which he gives as headings. Firstly:

> Susceptibility of the ear. Apparent passivity and absence of interest of the same. Indifference.

The attempt has been made to produce neutrality in listening and this was fully in accord with what is referred to here in the expressions of passivity and indifference as the foremost qualities of the ear. The second step:

> As opposed to the eye, hearing is a mute sense

grasps the necessity of inner stillness which has already been mentioned as a preliminary. The more someone really wills to listen, the more silent, that is to say, the more selfless must he become, saying nothing himself. On the other hand, the more he wishes to take in of the surrounding world through seeing, the more strongly will he feel drawn out by what he sees.

But the characterization 'mute sense' can be understood in yet another connection, towards which a further step must be made in the act of hearing.

When neutrality and stillness have been established, we may ask about the effect or, in other words, the forming power of the note. We can start again with middle C for this exercise. What mood is induced by it? This question is not easy to answer. We do not really know what is intended and what we should observe. At first it is good to ask about quite straightforward familiar moods. Is it a sober or a cheerful sound? Does it summon us to activity directed towards the outer world, or to composure and reflection? We begin to notice that it has a decidedly sober character of composure. It calls for concentration and a gathering together of one's thoughts. It directs us towards an inner listening. We are not easily swayed, not easily moved or stirred into a questioning attitude, but tranquil and self-confident. If we ask what it requires of the physical body, it is always a strong upright posture. An element of clarity and control flows from it. A person who has this attitude will be a composed ego-personality, equal to life, self confident and calm. No other note has the same effect of summoning the listener to be dependent on himself.

Such preliminary discoveries, which can easily be experienced by everyone, are sufficient to bring about an understanding of why it is just this note which, in general, has the function of keynote. It has been pointed out already, with regard to the striving for an individual method seen in every leading personality today. It should be observed that we are less concerned here with an expression of subjective soul experience, acquired through earthly circumstance, than with the cultivation of an art which can become the language of the higher ego-being established within the cosmos. C as keynote for the future means the conscious reunion of the self with cosmic and spiritual realities, so that we can be guided by them in all we do, in all we absorb, in all we shape and fashion. It is clear that such an art of music cannot thrive without transforming the whole human being, without him acquiring deeper faculties of soul and greater sensitivity.

A useful aid to these studies is so-called movement-drawing. While the note is sounding the listener should try to sketch the course of the movement with a broad crayon on a blackboard or a big drawing-block, following the movement with his arm. It will be noticed how very attentive he must be, how frequently he has to make corrections, before the diagram corresponds to the actual experience. This change from hearing to another form of artistic expression is a wonderful exercise in developing clarity about the inner movement of the sound. It corresponds to the development of consciousness mentioned by Novalis as that of the inner sculptor who lives as the polarity of the musician.

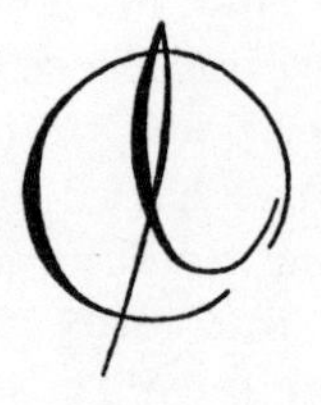

A figure such as this is often made for the note C: the stream of the upright force from below upwards and from above downwards, the gathering together and the resting within. In the second volume of this work it will be possible to discuss the movements experienced through qualitative hearing. There is no indication here of pitch. We have entered a completely new world, in which new laws are found. We no longer hear the external sound but follow the stream of movement, the dynamic rolling together and dispersing, the active or passive attitude of the soul to which the note guides us. To use the expression given by Rudolf Steiner in his first lecture on music to teachers, the sounding of the note in the air has been overcome. (Stuttgart, 7th March 1923). The preliminary audible sense impression mediated by the ear is there — it must be there — but the attention of the listener is directed towards what lives within. It is the first stage of the transformation which leads from the acoustical impression to the more spiritual and ethereal living movement of the sound, the first impression of the unique activity and intrinsic power in the note itself. It is a guide to a further understanding of what Goethe wished to signify with the expression 'a mute sense'. The quantitative factor is silent in order to make way for the qualitative element.

This opens up something which is of basic importance for all things musical. In going from this dynamic hearing of the single note to the simplest succession of notes — for instance, to a short rising and falling chromatic line — one notices that in many cases the dynamic hearing no longer coincides with the pitch. The step from C sharp to D, which is seen to go upwards, is for ethereal hearing a release in a downward direction and the movement from D flat to C seems to rise. The strong grasping of the self in a fourth from the keynote completely effaces the sensation of rising in pitch, and there are many more examples. It is a first experience, and for many a staggering one, that the outer hearing no longer always coincides with the inner. In other words, the first step in the transformation towards the inner tonal sense shows that it is impossible to grasp the true nature of musical phenomena with quantitative hearing alone.

These things throw light on interesting facts. It is well known that those who are hard of hearing, or even deaf, listen with pleasure to music. The author lived for a time with an almost totally deaf gentleman, whose great joy and relaxation in the evening was to have Beethoven's music played to him on the piano, or to play this music himself. In another case of almost total deafness, the person in question sat in the back row at a concert, and then after it had ended, gave a remarkably sure judgement on the playing: 'This soft passage, or that change of expression, was wonderful', and so on. Once when a music course was being held, it was requested than an attempt should be made towards etheric hearing with a girl of about sixteen, who had been deaf and dumb from birth because of an injury to the auditory ossicles. The evening before, the child had sat through a concert with hands outstretched, with palms open and in great excitement had then given to understand: 'I am not deaf. I can hear a tremendous lot.' She thereupon made large diagrams with interesting movements, without knowing anything at all about these things. Then she was asked to draw on the board the notes she had indicated she felt on her body. The following gives exact copies of her drawings. Without regarding how far the movements correspond to the nature of the different notes, what she — in her handicapped and somewhat sick condition — indicated was the truly remarkable fact that here, in spite of deaf ears, distinct sensations of movement were felt.

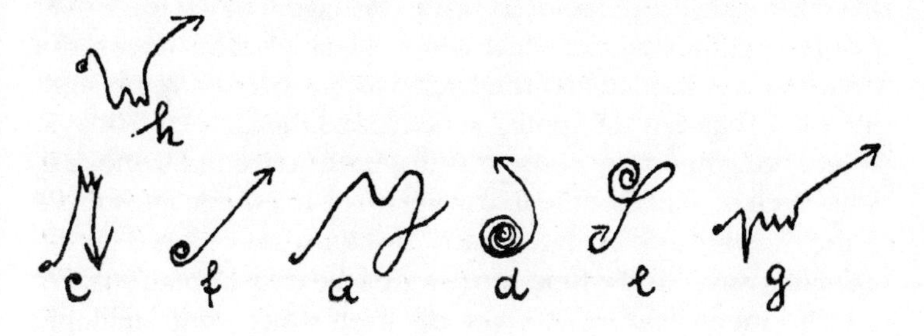

The lemniscate of the notes F-A-F-D-F was heard in the following manner:

It may be seen how the child grasped the movement around the F just as she had grasped the single notes. In such experiences a realm of music-therapy opens up which has so far been almost completely ignored. In the case of this last lemniscatory form, the word 'wonderful' burst from the child in her deaf and dumb language as she walked from the room, poised and upright and with a swing in her step.

Another indication by Goethe from his 'tabulation' is relevant here. The third, fourth and fifth stages will be illustrated later on. But here we anticipate what he says in his last paragraph. He says:

> In the case of the ear, we must pay special attention to its guidance, which works in a thoroughly stimulating and productive way. The productivity of the voice is roused, stimulated, enhanced and diversified. The whole body is stimulated.

The guidance which is here referred to embraces two organic systems: the productivity of the voice — hence the larynx — and the whole body. A slight indication of both of these was given in the outbreak of the word 'wonderful' and in the altered gait. Both are known, particularly in the case of children, as effects of music that are not always pleasant or easy to assuage. The ear leads over to other organic systems, which become bearers of an inner sense of sound. It is particularly the back which is ever more brought into play, that 'lyre of Apollo' so sacred to the Greeks. Today it should be brought to a consciousness both active and living, and it may well be said that the following up of an etheric movement — the drawing and bringing into consciousness of forces working in this way — is the first step towards the transformation from outer to inner hearing. It is the ear itself which, with infallible certainty, guides the feeling towards the place where otherwise unconscious experiences are gradually grasped and comprehended. It is in this connection that the first experience of the note C is so richly informative: the ear guides, through the power of standing into the back. The head, bearer of thinking, is raised in order to unite with heavenly space, that cosmic space out of which the note resounds. And, anchored to the earth's centre, the movement streams downwards and so reveals the world-uniting being of music.

Chapter Four

EAR AND LARYNX

Even when the outer organ of hearing has been damaged or lost it has been shown that there can still be a deep qualitative musical experience. This substantiates Goethe's third statement that the ear is 'only part of a sense'.

Such a cogent remark is hard to understand at first. Where is the other part of the sense? This mystery has already been touched upon in various ways. In the chapter on instrumental music, when discussing the human voice, it was stated that the singer or speaker goes out with the sound into space, whereas in inner hearing he receives the sound out of space. These two events live one within the other. Larynx and ear form one organ of simultaneous doing and hearing. The child's imitation of noise as well as of speech demonstrates this relationship. Rudolf Steiner, in his theory of light, enlarged in a scientific way on this Goethean statement, saying: 'The will-like element pulsates through the larynx, and the more intellectual sense-element goes through the ear.' They belong together and must be regarded as a whole.

The first exercise described in the preceding chapter indicates the possibility of penetrating into these processes with understanding. In qualitative listening, the inner etheric dynamic form of movement is heard and an attempt can be made to hold it in movement-drawing. It may be referred to as the form at the basis of the sound. It can also be recognized as the will-like gesture, pulsating through the larynx, which unites with the ear to bring about the totality of the sound. The first step in qualitative hearing opened up another facet of the ear. It had more of a receptive character; the second is more active, moulding in an etheric and plastic way.

Since the larynx inaudibly and unconsciously carries out this function, it is evident that arbitrary, wrong handling of the organ leads to movements that are false and injurious and may damage both the singer and his voice. This is the reason for loss of voice and the tragic ruin of many a born singer. The methods of present-day voice training are one-sided, working not from the spiritual into the physical, but through arbitrary bodily training which all too often results in injury. The movements forced upon the larynx are non-musical and can damage the organ permanently. The first rule is to train the larynx by imitation. The teacher must demonstrate and his singing must be musical, must be guided purely by hearing. This means that he must begin with the etheric in hearing as well as in voice production. As the pupil listens to the teacher, his larynx moves in sympathy, he practises in this way in all his singing and speaking, accepts all that is presented, whether good or bad.

After this first study of the movement made by a note we return again to the C and gradually become aware of something else. It is not participation in the movement alone that fills the soul, not only the experience of becoming upright, not only a self-enclosing concentration turning towards the inner world. Gradually, definite and always similar feelings of sympathy or antipathy arise. The formulations of the experience go over into characterizations more of a soul-nature. Previously it seemed that the qualitative perceptions of movement were grasped more by an inner limb-system; but now in listening the fullness of receiving goes over into the heart. The force of becoming upright, or, in the case of other notes, the fluidity, lightness, firmness, weight, warmth and so on, are all characteristics taken from the world of the elements. They reveal something of an objective nature, reveal the etheric moulding forces in the way they work as life-functions within the note.

But now, in this force of becoming upright, feelings arise that go deeper — self-confidence, courage, and joy in activity, proper to an upright person; but also loving, protecting, enveloping powers of soul. The head, in its freedom, gives surprisingly distant vision and a feeling of awe and devotion; a firm anchorage below gives earnestness and a feeling of responsibility. And above all the pupil knows that he does not possess this but must acquire it. The true nature of this ego-note speaks to inner hearing. A part of the higher, the heavenly man resounds, and his words are understood within the heart. What Goethe speaks of — in the part on *Acoustics* in his *Theory of Musical Sound* — as moral enthusiasm acquired through the senses has to be enkindled and is experienced spontaneously. It is only that the soul of man is generally not sufficiently open for a spirit-dialogue in music that has taken its course in the twilight of the unconscious without rising into the light-filled region of morality. As a result, it cannot be condensed into strong, morally determinative impulses, as is necessary in the conditions prevailing today. But in qualitative listening we open a door to the spiritual through conscious work. The revelations which stream from there as gifts of the spirit are saturated with will and can work back morally onto the ego-forces. So music, in the hand of man, will become educative in the deepest sense as in previous centuries; but now he will take over, in absolute freedom and with individual responsibility, the priestly guidance of those former times.

When the heart of man lays hold on the deep inner nature of the note, and he is led by the stirrings of his soul to spiritual dialogue and understanding, he gradually makes a pleasing discovery. A new kind of absolute hearing arises in him. The exercises in qualitative hearing lead to subtle reactions and give sure knowledge of the nature of the phenomenon. Just as we always recognize an acquaintance when we meet him so, as time goes on, a note can be recognized by the way in which it speaks. For this there are also exercises. Closing one's eyes, one can strike this or that note in the middle octave and try to identify it by its effect. Or, one can call up in the soul the bearing, the nuance or shade of feeling of C until one feels C-like, and then gently hum the note which arises. In time the C will sound ever more clearly. If later on one learns to know the organs which correspond to the different spheres of sound, this will be a help. A new kind of perfect pitch develops, but not in the sense of an inborn certainty which says nothing about the true musical nature of what is heard. There is now a kind of flowering, like a heartfelt relationship, a weaving together, a certain unmistakable knowledge of the nature of the note derived from the experience of its living effect. And because this relationship was learnt of listening, it always brings new experience and new knowledge — gifts of the spirit without ceasing, inexhaustible as life itself.

To finish this chapter let us look into the future. There has been statistical evidence for decades that the range of hearing is shrinking. Many people can no longer take in the extreme positions below and above the staves, far less distinguish between the sounds. It is not only the excessive demands made on the organ of hearing and its over-stimulation through the turmoil of everyday life. Think of the street noises and the continual noise of vehicles; think how many people have to spend their working day in factories full of gigantic machinery, how many work among twenty or more type-writers, so and so many radios, etc., etc. It is not only the mania for continually scourging our nerves through music of the most questionable and over-stimulating kind; the media play their part in the ruin of this human faculty. Without wishing to stand in the way of evolution, one has to admit that vestigial organs are regressing — as for example the pineal gland, which in earlier times was at a higher stage of development and more active. It is justified to see in the transformation of hearing from a quantitative to a qualitative kind a means of healing which will bring about a change in the future. Just as the deaf and dumb girl, without being able to receive the actual sounding of the note through the medium of air came nevertheless to a musical experience, and the healing of one hard of hearing has also been brought about by this means — so might a further cultivation and spiritual development of these possibilities bring about experiences, the necessity and value of which has so far not even been imagined. The ear is indeed only a part of a sense. What tasks lie ahead in the conscious cultivation of the other part, the larynx?

Chapter Five

REACTION AND DEMAND

Goethe's fourth stage opens up an entirely new chapter for the future of hearing. He writes:

> To the ear, as a lofty organic being, we must ascribe reaction and demand; whereby the sense alone is capable of understanding and grasping what is brought to it from outside.

The expression 'reaction and demand' refers to the fact that the process of hearing has not yet been fully comprehended. And the characterization of the ear as a lofty organic being means that we are no longer concerned with the usual organic procedures, but with those that border on the higher senses, that is to say, those on the threshold of the supersensible.

It is good to start from practical experience and the previous exercises point in the right direction. We start again with the single note, with middle C. Listening to a single note demands concentration and rouses the feeling of grasping a focal point within oneself. In the first exercise in acoustical hearing this came strongly to the fore; one centres as onto a point. A subtle attentiveness to the inwardly perceptible effect — not of the qualitative nature of the note, but of concentrated hearing — shows that with this effort of concentration the soul expands as it were to the circumference, as if it had passed through the celebrated eye of a needle and created the opposite pole. For, without losing hold of the central point, there is a feeling of growing into space, expanding and creating a periphery. Something can be felt of what Goethe called 'reaction', which through polarity creates a whole. Something similar has been mentioned in the first part of this work concerning the inner demand of the deep bass for a complement in the treble as an opposing force, thus creating equilibrium.

These experiences in the realm of hearing bear a resemblance to the phenomenon of complementary colours in the realm of sight. Goethe took special interest in this and makes deeply penetrating remarks about it. In the didactic part of his *Theory of Colour* he says:

> The eye cannot and will not remain one moment in a specific condition identical with the object. Rather does it need a kind of opposite, putting one extreme against another, centre against centre, binding together opposites, gradually making of them a whole, not only in time but also in space.

This producing of opposite factors, the synchronization and the reciprocity of a passive and a creatively active process, occurs in every sense-activity. It appears in the complementary action between ear and larynx, the more intellectual sense-like receptivity of the ear complementing the pulsating, will-enfilled principle of the larynx. The element that unites passively intensifies until the need for reaction arises. It is something like a reflection between the qualitative sympathetic experience and the creative counter-thrust which the soul produces inaudibly. In this connection we can add the following impressive sentences out of the *Theory of Colour*, and make full use of them for the activity of hearing. Goethe speaks of:

> the silent contradiction which all living things need to express when faced with some particular situation. Inhalation presupposes exhalation, and the opposite. It is the eternal formula of life which finds expression here. As soon as darkness is imposed upon the eye, it requires light. It needs darkness when given light, thus showing its living quality, the right to grasp the object by bringing something opposite to it, as complement, out of itself.

In the case of the eye, the organ that takes in the external physical world, this creative process appears as the etheric complementary colour, not in the physical, but on the supersensible boundary of the physical. The ear absorbs the inner being, the soul-expression, through outer perception; and the creative counter-process with which the complementary nature of man answers is not a physical sound of definite pitch, but (to connect up with the example of the low C in the bass) he creates, over against the soul impression of firmness, weight and darkness, the demand for light, levity and 'star'. One can proceed to trace and seek out the corresponding sound in the realm of the audible. For example, the experience of the low C in the bass calls forth as inner demand the C two octaves above middle C. The creative counterpart of what is heard arises as the soul's demand, without any idea of pitch in the realm of the inner tonal sense, just as the after-image in the eye belongs in the etheric to the sense-conveyed moral colour-perception.

It is evident that the activity of hearing, freed from the purely acoustic experience and guided ever more deeply into the spiritual and qualitative sphere, demands a polarity between the outer sound and the inner response. This may be a movement, an inner picture of nature, a strong feeling or something else, but it arises from hearing. Submission to this inner process gives to the outer activity its true musical substance with compelling insistence. One could say, purely superficially, that this is in any case there. But we must not forget that it is not a question of the usual subjective 'moods' that come and go in any case with every artist. These experiences are objective and the phenomenon expresses its own nature. They are revelations of music itself and not human fantasies. It becomes increasingly clear while working that all external activity must be guided by these revelations. The inner activity determines and fills ever more and more the 'how' of the external action, streaming out from the spirit to control the body and bring the music to life.

The following exercises are given to illustrate this. We begin by listening to the note. One focuses on the note as the central point and brings to meet it the concept of periphery. The further this feeling for periphery expands, the more will the kernel of the note be filled. It will be surrounded by a warm living aura. If it is regarded only as a central point, as pitch, it will not transcend the character of a strongly contoured, immovable building stone of music.

Something similar can be experienced if one sings the note as a keynote with a real feeling for the ground under one's feet and over against this imagines the octave. The experience intensifies in the soul until it becomes a clear, inner conception of the sound. The same exercise can be practised from the higher C, regarded as octave, by imagining over against it the keynote. In both cases it will be noticed that the keynote overcomes a certain flatness and starts to soar, filled with a light-giving force, while the hovering of the octave acquires a kernel, found without it losing its transparency.

In connection with the fifth and fourth the following exercise is valuable: the hearing of the fifth C to G (a) is felt in a certain way as moving upwards. After a while, the strength of the fifth from C to F downwards comes as an inner counter-claim, and must be kept in mind by singer or player to keep the balance.

The inversion, from C downwards to F as physical element, with the transparency of the mental image of C upwards to G modifies and fills out the one-sided character of the actual sound. Exercise (b) shows the corresponding processes with the interval of a fourth.

In the sphere of harmony, such studies can be made with alternating chords of tonic and dominant, of dissonance and consonance in the major/minor system, in so far as they have distinct tendencies. The tendency to movement peculiar to every such harmony is like the consonance of repose connected with (a) and (c) or the dissonance of further movement (b). This living concept, when put into practice, gives the most astonishing variants and changing shades to what is actually sounding.

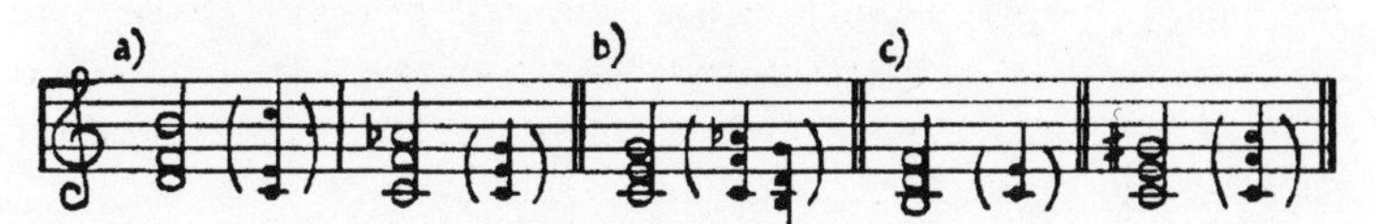

This basic law of simultaneous action and reaction was probably the reason why the Italian master of Bel Canto advised his pupil to imagine the depths in a high sound and the heights in a low sound. And that same law holds good in all exercises relating to loud and soft; for instance, the counter-concept of a feeling filled with light and lightness in the case of a heavy forte or the opposite with a soft piano. All hardness or pressure on the one hand, or loss of tone on the other, is alleviated through the summoning up of the opposite phenomenon, giving colour and depth.

When Goethe, in connection with reaction and demand, speaks of the lofty organic nature of the ear, it can be said that a fruitful realm of spirituality opens up. The path taken here in The Transformation of Hearing according to Goethe's Theory of Musical Sound has led from the receiving of the acoustical pitch to the development of movement within the sphere of the forming forces. By this means the life of the soul is enkindled and takes the essential revelation of what is heard as a challenge to man to make the creative counter-thrust, which springs from the power of his ego. With each of these steps hearing withdraws more and more from external sound. Activity is transferred to inner intensification. This does not mean that the connection with the requirements of the physical are lost. It is an absolute reversal of the usual method of working and it is impossible to emphasize it enough. Ordinarily the physical faculties are exercised and trained in external activity, and one notices only when it is too late that physical faculties as well as vitality of soul have suffered damage. But in this instance one works primarily on the deepening, the spiritualization, of flexibility and reaction in the soul, and is guided from there into the physical organs of expression. Standing on the threshold between two worlds man awakens, through the consciously trained totality of concept and action, of spirit and matter, of the audible and the inaudible, to the mystery of the unity of all polarities, 'the eternal formula of life'.

Chapter Six

ONCE AGAIN THE GUIDANCE OF THE EAR

It is wonderful to see how Goethe builds up and expands organically the five guiding sentences about thc car. The precision of his expressions and the way he places them in the sentence enable the keen reader to find a way of deepening his understanding. To Goethe the remarks about the guidance of the ear are apparently something so self-sufficient and important that the indications build up to an almost exciting climax. We give the text here once again.

> In the case of the ear, we must pay special attention to its guidance, which works in a thoroughly stimulating and productive way. The productivity of the voice is roused, stimulated, enhanced and diversified. The whole body is stimulated.

It is a very striking contemporary phenomenon and even a cause of anxiety, that people cannot really listen to one another. The person with whom one speaks is often far away with his thoughts, his eyes and his interest — often very far away. Our words ripple along somewhere or other in space without reaching the other person at all. And the answers, also, seem often to come from a distance and have no true inner connection with what has been said, giving the impression that in ordinary social life the ear seldom leads to the fully conscious ego of man. This is not the place to go into these difficulties, but one may well say that Goethe had his reasons, looking forward in a prophetic manner, for giving so much emphasis to this last remark about the guidance of the ear. And in this connection it is worth drawing attention to a remark which Eckermann reported after a musical performance.

> 'It is curious', said Goethe, 'whither the most advanced technology and mechanical science lead the new composers; their works are no longer music; they go beyond the level of human feelings; one can no longer support such

> things with mind and heart. How does it seem to you? To me everything remains suspended in the ear. ...None the less the Allegro had character. This eternal whirling and turning brought the witches' dance of the Blocksberg before my eyes, and so I found something with which I could support this very strange music.'

From this two things are clear. The purely external technical moment remains 'suspended in the ear'. But Goethe wants his heart to be involved or to have an imaginative picture arise. Only the latter can justify the music in the above case. Although the picture here is not a pleasant one it leads to the inner realms of the human being. A bridge is built from the world of the creator to the heart and mind of the listener. No abyss, no emptiness any longer separates the one who gives from the one who receives.

There are two things stemming from the guidance of the ear, 'which works in a thoroughly stimulating and productive way'. It is a feature of a hearing that 'remains suspended in the ear', that does not go beyond mere acoustics, that it leaves the hearer apathetic, uncomprehending and disinterested, as though he were separated from the event. One could almost say he sleeps through it, he is excluded as a human being. That actually means he does not hear. His waking consciousness is either not there at all or is only half there, as in a dream. This so-called hearing does not reach man's inner being and therefore cannot work as a stimulus. A fully alert ego is essential in order to create the necessary basis for the experience of this final, fifth stage of hearing. But an alert ego leads to openness of heart and readiness to receive. It is a pre-condition of selflessness. Then one starts to become inwardly alive, as described in the exercises on the transformation of hearing. One sphere of man's organism after another is not only stirred, not only comes into motion, but is kindled into productivity. What does Goethe understand by this talent of 'productivity'? He formulated it clearly under the title 'Theory of Singing' which runs parallel to the directions for hearing.

> Singing itself is fully productive. The natural disposition of the outer sense and the genius of the inner sense are required throughout.

Such a statement is of great interest today. In those times what was referred to as 'genius', as a highly gifted talent, was an unconscious union with the divine world-order. Man was gifted, endowed by the spiritual world, although he himself was not always conscious of why such thoughts and creative impulses took hold of him and directed him with such compelling force. Higher guidance spoke through him. And it was able to do this, because the people of that time — think of the spiritual tide of the Romantic Age — knew they were still in union with higher powers, knew they were striving towards the spiritualization of man, a striving which, in the sphere of music, was still fully nurtured by forces of soul and mind and began — for instance in Beethoven — to seek universality in the subjective experience of the ego. When Goethe presupposed the productivity of the 'genius of the inner sense' there stood before his soul this unconscious and yet quite certain union with the spiritual background of music, the intuitive knowledge of everything that wanted to stream into music unconsciously. It was to him a matter of course that with outer hearing a 'natural disposition', that is, a sound natural talent, must be there. And even today a well-structured, good, guiding ear for music is still necessary.

But since those times conditions have changed to such an extent that it is no longer possible to take for granted the gift of unconscious spiritual union in the Goethean sense. Outstanding capacities of talented artistic personalities are there to be sure in distinguished measure in the sphere of instrumental technique. Yet, was that not precisely the sphere which remained 'suspended in the ear' and which led to the imagination of the Blocksberg? One must not think that it is no longer the case today. On the contrary! But the spiritual background is no longer within the range of human consciousness. 'Genius of the inner sense' as the basis of true productivity, of true creative talent, bubbling up from the spiritual wellsprings of music, is no longer given. It must gradually be regained in full consciousness, and sound hearing must also be reborn. The productivity expected from the guidance of the ear today is of a self-creative kind. It does not signify an unconscious gift of destiny but reveals the alert, morally-active higher ego at work. This means, speaking for the future: genius, not only in a technical sense, but in a deeply artistic sense, called upon to guide a humanity that is morally united with the spirit. It is different from the old type of genius, that was often not of high moral calibre.

Goethe himself did not wish to indicate a method leading to this new human realm, although in the course of destiny he had certainly experienced a schooling of the spirit. Wagner could not show the stages of development in his Parsifal between the end of the second act and the return in the third act. The possibility of such an awakened clarity in cognition was first revealed through Rudolf Steiner's Anthroposophy. None the less the four stages indicated in following up the guidance of the ear are astounding signposts pointing the way. One may surely transfer everything indicated here for the voice to every other field of musical practice. For is all that is done in this way not a wanting-to-sing?

Some practical directions can now be given, this time taken from work at the piano. They can easily be extended and used in other spheres. They cannot lay claim to being in any way complete but they have been used successfully through decades and may well be mentioned here. They deal with the method stressed at the end of the previous chapter of making the body technically pliable by deepening experiences and imaginations in the soul. As a basis, the first thirty exercises from Hanon's *Sixty Daily Exercises* may be taken. They imprint themselves easily on the mind and attention can be turned wholly inwards instead of outwards. They should not be worked at in the usual way, that is, as mechanical exercises. The following exercise is the first and the easiest.

One should remember that, to begin with, the change from acoustic to qualitative hearing led to movement in the realm of the forming forces. Solidity, fluidity, light and warmth begin to form the soul through the element of sound. For all artistic work it is important to start practising with this idea in mind. One should notice where the ear guides the touch physically, and should test, through attentive listening and by following up the activity, whether the character of the sound corresponds with what we had in mind. With which of the elements we begin depends largely on what musical experience and what form of expression is required, what one wishes to attain in artistic pedagogy or, in other circumstances, to use therapeutically. In these short examples the same course is taken as was previously followed at the end of the fifth chapter.

The fixing of pitch as such is a centring, just as there is basically a drawing-together in every solid. It is a question of bringing the note one hears externally in space into 'embodiment', as it were. With this picture in mind the ear guides all physical movements, without forcing them arbitrarily, out of a free position into the finger-tips, as if from outside, so that they touch the keys firmly but without being cramped. The stream which draws together through the finger-tips for a brief contact holds the key as if it had contour, then frees itself again into the released position from which it started (dotted line b).

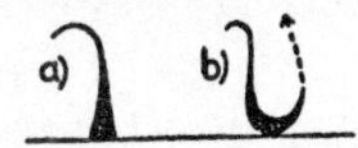

It is essential to experience the difference between an ordinary firm touch (a) and the touch described here (b). The touch (a), in keeping with the meaning of the word, comes out of a bodily muscular movement and presses the key down. The weight and pressure are physically generated through muscular action. But the musical note heard in space is as if taken away from the instrument, without the finger leaving the keys, and is held in crystal clarity, 'hovering' in the hand. It is as if a bell were rung and harshness becomes impossible. The exercise begins slowly, note by note, with a conscious loosening between the notes, then it gradually increases in tempo. The interplay between the striking of the finger-tips and the quick loosening is like the rolling along of small pearls of notes above the keyboard. The player does not 'slump' but is aware of a force of uprightness in his back and up towards his head. The ear leads to this with its musical demands: uprightness equals ego. And if Goethe speaks of the rousing of productivity, the feeling is truly that of being awake, leading from the ear to the ego in constant inner musical control and adjustment, starting with the purely acoustical production of the note and following the laws of being firm and awake from the inaudible into the audible.

The next step is the linking up of the notes with one another so that the forming activity begins to flow. We now do the Hanon exercises in accordance with the experience of 'water', following diverse imagery. In contrast to firmness, which draws in from outside, from space (a), we develop an attitude which makes of the sounds an inner stream, waving, flowing and dissolving.

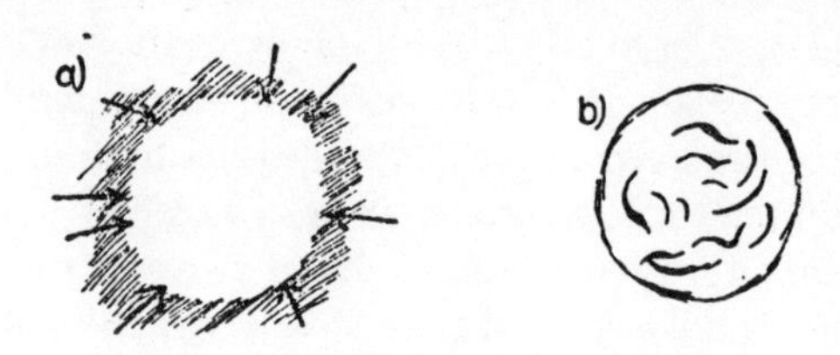

This wateriness, this releasing of everything into movement streaming along the keys, but with a certain heaviness, is very difficult for many people today. Everyone seems forced into a wearisome form of life and the attitude has become second nature. Whither does the ear lead? It is not restricted as regards place; it leads to complete bodily relaxation. It leads into a heaviness which often gives the feeling of sinking through the keyboard and playing under it. A flowing form of movement emerges from the music. It is not the individual notes which are outlined but the form, which is artistically heard and experienced. For this the exercises in Hanon with their concise motifs running a repetitive course, offer a fine foundation.

The ideas and pictures, summoned up inwardly as water beings — sea, streams, brooks, waterfalls, fountains and other such things — conjure up more and more the flowing character of sound and give a beautiful legato. Goethe wrote 'stimulated' in second place after being roused — stimulated to inexhaustible new forms of musical life. The sensation of playing, without any hindrance in the hand or forearm, is only of water, feeling the flow in the body and a heavy horizontally-flowing connection with the keyboard, just as the nature of water always has the tendency to fall and connect with the ground.

This flowing heaviness is relieved by the next step connected with the element of air. As a leaf seized by the wind, so does this listening now lift the player in idea and feeling away from the keyboard and out into space. The arm is not guided from within, but is wafted hither and thither without any weight, swinging in the air, body-free in the sense that the body does not play, but is played with by a breath of living air.

Productivity is truly 'enhanced' in the Goethean sense in so far as this weightless wafting in the air is filled with every degree of emotion. From storm to the most gentle zephyr with divine immanence, ideas and experiences can be called upon, through which the continually improving ear can grasp the appropriate physical organs, and lead to a drawing together and loosening under constant control. The feeling seems to come from outside, move through the physical organs and shape the unfolding sound in piano as in forte.

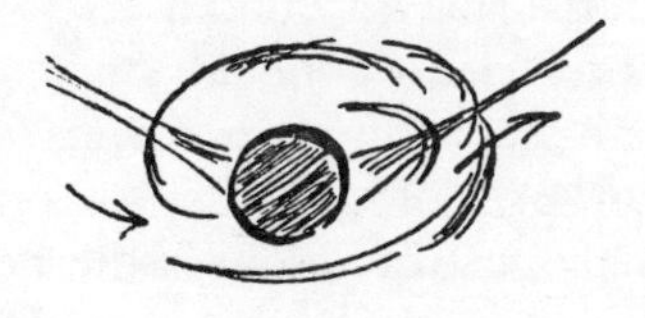

It can be felt that arms and hands in close association with the music can be worked upon and trained through a breathing determined by the demands of form, theme, motive or gradations of tempo.

And now concerning 'diversification' through the guidance of the ear. Warmth can be grasped as an effective formative force. But all experiences connected with this are drawn from the centre of the heart. Far-reaching exercises can be made here. Warmth, experienced as flame, brings to maturity an impulsive force, a will-enfilled possibility of intensification and 'getting a hold', whereby the sensation of playing is led from the ear into the lower limbs. But warmth as tender inwardness holds back all movement in prudence and tranquillity, and plays from the heart towards the inner being. Warmth streaming forth, or glimmering warmth, as the smoke of sacrificial incense upon the altar, or a passionate welling up of the blood — there are innumerable variations which play from without and within. One thing can be observed: the louder it is, the less does it give. But the more it is held in tranquillity within the heart, the more it is experienced as outstreaming. Here all the gripping and subtle tones of the heart are achieved, which give to artistic playing unforgettable value and beauty. It is not a question of any special technique. It is only a question of listening and of a quite intensive feeling for the organs to which the ear leads, in order to speak subtly and out of experience. One practises flexibility of soul, practises on the power of the creative idea, practises the summoning of heart-warmth — then the body is controlled and is blessed with diverse new faculties.

In a similar way it is possible to play in the element of light — light as radiance, light as cosmic weaving, light also as inner clarity and comprehension. Here we meet with problems of transparency and audibility of parts when playing meditative or polyphonic music. The ear guides into the finger tips again; and it is always valuable to direct attention away from the instrument and to 'sketch' in the space around it.

The most subtle and most difficult studies in transformation, of combining and dissociating various kinds of playing follows on from here. We can speak of admixtures of tone, by which the ear stimulates and makes use of various bodily bearings. It demands variety on both sides, on the right and the left between melody and accompaniment, and in polyphony the real will to give plastic shape and form. Light and water can play together, warmth change into light, solid play with spray and so on, streaming through each finger of the hand differently and, above all, learning to direct the play between distances of space and closeness to the instrument.

These last remarks indicate what is of utmost importance: to include space in playing. Hearing in space links up the performer with the instrument in an all-embracing unity. Depending on the requirements of the performance the player will turn more away from himself, giving shape outwardly, or will turn more towards himself. If air is the bearer of musical sound it is clear that the inclusion of the surrounding air must be among the most important requirements in playing.

It can be understood that this listing of ways towards the overcoming of technical demands must appear curious and unlikely to present-day consciousness, used as it is to physical training. Nevertheless, what is impossible today is possible tomorrow. And, for those who have suffered because of their love of music at the present time, perhaps a glimmer of hope will arise for the future.

Chapter Seven

THE LYRE OF APOLLO

Goethe's final statement comes almost as an appendage:

The whole body is stimulated.

The truth of these words has already been emphasized in the passage about the different stages of development. The guidance of the ear leads to the most diverse physical demands and ways of working, but something needs to be said about this short concluding remark.

In the course of the suggestions made about exercises one soon notices that, in addition to the basic attitude, each of the musical elements has its own appointed place in the body. An interval of a third is played differently from that of a prime or a sixth. Scales are incorporated into the human being differently from harmonic structures. A minor scale requires a different way of playing from a major, and so on, so that gradually the feeling arises as if there were an enchanted dancer, who captures the music heard in space and incorporates it into the body; but instead of leading it over into movement of the limbs, leads it into forms, into colouring and fullness of sound. In the case of the dancer, the limbs become ear in order also to become organs of expression, as if taking over the function of the larynx. For that reason all musical experience in olden times was intimately linked with dance. But what did this bring to expression?

In this connection, one should remember the first part of this book. It was stated that formerly humanity experienced music in a state of ecstasy, as the working of forces out of the whole cosmos. 'It was the ruling of the gods that resounded.' In the state of complete openness to the world — clear-sighted, clear in feeling, clear in hearing — in which humanity then existed, stellar forces and movements streamed in on the pathway of music and dance in the service of the gods and was mostly ritualistic. The organs had not yet hardened as they have done now. It is important and also interesting to hear what is said of this out of research through spiritual science. In his book *The World of the Senses and the World of the Spirit*, Rudolf Steiner writes:

It is very illuminating for our knowledge of the human being to trace back the development of the ear. For in its existing condition human hearing is really only a shadow of what it once was. Today it hears only the sounds, or the words of the physical plane expressed in sound. This is in a way a remnant, for at one time the powerful movements of the whole universe flowed in through this instrument. Today we hear only earthly music through the ear, but in olden times the cosmic music of the spheres flowed into man; and as today we clothe words in musical sound, so was the cosmic word once clothed in the music of the spheres, and St John's Gospel calls it the Divine Word, the Logos. It flowed out of the spiritual worlds into all that can be designated as hearing in the earlier sense, just as only the human word and earthly music can now flow into it. There flowed in the heavenly music of the spheres that which the divine spiritual beings spoke.

The further one goes back into ancient times, the more there arises a picture of mankind developing from outside inwards. Man was, as it were, entirely ear, in the way already depicted. The shrivelled up, wrinkled organ of the ear as we now know it extended at that time inwards, undulating through the whole human being. The later process of reversal depended on the awakening of the I in the inner being of man, and found its culmination in the experience that, after the Mystery of Golgotha, each individual could find the Logos, the creative Cosmic Word, in his own soul. Man gradually awakened to the realization of himself as microcosm, able to create his own human music. All further human development in the higher sense is now a question of self-development from within outwards. Man becomes 'musical' in an entirely new sense.

The question is often asked by earnest seekers, and one should also often ask it oneself: What is meant by the word 'musical'? Although this question has already been considered, it may be asked again without hesitation. The answer lies not only in the fact that man is, in any case, well-disposed towards music and has a pleasurable relationship to it. It is more relevant, regarding the course of development described here, to answer the question: What does music ask of man? Has he a feeling akin to historical conscience? What faculties need to be developed in order to do justice through music to the course of history?

With this thought in mind, we may compare the representations of man in Egyptian times with those of Greek times. The former have about them something architectural. These figures, in their harsh impersonal severity and standing upright, look as if they were fitted together. Where they appear in a frieze as musicians, they are arranged geometrically in rows. The instrument is placed in their hands but it does not really belong to them. One has the impression that they dare not move. They keep still, directing their gaze into heavenly distances. And this keeping still is like a breathless, tense and tentative listening for what is about to happen to them. But what does happen? They are guided to themselves. Just as normally the child only begins to say 'I' of himself when he is about three or four years old, it was much the same with earlier humanity. Yet it is not so much a thinking as a first feeling of personality that awakens, and it is the physical body which is presented artistically as the earthly abode of this first feeling of self. The Egyptian felt as if banished into his solid body, which seemed to be formed in a crystalline way by the divine harmony of the spheres, and he conjured this experience into his figures, temples and friezes. These figures are static and, like obelisks and columns, stand between what is above and what is below, revealing that which is the garment of the human I in the most austere, immobile upright posture. It is as if only when they were silent and motionless could they hear the mighty voice of God summoning them to egoity.

How entirely different is the picture of the Greek flautist on one side of the throne of Ludovic in the National Museum at Rome. Sitting resigned in calm submission, inactive, listening and relaxed, she gives herself up completely to the streaming of sound through her own being. Music has already become inner experience to such an extent that all her limbs in their harmonious symmetry grasp this selfhood, entwine, as if they were woven together. The feeling of a happy interplay between curving and stretching, holding and relaxing, is that of the music whose mysterious enchantment was heard. Instrument and player are one, both animated by the same stream of the breath. Even the cushion is adapted to the melodious streaming form of her body. Does this not point to entirely new faculties having evolved in the hearing and forming of music during the centuries between Egyptian times and Greek? There still sounds, almost as if in a dreamy, remembered state, Plato's *musica humana* — an echo of the harmony weaving between body and soul.

The Flute Player. National Museum, Rome

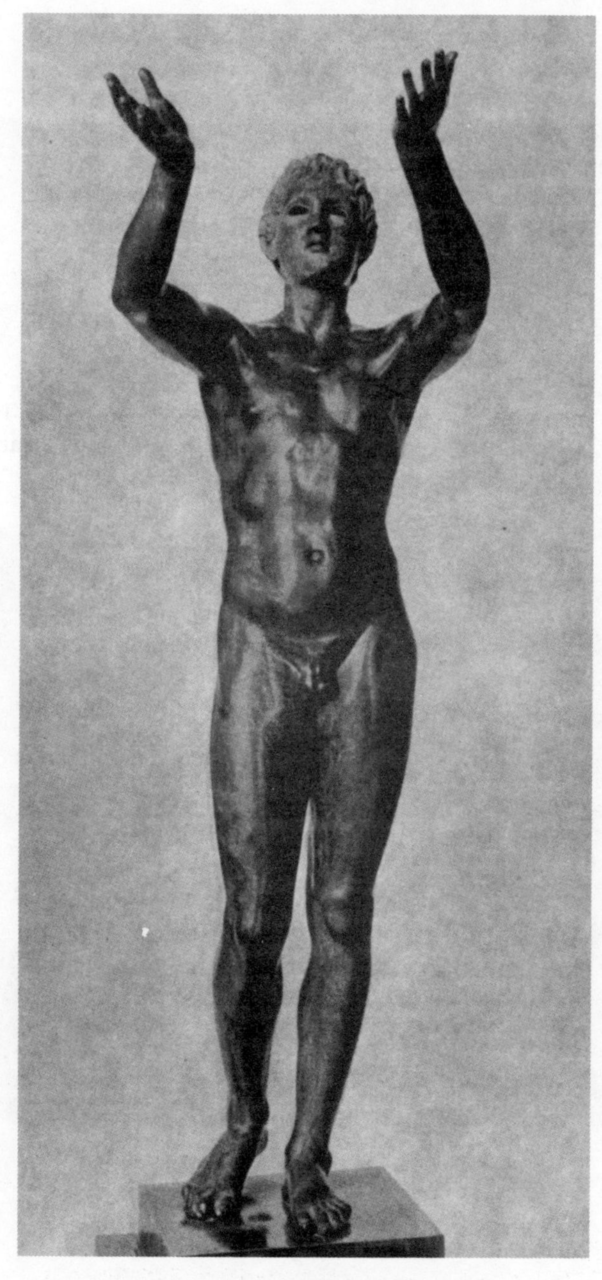

The Praying Boy. Antiquarium, Berlin

But in this picture the force of uprightness seems to have been lost. The human being does not seem so awake, does not stand firmly like a pillar, as in former times. Rather does a gracious breath of youthful dreams play about the whole figure. The vitality of an incredibly relaxed nature is portrayed in the back, as if all listening were concentrated there. And let us look thirdly at the *Praying Boy* in the Museum of Ancient History in Berlin. This statue might almost represent the young Apollo! It is inspired by the gesture of turning to the light, secure and yet swinging, stepping serenely over the earth in a beautiful upright posture. There stands man, the ego-forces streaming from the crown of his head to the soles of his feet. One cannot but think: He resounds! In the deep harmony of his being he is music. He is no longer in a dream but has awakened with joy to himself and to the beauty of the earth. And the inner music of the boy is the foreshadowing in his whole body of the mystery of the zodiac and the planetary powers out of which he is formed; the knowledge of the divine word still pulsates in his blood and vibrates in his nerves. He feels unfolding in his blood the life of his ego, and in the sensitivity of his nerves the whole world of feeling. He holds himself up, raises his gaze with an inimitable gesture of the arms, expressing at one and the same time surrender and acceptance, promise and gratitude. He reveals the divine and human wonder of the unity of World and I, standing there as a perfect picture of creative man, at rest within himself yet proclaiming the true meaning and content of his life of soul.

That was the great experience of the Greek: to know himself within himself, founded in divinely-willed beauty. All works of art handed down to us show this unique, beautiful and dignified composure, often touching us as a faraway ideal. And yet, how close to life in every way! Because, as human beings they had found themselves, the gods could now approach them closely and be represented in human form. Yet it was inevitable that here also, not only in the north, a twilight of the gods occurred so as to make place for the one god, the Logos, in the human soul. From now on this is the focal point in which heaven and earth, spirit and matter can 'in unison rejoice'. Hope of man, hope also of the gods, hope from which music, as the youngest and from now on independent art, could be born — nay, must be born!

It has already been mentioned that the Greeks called the whole system of the 28-30 nerve strands connected with the brain and the spinal cord, the 'Lyre of Apollo'. This was not merely a poetic imaginative picture. It indicated in actual truth that to them the impact of musical sound was perceptible in the spine, passing through the whole length of the individual nerve fibres and then through the whole body. One surmises something of the earlier ear, extending over the whole being of man. It is like a residue of an erstwhile openness, a last portal through which the whole human being felt himself encompassed by the world of sound. And how marvellously was this 'ear' in him constructed!

The number 28 - 30 was an indication of the phases of the moon during the course of the twelve months of the year. But the months have the number 12 like the nerves in the brain. In the 12 there was always a connection with the working of the sun in its course. In this interaction of the 12 with the 28 - 30 nerves of his earthly body, in this interplay — permeated cosmically by the forces of sun and moon — the Greek felt himself musically as soul and spirit, just as we, by means of the ear, can break through to a conscious, qualitative experience. At that time they said: 'Apollo plays me within myself... Apollo's world is my world'. To this the Greek was committed. But what do we experience today?

A new culture has arisen and humanity has changed. As the organ of clairvoyance, the pineal gland — this former cosmic eye of humanity — has gradually closed and withered, so has the 'ear' in the spine hardened and become impenetrable. It has shrunk into the small sense-organ we know in the head as the ear, which is linked with the larynx. With this knowledge we approach the question of human musicality, or historical conscience. What faculties are to be regained in the light of development from the time of the Pharaohs up to our present time and beyond? The answer is clear. What was at one time bestowed upon childlike man externally by divine powers has to be acquired again through free inner work by the human being of today. He has come of age, is individually responsible, is the bearer of the I. And if the lyre of Apollo was described as the portal through which the whole human being could feel himself connected with cosmic sound, then for the culture of today — of the future — it means that the hearing in the spine is to be reawakened. But this hearing is ethereal, not physical. It is related to events of soul and spirit in the realm of the inaudible and is complementary to physical hearing. But how should this be developed?

The way has been indicated in the exercises given for the transformation of hearing, a way based on the spiritual factor in man. If in earlier times the laws of the earth were read supersensibly from the stars, man must now understand the laws of the stars, that is, of cosmic music, within his soul. There arises a great conscious spirit-orientated breathing-process between the inner and the outer. There arises the qualitative experience of music in connection with the relationship of the soul to itself and in the relationship of the soul to space. Minor and major attitudes alternate — a drawing together and a drawing apart. Goethe's systole/diastole becomes the basis of all living development. The ether ear in the spine awakens in the same measure as the experience of cosmic music in the inner being of man makes it possible for spirit-forces to flow through him. This is not an abstraction superimposed upon music as something alien to its nature. One simply adopts an ancient law in the making of music, but now in the play of ether forces and not in the physical alone.

Dr Guenther Wachsmuth, in his book, *The Etheric Formative Forces in Cosmos, Earth and Man*, describes a fourfoldness of such cosmic forces, two tending towards the solidification of matter, the other two towards rarefaction. He calls the former sound, or chemical and life ether, the latter light and warmth ether, and on this scientific basis makes the following statement:

> The sound which we perceive with the senses is the result of a conflicting activity of the chemical ether with the light ether for the solidification of substance.
> The constant vibrating to and fro of the substance of air between rarefaction and solidification in a particular place is, for us, sound.
> The physically audible sound is the cry of matter compelled to solidify.

Here we also find the interplay between contraction and expansion, between a minor and a major process. Here there is also a rhythmical breathing and interweaving of polarities, of that 'strife' which Heraclitus called the father of all things.

This new ether hearing of the future is trained by qualitative study, by combining the 'becoming dense' experience of the I with the rarefying processes in space. All this presupposes an inner self-creative activity, with the fine nerve-fibres of the spine and brain as the bearer of thinking and the solar-plexus as bearer of supersensible stellar forces awakening to new activity. The power to stand upright, of thinking and unity with the world-all, make man in truth human. They give him the faculty of speech and sound, of musical utterance arising and working in accordance with his higher genius.

When Goethe, summing up his observations, formulates his crowning statement:

> The whole body is stimulated,

he makes an inner connection with the totality of man as a being of soul and spirit. It is the realm of the ethers, the region united with the body and yet not purely physical, which is the threshold to pure spirituality. This was known to Goethe. He tried to point it out in all his work in striving for a moral awareness of the phenomenon through the senses, so that on the one hand man recognized in himself the inaudible quality of the spiritual nature of hearing, and on the other, in the quantitatively audible, the descent of this spirituality into matter. If one feels a musical sound — for example an interval — as warmth, a relationship to the loving heart arises. Light will lead to an imaginative, regulating and harmonizing force, and so on. For all these fine differentiations the living reaction of the back is the receptive ear, the portal opens again to the world of Apollo, to the world of the Logos. In his work for the future, man and his music are transformed, so that, in Guenther Wachsmuth's words:

> Sound can be transformed from lamentation into joy.

That is the new musicality required by a historical conscience: the bringing to life and experiencing again of the 'Lyre of Apollo'.

Chapter Eight

THE HUMAN BEING

Self-creative work in the realm of music is not possible without the question arising: What, in addition to artistic capabilities, happens in a purely human way? What moral demands are made? What is awakened and what changes through this kind of schooling? In considering the future and the increase in productivity in the Goethean sense, it was mentioned that genius would become a fully conscious moral and human affair linked to the spirit, unlike what it was in the past. What powers can be developed through the exercises we have given? These are questions which in the end will stir the interested reader into action. With that in mind we shall follow this through again.

First and foremost it is a question of freeing oneself from what is customary. For most people this is difficult, if not impossible, for it demands a degree of impartiality, of freedom and of courage, which can by no means be taken for granted. From childhood on we live in an established educational system, in peculiarities of race and family, which determine temperament and destiny and set us from the beginning on a certain path of development. 'One' does, thinks, feels as a normal human being, thus and not otherwise within the social structure, and incorporates into one's being from infancy onwards habits that become second nature. An above-average personality is needed and a sure inner feeling for truth, if this 'one' is to be freed from the tyranny of this second nature. In addition, in the realm of music the mentality of our age determines the education to which we must accommodate ourselves in order to attain any standing in the usual sense.

The position, in general, is that only after a somewhat exhaustive period of study within which one begins to notice the harm and injury due to training, does the possibility of trying something else arise. And who, nowadays, has the strength or can afford to start again from the beginning and give up all that has already been acquired and apparently achieved? Here the first moral action is required, the first truly free act, determined not externally but from within. It is not hard, and there is nothing remarkable in acquainting oneself in passing with the trains of thought and the exercises given here, amongst many other methods and stimuli. But it requires renunciation, perseverance, courage and inner freedom, to start afresh from nothingness and, in face of all that is customary, to follow such a path of transformation.

Then the work of still, selfless listening begins, the moral demands of which must be repeatedly emphasized. This cultivates powers of dedication, selflessness and awareness. It is necessary to make a fresh beginning over and over again, to forget, and live as in a first primordial experience. This means keeping one's own self free and flexible, letting nothing become rigid, so that the soul may stay young and open to learning something new. There might even be an unexpected and hardly credible wonder. Infinite as life itself is the variety of musical elements and forms before which we stand, and we must learn not to be overwhelmed and not to lose courage when faced with an abundance such as this. We know ourselves to be living in the stream of what will come to be, where all that we possess passes away in order, perhaps, to make it possible to rise again on a new level. It is a question of patience and trust which in the end become great helpers.

And we need these helpers! For it is the path of the I, the ego, that we have chosen to tread. That means it must be taken alone, not only in face of difficulties but also of one's own achievements. Basically no one can relieve another of anything—often not even give advice — for everyone's experience is different. A poem by Christian Morgenstern speaks poignantly here.

Journeymen to truth journey on their own; none can be companion to the other on the road.	Die zur Wahrheit wandern wandern allein, keiner kann dem andern Wegbruder sein.
For a while we seem to travel together as a host: but in the end we notice that everyone is lost.	Eine Weile gehn wir — scheint es — im Chor, bis sich endlich — sehn wir — jeder verlor.

Even the most loved one	Auch der Liebste ringet
seems somehow to err,	irgendwo fern...
but he who keeps on	Doch wer's ganz
to the end	vollbringet
wins through to his star,	siegt sich zum Stern.
makes — himself	schafft, sein
en-Christened —	Selbst-Durchchrister,
new ground in God,	Neugottesgrund,
and is welcomed by his kindred	und ihn grüsst Geschwister
in eternal brotherhood.	ewiger Bund!

But loneliness, rightly experienced, bestows powers of love and sacrifice. Dying into a freely chosen task happens in the light of Venus, of cosmic love. It is a path under the guidance of the Logos, the Cosmic Word. The truth of Goethe's words about dying and becoming is apparent at every stage. That zero point of many deaths is known and confronted repeatedly with its dreadful nothingness — the path into the sphere of the Mothers, which has to be trod if the All is to be found.

The words seem almost too grand. And yet — after the conquest of self and selfless inner emptiness — when the nature of a musical structure begins gradually to appear, when the reality and efficacy of world-forces become perceptible, when man awakens to his own centre and responds by his own creative activity — what is that, other than the beginning of a revelation of the cosmos? The greatness and the wonder of cosmic being is nearer than one dares to believe. And a great part of the work consists in winning back the steadfast consciousness of cosmic man which a materialistic age has shattered.

But then in the continuous 'Let there be!' arises the light of new knowledge. This is as yet but dimly realized. One hardly goes through sacrificial death without seeing through all that is death-bringing, however interesting the garb, however all-too-wise, profitable or seductive. It is not by chance that the present time is spoken of as a 'Michael Age'. But the dragon, which must be recognized and overcome, belongs to this picture, just as it was with Apollo. It is justifiable to speak of the present age as an age of coming to grips with evil. The archangel with the sword is the bearer of cosmic intelligence. It is entirely in keeping with his nature that when the connection with the music of the spheres has been found, all earth existence is illumined by the light of its truth. This means that all earthly darkness is pitilessly recognized as such. A moral problem arises, for the solving of which a high measure of loving understanding and wise caution is required. For the most part it is essential for the rebuttal of evil to oppose it with positive forces, with the good in one's own soul. The actual field of Michael's conflict is the soul of man. Triumph or defeat is experienced there. One either conquers prevailing demonic tendencies or surrenders to them. A clear knowledge of external things indicates the path which leads to the inner being. In some way or other evil nestles in every living person and is in the deepest sense the spur towards true clarification and the finding of one's own inner stance. In recognizing this all sinister events are relegated to their place and their limitations can be turned to positive good.

A musical example as a sign of the times may be indicated. To many people it is clear that excessive listening to the media has a decidedly injurious effect, particularly on the ear. Not only the alarming destruction of aural forces but also lack of interest, lack of attention, difficulty in concentration — all this is brought about in no small degree by the continuous aggravation of the organ of hearing. One simply does not react to it at all; one does not listen! There would be little sense in battling against these 'cultural phenomena' for they have their mission in the world. But it is of the highest importance to pit against this destruction of physiological and psychological faculties a conscious daily rebuilding, as has been suggested here, for example, in the exercises. The faculties trained in this way have the power to guard against injurious influences. They will fend off an attack, because forces acquired through inner exertion act like a mirror, in which the true nature of everything is revealed and can be assessed according to its value. As pupils of Michael we stand in our time, or perhaps against our time but — we battle for our time.

With an attitude such as this we already stand in a region of soul which guarantees a connection with the full spiritual background of music. It must be admitted that there are many people who are not able to have any relationship to a true spiritual state of being, any more than to the Archangel Michael. But perhaps it would not be so difficult to re-acquire the relationship if they were free of their connection with confessional and ecclesiastical habit and many of the artistic representations of our present age. No one who is truly awake and lives in the present with a moral outlook can avoid the impression that a spirit of courage and clear, objective powers of intelligence are needed in order to cope with the tremendous conflict of polar forces working from above and below. The imaginative picture of Michael with the dragon is a true, living picture with which — as in Goethe's experience with the Blocksberg — one responds creatively in mind and heart to contemporary events.

It is ever more understandable — indeed, it is even self-evident — that musical work which finds its starting point and its anchorage in the spiritual, grows far beyond personal necessity and gratification. It will become a social, a human concern, for which one pledges oneself to work. And moreover, it is not arrogant or far-fetched, but only felt and spoken in truth, if one learns to know oneself as the mouthpiece of spiritual cosmic forces. If one experiences, for instance, firmness and form in a note, as shown with the first Hanon exercise, if one comes to a confluence of all streams of movement, if one penetrates ever more deeply into the wisdom-filled harmonic relationships of music — then the soul, in complete stillness, will know that the spirit-forces of *form*, the spirit-forces of *movement*, the spirit-forces of *wisdom* are at work. Then it is not only earthbound man that expresses himself, but cosmic forces work through him, once he has prepared himself in full consciousness to be their mouthpiece and has replaced through his own effort the dwindling forces of genius.

The second part of this work was headed: 'The Transformation of Hearing'. Work on hearing brings about a deep transformation in keeping with the nature of music, which has been recognized from earliest times as an educational element of central importance and as such has been sponsored by responsible leaders of mankind. In earlier times it was directed by priests for the well-being of humanity, but now it is taken in hand by man himself, and it is left to his freedom and his insight to exercise his musical activity in a priestly and healing way.

This unique artistic possibility of leading man to the divine, morally-creative kernel of his being has in some measure been experienced by all great personalities. Arthur Schopenhauer in *The World as Will and Idea* writes that the musician hears directly 'the pulse-beat of the divine will flowing through the world'; he stands closer to the heart of the world than any other artist, for 'to him it is given to represent cosmic will itself'. If one takes such words in earnest, they can be quite startling. For they say neither more nor less than that music directly reveals the nature of the divine will in life itself. Not merely a blind will, such as rules in nature, but love and creative dedication and powers of sacrifice, from which in every moment a universe arises, presenting a reflection of the creator — this is captured in the hearing and outstreaming of musical sound. One should learn to grasp it more and more consciously in order to do justice to music, to humanity and to the divine will.

Goethe probably had a feeling for this when he wrote:

> He who does not love music does not deserve to be called human; he who only loves it is only half human; but he who practises it is wholly human.

To practise music — does that not mean to be beholden to it, to give it, inasmuch as one is able, the necessary subjective-inner and objective-outer space in which it can live?

PART THREE

THE INTERVALS

Chapter One

BY WAY OF INTRODUCTION

In considering the intervals we shall follow up the principle of this book and start with the seven or eight stages of the major/minor system. The twelve-note system, dodecaphony, will be considered in the second volume of this work. It is not possible to support anything of the future without first having treated exhaustively what comes from the past, without starting from it, and — in full understanding and with reverence for its eternal value — finding the starting point from which the way opens into the future. If one would speak in this sense of the qualitative experience of the intervals, then that presupposes entering deeply into the nature of the seven basic notes of the major/minor system. The particular nature of the seven intervals is revealed through the extent to which one gets to know the character of the single notes — C, D, E, F, G, A, B — and the forces working in them. Just as the painter must come to terms with the impression the colours make upon his soul, and the poet has to experience the sounds of speech and the effects they have if he is to work with them artistically, so must the musician come to terms with his sounding material. One should not think that a study such as this is too elementary, uninteresting or even primitive. For here the very nature of man will unfold in all its possibilities, in every shade of soul. Qualitative knowledge of music goes hand in hand with self-knowledge and this can expand to world-knowledge.

The image of man heard musically in this way is not merely subjective. It is not the everyday person, with all the commitments and inhibitions of his earthly destiny, but the prototype of man that is gradually revealed, as a thought of God awaiting discovery and perfection on earth. Comprehensive laws and norms are imprinted into the listener and are the same for everyone. In this lies the social value of this work. In these activities and in the practice of this art, all participants are attuned to each other. Their united glance to their higher divine origin becomes light, becomes a bond, from which life-forces can flow.

From our repeated concern with the note C it should be

apparent why it is so important as keynote for our present-day culture. In this connection, our contemporaries must learn to acquire a deeper and more understanding relationship to it. The pronounced ego-like character peculiar to this note, the force of becoming upright which it conveys, its stance in both an ascending and a descending stream, creates the right basis for contemporary musical activity. The more one surrenders in true meditation to these experiences, the more surely will there arise a deep and genuine feeling for what is musical: enclosed within oneself and yet linked to the universe. No other note makes this so penetratingly clear — and nothing else will really suit contemporary musical experience in the same way.

If this note is struck twice in succession in a steady tempo, the movement of the interval is like a self-comprehending gesture, a foundation. This is a first standpoint, a beginning, to which everything else refers. It is the prime, the relationship of a note to itself. And one notices that this interval receives its specific character from the very nature of the note C.

The next note D has a completely different effect. It is good not to hear it immediately after C, but as far as possible unconnected with it, on its own. We should begin afresh, thereby avoiding the objection often put forward that, following on C, one would hear the D from the beginning as an interval. The soul immediately feels freed from an enclosed and static condition. 'Moved', 'friendly', 'questioning', 'wanting to go on', are the characterizations always given at this point. The movement, the gesture, is almost without exception an open wave or a lemniscate. And this also indicates the nature of the interval of the second when the two notes C and D are heard in succession.

In these studies the difference will gradually be noticed between the movement of a note and that of an interval. In the case of the single note the listener concentrates on its inner life, wants to know it, and listens with focused attention entirely to it. In the case of the interval, on the other hand, it is the movement between the two notes which is of interest and which we must follow. The keynote determines the sphere of experience in general, while the note forming the interval expresses the relationship of the two notes to each other. For the keynote C, the note itself and the interval are as one; they coincide qualitatively. But an interval may be transferred to any note as its basis. The

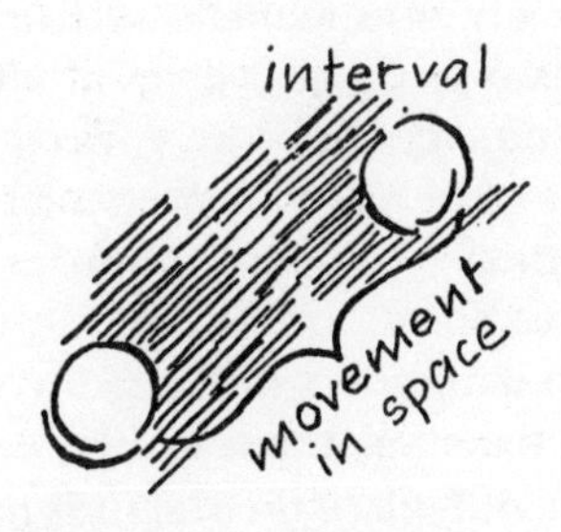

effect of each of the seven basic notes is always revealed in it: each interval of a second will have something of the note D, each third something of E, each fifth something of G, and so on. But one cannot transfer the individual nature of these notes and say for instance that A is the same as D. In these differentiations absolute clarity must prevail. In a later section we shall discuss transposition. It is clear that the movement inherent in the note, and the movement of the interval in space are two aspects which speak in different ways, and yet belong together.

After D the E reveals a more enclosed character again, related to the self. 'Moved' is often stated here but an element of warmth and light enters in, touching the listener in a more intimate way, like a stirring of the heart in contrast to an outer movement in space. It is this inwardness which constitutes the nature of the third and makes it the exponent in the triad of the intimate soul-impulses. All music from the time before Bach until the beginning of the twentieth century, music which reveals an obviously subjective character emphasizing soul-qualities, is for this reason defined by the third as major or minor.

In listening to the F two things are heard: on the one hand a beautiful inner warmth but covered over by a kind of crystalline firmness. A triangle with the apex pointing downward, or a spiral rolling inwards with strong emphasis on the centre are the forms of movement most often found in this note. There is a foreshadowing of the nature of sacrifice, which encompasses the greatest love and the passage through death at one and the same time. It affirms fully the grasping of the earth, but also the passage through the world of solid matter. This brings about a close into which every movement flows. In it the ultimate spiritual principle of the nature of sacrifice lies hidden. This was the reason why in the Middle Ages the note F was said to be the note of Golgotha, the note of Christ. The interval of the fourth between C and F is determined by this in its movement. It contains a crystalline power of form and strong concentration, yet there streams through it inner warmth and force of will. It is probably for this reason that all children love it.

In the fifth place there stands the note G. The spiritual quality hidden and held back in the F is now fully revealed in this sphere. Every relationship with the earthly seems overcome in turning towards the light. Even if it is carried and held by stillness and, one might almost say, wondering earnestness, its character is mostly grasped as a ray of light or as a spiritual power of form. This is imprinted wonderfully in the fifth which, like the octave, has the effect of being translucent, as if rounded off in spirit-expanses of light. But how little the present materialistic age is able to fill such an interval with spiritual substance is shown in the often-expressed opinion that it is empty. It would be better to say that it is bereft of matter.

The experience of the A sphere, following on after this portal to spirituality, releases a weightless, happy feeling of bliss. There is hardly anyone, whether young or old, who can deny this. What moves the E as inwardness swings freely here through cosmic space without losing itself. The Sun-relationship, harmony, is felt without question — harmony in so far as both rest and movement sound at one and the same time; centre and periphery come together proclaiming that in this note and in the interval associated with it, the sixth, the soul touches that realm of pure spirituality where the polarities of earthly existence are held in divine equilibrium. The gestures found here are always large and swinging, yet of harmonious measure.

When the note B sounds, the soul is as if rent with startling force from the bliss of the A sphere. It is not allowed to tarry and there is unremitting pain. There are people who cannot listen to this note for long. They feel a cleavage, or a scattering, to which the soul is unequal. The interval of the seventh can almost be welcomed in gratitude, because all that cannot quite express itself in the single note becomes clearly audible. Two worlds struggle with each other: the feeling of the keynote holding fast in the earthly and the endless yearning for the spiritual fulfilment of the octave. After the blissfulness of the sixth — standing between the I and the note of the sun — this seventh degree is experienced, before the finding of the higher ego in the octave C, in uncompromising clarity as pointing to the crossing of a threshold. Standing firm and binding the earthly nature of the depths, it is a reality which must at all costs be heard. On the other hand the true reality of the upper sphere lies not so much in the seventh itself, with all its discrepancies, but in the spiritual octave, standing resolutely there, as promise of a resolving consonance. This simultaneity of a physically audible keynote and of a concept of the octave, living beyond the seventh but as yet inaudible, constitutes the mystery of this seventh note and its interval: a mystery which, unsealed, lets the being of man ring out in full dramatic suspense. It is the life-situation of the present. The attainment of the octave is for most people a hope for the future, an ideal working out of the spirit as an impulse of the soul, but it is rarely imagined as a stage already achieved.

A new cycle of life begins here with the notes ringing out on a higher level. If the octave becomes a new beginning, the intervals that follow remain the same, but the higher pitch gives to them a lighter, more spiritual colouring. It has been customary until now to regard them in this way. How far this sevenfoldness is in accord with the cosmic spheres of the planets will be discussed in the second volume.

The question now arises: How is the soul-being of man reflected in the realm of the intervals? How do the laws of the ego resound there? It is customary and justifiable in this connection to look upon the soul as threefold. Will, feeling and thinking are the forces within which its life unfolds. But in truth this picture is inadequate, one-sided. It does not do justice to the part played by the ego. For this lives not only in the three separate parts, but in holding them together, in harmonizing the three in an over-ruling unity. One can speak of a condition of equilibrium in these three forces, which the fourth both embraces and penetrates, so that it is in this fourfold condition of will, feeling, thinking and equilibrium that we first come to an overall picture of the human soul and spirit.

The following example gives the intervals from the unison to the octave, sounding harmonically.

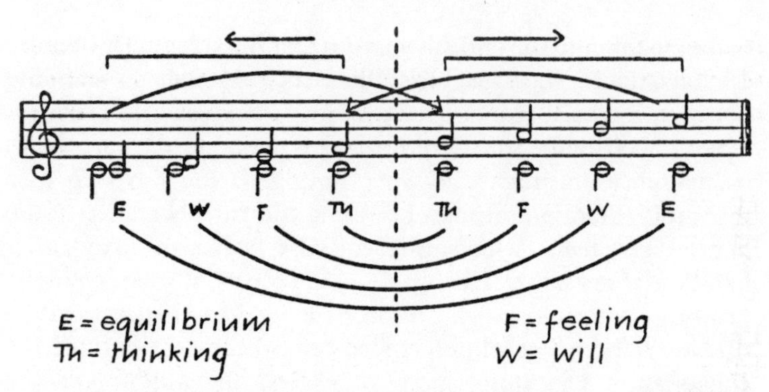

In assessing their relationship to man from the viewpoint of qualitative listening, one is compelled to take into account a twofold aspect. The first, and hitherto customary one, inclines to the classical experience. But the second takes into consideration the altered state of soul in present-day man. The comparison is interesting, and it is important to deal with it. Classically, in unison and octave, the power of equilibrium is felt flowing through them, creating out of two poles the truly perfect consonance. It points to the ego, on the one hand in union with the earthly, on the other as expression of the eternal world. It is a heritage of the church modes and of Ancient Greece, with the notes moving through the octave and the ego holding firmly at the beginning and the end. In keeping with their perfect harmony the unison and the octave are called perfect consonances. This twofold orientation shows two groups of intervals, the unison up to the fourth with its strong grasp of the earth and consequently also of the realm of death and the readiness for sacrifice. The upper arrow on the left indicates that the interval of the fourth belongs below. On the other side is shown the upper group from the fifth to the octave as the realm of the spirit and the arrow to the right points upwards.

We see that both the fourth and the fifth stand in the middle, form the true centre, and it is the passing over from one group into the other that is the most vital moment of all. Not to remain in matter, in the realm of death, but to bear so much warmth that a resurrection in spirit can follow — that is the main task of the human ego. In perfect consonance with the earthly, yet also attaining a perfect consonance with the spirit — that is an act of free will from below upwards, a gesture of love from above downwards (see the two curved arrows). All these are facts which lie enclosed within the spiritually determined course of evolution in a completely objective way. They have their root in a sphere that can be attained only by way of thinking.

Accordingly, the diagram bears in both these central places the Th of thinking; in the case of the fourth with the indication of will upwards (+W) and with the fifth, of feeling downwards (+F). In both instances the wonderful feeling of enclosure is felt as a perfect consonance, even if it is not a unison.

The inner steps in both groups bring something like a subjectively moved life into the frame which goes beyond the personal, of unison to fourth, and fifth to octave: the second and third in the terrestrial realm, the sixth and seventh in the spiritual. One sees with growing amazement how a harmonious structuring holds the whole together. The perfect consonances — unison, fourth, fifth and octave — constitute a kind of static framework. They are resting sounds, determining the structure of the seven-note system.

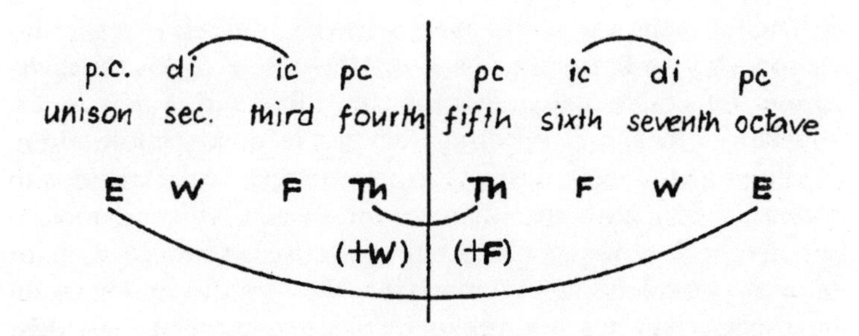

p.c = perfect consonance. ic = imperfect consonance.
di = dissonance

They should be heard often and practised, sounding together in harmony as well as in melodic succession, as in the example given, first as at (a) and then as at (b). The overlapping into the supplementary sphere, from the earth-ego into the spiritual, then from the octave down to the note of sacrifice as in the third form of (b), is a wonderful mutually supporting structure, up to the head and then down to the feet, feeling its way through to the power of the upright.

In contrast to this, the four inner intervals have the effect of being sounds of movement; the interval of the second, open and questioning, has its opposite pole in the seventh. Previously they were both sounds which could not be at rest within themselves but which found their true release from tension externally. At this point, however, one can see the progress made by mankind beyond these forms of experience derived from classical times. The major second is basically no longer a dissonance but has become a pleasing sound. It works, as we have already indicated, for many people like a gently moving, iridescent surface of life-giving water. Concerning the seventh we have already pointed out many details. The strong inner friction to be experienced in the second, in which one feels a connection with the tonic — almost becoming drawn into it — changes here to an external tension, compelled towards two opposite poles. This major seventh is really the only interval experienced as dissonant today. In spite of this, it is so deeply in keeping with the spirit of our time that it holds a privileged place in present day musical life, more privileged than the consonant sounds.

The third and the sixth, on the contrary, nowadays regarded as too soft and romantic, are on the point of losing their former musical values unless they are filled with a new inner substance,. This will be discussed in the next section when dealing with the second aspect of this structure. In the traditional classical sense, both are still beautiful sounds, which in no way stir up the listener or rouse him but envelop him in an harmonious mood of soul. But in so far as they indicate a subjective, heart-filled character they are experienced as consonances, though imperfect in contrast to the others.

All who follow present-day musical life attentively and with an previous centuries have undergone a transformation in the souls of our contemporaries. Very much more than formerly the question of intervals has become one of equilibrium at all stages. Instead of listening with the earlier comparatively unequivocal attitude, one now hears them in two ways, depending on whether they mingle with each other or thrust each other apart, so that it is a question of finding and then holding one's own true centre. Resting sounds are rarely bestowed any longer as a matter of course but must be acquired. That is to say: musical life is no longer only a question of soul but demands an alert activity of the spirit. It no longer suffices for modern man to be rocked gently into a dreamy condition, relaxing and recovering from the cares of the day. Whatever, according to circumstances, music may do to him, it only begins to interest him when he feels a challenge to inner activity and understanding, in which something new will live. This completely different relationship to music cannot be incorporated into the classical scheme already mentioned. The being of man was wonderfully and organically enclosed as a whole, but for modern times that no longer suffices. One may regret this. But who knows whether there may not lie in the lap of a transformed state of consciousness the seeds for a new flowering in the future?

It has been stated that among the seven basic forms, the major seventh is now the only dissonant interval, and perhaps, just because of this, it assumes a privileged place in present-day musical life. In the realm of chromatic alterations further dissonant sounds can be made but these are deviations of the seven-note system. They cannot be taken into consideration here but they may be considered later on. Because of the singularity of the seventh there is justification in ascribing to it a central place in the whole. The arrangement of intervals in a modern sense must take this into account. Instead of a balanced symmetrical orientation between the unison and the octave, the structure will be formed with the seventh as centre, on either side of which the intervals complement each other. The seventh points beyond the octave to a region of wider intervals we have not yet considered and towards which modern man is striving. This is more justifiably the case because, in fact, the spirit-sphere of the octave starts to sound within the seventh. The real threshold of experience between the earthly and the spiritual is formed by this central between the earthly and the spiritual is formed by this central sound, which embraces greater expanses than, for instance, the crossing over from the fourth to the fifth within the octave. Man unfolds beyond the earthly limitations of his self and, for this reaching into the world of the transcendental, he needs new forms of expression. The consciousness of today demands the unfolding of a series of intervals above the octave, which are supplementary to the smaller intervals below it.

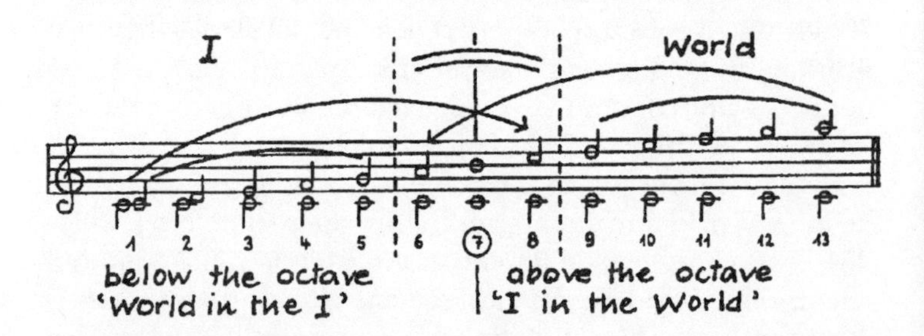

The first sound on the threshold to the spiritual sphere (indicated by the dotted line) is experienced here in the fifth and leads into the experience of soul-conditions with polar orientation: the sixth with the differences of inner and outer, rest and movement held together as yet in harmony; the seventh, in which the duality sounds like a division, a painful discrepancy; and the octave which, as the first step on the far side, can bring these worlds into harmony again through the power of the higher ego. With it a second gateway opens, now on a higher level (indicated again by a dotted line), leading to five further stages from the ninth to the thirteenth. In this way, sixth, seventh and octave form an inner space, the centre (shown by the upper double curve) of a soul-force enclosed on both sides. If one can speak of the 'World in the I' for the lower part — a world still enclosed within the inner being — then this diagram reveals with the new upper region the full possibilities of the 'I in the World', in so far as the expansion into the 'World' is understood as a vigilant, fully conscious listening which overcomes the subjectivity of the individual inner world. It was the sphere of the sixth, C to A, which enabled the 'World' to come to life for the first time, and one sees the relationship between 'I and World' overlapping in two great arcs: the I from the keynote to the octave (first to eighth stage), the World as if sounding towards it, from the thirteenth to the sixth (thirteenth to sixth stage).

If we scrutinize the diagram relating to this, mainly in relation to the question of consonance and dissonance and the soul forces in them, then certain things become apparent: firstly that the relationship of our contemporaries to music is based in an amazing way predominantly on consonance; and secondly that a very much more pronounced division, a kind of contrast in colouring, is experienced in each of the intervals. These are not as clear and straightforward as formerly.

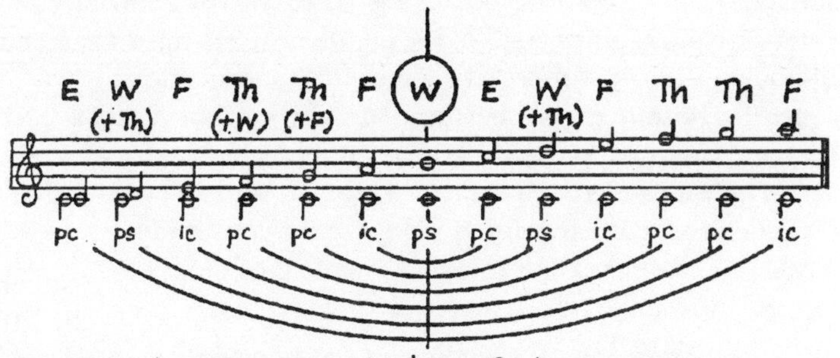

Unison and octave have retained their harmonious character as perfect consonances. But in this connection a significant difference from the former classical diagram can be experienced in the octave. The feeling of perfection, rounding off and crowning the whole, gives way to a feeling of transition, which has the character of a threshold to a still wider and lighter sphere than that of the fifth, and it no longer has the value of an attained goal. The octave has drawn closer to man. In connection with the first musical example it was stated with complete justification that the attainment of the octave is for most people a hope for the future, an ideal working out of the spirit as an impulse of the soul, working deeply in all reality but rarely imagined as a stage of development already attained.

This feeling of finality was experienced as a surrounding firmament. But, where this interval sounds in the course of a diatonic twelve- or thirteen-note tonality, the step must be taken of feeling the 'firmament' not only as representing a distant heaven but of drawing this promising sphere beyond the earth right into oneself. A demand for profounder forces sounds. The higher world to be awakened within oneself demands in the diatonic the schooling in intervals beyond the octave: work on the ninth, tenth, eleventh, twelfth and thirteenth is needed. In musical composition the ninth and tenth have been in use since the time of Bach. It is now only a question of bringing them — and the wider intervals — as a matter of course into closer qualitative experience. It is a question of not only hearing them externally but also of filling them with quite objective soul and spirit substance, just as one does with the stages below the octave. An extension such as this leads to the eighth note losing its character of finality. It is now more like a moment of transition.

It must be understood that these steps beyond the octave are not easy and not readily accessible. They must be worked at in a new way. This intensified, self-creative activity in soul and spirit will be especially concerned with not losing its connection with the keynote. Only this can ensure an awareness of the ego which will prevent the listener from being carried away. This relationship need no longer be a feeling of suspension and a supporting centre, as was already contained in germ in the sixth and seventh. A feeling such as this is attained by systematically training oneself to hear with dual consciousness both components of the interval, the lower as well as the higher. This means, in their polar reality over against each other and at the same time in combination with one another, not only experiencing the interval from below or above, but out of the centre between them, in which the polarities begin to cancel each other out. In seeking both components, the lower note as well as the upper, and hearing them simultaneously, it will gradually become clear that neither 'guides' or 'attracts' in any one direction. This isolating of the notes clarifies the feeling to objective neutrality, reaching the realm of freedom in soul and bearing within it all possibilities — the very condition required in life today. It will become apparent from this inner work that, beginning with the octave, upper and lower begin to interpenetrate and to cross over each other. The depths light up, the heights weigh down, and the interval of the octave gains new significance.

The next step in the sphere below the octave, the major second, has changed for us today. The comments relative to this in the fourth octave of the series of overtones indicated that in our present time, in contrast to earlier times, we feel it as a consonance. It controls and satisfies contemporary requirements in quite an astonishing way. When, for instance, a straightforward triad is avoided because of the gentle nature of the third, it is nothing unusual to insert a second. The vibrating and quickening qualities of this interval do one good. Music goes deeper than the soul element into the vital forces and functions of one's whole organism. There is a more intimate identity with the element of the second, and what was formerly experienced as friction with the keynote now becomes inwardly flowing life. In these flowing forces is revealed the divine wisdom which encloses and combines all that goes to make up an organism and which is accessible to man in thinking and in his striving for knowledge.

This sphere discloses an evident cleavage: even if the major second has assumed for modern consciousness the character of consonance, the minor second still keeps for the listener its earlier experience of dissonance. The difference between 'major' and 'minor' leads to a sharp differentiation between the dissonant and the consonant forms of experience. It needs to be described in a way in which reference is made to both poles. This would be satisfactorily achieved if the sphere of the second were described as polar-sound, (ps) in which the word 'polar' allows for the opposite experience of the dissonance of the minor second. The will-character which befits both these forms of the second is, in the case of the major, associated with the consonances only through the modification 'with thinking' (W+Th).

In the sphere beyond the octave the second becomes a ninth. The expansion of the soul which becomes possible after the threshold experience of the octave reveals a new environment. But how different it is! It is not so much a questioning element, as was the case in the interval below the octave, but much rather an energetic will element which determines the necessity of grasping something beyond the self. One is more dependent on an inner hearing-in-anticipation, sure of its goal, than is the case with the second, which for nearly everyone is simply there. But here nothing comes on its own. A true and clear spiritual goal must sound inwardly if the new spiritual sphere is to open up, giving shape and form to the ninth. And, like a light leading onwards and illuminating the path, this ninth must be held consciously in suspense with the lower keynote.

In classical times the ninth was an experiment of the utmost daring and it was seldom used except by the greatest composers. The range of experience was kept within the octave. But today, when the transcendental world knocks at the door in phenomena by the hundred, such wide intervals are an obvious means of expression. What is it other than a negative ninth when a consciousness bound to matter introduces flights into space and research into the atom, which burst open the bounds of the earthly — albeit with insufficient intelligence — and shatter the wise structure of the world? The extension of consciousness beyond bodily constraint, which should happen in spirit, takes place in an alien sphere. The task of a conscious, healthy crossing of the threshold to the spiritual is at this very time placed before us. The feeling for the ninth is wanting to develop.

For this realm also, the description polar sound is suitable. We have to summon up an enhanced alertness and activity of the Will (W); and a 'plus Th' is also correct, for each crossing of the threshold beyond the experience of the octave connects the soul musically with the expanse of cosmic thought.

The third as interval within the octave stemmed from a feeling of joy or sorrow, from being beyond oneself or more within oneself, a more active or a more receptive element of soul — this all determined from an earthly point of view.

The tenth, however, lays hold on all that could be referred to as the element of personal destiny within the octave and as the actual question of harmony or disharmony at that stage. Here, the bond with the keynote is no longer so burdened with tension and weight. Both spheres unite as a matter of course. Something like a reversal process between inner and outer begins to resound: just as in the geometrical diagram so often referred to, which was given in the chapter on the complementary series, there is an interchange of experience between the lower and the upper sphere. A previous major experience of the third sounding as tenth, in spite of its high position, is much more enclosed; even though far off, it is rounded off within itself, as if it would pass itself off as minor. On the other hand, the E flat of the high position, in relation to the C lying a tenth lower, bears within itself an activity which lends to the interval a feeling of tension and anticipation. One could imagine it to be D sharp. Feeling (F) may also be connected with the tenth in spite of the difference in colouring it bears as the major C to E or the minor C to E flat. Subjectivity of feeling remains the same as with the thirds, and it is included as an imperfect consonance.

In connection with the fourth, which becomes the eleventh above the octave, it has already been pointed out that modern man is united with this interval by a strong personal feeling. Is one still justified in referring to it as a perfect interval? Certainly in pure form it is now as it was before, a grasping by the will of the earthly. But in contemporary music — and probably also for the music of the immediate future — the fourth in its augmented form as the tritone C to F sharp begins to play a role which is more decisive and central — even if it is still controversial — and one may well ask why.

In the seven-note system it divides the totality of the octave in half, spanning the strong contrast between the intervals C to F and C to G by a radiant force directed towards a goal. An inner light bursts forth, showing the way to the spiritual threshold of the fifth. Light begins to penetrate matter. It is understandable that in the circle of the twelve the tritone becomes the diameter, an axis which unites the opposite poles and in this way holds the twelve notes together. This tendency of the fourth to transcend itself, to become the exponent of an ego-force which makes of itself a boundary and at the same time gives the direction towards a goal, does not indicate any abandonment of its character of fulfilment. It only means that this enhanced feeling of self becomes a centre where the spheres of earth and spirit meet and sustain one another. This tritone is like a light-ferment handed over to the earth. The description of perfect consonance (pc) still holds good for the interval of a fourth; and the relationship to the soul-forces of thinking (Th) plus the contribution of a pure will towards the spirit (+W) is also justified here.

As with the fourth within the octave, something new arises in the eleventh above the octave. The relationship between the keynote and the note forming the interval can be experienced differently from stage to stage in this upper sphere through the suggested exercise of experiencing the two sounds in their polar reality with dual consciousness, in opposition and at the same time in combination each with the other. In the case of the ninth, the relationship to the keynote was experienced clearly as suspense, the notes sounding singly over against each other. In the tenth, on the other hand, a beautiful blending arises as a matter of course between the lower and the upper note. In the eleventh, the lower C — the exponent of earthly existence — which left its mark on the fourth, drops away. A life in pure spirit begins and, corresponding to this, a feeling arises that the intensity of experience is concentrated in the upper note while the lower note seems to disappear. In the case of this interval, it is no longer important to be reminded of the ground beneath one's feet. The human ego musters new strength in this unaccustomed interval of the eleventh. In the eleventh the ego of man seems to garner new strength. Once again a reversal takes place; the firm composure of the lower, earthbound fourth begins to expand centrifugally, outwards towards cosmic man. Because of this one can speak of the eleventh as a perfect consonance and connect it with pure thinking (Th).

A similar cosmic element is revealed musically in the intervals with the fifth. The fifth within the octave has acquired a new character for our prevailing musical feeling. Emptiness is hardly the right word any more. Rather, the state of soul of the early Middle Ages, the organum age of singing in fifths, has come quite close to us again. The revival of this old music, which stems from the mood of the fifth, demonstrates this. In our diagram, this interval can be called a perfect consonance and the soul-force of thinking (Th) can be combined with a 'plus feeling' (+F). The fifth has become much more a personal possession than it could have been in an earlier age.

Today this interval has special significance, especially in the two chromatically altered forms, the diminished and the augmented fifth, C to G flat and C to G sharp. C to G flat is the middle of the octave, enharmonically united with the tritone, creating a point in which balance is held between a striving to the light (C to F sharp) and an inclination towards the depths (C to G flat). But C to G sharp, the augmented fifth, leads with intensity to the crossing of the threshold and orientation beyond the octave.

The twelfth, in this realm beyond the octave, brings us closer to the completion of the scheme. As in the case of the fifth below a new orientation occurs. Gently, no longer in a dominating way, nor dropping away as in the eleventh, the keynote C sounds again in the depths of the interval. The circumference of the inner being expands towards bringing about a twelvefoldness of sound. It forms a new totality. This penultimate interval gives an incredible impression of light, which in its pure form reveals the character of a perfect consonance (pc+Th). In the upper sphere one prefers to leave untouched the objectivity of the pure form, which does not readily admit of a chromatic augmentation or diminution. The signs for feeling (F) and for willing (W) are not applicable.

As with the sixth within the octave, the transition to the thirteenth beyond the octave is of special significance. We have already spoken at length about the sixth and a repetition is not necessary. The connection with the sphere of feeling (F) is clear and it qualifies as an imperfect consonance (ic).

The thirteenth objectifies this quality in so far as it mediates an experience similar to that of the octave in the sevenfold order. It is at one and the same time an end and a beginning — it alters and becomes the beginning of a new series of intervals from A to the F in a higher octave. But this new structure bears a different character, for its intervals have partly other values. Just as in the classical diatonic system from C to C one embraces the whole range of musical sound from the depths to the heights in seven or eight octaves, so does there emerge here in four patterns of twelve, that is to say of thirteen notes, a complete structure of forty nine steps.

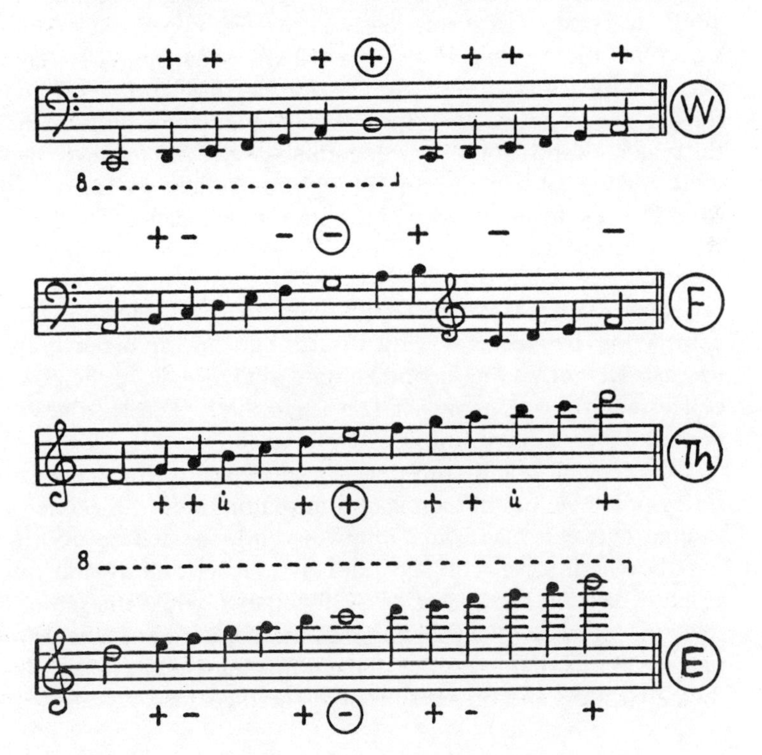

It would lead too far to enter into a detailed consideration of these four basic forms. Yet even a brief survey will reveal that their structures and moods differ, both in the scale and in their intervals. But the thirteenth note of these scales, be it major or minor, brings a kind of conclusion which at one and the same time opens up the possibility of continuing in another kind of way.

In times such as ours, when the twelve has to take over from the seven, it will be important, even within the pure diatonic — not only chromatically or with semitones — to approach scales and intervals corresponding to and grounded in the phenomenon. A comparative way of listening shows each of the four forms in their totality to be connected with one of the four soul-forces. These are determined by the separate intervals, which incline more to major (+) or minor (-). The first scale from C upwards shows, around the central point of the major seventh, a picture of only major and perfect intervals. These can be experienced with full justification as laying stress on the will (W). The second scale from A is far gentler, with two major seconds in addition to the perfect intervals and the five minor ones. The seventh in the centre is also minor. This scale can be said to lay stress on the feeling-forces (F). The third form is burdened with tension and conscious of its goal; two augmented fourths, with the major seventh in the centre, emphasize the will towards the light. A living consciousness (Th) rings out. Finally, the last form from D gives the experience of a wonderfully balanced equilibrium (E) around a minor seventh. All four forms take their course breathing as it were between a major and a minor mood, revealing the fundamental law of life between expansion and contraction, between a striving towards light and an inclination towards weight. In the second volume of this work, in the part concerning the twelve, we shall return to this and endeavour to penetrate more deeply into the whole realm.

We must still briefly consider, in connection with these four series of twelve or thirteen stages in diatonic form, the interchange between major and minor sevenths as central point. Exactly as in the case of the second, a division appears. The major seventh has still the character of dissonance while the minor seventh, for present-day feeling, has the colouring of a consonance. Chords of the seventh of the following kind have lost all their sharpness and the tension of dissonance.

As in the sphere of the second, one can distinguish between a more dissonant or consonant character and speak of a polar sound, whose emphasis on the will-quality is modified by a 'plus feeling' W(+F).

These distinctions of major and minor lead as a matter of course into the realm of the chromatic. With time attention must be paid to two distinct aspects in the structure of intervals. But first of all we must go back to what was customary in classical music.

Man's relationship to light and gravity, the power to raise his body into an upright position between the firmament and the centre of the earth, illumines all things musical in polar interplay. In the colouring of sounds (chromatic means colour) whether lightening or darkening, this law of life finds spontaneous expression. Sharp and flat, tending towards the light and inclining towards the depths, are chromatic extensions, are bearers of definite functions in a definite direction, exponents of the principle of breathing. Extending into double sharp or double flat, one finds the resultant fivefoldness of each note still musically determinative today, where the connection with the seven is maintained. The raising or lowering of pitch, of sharp to double sharp, of flat to double flat, essentially links up with all that is connected with the centrifugal or centripetal forces of the ego.

At this point it is worth listening again to these different experiences in the single note, even if they are thought to be known. It will be found that in the extension from sharp to double sharp, or from flat to double flat, it is not a question of increasing or decreasing tension.

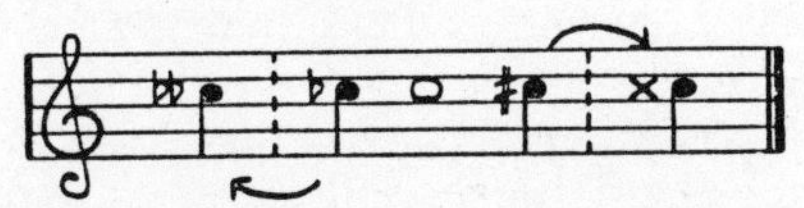

Much rather does one perceive something like a leap between the simple and double alterations, as one moves into regions of light out beyond oneself, or into the mystical darkness of one's inner being. In both cases it requires something in excess of one's own forces which cannot be given simply by sharp or flat. It is necessary to reach beyond oneself until a more spiritual aspect of soul is attained in order to accomplish this raising or lowering. They are the sound-forms of a modern consciousness striving to gain access to a higher and a lower nature at one and the same time. In this connection it is interesting that both these extreme chromatic forms first appeared about the middle of the eighteenth century. The note achieves a range of four semitone steps, equivalent to a major third, and accords beautifully with the major and minor systems.

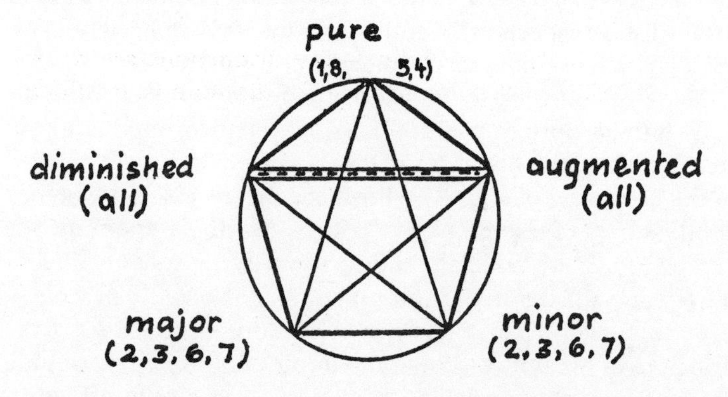

The former differences in the chromatically-altered intervals, in keeping with the soul-forces activated and expressed in them, require a division of five, making a distinction between the perfect consonances, the imperfect consonances and the dissonances. The latter, the 'moving' sounds of the scale, grasp all possibilities in the soul with their major and minor distinctions, as well as with the gradations of augmented and diminished intervals. On the other hand the 'resting' sounds, in their absolute objectivity, bear the unalterable character of 'pure'. No major or minor variation is possible. In so far, however, as this sphere is accessible to man's insight, they merit the terms augmented or diminished when expanding or contracting. The diagram above shows this division in the form of a pentagram. The overlapping which occurs in the transformation of pure intervals destroys in a certain sense the original purity. The wonderful character of the unison resting within itself, for example, in the case of the prime and the octave, becomes strongly dissonant.

If one were to go beyond this, from C to C double sharp or C double flat, then the perfect consonance would move from its static exactitude and slide over strongly into the movement of the second. But fifth and fourth go over into the sounds of the famous tritone, C to G flat and C to F sharp, while on the other hand C to G sharp and C to F flat are more akin to the minor sixth or major third. But apart from that it is right to say that the perfection is annulled.

It may well be asked whether these distinctions are really audible, or whether they are imposed on the sounds. It will be found in comparing the seven basic notes with the five chromatic intermediate stages that there is a distinct difference. They carry a disunity within themselves from the start, vibrating between tenderness and tension. One or the other certainly predominates, as the following shows.

Only G sharp and A flat are equal. The predominant character of sharp or flat is traced back to the enharmonic within the note. Each note except G sharp/A flat, embraces a threefoldness — sharp, flat and a double alteration, either double sharp or double flat: e.g. C-B sharp-D double flat, C sharp-D flat-B double sharp, E flat-D sharp-F double flat, and so on. The double sharp or double flat in the note gives it its decisive nature: in the case of C sharp the B double sharp, in E flat the F double flat and so on. The diagram overleaf shows a chain of intervals which, when experienced qualitatively, gives a differentiation of the twelve tempered notes into 35 which overlap. It is one of the exercises in this chapter to make these variations within the individual note one's own. They introduce into music the chroma, the living colour. One must distinguish quite clearly two different things: firstly, all twelve notes show a twofold lighting up or darkening down and are differentiated in a fivefold manner, following one

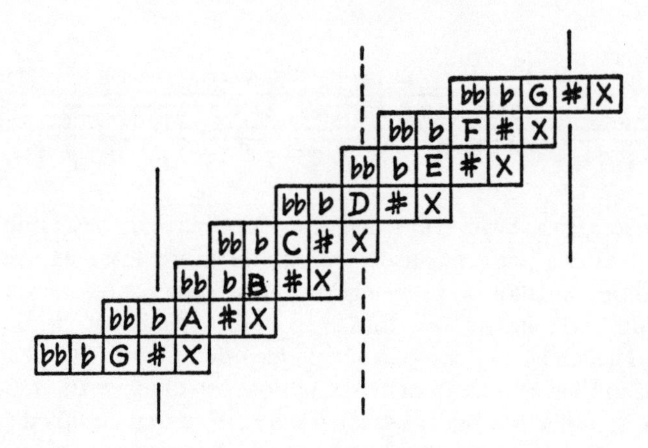

another as it were horizontally in time. The vertical spatial element arises out of the fitting into one another and the overlapping of the chromatic. Secondly, there is the transference of these differences to the being of the interval, so that a double transformation does not conform with a perfect consonance in its more static character, but only a simple one above or below.

The chromatic alterations of the 'moving' sounds ring through all the subjective transformations of personal life. Fundamentally they breathe between the active and passive of major and minor, turning more to the surrounding world or more into oneself. With the augmented and diminished forms they acquire the shading of the neighbouring interval above or below:

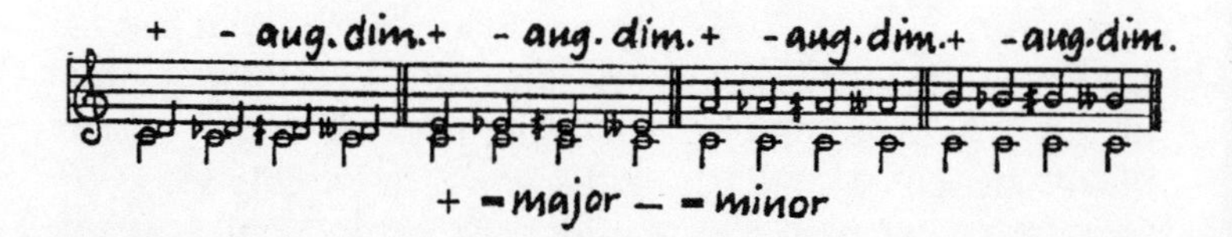

C to D sharp takes on the colouring of a minor third, C to D double flat that of a pure prime, C to A sharp sounds similar to the minor seventh, C to A double flat corresponds to a pure fifth and so on. Here also the dissonant sounds, like the second and the seventh, become consonant, thirds and sixths as imperfect consonances tend towards pure or dissonant sounds. As these intervals are 'moving' sounds the changes do not break through their own sphere.

But what happens to the laws of chromaticism from this point of view? The altered experience of the intervals (pages 146 and 147) reveals that at the present time new soul forces are at work and demand other tonal-structures. These can be illustrated by the heptagram, the seven-pointed star, in which besides the perfect and imperfect consonances the cleft dissonant intervals of the second and seventh are indicated as polar sounds.

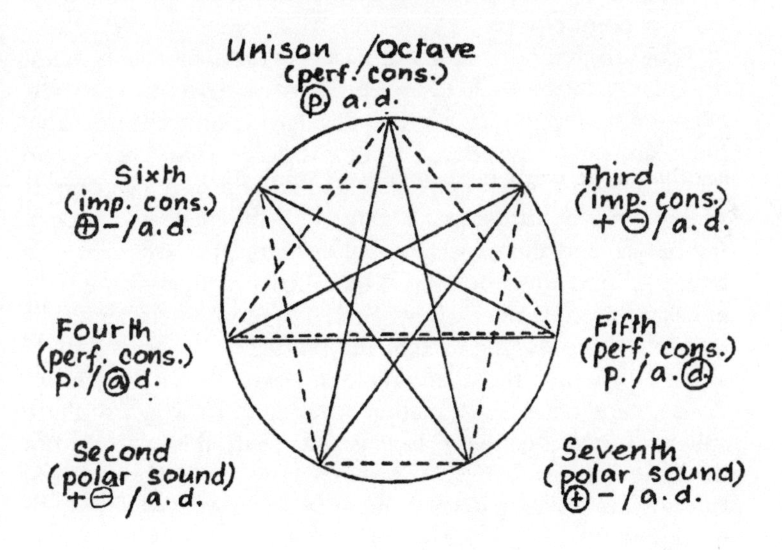

The chromatic alterations remain the same as in classical music. But gradually the experience comes through that each interval is expressed most clearly in keeping with its own nature in a definite constellation. Prime and octave, as bearers of perfect harmony in equilibrium of soul, express this most clearly in pure form, while the fourth and fifth become an enharmonic unison in augmented and diminished form. The sixth registers in major form the cosmic distances peculiar to it in feeling, while the third expresses its inward quality beautifully in minor mood. The original dissonant quality in the realm of the second and the seventh is kept most purely as minor in the first instance and as major in the second. Feeling does not err if one senses in this seven-pointed star a more comprehensive picture of man than previously. It gives to the whole aspect of interval a meaning which can only be verified through practice.

The overlapping of the intervals (page 158) leads to a musical phenomenon which is the cause of much dispute today — that is, the enharmonic. It has already been mentioned in the chapter on the overtones in considering the opposite streams of movement with their stratifications, constellations in space, quarter-tones and the fifth octave. We shall investigate it now from another point of view.

Tuning by temperament, not least with the piano, has brought it about that the difference between sharps and flats has gradually been eradicated. C sharp and D flat, having one and the same pitch, are today considered to be the same note. There is no longer any distinction between them and they are used pretty well at random. But if, proceeding from the qualitative aspect, the nature and the experience of an interval is accepted as a reality — and this book would awaken just this — then the enharmonic must not simply be swallowed up by the similarity in pitch. Intervals originate in the mutual relationship of two sounds, whether these are melodic, harmonic or rhythmic. Consequently it is not a matter of no concern which of these spheres sound together. C to E as a major third is in reality not the same as B sharp to E, D double flat to E, or D double flat to F flat, or, even B sharp to F flat and so on. The sound which is built up out of the upright nature of C with the warm inner movement of E, is quite different from a B in its painful tension being raised to B sharp and working together with a darkly moving, fluid D double flat. Still more subtle are the differences which arise in the case of B sharp to F flat, or in the interval D double flat to D double sharp. The example given here shows some such differentiations, giving in each instance a different interval.

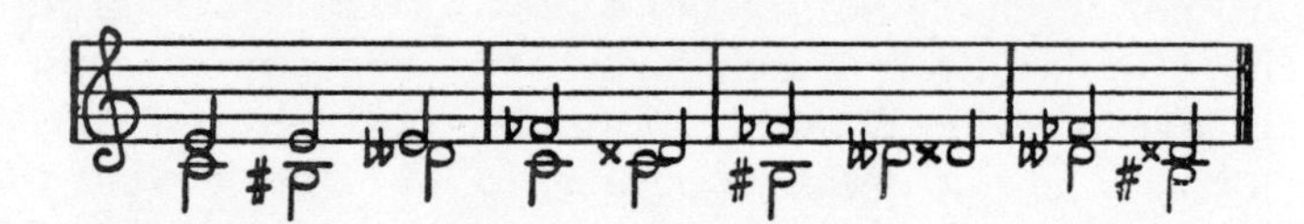

One sees that in theory the same interval can expand to a relatively simple augmentation or diminution and a double or even a threefold intensification. In practice, these are questions for the future, for, in order to hear and form such subtle distinctions, we must first work consciously on a new supersensible etheric organ within the self.

We should not shrug off these niceties of musical versatility and possibilities of expression with the words 'abstract' or 'hair-splitting'. This they are only so long as we are not capable of experiencing them qualitatively. A subtle and penetrating wealth of feeling arises in them, such as has not yet been foreseen. It would be equal to a process of death if these colourings were to be obliterated arbitrarily from musical experience and if there were no further development in this field. Rightly formed through hearing and applied in composition, they would fill the need for a new stimulus of the most far-reaching kind, and would offer a spiritual counterbalance of a powerful and health-giving nature to experiments of a mechanical and electro-acoustical kind alien to man.

Attention to these phenomena and schooling through them points the way clearly into spiritual realms and is of relevance to the contemporary musician, and is relevant also to the historical conscience mentioned in the 'Transformation of Hearing' in connection with the re-creation of the Lyre of Apollo. In the second volume of the present work, in considering the 'Seven in Music', this matter will be taken up again.

A brief glance may now be cast at the question of transposition, for with the enharmonic we are already there. The comprehensive elucidation of this question will be found in the last part of this book in 'The Nature and Activity of the Keys'. But in so far as the keynote and the basic intervals form the starting point of investigation into the nature of the keys, it may also be mentioned here.

It is often said that a fifth is a fifth, no matter where it lies or which notes constitute it. This remark is but a half truth. The experience of the interval as such is the same, but the shades of feeling which lie within the component sounds are different. These evident deficiencies in the more subtle musical distinctions may well be attributed to the obliteration of values through tuning by temperament. This needs to be clarified here.

Four intervals are given here in comparison with the basic

form on C. At the beginning of this chapter it was shown that in the playing together of two notes to form an interval, the lower note determines the sphere generally speaking, while the note forming the interval expresses the relationship of the two notes to one another. Attention to the lower note determining the sphere in the above example point to the following: C to G in relation to E flat to B flat sounds more static, more secure and more unequivocal. The nature of this keynote dominates the relation to the G. In the case of E flat to B flat, on the other hand, a gentle inwardness prevails. The love-filled, downward-inclining B flat, whose movement one might almost pursue to a still deeper stage, and the inward E flat, as basis, give a much gentler feeling to this fifth. In the following two intervals of a major third C to E and D to F sharp, it is clear that the latter is more intensively active than the former. The light-filled raised F introduces a tension which is borne by the questioning element of the D. The two sevenths are different essentially in the sharpness which operates strongly from the F, while in the case of the seconds it is clear that the different spheres of the lower notes, whether heavy or light, are experienced in the C and the G. These distinctions are certainly not a matter of difference in pitch. B to D sharp, for instance, sounds definitely brighter than C to E, because B and also D sharp are, as sounds, more intense — that is, through the sharp they bear within them more light.

The same holds good for the two fourths in the above example. In the movement presented graphically, there would, in hearing, be similar differences, as if the basic form (a), were transformed each time into one of the others without losing its original tendency of movement.

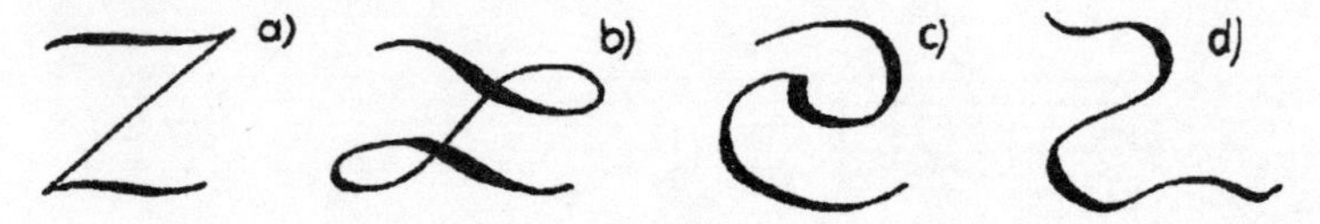

The word 'love' indicates a definite soul-force, but never will two people express it in the same way. This is a truism not yet carried through to its logical conclusion in the world of music. It would mean not only an inevitable demand to proceed to true clarification of the intervals, but would also make it impossible for a properly schooled listener to dispose of, to put aside, to interchange at will, the single forms which spring from a deep spiritual foundation. If attention is paid to a person's peculiarities, why should it not be so here, where it is a question of experiencing the reality of living spiritual forces?

In conclusion, and at the same time as transition to the next chapter, one thing must still be mentioned which has not yet received sufficient attention: it is the distinction made between an interval regarded melodically — the notes following on after each other; or harmonically — the notes sounding together; or in the rhythmic relationship of notes one to the other. As each of these spheres lays hold of a different part of the human being, the melodic the head-system, the harmonic the chest, the rhythmic the limb-system, it is evident that a clear distinction may also be experienced and raised to consciousness in the intervals. For in so far as these systems are connected in soul with thinking, feeling and will, they each disclose an essential body of law. The next chapters will be devoted to these questions.

Chapter Two

THE FORMING OF MELODY THROUGH THE INTERVALS

Once the basic intervals are so imprinted upon the listener that they can be recognized unerringly there will be a completely new living experience of every work of art. This imprinting occurs with amazing rapidity, much more so than by purely acoustical means. It enables a person whose soul is alive — that is, whose soul is in movement — really to live with music, whether as listener or performer. In the course of time something like a new absolute pitch develops from which the note is recognized by its spiritual nature.

Clearly this is especially important for performance. The intervals are best made one's own through personal activity. They should awaken a feeling of responsibility towards what has been heard, and enable the performer to give a new and spiritually guided rendering, whether instrumentally or vocally. This is the next step required of qualitative hearing. There is a unity between ear and larynx, listening and activity, impression and expression, and this should be taken seriously right from the very beginning. One should no longer simply make music in the usual way, with technical mastery and a grandiloquent musical joy in one's own performance. To play, to sing in the true sense means to be creative. But how far one has become divorced from this awareness has already been indicated by the distinction made between a creative and an imitative musician — Prometheus and Epimetheus! But how will Epimetheus become Prometheus? By transforming himself into what he wants to play. He must really be that which he plays. He must consciously produce the language of music objectively, in a fully human way, and do only this, without momentary moods and personal interpretations. A beginning has to be made with the simplest things, for this challenge is not an easy one. It makes a great difference if these preliminary studies are done adequately, not only in body but also in soul and spirit. For here music begins to be raised out of the 'beautiful semblance', out of the 'as if', into full reality. And out of this newly created vitality it can once more become truly objective in the sense of the Orphic age: Prometheus created anew!

It is in this sense that the ensuing suggestions should be followed.

It is good to begin with the single notes that are to be connected. In order to school a certain mobility of soul, a capacity for transformation, the following simple exercises are suggested. They can always be supplemented. Firstly, the transformations through the scale: the bearing of C gradually changes to that of D.

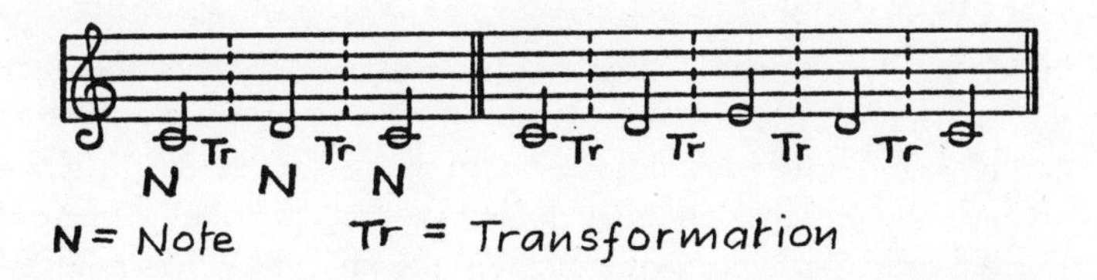

(N, the bearing of the note; T, the transformation to the next note.) Only when this new bearing is established within the C is the D to be sounded, not before. It is also important to take care that the bearing is fully established before beginning at all. Usually it is played according to a certain routine, superficially, without any inner participation. The exercises should be continued until the whole scale is mastered in gradual transformation from note to note and the character of each sphere has been distinctly formed. It is especially important to pay attention to the complete change from firmness to brightness between F and G, and also from the painful nature of B to the restfulness of the octave C.

As the next step these transformations can be made in any chosen succession of notes, but without making the movements of the intervals.

It is rather like the sensation of flying through cosmic space from one starry sphere to another. A beginning can be made by experiencing the first sphere; then gradually allowing the next sphere to take over until union with it is achieved.

After these loosening exercises in transformation, which develop the feeling for connecting the notes as well as for the movement between them, one may go over to the forming of intervals. With this aim in view, everything available in this connection should be used in individual studies, and it is important to be familiar with this before proceeding to artistic work. Alertness and vitality of soul are not so easy to acquire. Often in a state of sheer despair the inclination arises to fall back into a certain dreaminess in musical matters. Qualitative practice makes high demands. New capabilities and organs have to be developed, old habits have to be overcome and above all indolence, much loved as it is, must be conquered. The stronger the connection with what is customary the more energetically must the awareness of a new kind of activity be sought. It is a matter of course that everyone who is to some degree musical can play and sing these familiar, and as it were inborn, intervals acoustically. But then in the ordinary way only the pitch is grasped. For the most part training is directed towards the achievement of purity in this respect. But here it is a question of the nature of the movement from note to note. It is not the note as such that is important — though of course it must be pure — but what is experienced in the soul between the notes. In this the true life of music is raised into the spiritual and inaudible, and is united there with the creative ego-centre of the performer. That is what matters.

Some short examples from various works of art can now be given. For the study of purely melodic intervals the polyphonic style is especially suitable. The wonderful themes and motifs of medieval church music provide good opportunities for work that is calm, pure and inwardly alive. It is best to practise first without the text and then afterwards to enliven it with the words. Here is a study in the interval of the second from *Domine Deus* by Orlando di Lasso.

In it the steps from note to note are practised and the note reached as second is changed in feeling, in order to create the second to the next note. This transformation in the note is important as a study alternating between rest and movement, between grasping the ego and stepping out into the surrounding world.

A flowing exercise with the second, which brings to the fore the unifying element of this interval, is the *Agnus Dei* of Josquin de Prés (16th century).

Here it is the fourth from A to D, both rising and falling, and the octave in 'tollis' which particularly have to be formed, in contrast to the otherwise flowing succession of notes.

In an 'Adoramus' motif, also from Orlando di Lasso, it is important to give expression to the fourth and minor second in '...ramus te' and to the wonderful upward glance of the soul in 'Christe' — a completely light-filled dematerializing of the fifth and also of the whole Divine Name, which embraces a sixth.

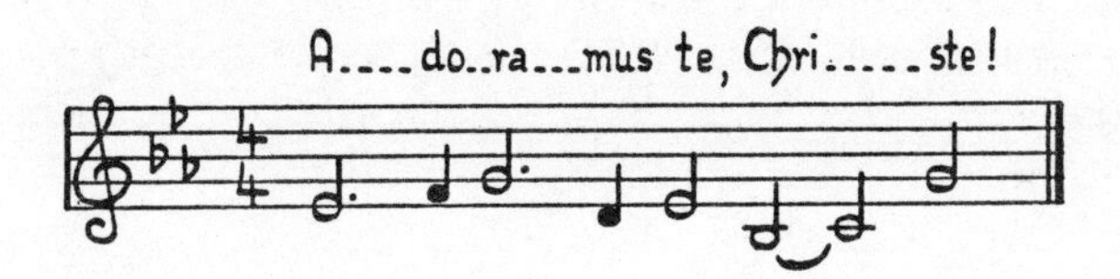

An exact imitation in the experience and movement of a motif between tenor and soprano may be practised in the following short motif by Samuel Scheidt.

The musical experience and not the declamation of the text stands in the foreground. The being of Christ is felt again through the rising fifth, to which the tranquil movement of the second, outwards and back again, resounds like a sympathetic vibration of the heart.

Another short Scheidt motif between higher and lower instruments sets the task of distinguishing and balancing out inwardly the contrast between D and E flat above and G and B flat below, a minor second above and a minor third below.

A study in the constant interchange of theme and imitation between two recorders is found at the beginning of a *Fantasia* by Orlando di Lasso.

These four successive motifs, where in the fourth — the last — the low voice brings a sixth instead of a third (x), are interesting because the polyphony of the intervals and their contrasting melodic direction is not only important according to the notes, but because it can also be formed qualitatively between the notes bringing about an unexpectedly lively spatial interplay of the voices of a wonderful transparency, or, one should rather say trans-audibility.

In concluding these short examples of pure polyphony, in

which it is never a question of vertical harmony but only of an interplay of the horizontal lines, let us consider a little reveille by Karl Marx, a splendidly cheerful study in fourths and fifths, in which the up-beat character of the crotchet must not be confused with the first beat of the bar.

All the previous examples have been chosen intentionally because they are easy and satisfying in themselves and are therefore accessible to everybody. It is left to the option of the serious reader to seek out or write other exercises according to individual requirements and questions which arise. From such short studies and their gradual elaboration it will be more and more noticeable how the transition into the artistic sphere is accomplished without coercion in all fields of instrumental music and song. An amazing abundance of new, subtle, pliable and colourful tone qualities emerges in spite of an overall simplification.

In a qualitative study of the basic intervals such as this, work in the melodic element requires the incorporation of chromatic differentiations at this stage. Care must be taken that in spite of the tension in the sharp, or the relaxation in the flat, the true nature of the note is not lost. In addition to the first exercise on the structure of the scale we must now take the chromatic from C with the

two kinds of endings, (a) and (b). The tension to A sharp, and still further to B natural, is difficult to begin with for most people, so that the gentler use of B flat is better. If, however, this exercise is carried out as far as the octave, one will notice that at first the ending is not quite pure, but either too high or too low. These variations usually occur between the fifth and the sixth steps. In this upper sphere it is more difficult to find the right degree of tension. Below, the closeness of the keynote gives a firmer footing. This 'chromaticism' can be varied rhythmically according to choice. The main thing is that between the brightening-up and the transition to the next step, a quite lively interchange of tension and release is audible.

The opposite exercise is downwards in flats.

The little lemniscate, A flat-G-F sharp-G around the fifth, must be made with care, as also the diatonic transition into the lower region of F.

The trends in the movements of chromatic alterations should be studied in a motif that is more free. In face of levelling out in this sphere it is impossible to take seriously enough the necessity of listening closely to this inner will of chromatic and enharmonic changes and following them through. In the study of phenomena it is a matter of clearly understanding the intrinsic nature of each phenomenon. Whether one follows this inner will in practice later, or not, is quite another question and lies within the free choice of the artist. All the laws of formation in the seven-note system are founded on this inner will of the elements. In this lies the beauty and the grandeur of the creations of former times, and it is the task of the future to include these manifestations of the life in phenomena even in newer kinds of musical experience and in new tonal systems. In the following motifs (a) and (b), transformations are borne in mind which lead into the enharmonic:

C sharp to D flat in the first exercise, F sharp to G flat, and especially the change in the note B flat to A sharp in the second. It may seem that such studies should not be made on the piano. Yet this is a deception, as in the case of other instruments one usually helps oneself with a slight alteration of pitch either upwards or downwards. It is better to keep to the tuning by temperament, and to attain the character out of the inner intensity of experience. Such efforts on the piano produce beautiful variations of touch, and also living colours in other instruments, and especially of course in singing.

The distinction between minor and major and between diminished and augmented intervals leads, in the seven-note system, almost involuntarily through the change of direction from a minor tendency to a major one. An experience arises similar to that between seventh and octave and is not lost through transposition: an inner resolution sounds inaudibly, giving the next stage, and it does not matter so much whether this is actually audible or not.

This emerges most clearly in the augmented and diminished stages, because they contain the greatest tension. They are especially difficult to sing and can be formed purely only when the idea of the relevant resolution stands behind them.

This relationship to the seventh exists within the rising tension of every sharp; while every flat has the tendency towards a minor second, which has the same significance as a major seventh downwards. It is evident that rising chromatic progressions, simply as successions of semitones, might seem to be soaring away, while when descending they tend to weigh down. Oscillation between these extremes gives to the whole field of the chromatic the imprint of drama and suffering. It is no wonder that in Mozart simple little turns and appoggiaturas indicate a playing in the light, a dissolving of contours that are too firm, while with Beethoven it is the appoggiaturas that underline the striving element of the ego. Richard Wagner, with his intuitive genius, knew very well that by the chromatic quality of his Tristan he opened the gateway to a world of longing and a search for redemption through supersensible man which today rules everyone's inner life.

This seeking element looking outward, questioning inwards, lives also in the theme of a little 'Chromatic Invention' in the third volume of Bela Bartók's *Microcosmos:*

The looking backwards and upwards in the G sharp to A, the harsh change to E flat and D, then the embracing of the middle notes in this space of a fifth, it is as if the heart were vibrating to and fro between G and E. Moreover the indication 'Lento' enables the theme to be recognized from the start as that of a soul entangled and deeply tortured by questions and contradictions. The mood of the seventh rules here, perhaps also that of the questioning second.

This last sentence touches on an aspect of interval which should be mentioned and brought to consciousness: it is the interval-mood, which as such extends over and encloses a whole piece of music. Just as certain intervals have governed whole cultural epochs (Part One, Chapter Two), because they emerge from a certain state of human consciousness, so, on a smaller scale, a certain frame of mind may prevail throughout a composition and be characterized by certain intervals. Without doubt one can feel that a pentatonic bears an objective mood — free, detached, unearthly and light-filled — which befits the fifth. Over a lullaby by Brahms, over all his work, lies the third, as it does over the whole romantic period. A Träumerei by Schumann is inspired by the minor third, intimate and directed towards his inner being, while, on the other hand, Beethoven lives in the strong impulses of fourth and seventh. Pursuing these thoughts it will gradually become possible to hear with considerable certainty which interval determines the composition under consideration, even if it is not stressed as such. In this way the performer has another opportunity for giving objective, artistic shape and form to the work in hand. A piece, played in the mood of the keynote in so far as this is harkened of the music — that is, resting and enclosed within itself from the first note to the last — will evoke in the listener without fail an ego-awakening force. This shows the realm of the intervals in a comprehensive way, and in the fourth part of this book, concerning the keys, it will be shown in greater detail how an interval determines mood.

Everything concerning the forming of melody through the intervals and the spheres connected with them has been touched upon here and goes well beyond the usual way of dealing with this matter. Apart from accuracy in the rendering of the notes, piano or forte, faster or slower, animated in soul or established in body, the appeal must be made above all to a spiritual forming of the material. The step to be taken is to move from permeation by soul to permeation by spirit — not 'spirit' as understood intellectually, but in the Goethean sense as the living manifestation of a revealed mystery.

What more can man attain in life
than that God-Nature is revealed to him?

Chapter Three

THE HARMONIC INTERVAL

In the previous exercises all listening was determined by the horizontal — that is to say melodic element — and something like a musical thought-process lay in the tracing of law and beauty. It is the mark of the true art of melody that it reveals this 'logic'. In the scale, as the prototype of the melodic principle, one can feel how every newly-achieved stage conceals within it the seed of the next stage: the keynote with its static condition of calm composure is none the less experienced as inwardly filled and promising much, just as one feels that the ego in man has many things to say of great import. But this wealth that is contained has the tendency to open out, to stream out into the surrounding world in the second. This movement is then held back again. The third arises harmonizing all that occurs between inner and outer, so as to produce out of its own being the strength of the fourth, with its readiness to sacrifice itself into the earth. From this innermost centre comes the breakthrough to the light sounding in the fifth, just as an Easter morning follows each Good Friday. And just as within every death there dwells the seed of a new life freed from the body, as in the transition from the fifth to the sixth — so does this finally grow into the life of a seventh, between two worlds. Harnessed in this way in the struggle between polarities, the soul must take hold of itself in its own centre, must ripen towards the perfection of the octave. *Ninth* and *tenth*, in harmonious succession, make a new beginning beyond the octave, a new beginning determined by the higher ego, new-born in spirit to a new cycle of life.

To make this distinction between the experience of the melodic and the harmonic principles clear , some examples of this musical logic are now given, in four fugue-subjects out of the second volume of Bach's *48 Preludes and Fugues*. This kind of artistic analysis can be practised in any literature of quality. The first example, in B major, is one of a rare harmonic balancing process, which sounds in a complementary question-and-answer form.

Like two people in conversation, in which the second confirms the first one's thought and even enters deeply into his whole range of ideas, so do both these thirds merge in the third bar in the cosmic expanse of the sixth. This experience of the sixth has already been sounded by the chiming-in of the first answer from G sharp, the sixth step from the keynote. In continuation it is taken up as an interval, in order, in the fourth bar, to run back again from the octave, filled with the clear logical course of the scale.

The second example is in D minor.

It rushes hither and thither in an agitated triplet-form, upward from the keynote to the fifth. The inner logic demands a mollifying counter-event, which descends from the octave to the fifth, without agitation, but in semitones restraining the storm from the depths. This crossing-over of the fifths D to A upwards and D to G downwards stresses the static principle of the key, as has already been described in Chapter 1. The seed of the concluding cadence lies concealed in it. A kind of ending comes logically in the emphatic tonic triad. That this ending is still open in feeling is shown by the ascent to the fifth, A, and conforms truly to the nature of this interval. The strongly emphasized firm chromatic eases off a little and refers back to the beginning, which hurried through the steps of the triad.

The third example is in F minor:

It brings, in connection with a descending fifth which stresses the keynote emphatically, the sound of a diminished dominant which remains tensely on the leading note. Both figures develop in a downward direction, in keeping with the minor character. But now the soul demands the opposite: it sets the movement free and it runs between the opening motifs, F to D flat and F to C. Firmness needs relief as inbreathing needs outbreathing and the depths require the heights. What complementary man does inwardly is done outwardly here as the logic of development. If these musical and melodic laws were not satisfactorily fulfilled, it would make the same impression as a person thinking and speaking disjointedly. A good continuation, an artistic construction of the fugue that follows, is largely dependent on the clarity and logic of the basic theme. Here we can grasp the relationship of thought and music, shown in the first chapter of Part I to be absolutely essential.

To end with, the subject of the B flat minor fugue:

a steady and emphatic step of a second points towards a rising tendency, but before that it is led by a diminished fifth downwards back to the tonic. Then, however, it is no longer held back: in a three-crested wave it rolls upwards and is caught in the open fifth above and — as if inwardly still quivering — is checked in the third by way of a diminished fifth downwards. The three decisive rests also belong to the nature of the second, which dominates the whole. Like a spiritual drawing of the breath, they fill the expanding stream with energy.

The musical structure of the themes is divided into two, three and four parts. This is sketched into the musical examples and underlines the totality of the musical idea which is carried through in the working out of the fugue. One sees how the experience of the interval from the melodic point of view always seems connected with thinking.

The whole thing is quite different if the notes in the interval are sounded together. It is not, as with melody, the laws of movement that are felt in passing from one note to another, so much as tension and relaxation in various forms. There is a spatial principle in notes sounding simultaneously. The relationship between the notes no longer depends on the way they follow each other, it is no longer an organic transformation corresponding to the laws of thinking. The harmonic relationship is determined more by feeling. The difference between consonance and dissonance is in accordance with feeling. The notes attract each other or thrust each other apart, are mutually sympathetic or antipathetic, enclose themselves inwardly or cleave apart externally. As a collective whole they appeal to the feelings and are felt directly within the heart, not as with melody within the head. They are best practised by two people singing together.

In this connection it is important for each to listen to the other. For example, in the singing of a third it is not so important that each singer sings his note, as that the keynote listens to the third and the third listens to the keynote. In this way an inner fusion comes about and one's own note, in consciously feeling its way and holding its own, becomes much more plastic. One discovers through these studies how difficult it is to bring into perfect accord an octave or a unison vividly experienced from both sides, so that both blend right into the very tone of the voice. Or how far from easy it is when singing the interval of the second not to be drawn back into the keynote, which must not falter. To listen to each other, that is, each to feel at one with the other, is of fundamental importance for singing together in harmony.

From this, something else arises in relation to artistic performance distinct from the purely melodic. The following short phrase would be from note to note a succession of keynote, second, fifth, third, second, third, third, second.

But harmonically, based on the C of the lower voice, we have the following intervals: prime, second, sixth, fourth, third, fifth, seventh, octave. It is a question of style to determine which is preferable. This difficulty did not exist in medieval polyphony.

In addition to the studies of metamorphosis in melody (page 165) let us work out a similar process at a new stage. The following opening of a vocalization by Sieber embeds the interval on the first beat of the bar in a quite definite vertical relationship to the keynote of F major.

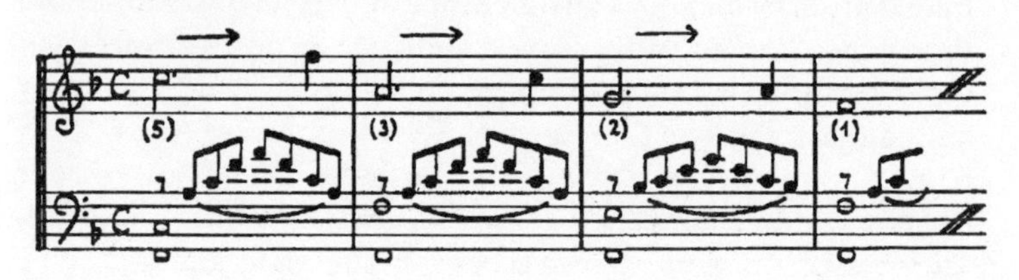

It is a progression downwards from the fifth by way of the third to the second and to the keynote. At the same time the melody sings an upwardly inclined horizontal line: a fourth, a third and a second, then to the keynote. (See small arrows above). A transition must therefore be made from the vertical to the horizontal interval in exactly the same way as previously described — only here it is the movements of the intervals that matter, in contrast to the earlier studies into the nature of the notes.

In the course of practice it becomes ever clearer that the experience of intervals in harmony indicates an embedding into or an adaptation to a determining key. This is represented in the classical cadence form of tonic (T), subdominant (S), dominant (D), and tonic (T), the triads on the first, fourth and fifth steps of the scale (a), or the fourfold dissonance built up on them (b).

For the present day this succession of chords has apparently become devoid of interest and is outmoded. But it is built organically into man so deeply and is such a life-bearing, cosmic-spiritual reality that, especially in the compositions of the classical masters — Bach, Mozart, Schubert, Beethoven and others — it has timeless value, and the normal, unencumbered being 'Man' always responds to it with his heart. Whoever listens qualitatively to this harmonic succession will recognize in it a wonderfully health-giving breathing between the minor-like movement inwards and the major outwards, with the tonic in between providing the resting central point. This breathing experience has been lost: it no longer determines the form of composition in modern music.

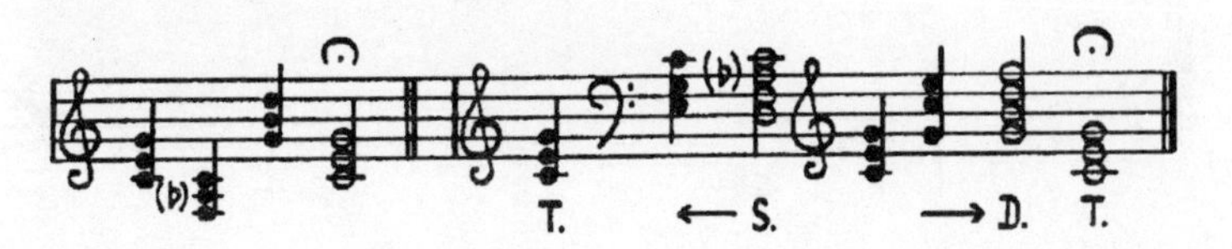

But there is no doubt that the deeply moving effect of quite simple forms is often based upon it. A rich field for renewal lies here. The conscious transformation from rest (T), to relaxation (S), to outward tension (D) and then back again to rest (T) is not easy for most people. It awakens them out of their much loved, comfortable, dreamy self-indulgence!

As all seven notes, and especially their intervals, are included in these cadential phrases, they are connected without exception to the immanent tonic sounding within them and so acquire their character and their tendencies of movement. This is shown in the following example.

The fifth as the dominant tends towards the keynote or octave, the seventh in its dissonant tension also to the octave, the second with its variable lemniscatory nature tends in both directions, and the fourth moves to the third. The same rules, determined by their essential nature, prevail in the subdominant intervals.

Schubert's cradle song *Schlafe, schlafe, holder, süsser Knabe*, is built on a continual interchange between tonic and dominant. All the intervals of the melody are related to the keynote A flat, not to the bass note. Attention to this, and the relationship of the melody to repose and tension means that the rocking comes into effect convincingly.

Not only is every essential step to be taken as interval, but the whole phrase bears a harmonic character. For instance the fifth, B flat falling to E flat on the word 'Knabe', does not need softening, as one usually hears it, but it tends towards the next bar. This simple song provides a beautiful study for listener and player alike.

Brahms' cradle song *Guten Abend, gut' Nacht* includes the interchange between tonic and dominant in longer phrases. The mood of the third lies over the whole exactly as in Schubert's song. Four bars' peace, four bars' suspense; in 'Morgen früh' — a brief plunge into the inwardness of the subdominant; 'wenn Gott will' — the peace of being watched over; 'wirst du wieder geweckt' — the expectation of the coming day — this is the course it takes. It is quite tender and yet a stroke of genius when Brahms places the turning inwards of 'Morgen früh' melodically into the rising octave. The necessary release from tension in the sphere of the subdominant is a wonderful complement to the rising major interval which, as keynote and its octave, sums up all the events of day and night: that is, every experience both earthly and spiritual. It is usually sung in a much too extrovert way.

An essential exercise in connection with the harmonic interval is to form, with a sustained note in one voice, the intervals in the other voice moving against it. Exercise (a) and more particularly (b) bring studies in modulation in the interplay between minor

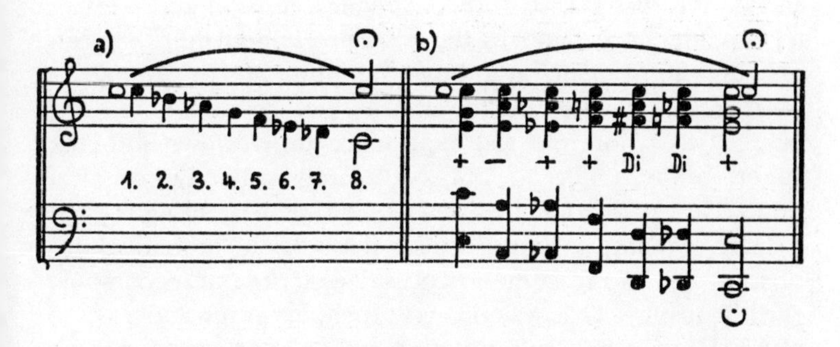

and major and dissonant harmonies. (Minor = -, Major = +, Dissonant = Di). In these studies — allowing again for individual needs — there is something like a melody in the note itself — the absolute musical expression of what arises in the soul of man as a melody amidst the karmic events into which he is placed.

After studies of movement in the single note, a beautiful

passage such as this out of Brahms' *Sapphic Ode* would be given the necessary tension without having to bring it to expression in a crescendo. It is not a forcing of the tone, but a living within the note which produces the right effect. One often has the impression that the composer would like to bring these inner processes closer by emphasizing forte and piano passages.

With these harmonic intervals everything depends on reciprocity, upon 'each one hearing the other'. It is a matter of feeling the way into the sustaining mood of the surrounding harmony; of recognizing and giving form to the interplay between major and minor, dissonance and consonance, tension and release; it is a matter of recognizing the breathing interchange between rest and movement, and how the pure life of feeling — pleasure and displeasure, joy and sorrow — sounds within the heart. This whole musical experience drops down into the sphere of the subjective soul, as was fully justified in classical times. The ego of humanity — awakened in the Greek Age — had to learn to define its limits through thinking and other qualities of soul, and had to come to an understanding of its personal earthly destiny. That was the case then, and even today these musical works are truly timeless, in so far as man learns to immerse himself in their beauty selflessly and creatively and not merely with romantic enjoyment.

So, not only as an exercise, but as a true pearl of artistic creation, a song like *Der Ton* by Peter Cornelius, can still move us today. It embraces in the most subtle way all those laws we have just been considering.

The note itself — B as the fifth in the key of E minor — allows the sphere of the dead beloved to rise up in the heart. It is as if her soul is listening down into the melody resounding from the earth, and absorbing it into herself. One experiences it taking part in the dramatic climaxes and refinements of all the modulations until, in the redeeming E major, the earthly person is so filled with light that the one who has died can be united with him.

The second song following this one is also on the note B — *An den Traum* — but this time experienced as the sphere of the octave in B minor. It may also be worked out in its timeless depths through listening intimately to the interchange between the voice's note and the melodic accompaniment surrounding it with its harmonic transformations. It may readily be assumed that the great grief experienced by Cornelius in this death loosened his soul to a quite special transparency, through which — in word as well as in musical sound — pure spiritual experiences were able to stream through him, so as to find — perhaps unconsciously — expression in such a unique musical response.

Chapter Four

INTERVALS IN THE TWELVE-NOTE CIRCLE

A feature of the transition to present-day music is the fact that the world of the seven, the major/minor system in the classical sense, is gradually giving way to the predominance of the twelve. This reveals a law of life: time tends to become space. Seven is the number which governs all things temporal. Within it, processes of growth and change give rise to sound. The structure of the scale and the intervals formed by it has made this clear in relation to man. The chromatic stages were still derived from the seven-note system. But all things temporal, all flowing and growing, bear the tendency to become fixed. One may say 'form', 'shape', 'space', 'body', or even 'memory' — time will always become space, whether in the earthly or in the transcendental sphere. But the laws of space are subject to the number twelve and create boundaries, outlines and forms. Cosmically seen, it is the world of the wandering stars and the sphere of the fixed stars that are mirrored musically in their differing ways.

This transition to a new tonal system of the twelve has been manifest since the end of last century, and is based through and through on a transformation of consciousness and of musical outlook. More detailed discussion of the laws of the twelve, and also of the seven, the three and the one in music will be reserved for the second volume of this work. At this stage there will only be some basic indications. It is not only a question of considering the twelve-note system of Arnold Schoenberg or Josef Matthias Hauer. They are but the most extreme advocates, whose one-sided tendencies await many modifications and a mature process of clarification. Even Richard Wagner, with the breakthrough to chromaticism in his Tristan, Max Reger with the dissolving of a prevailing tonality in continuous modulation, Claude Debussy, Bela Bartók, Paul Hindemith — to mention only a few — all these live and create musically on the basis of the dodecaphonic nature of the octave, although they still acknowledge, and have recourse to, the customary major and minor principles.

If one speaks in this way of the twelve as the number defining space, it is also consistent to speak in connection with this of a delimitation of each of the single notes. These appear, to begin with, quite independently, each resting within itself like an object in space, for which reason they have been called 'objective'. This is only given as material, like the colours on an artist's palette. In accordance with the principle of setting limits, the twelve semitone steps of the octave appear in a circle corresponding to the zodiac, regardless of whether we are speaking of sharps or flats. In carrying these matters to a conclusion it is necessary to speak of a thirteenth step in which, exactly as in the octave, ending and new beginning coincide.

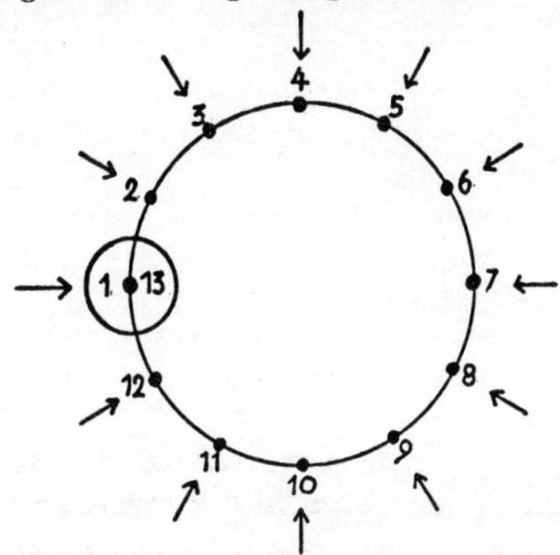

This matter must be considered from three different angles. Firstly, the laws of space, unlike those of time, work from outside giving shape and form, from encircling space in towards the periphery (see arrows). Secondly, these twelve places conforming to the zodiac are not individual stars, but constellations of fixed stars in contrast to the moving planets. One can understand them not as twelve single notes, as in the structure of the seven, but only as constellations of sound. The diagram (page 158) in which we were able to distinguish thirty-five notes interlocking with one another comes to mind again. In this enharmonic, in this harmony within the note, forms can be heard, so to speak, which unite with one another out of the threefold nature of the note. In this threefold way the essential point is that the temporal element of the seven moves in the twelve in two opposing streams of sharp and flat, of active and passive, of a rolling out and in, which meet in the middle note as if held there. But the twelvefold nature of the diversely working forces, which stream in from encircling space, gives special importance to the musical reality of one of these three components, and places it in the foreground.

What is this musical reality? The answer, as a third essential factor, is connected with what was revealed through the overtones and the complementary series. These were built up from the keynote C and both together yielded — if one does not include the repetitions — thirteen notes: from the partial series, physically audible and sounding with the note C, G, E, D and B and, from the descending series sounding in space as exponents of an inner counter-event in soul, F, A flat, B flat and D flat. Added to this is the enharmonic crossing-over of F sharp and G flat, which meet in one place and in the circle provide the axis to the keynote; A and E flat are included as representatives of a spirituality completely inaudible.

This structure, conforming to the law of over- and undertones, does not adjust, as previously, to the circle of fifths, but to the succession of semitones. It gives the following picture (a).

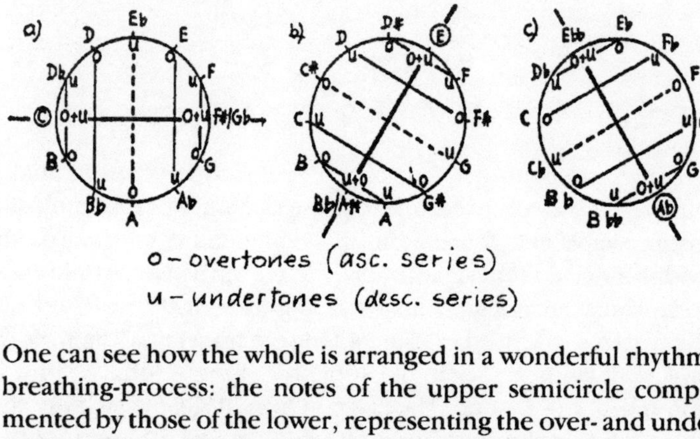

o – overtones (asc. series)
u – undertones (desc. series)

One can see how the whole is arranged in a wonderful rhythmic breathing-process: the notes of the upper semicircle complemented by those of the lower, representing the over- and undertones (connected by lines). The central dotted line unites the two exponents of the inaudible. This law of a true tonality is revealed as a musical reality from each of the selected keynotes. Take, for example, the structure from the note E in (b). One finds in the over- and undertones no D flat, E flat, G flat or A flat, but from this note, C sharp, D sharp, G sharp and A sharp. The impelling force of these notes follows the stream of light and not, as in the case of C, the stream of gravity. The picture of the tonality of A flat as the third example (c), shows no sharp notes at all, but several double flats. It is evident that each step is different with each keynote. D flat, the second step from C, becomes the tenth from E as C sharp, and appears in A flat as the sixth, and so on. From these brief indications, which will be treated in detail in the second volume, it is already clear that the twelve-note system and the enharmonic are closely connected. By eliminating them one arbitrarily erases a law of life and renounces subtle possibilities of expression for the future.

Various questions arise. In what way do the customary intervals create form? How can one prove that in this way they play a predominant role in modern music? And furthermore: How is the impelling force, the trend of the individual note revealed and where does it lead? In so far as the intervals become dissonant, to what resolution do they point? Then the third question: From what point of view should this arrangement be seen?

In connection with this, let us recall what has already been stated about contemporary, not classical, experience. A focal point was found in the interval of the seventh and was developed in both directions. Working outwards from one's own centre, which stands between polarities struggling for equilibrium, we proceeded from a central note orientated in two directions, and shall apply this principle here. It is obvious that this central note must be the keynote of the tonality and also of the basic arrangement in the foregoing sense. The note C is taken as centre and everything develops from there in two directions, upwards and downwards until the circle closes in the opposite pole with the enharmonic F sharp/G sharp (see arrows).

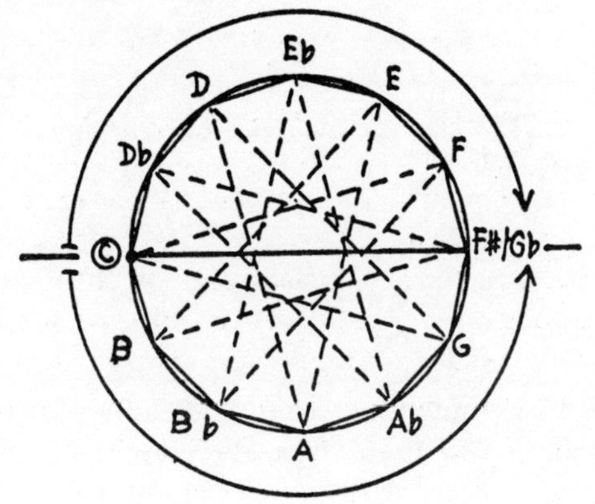

These points, connected with one another, form a dodecagon. If in this one seeks out the circle of fifths it is found in the twelve-pointed star (dotted lines). In the first arrangement the twelve semitones appear as a succession of minor seconds, whether diatonic (C to D flat) or chromatic (C to C sharp). It is clear and needs no further comment that these control our contemporary musical scene to a far-reaching degree.

The next form of interval from C is the major second and it makes a hexagon in the circle.

Starting from the middle C (a), or G (b), we find all twelve notes in two hexagons. Moving round the two interpenetrating hexagons we find they each give a whole-tone scale (c) from C to B sharp, and from G to A double flat. This brings to light how closely the twelve is connected with the enharmonic, especially if these intervals are followed through in reality and not, as so often occurs, made to jump in a diminished third from G sharp to B flat upward or from D flat to B downward (x in (c)). Just as in the case of the first forms unfolding from the centre, the augmented seventh from C to B sharp, regarding pitch, could be seen as an enharmonic octave. In truth it does not reach the harmony of the true octave, but only assumes the sound of it in the tuning by temperament.

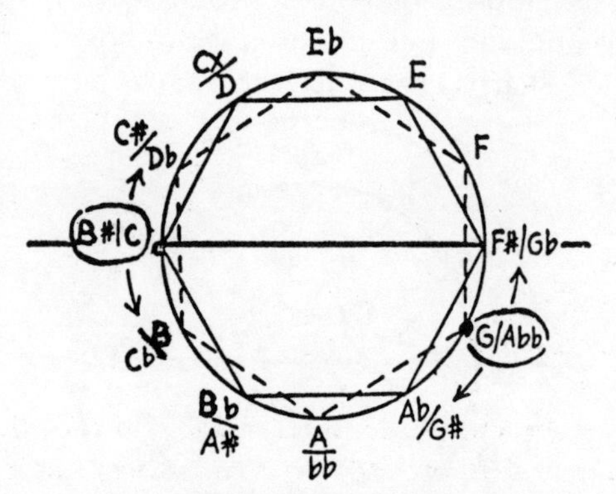

What makes this whole-tone scale so essential for the present time is the tritone formed in every direction: in C to F sharp, D to G sharp, E to A sharp and F sharp to B sharp upwards, as well as in G to D flat, F to C flat, E flat to B double flat, and D flat to A double flat downwards. The same principle also holds good in the form given from the centre, between mid-point and periphery on either hand: C to F sharp and C to G flat in (a), G to C sharp and G to D flat in (b). The essential nature of the second, not enclosed but vibrating within itself, is intensified here to a succession of notes which give melodically an unprecedented straining and wanting-to-go-beyond, and reveal a structure of five major thirds, four augmented fourths, and three augmented fifths. If, in this connection one thinks of the contemporary structure around the seventh (page 147) and the seven pointed star (page 159), it will become clear how the whole tone, as a polar resonance within the twelve, must be recognized in a new way as a guiding factor for present-day consciousness.

If in both these forms of minor and major seconds one has the melodic principles of the present age — that is, the series of semitones and the whole-tone scale — one must now consider, as representatives of the harmonic principle, the minor and major thirds. They appear as C - E flat - G flat, the first, fourth and seventh stages upward, and C-A-F sharp, the same stages downward. They join in the enharmonic opposite pole, as if sounding in unison, but in truth concealing in this unison the interesting experience of a threshold to the region beyond the octave in the diminished ninth, F sharp to G flat.

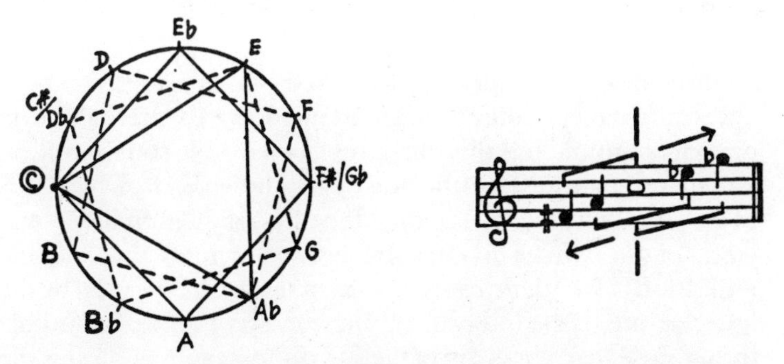

On the spur of the moment one says: the chord of the diminished seventh, and is inclined to brush these intervals and harmonies aside and avoid them as too weak and sentimental and not sufficiently modern. They occur in each direction three times within the complete circle. Experienced, however, from the qualitative point of view, they bear within them a tension and a dramatic quality such as occurs in hardly any other place. These minor thirds and diminished fifths oppose each other in the struggle for light and darkness. The minor third, for instance, is the experience of the inner world. For modern man this is no longer harmonious, tender and intimate. The fully experienced structure of these harmonies should expunge every recollection of the sentimental and the romantic. Such exercises reveal whether and to what extent one can overcome the customary external impression by a new, creative will. It can be done.

With this dramatic sound of the minor thirds one also stands in the middle of a threefold structure of diminished fifths: C to G flat from below, and, in the combination of the upper and lower middle notes, A to E flat as well.

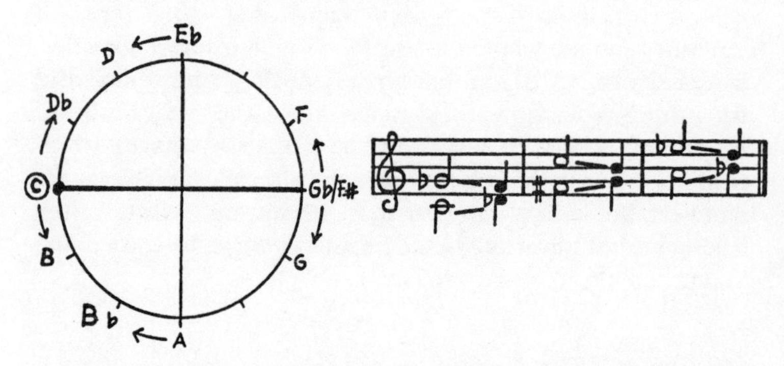

All three bear the quality of diminished — that is to say, experienced qualitatively, they have a tendency towards internalization or concentration. It is this that gives to the whole sound its firm, articulated nature. Like the square or the cross in which it is placed it represents the realm of the physical. Within the framework of the twelve it must be borne in mind that audible indications of tendencies are not, as in the seven, dictated by the inner nature of the interval. On the contrary they make audible the impulse that works out of the surroundings and indicates the direction from which the interval sounds. G flat and E flat, like all flat notes, belong to an inrolling stream and take their bearings from below, while on the other hand F sharp points upwards to a stream of light. From a standpoint which strives fully to understand musical phenomena in their purity and to restore them to their own true nature out of the confusion into which they have been drawn — partly through tuning by temperament — it is not possible to share the views expressed by Paul Hindemith in his *Treatise on Composition.* Starting with the tritone he says:

> From time immemorial this name has been borne by the augmented fourth, corresponding to its formation of three whole tones following one after the other. To its enharmonic, the diminished fifth, this designation is not relevant. But because of the established usage of chromatic and enharmonic structures, only on manuscript paper do we make a distinction between the two intervals, so that I do not hesitate to include under the term tritone both the augmented fourth and the diminished fifth.

The intervals of the major third, heard as the dynamic which lay concealed in the augmented fifth, now come to the fore in the harmonic principles of the circle of twelve. They create an equilateral triangle from middle C. If one allows this augmented triad to work in its wonderful harmony on both sides of a central note — not built up on a keynote — then the feeling for any decisive trend towards one side or the other is gradually lost.

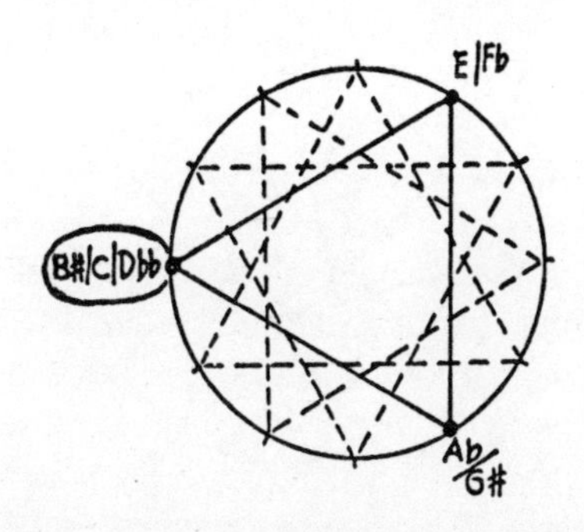

It works more and more as the heart-structure of the twelve at rest within itself, opening the soul without straining it. It stands even more strongly in the play of the enharmonic. Unfolding in both directions two other combinations of sound arise which finally reach the C either as B sharp or as D double flat.

Four such triangles lie in the circle, each having a different mood. For present-day musical perception their use no longer signifies a one-sided tension, but is rather the expression of an objectively maintained strength, just as the balance between thinking and willing is held by the central position of the heart. And each time the tonality in the circle changes with the middle note, by which it is determined.

The rules of rhythm start to sound in the ensuing forms: rhythm in the sense of E. Hanslick, who makes the following distinction:

> Rhythm at large as the concordance of a symmetrical structure, and rhythm in detail as the alternating, regular movement of single members in measure.

In the case of the twelve it is a question of 'rhythm at large'. The five semitone steps to the sixth stage, up to F, or down to G, if continued, produces six fourths in both directions.

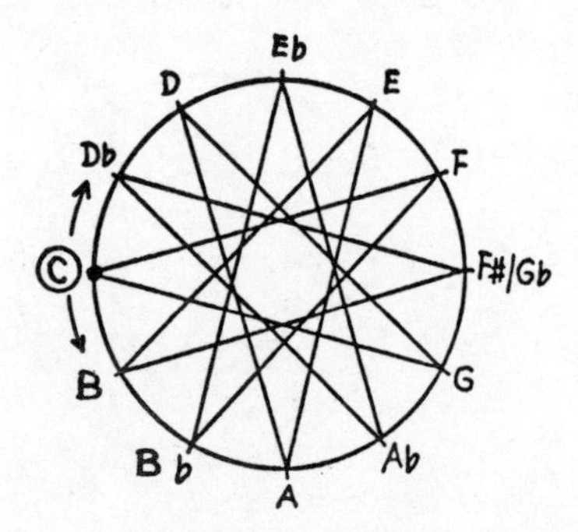

If these fourths are connected they create the figure of a star — that is to say, for the first time the feeling for the middle, that was enclosed as centre in the augmented triad, is now circumscribed in the structure of the twelve-note circle. The points of the star sketch the periphery of the twelve, forming an outer boundary.

The principle was characteristic of the fourth from the beginning, and confirms even here its character as do also the darkened flat notes inclining downwards in the rising series. A state of being enclosed within the self is proclaimed — the 'World in the I'. The 'concordance of a symmetrical structure' has found its cosmic symbol — the star formation draws inwards. This profound desire to lay hold of oneself in the centre of one's own being is the attitude of our contemporaries. No wonder that sounds connected with the fourth, with their peculiarly austere character, tend to prevail. The range this star encompasses is five complete octaves, closing enharmonically. The seventh step in the twelve, the tritone from C up to F sharp over against the C down to G flat, is like the rhythmical movement of a pendulum, allowing breathing and pulse-beat to sound again. It is clear that this name, drawn from the seven-note system, is no longer in place. It would be much better to say 'septone'. It is the seventh step in the sphere of the twelve and bears the nature of the seventh, whether as F sharp or as G flat. The axis which it forms in the circle, swings to and fro within itself, reaching C as B sharp or D double flat.

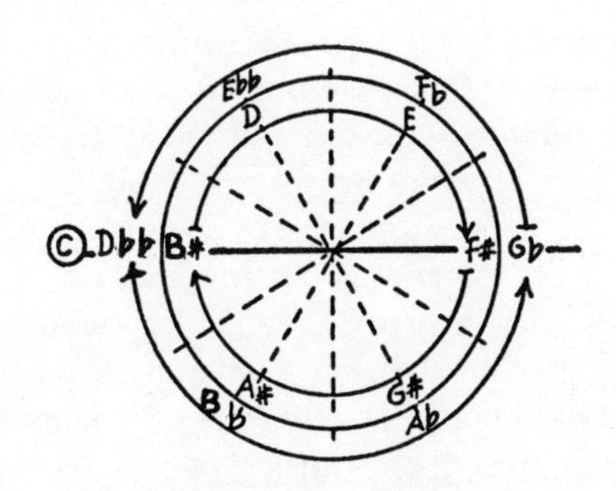

The inner upper semicircle from C to F sharp strikes back in the lower one from F sharp to B sharp, while the lower one, C to G flat is balanced out above by G flat to D double flat. As with exhalation and inhalation the circle in its entirety makes the form of a spiral.

At this point it is proper to insert a few words about the distinction between the enharmonic octave and the true octave. The name octave is dictated here by the acoustic point of view; it sounds 'as if' without really being. This double tritone coincides with the thirteenth, from which a new circuit can begin at a higher level.

This thirteenth step concludes the series of twelve and at the same time is a new beginning, exactly like the octave in the seven-note system. It is also characteristic of the tritone that one should inwardly hear its resolution in the eighth step. The second swing of the pendulum — back to the higher sphere — is audible, though only approximately right: the higher ego, the actual substance of the octave, sounds as an augmented seventh. A kind of unison arises, not within the same sphere of sound, but between two different ones. An element arises in outline and it can only come to life where a centre is formed which can, in the truest sense, rest in the balance between polarities. To this end the tritone calls out, in holding both sides together, to become similar to the octave. From this point of view it is no longer the 'devil in music', the 'glistening companion', as an earlier state of consciousness described it in another musical system: namely, that of the seven. Here it has become the resounding axis which maintains the structure of the twelve from each region of sound to its opposite: exponent of the force of a higher ego. Its inner tendency of movement, supported by the place of the sound in the circle, is always expanding and moving on. All four basic forms of the axis C to F sharp, C to G flat, lead without exception to the greater span of the sixth and from there to both neighbouring axes (see dotted lines). For the best of reasons this interval preponderates in present-day musical consciousness. But to do justice to it in an objective way it must never be confused with the opposite tendency of a diminished fifth.

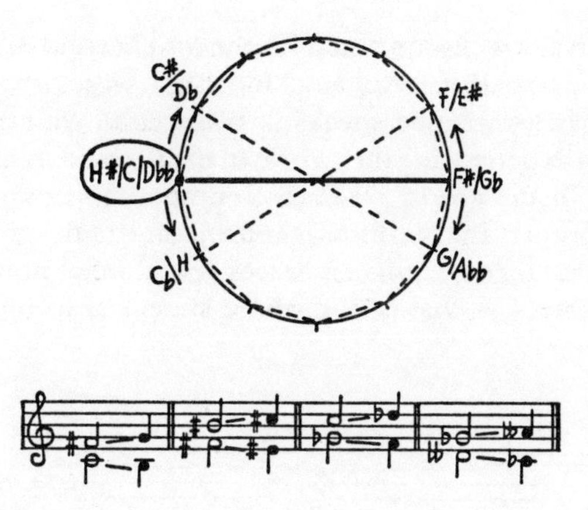

The above diagram, with its step by step formation of ever new axes, points to a new beginning in the original circle of semitones. The succession of twelve semitones as minor seconds sounds from axis to axis (dotted lines), this time arising out of the immanent will of the tritones which the external influence of this region of sound comes to meet. It is a not yet audible structure and is followed up inwardly as something spiritual — the new twelve-note circle is heard spiritually. From now on one follows step by step the changes in the spiritual counter-event, the will of the respective interval.

The next step beyond the axis C to F sharp, C to G flat, leads into the wider intervals, which it is customary to describe as the inversions of those we have already been through. Here they are seen in their true value. In contrast to the star of fourths, in which at each step something enclosed rings out as 'World in the I', one experiences here from fifth to fifth a continual aspiring towards the next fifth.

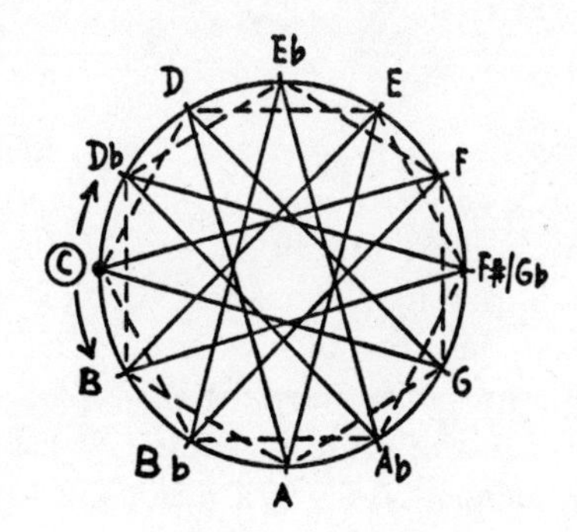

This interval will always reach for the fifth beyond itself on the far side of the periphery and include it, as it were, whether from above or below. If one speaks in connection with the star of fourths of experiencing the 'World in the I', one may speak here of the 'I in the World'. We have emphasized how this truly cosmic sound of the two fifths is appropriate for the present day. The whole range of fifths embraces seven enharmonically enclosed octaves — that is, the whole system of readily audible sound.

If one connects up the sounds aspired they describe (see the arrows pointing towards the crotchet) the two interlocking hexagons of the earlier whole-tone scales. They are drawn with

dotted lines into the diagram (page 195). In the case of the seconds this was a series of audible sounds; in this case it is a complementary element impelled by the spirit.

The law of an impelling will towards the next step turns out to be important and right for each new interval. The augmented fifth upwards assumes in G sharp the same place as A flat; on the other side, as F flat, the same place as E. A flat-C-E was the constellation of the augmented triad of major thirds (page 191). The

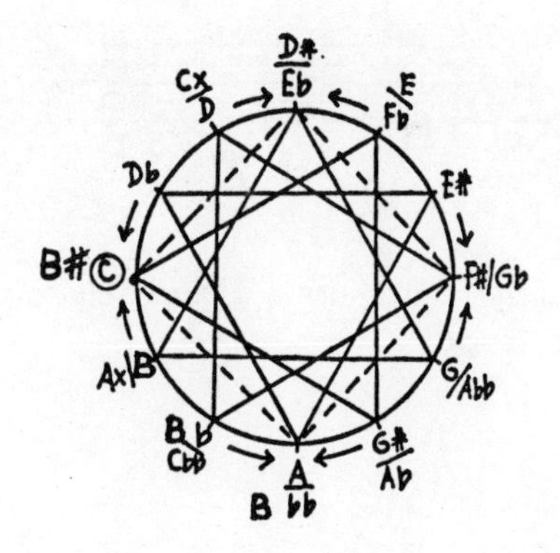

impelling will of the augmented fifths leads at this stage from G sharp to A and from F flat to E flat (a). The structure of augmented fifths on the opposite side, F sharp-C double sharp-B flat (b), moves towards D sharp and A, and enharmonically as G flat-D-C double flat, towards E flat and B double flat (c). One recognizes the square

of the minor thirds (top figure, dotted lines). The same trends in the triangles A-D flat-E sharp (d), and E flat-A double flat-B (e), lead to C-F sharp and C-G flat. Enharmonically D sharp-G-A double sharp leads to B sharp-F sharp. In their logical structure each is embedded in the enharmonic differentiations of each of the twelve notes.

The wider the interval, the more strongly does this enharmonic element determine the spiritual background. It was pointed out in the first part of this book concerning the over- and undertones, that in the realm of the enharmonic it is the constellations in cosmic space that count, and it should hardly be a matter of surprise that everything concerning the twelve must be linked with this realm of music. It is the same with the next step, which leads from C to the major sixths, A above and E flat below (a). These two places are also reached from the opposite pole as D sharp/E flat and A/B double flat (b).

The directions of the central notes, C and F sharp/G flat, point to B and D flat and G and F.

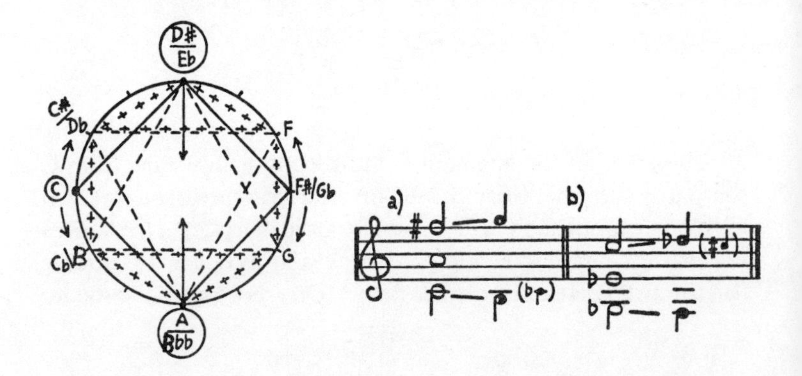

D flat and F, B and G, each make a triangle above and below with E flat and A, and form a hexagon. This structure of the whole-tone scale was, amongst other things, carried by three augmented fifths. The connection is found when the points of direction are joined (arrows) B and G with E flat above, D flat and F with A below, with D flat and B changing in the process to C sharp and C flat. The enharmonic determining of the spiritual background appears here for the first time as a change in movement, which underlines in C sharp and C flat the inner connection with the note C. It creates a kind of balance to the heaviness of the spheres of E flat and A.

The intervals of a second, previously shown in the two small triangles, E flat-D flat-F above and A-G-B below (Figure 108), are now taken up from C in an extended position as minor sevenths, B flat above and D below. Their impelling direction leads to A and E flat, but the strength of their movement is so intense that it leads on to an additional semitone, to A flat and E. These notes form two triangles of minor seconds, D-E flat-E and B flat-A-A flat, as background to the next and last form of interval. The C is

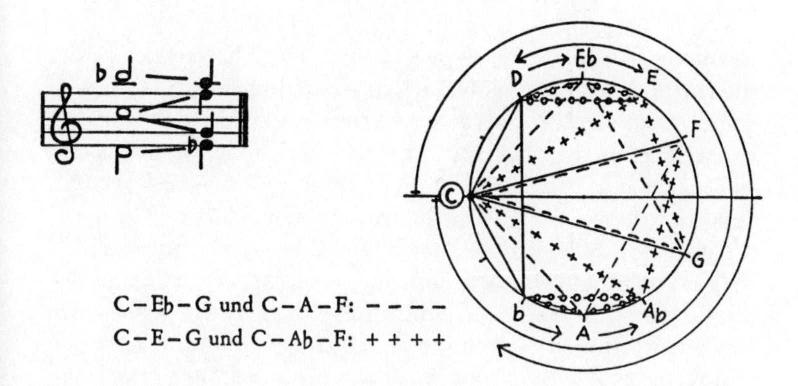

significant in leading to the fourth, F above and G below. It points to the circle of fourths working spiritually behind it and is connected with the dodecagram (page 192).

This opens the way to polytonality, which creates a harmony between the thirds above and those below.

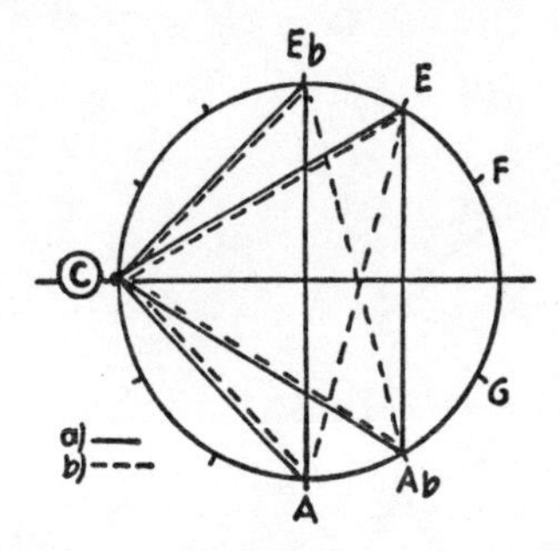

This musical factor of great significance is one of the happy surprises bestowed by intensive and attentive listening. It is important to realize that the twelve is concerned with laws of space, with the working together of various harmonies simultaneously. The fact that polarities hitherto regarded as incompatible arise at this point emerges through the method pursued.

Example (a) (page 199) shows the two basic harmonies of the diminished and augmented triads emerging from the step of semitone to whole tone; (b) shows the result of the B flat moving the whole tone to A flat; but D the semitone to E flat. The chord of A flat major arises around the central note C. The opposite, semitone above, whole tone below, gives the chord of A minor; (c) gives the reflections F major and C minor, F minor and C major. Polytonality is not a game leading to new enticing harmonies. It is a fact of evolution of the same order as the progress from the single note to the interval. Hearing simultaneously the connections of two harmonies to one other is shown here to be founded both musically and objectively. But there is one thing: polytonality can never be explained from a keynote, but only from a centre orientated in two directions. It conforms fully to the basic attitude of modern man.

The last interval in the twelve is the major seventh C-B and C-D flat. An inner bridge is thrown to the opposite pole, F sharp/G flat, which through the whole circle of twelve gave rise to the enharmonic form of the octave.

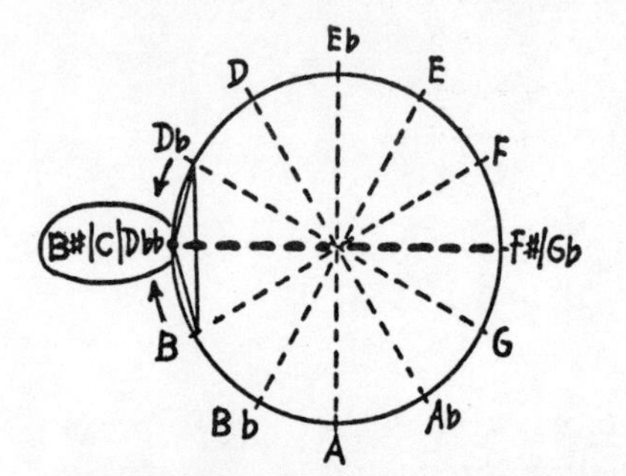

One has to remember how the upper and lower semicircle of the tritone swung back and formed a complete circle, reaching C from F sharp as B sharp, from G flat as D double flat. As well as the first two pure octaves this makes two enharmonic octaves from the pole of the tritone: C to B sharp and C to D double flat. Every place in the twelve is determined in four ways. The pure octaves rest in harmony within themselves as perfect consonances. The two enharmonic structures are seized by an impulse of will to go further: B sharp to its neighbouring C sharp, D

within itself. In the second case a new series of semitones would begin, building up on the basis of continual augmented sevenths, that is, of enharmonic changes of the octave.

But as this would go beyond the bounds of our present system of tonality from the third note, E double flat, on, it lies beyond any healthy method of practice.

This detailed representation of the harmonic intervals, especially in their connection with dodecaphony, was necessary in order to show that organically the seven can be incorporated into the twelve. We live simultaneously in the laws of time and space and can never be determined by one or the other alone. We must consider the close interweaving of the seven with the twelve if we are to penetrate into the spiritual background of music. The one-sidedness so prevalent in the world today, which leads to arguments about this or that, could be objectively solved on the lines indicated here, bearing fruit in every way. Much has been touched upon which leads over to the next chapter on rhythm, and from there the theory of intervals will be brought to a close.

Chapter Five

RHYTHM

In the light of musical history it is interesting to follow up — in keeping with man's state of consciousness from the Middle Ages up to our present time — how certain basic elements in music take the lead. With reference to the trinity of melody, harmony and rhythm, it is possible to follow a quite well-defined course of development. In the introductory chapter we were able to see how closely the soul-forces are connected with the intervals. This was discussed in connection with the expansion of the usual three into four — thinking, feeling, will and equilibrium. It was also stated that the trinity of melody, harmony and rhythm were connected with the different soul-forces; melody with thinking, harmony with feeling and rhythm with will.

The interesting fact emerges that music, starting from melody, becomes more and more intensively and intimately connected with man, lays hold of the harmonic element and then, at the present time, of the rhythmic element. At each stage there comes to the fore a more thought-filled character, or one more in keeping with feeling, or one emphasizing the will. The melodic principle, founded in Greek culture, in which it was particularly the thinking that underwent development, gradually unfolded in the West under the leadership of the Church of Rome, until it reached its Golden Age in medieval polyphony; this can be followed through from about the sixth to the thirteenth centuries. The guiding interval was essentially the second, then later the fifth and fourth. But it is the second — one should remember what was said concerning the overtones in Part One — which represents the logical element in music and which, still following the scale-structure of the Greek model, drew after it an abundance of diverse small intervals.

It was only with the infiltration of British influence into the Continent that the harmonic principle took over, giving expression through chords to major and minor. Here, in contrast to the South, wider intervals are found — thirds and sixths preponderating, even in melody. From this northern stream, which had its roots in the old Celtic-Druidic music of the bards, came another Golden Age from the fourteenth century on — that of the classical major/minor system. Determined harmonically, so that even the melodies were embedded within the chords, it gave the whole gamut of personal feeling in all those wonderful possibilities of expression which still go to the hearts of most people today.

But now, since the turn of the century, the ascendancy of rhythm in music seems almost like an invasion. A complete emancipation in this field is obvious. In the Middle Ages polyphony wove its web free of regular measure. Long and short notes, not in metrically equal repetition but in free melodic play, with one melody alongside another, gave life to the flow of music, until the element of regular measure was adopted with the stress on the first beat, standardizing and stabilizing melody and harmony. In carrying out the formal framework of thematic structure in divisions of four, eight and twelve, the relationship of breathing and pulse is combined with musical experience. The free rhythmic interchange between long and short notes in the melody fits into this organically. Feeling was never too strongly or unexpectedly shocked, not even in dramatic music. It was the harmonic principle, central to the feeling heart, which held sway and controlled everything.

It was precisely this regular breathing — a rhythm connected with the human organism — which had to be cast off. With the slogan: 'Be done with romanticism', 'Be done with what is physiologically given', a completely free play of rhythmic elements arose and, with the systematic avoidance of styles stressing feeling, thinking and will came to the fore; to begin with, freed from the middle region of breathing, it was driven into the region of the limbs. All forms of expression became problems of the day — beat, tempo, polarity, reflection, and so on. Jazz overwhelmed Europe, polytonality developed, a continual change of beat neutralized every connection with breathing, and the calm interplay of long and short notes found in earlier music was discarded in favour of an apparent arbitrariness. Modern humanity was subjected to the will-culture of its time, confronted with all these elements and with the task of adapting itself to them.

It is good to begin with the classical arrangement of the intervals. We find a division of the scale into two parts, each of four intervals, which can plainly be recognized as inbreathing

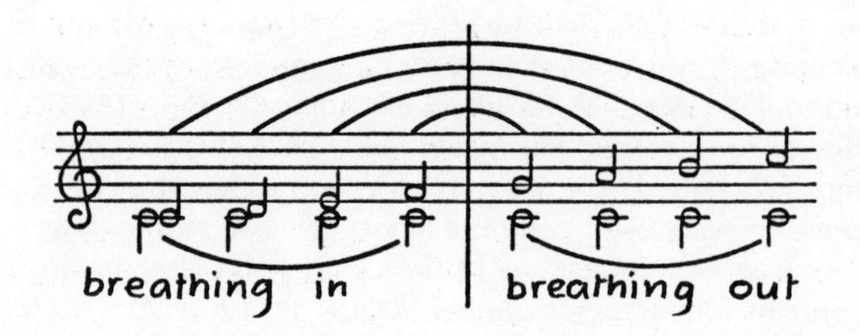

and outbreathing. One might also say a minor and major experience, contraction and expansion. In simple pictorial form there arises the primordial picture of breathing in the zodiacal sign of the Crab which, as a very ancient pictorial symbol dating back for thousands of years, appears in all cultures in a variety of ways.

Listening to the rhythmic curve in the above example, which can be extended at will upwards or downwards to three or more octaves, it will be noticed that a strong effort of will must be made where the change of direction occurs, that is to say, between the fourth and the fifth, and in the transformation of the octave into a new beginning — in the scale, between F and G and actually in the note C.

Here the relationship of rhythm to will is found, to a will which does not yet grasp the limbs as it does in the beat. When the inbreathing is complete attention should be paid to the change to outbreathing, to the opposite process. This process between the polarities of an inner and outer movement needs to be watched. It is strong in ego-force and lives between consolidation and dematerialization. We have considered the point at which contact is made with the rhythmic change in the octave. In qualitative experience it is important to seize upon this moment consciously with an effort of will and not to let it pass by unconsciously.

In connection with these preliminary observations of rhythmic procedure within the octave there is a fact which nearly every schoolchild knows in theory, but which has hardly been discovered as rhythmic experience: the distinction between the major intervals going up the scale, with the keynote as the note of reference, and the minor intervals going down the scale with the octave as note of reference.

The small arrow pointing upwards in (a) indicates the outstreaming, outbreathing process in major, with the major intervals reaching out ever further, while the opposite process is brought about by the minor intervals, which have a tendency to swing back to the octave. Particular attention should be given to this distinction in both the above exercises. The rhythmic breath is experienced in both directions of the complete scale, not in the groups of four. It is worth practising these exercises alternately in harmonic as well as in melodic form.

A melodic exercise such as this can be practised by every more or less musical person without difficulty and without thinking much about it. But what is the qualitative experience? It is customary to study the intervals from below upwards, in relation to the keynote. But in descending they are related to the octave. The experience is reversed and also the size of the 'intervals of movement' — the second, third, sixth and seventh. What is the significance of this? C to B, the minor second from above, in contrast to the lower major one C to D, has difficulty in freeing itself from the octave. It is drawn back so strongly, that one feels pressed into a similar state of soul as in the case of the seventh from below, C to B: the sphere of the octave sounds and calls compellingly. Then the minor third downwards is also experienced not so much as a third — intimate and turning inwards — but rather as a light, free sensation, resembling that of a major sixth. In the case of both the next intervals C to G and C to F, the fourth and fifth downwards, this is clear: the fourth from above has nothing of firmness but a light-filled element, free of materiality, such as was characteristic of the fifth from below, while the fifth downwards brings the true finding of the 'ground beneath one's feet', as was the case with the fourth upwards — and so on, with the sixth, seventh and octave downwards. One can say: It is not actually the interval that is experienced in itself, but rather the sphere supplementary to it, the complementary interval within the space of the octave.

Here again there is a kind of inversion: what was inward in the interval based upon the keynote is experienced from the aspect of the octave as the complementary external element. However inherently powerful this may be, the lower C is always there (interpolated above in small notes) and creates an enduring totality, which offsets with a beautiful holding counter-weight any tendency to float away or soar upwards.

One realizes that the minor intervals downwards do not bring about a true experience of minor. They all remain so strongly united with the complementary sphere and with the principle of light in the octave that they are illumined and carried along by a major-like quality. The external, audible minor movement gives rise to an inner, inaudible event in the soul. These laws will assume a significant role later on in the treatment of keys.

If we turn our attention again to the change of direction in the octave C, we find this connected with the upward and downward trend of pitch. This suggests changing this turning point into a centre and swinging around it in lemniscatory form. For listening it is better to begin with C, but in singing it is better with A or G. It is noticeable that from each central note the intervals above and below are different.

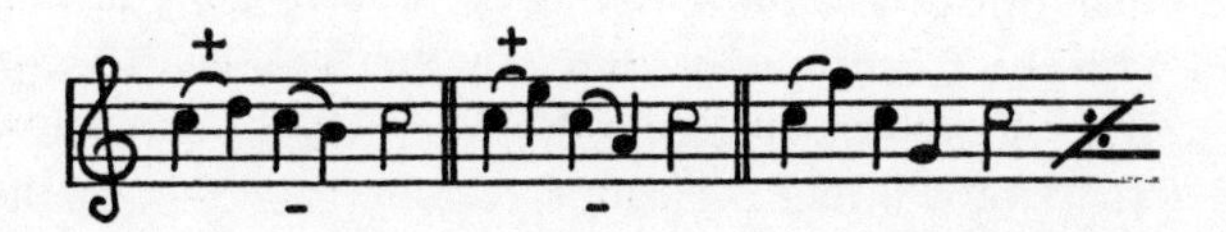

From C they are in a supplementary relationship; in the other cases, they are sometimes equal or vary from stage to stage.

One can go through an exercise such as this with all seven notes, putting each in the centre in turn. A new and deeper relationship emerges from the rhythmical lemniscatory play compared with that which was experienced as major or minor when working with direction.

At this stage attention must be drawn to the swinging of third, fifth and seventh around the note A. From this centre which is usually recognized as corresponding to the heart in man and to the sun in the universe, experience is led more upward and outward, or downward and inward, as felt in these three particularly significant lemniscates.

They link up with the statements in Chapter One regarding the relationship of the intervals with the soul-forces of man. The third, revealing personal feeling, plays closely around the note of the heart; the fifth, the sound of the threshold in crossing over to the sphere of light in the octave, spans a wider range: it lays hold of the heart out of a wider circle in both directions — man is united with the forces of thinking. Finally the seventh extends beyond the self, for which reason this lemniscate always calls up a real activity of will that is sure of its goal. Exercise (a) allows these three stages to be grasped directly from the heart; exercise (b) unfurls them on either hand as broken harmonies. The upper chord A-C-E-G clearly has a relationship to the spirit; the lower, A-F-D-B sounds in relationship to the physical. In the part on 'The Seven' in the second volume of this work these associations will be dealt with more thoroughly. Exercise (c) brings both harmonies into a combined form. In their breathing interchange, they exercise a beneficial and health-giving influence.

Attention to the basic scale simply going backwards showed that its intervals led to inner experience of the complementary intervals. Another lemniscate may be cast if one takes the exact reflection of the intervals.

With this, in spite of the fact that the descending intervals are also major, one can have a definite experience of minor. The basic scale upwards and its exact reflection downwards, studied repeatedly in its melodic course, or in the structure of its intervals, leads to the cental core of breathing rhythm in music.

Such studies in every form have a great healing and calming influence on the nervous people of today. One is always ascertaining the fact that nowadays almost everyone is ill and their breathing is somehow not in order. But the following example is a wonderfully harmonizing remedy which never fails to take effect.

The form of the movement can be illustrated in the following way

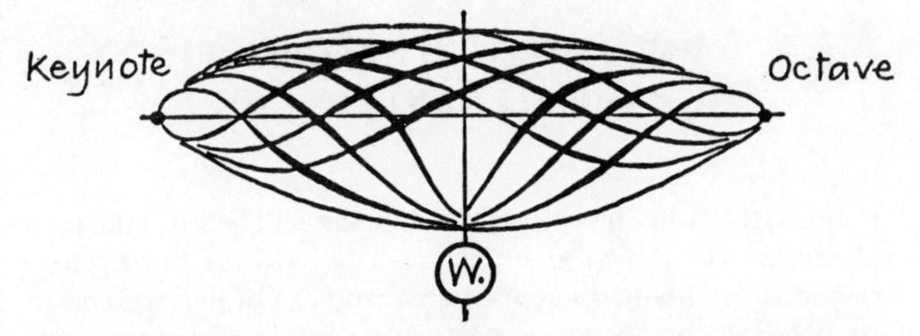

where the activity of the turning point (W) is connected with a swinging-over to the octave and must be formed consciously. If this does not happen it easily leads into a comfortable see-saw movement which does not strengthen the ego but leads it off into a dream.

The following exercise, carried out by two people around the sustained central note A, is of great value.

In this case it is essential that the continuous inner change between the bearing of a keynote and that of an octave in the central note A is experienced and made to sound. The other voice, however, which swings around this centre must be strongly anchored in it so as to hear in advance and experience accurately the interval above or below.

In this chapter on the lemniscatory reflections everything can be incorporated that has already been stated in anticipation in the previous chapter on the interplay in the circle of the twelve. Of special importance is all that lives in the rhythm of breathing — alternation between dissonance and consonance, forms of tension and release, tendencies of movement, interplay between the tonic and its two dominants and so on. We do not want to go into detail again here. The reader should feel all the more stimulated to find new exercises for himself in every field of music according to his personal needs. These rhythmic exercises can be carried out right into the enharmonic of each single note, quickened and quickening anew.

Chapter Six

THE NINEFOLD NATURE OF THE BASIC ELEMENTS IN RHYTHM

In this last chapter let us consider as a slight digression the basic elements of rhythm as such. There is a division into three, whose connection with man's being is clear and can be enlarged upon. It can be said that the straightforward, regular, continuous pulse-beat is the first of these elements. Connected with the heart and the circulation of the blood, whether fast or slow, it is like the becoming-audible of the life-force. It sets a standard as regards tempo and moves with regularity even when the notes are short or long. One might even imagine it could go on forever.

Metre is linked up with this, the rhythmic alternation of long notes and short. The normal relationship between them is one to two, one long to two shorts. Friedrich Hiebel in his book *The Gospel of Hellas* refers to the fact that the hexameter in its cultic origin was the foundation of all Greek verse. He writes concerning the division of the six feet into twice three which, separated by the caesura, arrive in the end at a point of rest.

> The three feet with the caesura provide a rhythmic unity, which is repeated in a somewhat modified form in the three following feet, with diaresis and rest-point, which comes as a matter of course at the end of the metrical line. The first three feet were spoken in a singing style, slowly, with the outbreathing stream of air, while the point of rest gave opportunity for inbreathing. A complete breath, exhalation and inhalation, corresponds to the three feet plus the caesura, that is with four rhythmic units. We know that each breath of a normal adult is equivalent to four pulse-beats.

The proportion between one long breath and four pulse-beats is revealed in the speaking of the hexameter. It is an expression of the human rhythm of lungs and heart.

It is clear that in the realm of music one should never confuse metre with beat. The former is connected with the experience of long and short and is a legacy from Greek times. The middle region of the heart, connected with breath and blood, lives in it, and regulates with this activity the whole physical organism. But beat comes from the North, from alliteration, and brings into music the contrast of heavy and light. It works into the limbs and impels the will. It is in accordance with this clear distinction that these two rhythmic elements may be employed educationally and therapeutically in quite different ways. The following twelve pairs of metre in their reciprocal relationship were, for the Greek, fundamental.

1)	pyrrhic		· ·	spondee		- -
2)	tribrach		· · ·	molossus		- - -
3)	iambus		· -	trochee		- ·
4)	anapaest		· · -	dactyl		- · ·
5)	amphibrach		· - ·	amphimacer		- · -
6)	bacchius		· - -	antibacchius		- - ·
7)	antispast		· - - ·	choriamb		- · · -
8)	smaller ionic		· · - -	greater ionic		- - · ·
9)	epitrite	I	· - - -	paeon	I	- · · ·
10)	"	II	- · - -	"	II	· - · ·
11)	"	III	- - · -	"	III	· · - ·
12)	"	IV	- - - ·	"	IV	· · · -

Musical metrical exercises, separated from speech and employed as phenomena for study, are best practised in scales or on triads. Care should be taken that a metre as a whole is heard and given shape in straightforward repetition on one note. Its very nature and its effect depend upon this objective, simple construction and steady repetition. If a melody is freely added to this,

(a) the effect is lost because the feeling-content is all too strongly emphasized. Concentration should be solely upon the experience of long and short, as in (b). The two examples show the difference. The calm movement in (b) leaves one free to surrender to the long measure as well as to grasp actively the short one. The fact that the long measure is not always the same is quickly realized. In the trochee (b) it has great calmness; one would like to be comfortably embedded in it. In other metrical forms there is a tension, sometimes an expansion in both directions and the short measure is experienced as an impelling heartbeat in the centre.

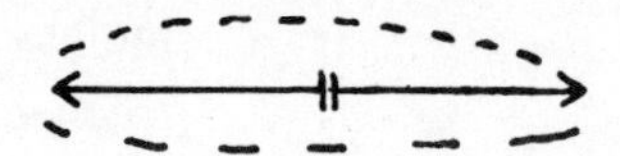

For the most part the short has to do with will, while the long has a contemplative quality. It is in this sense that the contrast of each single measure, as tabulated above, is infinitely life-giving and diverse in form. In the two columns of twelve each stands in relationship to the other in a similar complementary relationship as major to minor. Care should be taken that the relevant elements in the metre are stressed musically. Those beginning with a short note are better practised in major, while those beginning with a long note are better in minor.

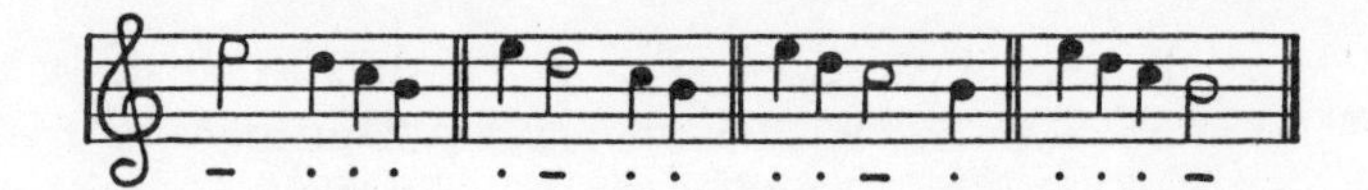

Of special interest are the studies in transformation in the epitrites and paeons in which, each time, long as well as short are given a slightly new shade of feeling.

But one thing must be observed with absolute accuracy; the metre must always start on its own, whether with a long note or a short. The short must never be taken as an upbeat. In that case the long notes would acquire a kind of heaviness from the downbeat and everything would move into another sphere. And something else should be mentioned: special attention must be paid to the transition from long to short and vice versa. That is the point where the ego can take hold, just as in the previous rhythmical exercises with their important turning points. It is a moment of special import in present-day schooling. The more one works qualitatively with this realm of metre in music, the more one will love it and be the less able to dispense with it.

If the metric element of rhythm is seen as being interwoven with the breathing, then beat strikes down into the limbs. Each of the metres has a quite well-defined formation, which in almost every form reveals a polarity as fundamental unity, a rhythmic breathing process. This is its nature, not yet quite attained in the two first pairs, the pyrrhic and spondaic, the tribrach and molossus. The pairs marked 3, 4, 5 and 6 bring the first simple polar forms while those from 7 to 12 are each constructed out of two basic forms. For example, the seventh pair combines iambic with trochaic to form two distinct new metres. The epitrite metres play with the spondee, the iambic and trochaic, the paeons with the pyrrhic, the iambic and trochaic. One experiences an activation of the breathing and flexibility of the ego, even if the way it is dealt with here is different from that in previous ages.

But with the growing predominance of the beat the breathing polarity in metre has been lost, and in many cases today beat is called 'measure' and measure is treated as if it were beat. The outstanding difference between them is that metre can make use of melodic differences in pitch. Musically every note is at its disposal, and for this reason rhythm is always experienced horizontally. In the case of beat, however, one speaks of the downbeat, and it is connected in feeling vertically with a repetition of the note or some kind of continuous ostinato. This pulse-beat, as 'the becoming-audible of the life-force', now adapts to the predominant feeling in calm or hurried units of measure, of a heavier or lighter kind. We must now listen to these differentiations, comparing a $^2/_4$, $^3/_4$ or $^6/_8$ time signature, these being the most usual in classical music. In general, $^5/_4$ or even $^7/_4$ have been brought into use only in modern times. They set man free from feeling too strongly connected with the earth element.

This last development made popular a continual change in the number of beats in a bar. But in order to compensate for a relative un-rest, a rhythm is often superimposed in great curves on the normal repetitive arrangement of a variety of beats in a bar. Bela Bartók, in Book V of his *Microcosmos* gives a little study concerned with changing time, in which an arrangement of $^2/_4$, $^3/_4$, $^3/_8$ and $^5/_8$ follow one another in fivefold repetition, and are then consolidated in a single breakthrough of $^6/_8$ in a double-forte interrupting a series of $^5/_8$ bars. The very interesting studies of the Bulgarian Dances in the sixth book carry the following instructions for time:

$$\frac{3+3+2}{8} \qquad \frac{3+2+3}{8} \qquad \text{or} \qquad \frac{2+2+2+3}{9}$$

The second of these (No.151) has a unique charm and is beautifully balanced.

The reflected first and third numbers enclose the centre one symmetrically and in this delicate change from a more agitated beginning and ending to a more sustained centre, they give to the whole a wonderful swing and peace at one and the same time.

To show how strongly a rhythmic process lies at the root of the most well-articulated musical principle of form, purely from the point of view of beat, entirely apart from any other musical content, two further examples may be given from modern and classical music. As a first example we offer a 'Song' from *Chamber Music for Piano* by Wolfgang Fortner. The analysis of the beat is:

$$\frac{5}{4}\ \frac{3}{4}\ \frac{5}{4}\ \frac{3}{4}\ \Big|\ \frac{4}{4}\ \frac{5}{4}\ \frac{3}{4}\ \frac{6}{4}\ :\Big\|$$

$$\frac{3}{4}\ \frac{4}{4}\ \frac{2}{4}\ \Big|\ \frac{3}{3}\ \frac{4}{4}\ \frac{2}{4}\ \Big|\ \underline{\underline{\frac{3}{4}}}\ \frac{3}{4}\ \frac{3}{4}\ \frac{4}{4}\ \frac{2}{4}\ \Big|$$

$$\frac{5}{4}\ \frac{3}{4}\ \frac{5}{4}\ \frac{3}{4}\ \Big|\ \frac{4}{4}\ \frac{5}{4}\ \frac{3}{4}\ \frac{6}{4}\ \Big\|$$

A first part of sixteen beats continually changing and yet held together, a middle part of ten alternating beats, the eighth of which is inserted as a protraction of the musical motif (double underlining), and then a repetition — and, intricate as it looks, it indicates basically a simple classical form of song! Polarity and repetition are fundamental principles of rhythm. If, according to this principle, one examines the foregoing summary of beats in relationship to the melodic line —

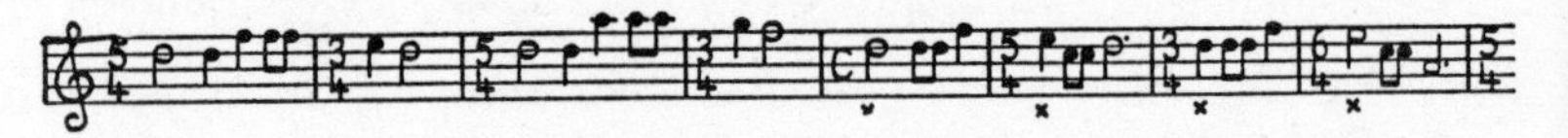

at least in the first eight bars, which are then repeated, the bass voice taking over the melody — one finds, in spite of the alternation, a beautiful polarity between out- and in-breathing, between $^5/_4$ and $^3/_4$, and quite a fine rhythmic variation in the next four bars: in the $^4/_4$ bar, the D at the entry of the theme is a minim and in the $^5/_4$ bar the E is a crotchet. Then there is an interchange: in the $^3/_4$ it is now the D that takes over the crotchet value, but then the E in the $^6/_4$ bar becomes the minim. The repetitive element, however, is sustained throughout. More examples can be taken from the simpler to the more intricate forms of modern times. They all indicate an endeavour to get away from an earlier architectural rigidity and bring about a more fluid, breathing movement without abandoning the structural element.

A composition such as that above, directs the attention forcibly to a further, not inessential, element — the bar line. What really happens from one bar to the next? Each time, it is an imperceptible grasping of the self, a pulling together and taughtening, in order to prepare for the emphasis on the first beat. It is the bar line which brings about a rhythmic interchange between the grasping of self and release in the course of movement. If the change of bar is as persistent and flexible as in the little 'Song' by Fortner, then the gesture of the bar line and the experience united with it is made easier because it is more obvious than in former times when the measure remained continuously the same. In comparison we may take a Mozartian phrase, and see how much more attention is required here. The feeling for the bar line prevents the 'weight' on the first beat from 'falling into the depths'. The grasping of the self is like a raising up of the self, from which the bar can be formed sculpturally instead of being ignored or over-emphasized. The second example, the prelude in C major from the first volume of Bach's *48 Preludes and Fugues*, will be analyzed at the end of this chapter.

It has already been shown that the basic rhythmic elements can be classified in a threefold way, which may then be extended. The pulse forms a focal point in the centre and is connected with heartbeat, blood and breath. It extends upwards into metre, into a realm of thought. The corresponding extension downwards is found in time, which is connected with the bar line. Here the rhythm pulsates into the lower pole of man, his limbs fired by his blood, testifying to a grasping of the will. But the will is guided and restrained by an element of clear consciousness. The grasping of the self in the experience of the bar line, and also in the many changes of time nowadays, requires well-considered guidance in order to work out the musical logic of the structure and all the turns and changes in movement. This justifies the (Th) of thinking beside the (W) of the supporting will in the following diagram.

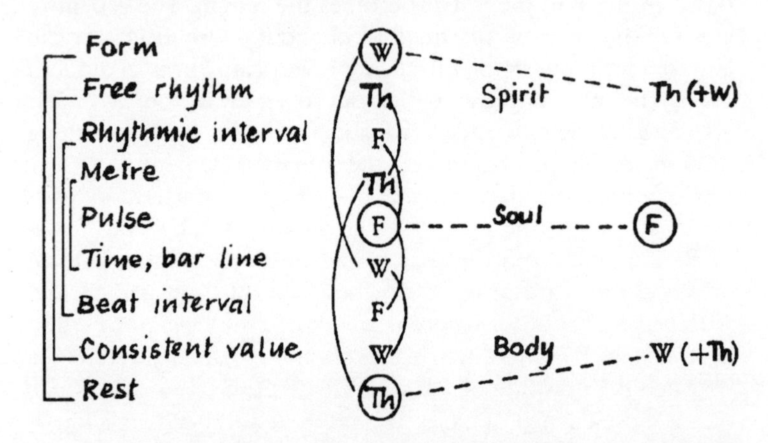

In the upper sphere the strictness of metre loosens to the rhythmic interval, to the free play of long and short notes which fits into the architecturally prepared framework of time through the caesura of the bar line. In the following example from Beethoven, Piano Sonata Op.31, No. 3, the language of the heart strikes up into the sphere of melody.

The rhythmic element with its melodic sculptural process seems to approximate more towards feeling, yet despite the changes of direction in pitch, the grouping of motifs and intervals of rest, as well as the tenser or more relaxed shaping of the different note values, it none the less bears within it the determinative will element. One can now truly speak of rhythmic intervals, for the time value from note to note is a continually changing one. All possible varieties of long and short, the dotted minims filling up the whole bar, the crotchets, quavers and semiquavers playing freely one with another, always calling forth a definite rhythmic experience in the duration of the note, the measure of a pulse in the crotchets (bars 3 and 5), the calm long notes, (bars 4 and 6), the restless questioning in the introductory motif with the rest, the semiquavers playing around, and the triplets charging ahead! If one practises this example only once on one note, without listening to melody or harmony, it is amazing what a stirring, rhythmic life is manifested in it.

The opposite of this, which can also be referred to as interval, deals with bar and bar line. It is enough to experience only once the following line of continually diminishing values without melody or harmony, simply as duration, in order to perceive how completely different in effect this example is to the one above. The continuous diminution by halving of previous values, making the interval ever shorter, does not produce a musical impetus to freedom, but on the contrary — despite external increase in velocity — a perpetual, almost cramping compression. In contrast to the previous rhythmic interval with

its play of movement in a given time, this emphasizes something leading rather to a standstill. It is the same distinction that has already been made but it is grasped here as experience. The interval, always diminishing in the proportion of 1:2, borne by the pulse and by the heavy beat, is connected with the bodily stress of the will — one might almost say, with the mechanical motor-force of an engine. The movement is sacrificed, as if to a death-process. The same process is evident as in the note F and in the interval of the fourth: an element of will, nurtured by strong feeling. This group of intervals according to beat and bar is usually practised by clapping or running. But this leads away from the really living element. The whole process ought to be made one's own in relation to breathing and out of the feeling for the process of halving.

Here, in considering division, an apparent contradiction is

In Part One, Chapter Two, the number two was seen as a determinative factor in the structure of the overtones arising out of a note, in that the number of tones was doubled from octave to octave. There was continual division within the octave. To repeat what was stated there:

> The law of division emerges as determining this sounding expression of man. All living, organic growth is controlled by division. And when this principle of the 2 is referred to as the number of the Son, that is, as the power of divine self-revelation, it is evident that the power of the Word — in fact of every creative human utterance — must stand under the banner of the Logos.

It is this reference to the connection of the division by two with the nature of the Logos that provides the key to the solution of the apparent contradiction. For with full justification one may speak of two kinds of division: of a splitting into two similar parts connected more with the physical, with its danger of approaching an abstract process of atomization in the possibility of endless division; and of another kind revealed in the breathing inner life of musical sound, which is not expressed in a mechanical beat, but rhythmically. It is worth giving this still further consideration.

Listen once more to the series of overtones. It has probably already been discovered that the need arises not to play the notes as if they were of equal length. It is better to play them in a quite unrestricted manner from octave to octave so that they can be written down as follows:

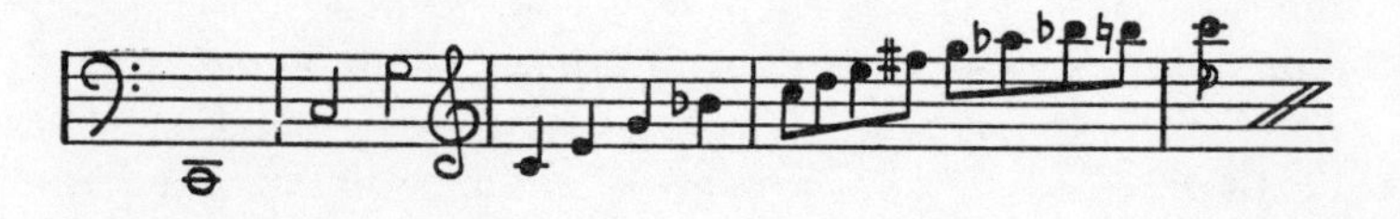

Of course this is not absolutely necessary. But it indicates a clear arrangement, dictated by feeling, of the law of multiplication which determines its course in time. A fifth octave up or down would be differentiated into semiquavers, a further one into demisemiquavers. It is revealing that this continuous multiplication never produces two equal parts. The point of division does not lie in the centre, but the second part is always smaller than not lie in the centre, but the second part is always smaller than the first. In the second octave it is clearly and plainly discernible: the fifth is a bigger interval than the fourth leading into the next octave. In the first of the thirds it can still be heard and experienced directly. From there on it becomes less evident, and the tuning by temperament eliminates these differences. The same principle of construction holds good for the succession of seconds, as well as for any intervals which may follow.

The following gives a picture of relationships in the series. Into the multiplying by two from octave to octave (dotted lines) — that is, one, two, four, eight, sixteen tones and so on — another series of three tones each is incorporated (black lines). If in qualitative listening these triads are compared, then, despite their differences, they all point to a construction showing a similar inner experience. One could speak of an outbreathing in soul and spirit, an expansion outwards, a major principle which is always followed by an inbreathing, a minor principle, a contraction.

The third tone coincides with the first of the following three. The continually diminishing intervals going upwards form not a similar diagrammatic principle to that of the subdivisions of the beat, but produce a wavy line, a picture of breathing life. Sketched as forms of movement they give the following figure:

The equivalent process in the complementary series in the grouping of tones and as a breathing process would be unfurled as follows:

It establishes in soul and spirit the reverse process: the triad begins with a minor and finishes off with a major bearing. So the whole process unites in two streams of breath in opposite directions. In the accompanying picture they are sketched as a regular interlacing principle.

In it the same fundamental form can be recognized as that of the breathing within the scale of the seven basic notes, which was given in the last chapter.

It is important to be quite clear that something of a dual nature, such as this, reveals either the sphere of death or the sphere of life, depending on whether it is grasped from the physical or from the etheric standpoint. The continuous even diminution of intervals revealed in the overtones, from a wide form in the octave to ever-narrowing smaller intervals up to the semitone, and possibly even further, indicates a continual ascent far beyond oneself. But experience in soul and spirit runs its course in an opposite direction. It is a continual movement inwards. A third is significantly more intimate — more personal, nearer to man, more subjective and tinged with a quality of soul — than the octave or even the fifth and fourth. In a qualitative way the series provides a transformation of experience from outside inwards; that is, the development of an increasing connection of the sounds with the self. The intervals imitate the path along which man passes in the development of his consciousness: from being embedded in divine cosmic space to existence in the centre of his own being, where the movements become ever more intimate and their differences ever more subtle. This would be valid in the highest degree for the quarter-tones in subsequent octaves, and even for eighths of a tone — the niceties of which the present-day is beginning to open up; they are fluid vibrations which are not experienced as distinct tones, but as a vibration within the note.

With this a kind of higher, fourth dimension is presented to the inner being, the reality of which reveals very fine gradations of sound. These require more spiritualized organs of soul. This internalizing towards the threshold of the supersensible world is reflected in the major as well as in the minor paths; in the partials of the note, as well as in the complementary series sounding in space. But in both cases it rests on the reality of the Logos Being, of the higher ego in the human soul. In this connection one may speak of a free rhythm: free in so far as it is a rhythmic interval-event which, weaving in the world of the absolute, is probably audible as the physical-etheric archetype of sound, but not yet compressed into the abstraction of tuning by temperament. Here 'the creative cosmic word' is revealed, which in its fundamental being, in its laws and its depths is, to start with, only accessible to thinking.

The abstract, lifeless division in the lower counterpole of the rhythmic diagram (page 217), is found in the length of the notes, which continually divide into equal halves. Under certain circumstances it would be justifiable to speak of a mechanical element, which mainly serves acceleration in the course of music. Yet these various rhythmic-interval gradations bring about quite clear and valuable qualitative distinctions, not only in an external sense. Where they dominate a composition, adhering persistently to a single value, they are the counterpole of free rhythm. And within them the whole mood of soul streams out with a gripping force; for example, the solemnity of a chorale sung in slow minims or the crotchet motif of Chopin's Prelude No. 20 in C minor, twelve bars

long and in phrases of equal length. Bach's *B flat minor Prelude* in the first volume of the *48 Preludes and Fugues* allows the rhythmic values to express the inwardly-striving soul drama with at least the same intensity as the concentrated melodic structure.

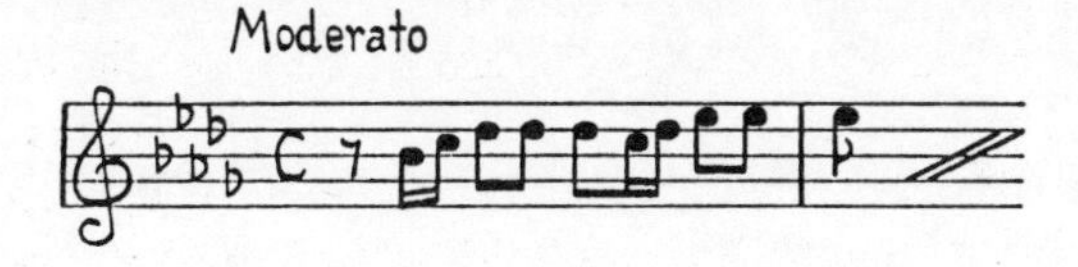

But it is often in the especially rapid and relentlessly surging phrases — for example Bach's *Prelude in D major*, also in the first volume of the *48 Preludes and Fugues* — that the small, but all the more intensely moving rhythmic semiquavers determine the character.

All musical compositions of this kind, however ingenious, ratify the mechanical motor element, previously mentioned with regard to beat. The continuous connection of the unvarying length of note demands an alert will, whereby the impact of the bars creates a significant reiterated measure.

Finally, consideration should be given to both the extreme rhythmic elements in the diagram — the rest at the lower end and the form at the upper. The rest is often called the 'dead' interval. This description is only possible in a time like the present, which takes as valid only what can be grasped by the physical senses, but which shows little understanding of the fact that it is precisely in all that is inaudible that the most important musical events occur. This is the case with the rest. If one plays a simple scale of crotchets legato, and then afterwards with quaver rests between the notes, there will be a great difference between the two experiences. It is clear that with each rest one is drawn away from the audible event. It is an experience similar to that of the bar line, where in the midst of the musical flow one pulls oneself together and the physical stretches into the upright; whereas with the rest one draws back each time into an inward listening in the silence — that is, more into the spiritual. This is also connected with the inaudible, accessible only to powers of consciousness in the sphere of thinking. Musically this silence is filled, depending on circumstance, with powerful stirrings of soul as though the thread of musical logic would continue on the far side of the threshold with the audible. The greater the surrender to this harkening of the rests, the more intense the consciousness that it is just there that the most important experiences take place, and that the audible course of the music is only one part — the half.

In this connection let us look at the Largo of Beethoven's

Piano Sonata Op. 7. The theme, at (a), is planned from the outset on this rhythmic interplay of the audible with the inaudible, and through this fact it receives much greater plasticity.

The dominant of the second chord wants to be more comprehensive, and this happens much more strongly by swinging through the rest from F into the octave G than would be the case if these two were connected. More space is introduced, so to speak. This process of coming back into the octave out of the inaudible is repeated immediately in the movement through the rest from the second to the third bar. It will be noticed, however, that this second inner movement through the rest is different from the first. The third, from D back to D, is different again, not far-reaching like the first, but more concentrated and more like a confirmation, in order to gather the whole process together in the suspended dissonance and in the *sforzando* in the fourth bar. Now definitely established in audibility this thought streams on in a melodious *legato* of four bars, which would never have had so wonderfully tranquil an effect without the previous activity of the rests.

Example (b), in a beautiful succession of melodiously flowing bars, shows the transition back to the first subject. The recurrence of the experience of the rest is prepared in that the chords and the succession of notes are loosened up and virtually broken through. Compare this with a playing of the passage without the rests, so as to ascertain the incredibly impressive effects.

In the next transition, (c), to the middle of the movement, bars 20 - 22, one is as it were twice thrown out by the short interrupting rests, in order to find the way back to a place of rest, again overheard in the inaudible. But this continuously-repeated plunging into the spirit-sphere of silence, in order to receive a creative impulse anew and to 'bring it down', produces not only a loosening of the depths but also the force to combine the linked and detached passages. Example (d) shows this, and Beethoven stresses this simultaneity of polarities through the indications 'semper staccato' for the bass, and 'semper legato' for melody and harmony in the upper voice. In every case it is a harkening to cause and effect between two worlds, between a soul condition and spirit connections, which can never be experienced in the audible alone with such compelling reality.

Similar examples are to be found in all musical literature. And this study of intervals is one of the most fundamental tasks: in rhythmic alternation to include the life of the rest with the audible sound, and to learn to fill it and control it with equal intensity. It will be found that this swinging between audible and inaudible in varying durations, shorter or longer, contains and brings to expression the most vivid moments of all; it is often a culmination. The rests are 'dead' only when one passes through them unmoved. Then they are like black holes which always have within them something of an ending, and for this reason, when playing the piano, they are often gladly disguised with the pedal. Fundamentally the same problem is displayed in this least of musical realms as in the fact of death — either it is truly the end, with the black hole of the earthly grave, or it will be the gateway to a new life beyond the light.

Consideration of the rest as an interval living between two musical poles — movement in the spirit and form in the earthly — leads over to the inner sculptor who, in the words of Novalis, lives in the soul of every musician. The spiritual 'figuration' spoken of there is to be found not only in the realm of the rest. In the audible flow of every composition the power of 'figuration' is revealed in the structure of its form and in the little breathing spaces between the motifs and phrases within it.

To conclude this examination of the basic rhythmic elements, let us consider the well-known *C major Prelude* out of the first book of Bach's *48 Preludes and Fugues*. In it we find the import and mastery with which Bach treated the structure of bars in relation to form. In keeping with the major/minor system we can listen to the structure of this piece in relation to the bars and from the point of view of harmony. The whole prelude has thirty-four bars, if in this matter one follows Bach and not the edition by Czerny, who inserted one more bar between bars 22 and 23.

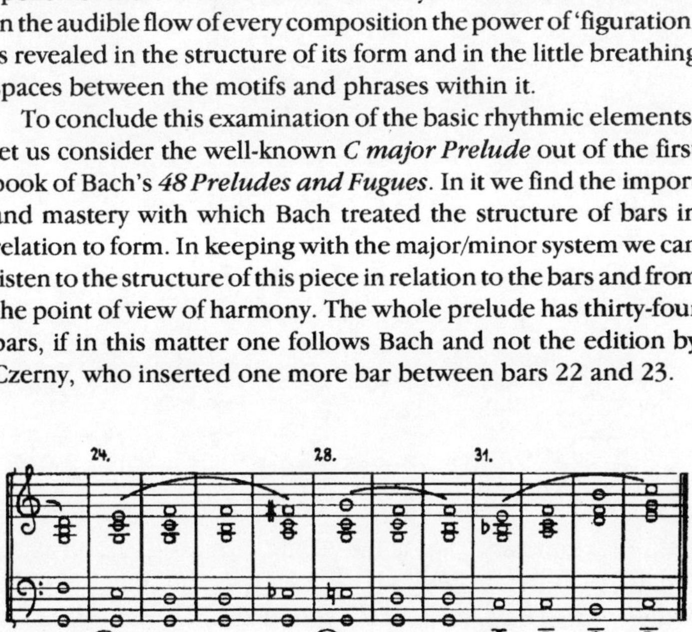

24. 28. 31.

D D T.

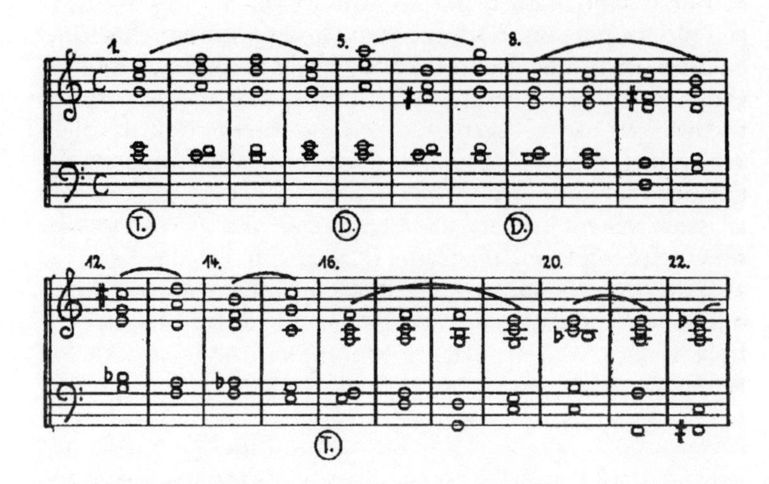

The analysis of the harmony is given above. One can summarize it from bar to bar in semibreves. Not only in harmony but also in bar-structure there is a wonderful, well-balanced pattern. The cadence on the tonic sounds three times —

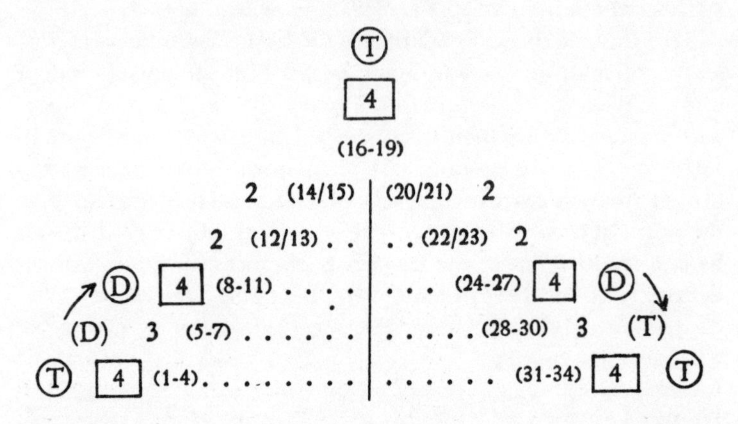

in the first four bars, (1-4) at the climax, (bars 16-19); and at the end, (bars 31-34). In between it passes over four times into the dominant (bars 5-7, 8-11, 24-27 and 28-30). These bars on the dominant can be grouped in sevens: at the beginning (see arrow) moving towards G major; at the end, from bar 23 onwards, expanding over a dominant pedal-point towards C major. Into this great, comprehensive rhythmic breathing, smaller sections of two bars each are inserted as links weaving between dissonance and consonance, flowing through this great architecture with life and movement. The fact that the harmonies in each bar are repeated twice — summarized as semibreves in the example — is an in and out breathing, touching upon the mystery of the relationship 1:4 between blood and breath which determines human life.

This wonderful structure in the pattern of bars gives to the whole work something like a framework, just as in man the bony structure is necessary for earthly existence. Out of higher forces of will, the musical life developing towards form is held together by this structure; but, unlike a dead skeleton, it inhales living breath. It is not to be wondered at that this prelude from the *Little Book of Anna Magdalena Bach* has captivated the hearts of the world. And the quiet religious mood which always embraces the listening soul is truly in accord with Goethe's words:

> Breathing is a twofold grace:
> To draw in air, and set it free.
> The former oppresses, the latter refreshes:
> So wonderfully is life intermixed.
> Give thanks to thy God when He oppresses,
> And thank Him again when He refreshes.

The ninefold diagram shows the relationship of the rhythmic elements to the soul-forces of feeling, directed towards the heart as centre, to *thinking* with a will-impulse, and to *will* with an element of consciousness. Going out from the pulse at the centre, two groups of elements correspond between the upper and lower poles: metre and time (bar), rhythmic interval and the interval of beat, free rhythm and the linking of time-values, and finally form and rest. It is evident that this ninefold arrangement has three groups of which one corresponds more to the spirit, one to the soul and one to the physical in man, held together by the I in the centre. Moreover, through qualitative listening we are led to hearing this great threefoldness divided again into three smaller parts, grasped by the soul-forces. The third part of this work, concerning the intervals, and particularly this last chapter on the rhythmic aspects, finds a proper conclusion in an appropriate picture.

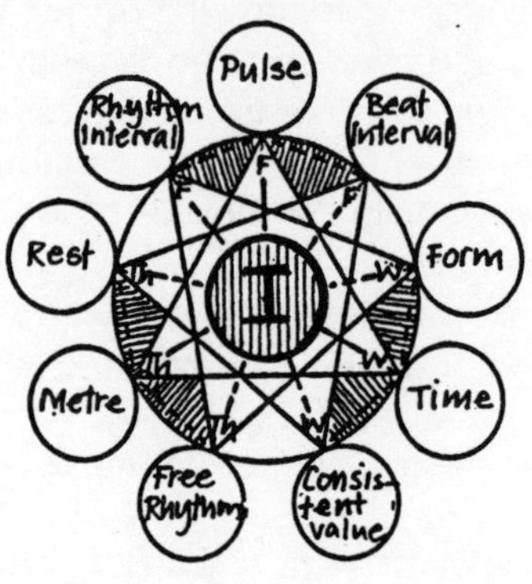

May its apparent schematic appearance be filled, according to the indications given, with ringing life.

PART FOUR

THE NATURE AND ACTIVITY OF THE KEYS

Chapter One

AN HISTORICAL SKETCH

After the young Felix Mendelssohn had visited Weimar Goethe wrote to Zelter:

> To me his presence was particularly beneficial, for I found my relationship to music to be still the same: I listen to it with pleasure, participation and reflection. I love the historical aspect, for who understands a phenomenon at all if he has not entered into the process of its development?

Goethe's attitude may serve as a guide in determining whether we should start by contemplating a composition, or start from the straightforward basic phenomenon of major and minor keys. It is one of the truly tragic symptoms of our time that feeling for the fine distinction of mood, intrinsic quality and efficacy of the keys has, in general, been lost. 'Practising scales' is a tedious process, a mere technical chapter in every musical study. A C major is different from an A major or an E flat major, not only through the fact that it has no key signature while the other two have three sharps and three flats respectively, but this measure of brightening or darkening places man in the polar interplay of light and heaviness and is something to which we do not normally pay attention. If, however, hearing and the experience connected with it were to be trained, Goethe's deductions about 'pleasure, participation and reflection' would live irrefutably in the soul. Listening to the constant forming and changing of mood can raise the study of the keys to a source of pleasure. Where an artistic experience strives to reach expression, where it aims at perfection, it can always be a source of pleasure. Does the perpetual discovery of the beauties in music not fill the soul with joy and interest? Fourteen sharp or flat keys in major, in addition to the initial key of C; the same number in the minor from A, and in these also the distinction between melodic and harmonic — do these not provide an abundance of lightness and heaviness, of brightness and darkness, of striving and rest? Forty-four subtle differentiations need the heart's participation in listening, as well as in performance. They will call up powers of reflection; they will softly and gradually rouse, with ever greater insistence, questions leading from experience to understanding.

The Greeks counted Clio and Urania, as inspirers of history and astronomy, among the Muses of Apollo. They were aware that the universe and the evolution of mankind were deeply connected and subject to universal musical laws. Goethe, 'the Olympian', felt he was touched by a universal breathing in the historical course of development. This points to a deeper understanding of major and minor keys and will form the content of Part Four of this book. In what way did they come about?

In this connection we must turn to the ancient form of the pentatonic as it prevailed in pre-Christian culture up to the middle of ancient Greek times.

However one plays these notes, whether upward or downward, with fewer notes or more, the listener will always find that it reveals a different basic relationship to music from that of the present day. To the modern listener pentatonic melodies seem to be free of all heaviness and firmness, like a happy child swinging in a spaceless, bodiless sphere of soul, carried and borne along by the breath of divine life. The basic structure is of a wonderful symmetry if one takes its bearings from the middle note, in the following case A:

A five note structure swings upward from D; another, similar to the first in all its intervals, answers in a downward direction from E. It is like a soul which opens to become a chalice so that something spiritual may be bestowed on it to bring about a perfect whole. This secret of life revealed through music has been known since ancient times in picture form through telling symbols. Of the three following (a),(b) and (c), (b) was the 'Tai-Ki' of the Chinese. It was a picture from the legend of the two birds Yang and Yin, from which six musical notes were heard, and experienced as if entwined in one another. The masculine Yang impulse was represented as black, the feminine as white. But both still bore an indication of the opposite pole in the shape of a black or white dot in the centre. The Greek 'Mneander-form' (c) shows the same life-principle in an interlocking angular form.

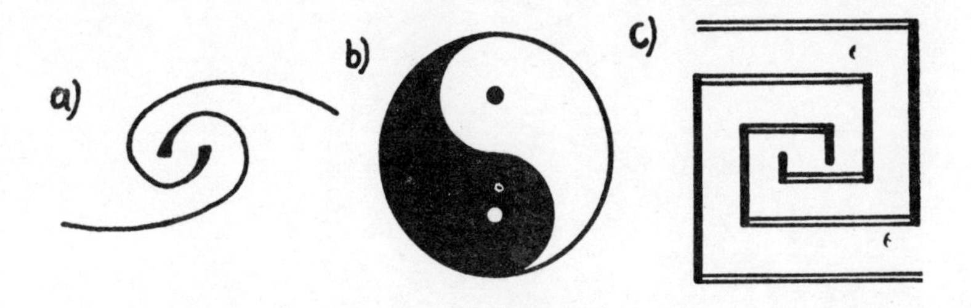

Listening to and entering into the realm of the pentatonic in this way, one cannot yet speak of a scale in the usual sense. If, however, one reflects that the totality of the chromatic notes in the octave, the twelve 'holy Lü' of the Chinese, were not arranged as they are today in a circle of fifths, but in twelve semitones, then

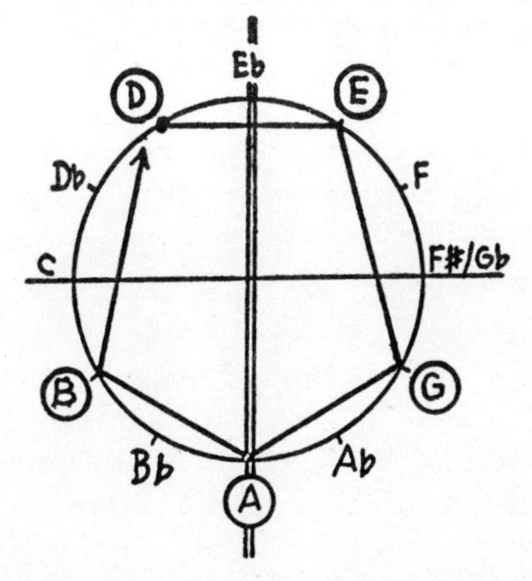

the above pentatonic D, E, G, A, B, would form a pentagon in the circle. The content of every pentatonic sounds as a cosmic scale, not devised by man but given by the Gods.

In his informative book *Singing Stones*, already referred to, Marius Schneider describes how the oldest traditions stemming from the Vedanta philosophy of India, as well as from China, bring a basic succession of five notes — C, D, F, G, A. Probably this has also been handed down in the musical history of other regions. The succession of fifths — F, C, G, D, A are notes which were experienced during that age as representing the five planetary forces: Jupiter, Mars, Venus, Mercury and Saturn.

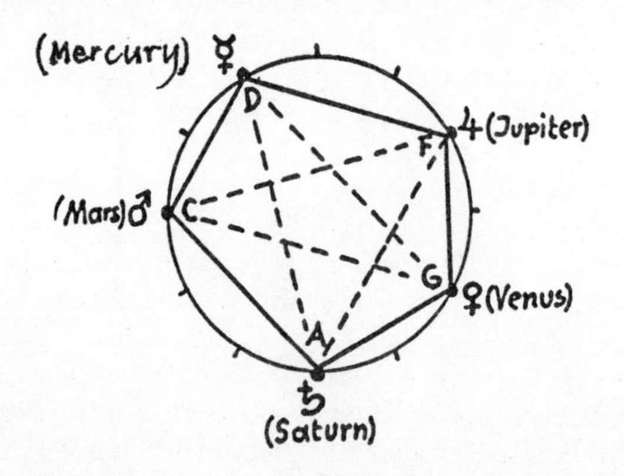

In the circle of semitones, a pentagon or a pentagram is formed again (dotted lines), the apex of which falls upon G, the Venus note of that time. And right through the golden age of the ancient Greek culture this wonderful pentatonic can be found, free of any tendency to establish itself upon the earth, the various forms testifying to a childlike nature being carried into spiritual spheres.

About the sixth century BC, as an indication of the beginning of a thinking consciousness, Pythagoras ventured to take the unprecedented step of putting number and concept in place of pictures. He arranged the notes in keeping with a mathematical foundation in a series of whole tones and semitones, and turned the pentatonic forms into a seven/eight note system. The Pythagoreans of the first Christian century report that on his long journey through the Mystery Centres of the old world, he spent twenty-two years in Egypt and was initiated there as a Theban priest. Like Moses in his time, he transformed the old traditions of his people. Consequently the swinging five-note music, loosely fitted together and for the most part without semitones, gave way to a calmly-stepping, enclosed structure, which for the first time may be called a scale in the true sense. One can imagine the shocks, the conflicts, and also the enthusiasm that such an upheaval evoked. This was all the more far-reaching in that through it a fundamental change in the consciousness of man and his relationship to music was disclosed. What had actually happened?

The pentatonic awakens in the soul something of a happy and unburdened childlike quality in that the notes, taken as a whole, yield an enclosed symmetrical pattern. The forces from the lower and upper sphere flow towards the centre. This is the reflection of a childlike being, which knows itself to be embedded in the interweaving forces of earthly and spiritual surroundings and surrenders to them. It was a state of consciousness which, for the Greek period, still determined the basic musical feeling of mankind. The awakening to the independent ego had not yet come. However, at the beginning of this new cultural epoch man trod the earth with a new self-confidence and self-assurance. Mythical consciousness gave way to a conceptual mathematical and philosophical way of thinking. Man began to know himself as a responsible being and he started to mature towards grasping in full the difficulties and problems of his personal destiny. Established within himself, he felt he was appointed to take over his own guidance and his own transformation; and that is a task which requires the newly-awakened forces of clear and logical thinking. The release from the world of the Gods had begun. Fully conscious of this coming of age, though still youthful and impetuous, he recognized himself as bearer and messenger of Promethean being. And it was music, within which he felt the cosmic connections still existed, which had the power to awaken strong ethical forces in him.

This newly-awakened feeling brought about a completely different form of music, and this is to be found in the Pythagorean seven-note system. No longer does anything surround the soul or enclose it. Step by step, in musically logical succession, the soul has to assume guidance and responsibility for the clarity of notes and intervals in mathematical ratio. Such an evolutionary step is always connected with the surrender of old forces and the difficult achievement of new forces. The birth of the seven notes denotes both a surrender and a gain. Even today, in listening to and experiencing the difference between a pentatonic and a

Greek scale, one can feel shattered as if one were empty or even impoverished. The portals of childhood close.

It takes time to grow into such a different state of mind, opening towards the earth so as to attain to the felicities and tasks of the newly awakening ego-consciousness.

The Pythagorean system of music may be examined from two standpoints. In his little book *Tonleitern und Sternenskalen*, (Richard Hummel Verlag, Leipzig, 1927), Felix Weingartner refers to something analogous to this. The one aspect, and presumably the older, is that of the seven stages. In this form two tetrachords, each of four notes — in the following example from E to A upwards and from E to B downwards — were connected by the central note E, which was placed in the middle like a sun-centre.

This gave a kind of heliocentric orientation. The general direction of this scale as a complete unit was experienced according to tradition in a twofold manner, (Albert Freiherr von Thimus in his work *Die Harmonikale Symbolik des Althertums — The Harmonic Symbolism of Ancient Times*). There was a sharp contrast between exoteric and esoteric. Exoterically the downward generally accepted form followed the feeling, then still alive, that music comes down from cosmic starry distances. Esoterically, secretly in the Mystery Centres, it was fostered in an upward direction. Here it was considered that in practice it awakened the forces of form-giving movement and prepared the way for the future support of these forces.

It is not possible here to go into the different versions of cosmic connections. Yet in relation to this present work it is essential to understand that the structure of the scale is no longer developed in the way of the pentatonic, centripetally from outside inwards, but centrifugally, from inside outwards. Considered in relationship to man's state of musical consciousness at that time this is deeply significant. For the awakening human ego then spread from the centre of its being out into the world, both spiritually and terrestrially. With this gradual expansion there arose a new relationship between the notes of the tetrachords on either hand — that is, the relationship of a complementary polarity. Observing the structure of the three kinds of Greek modes, the Dorian (a) with the central note E, the Phrygian (b) with D as centre, and the Lydian (c) with C as centre,

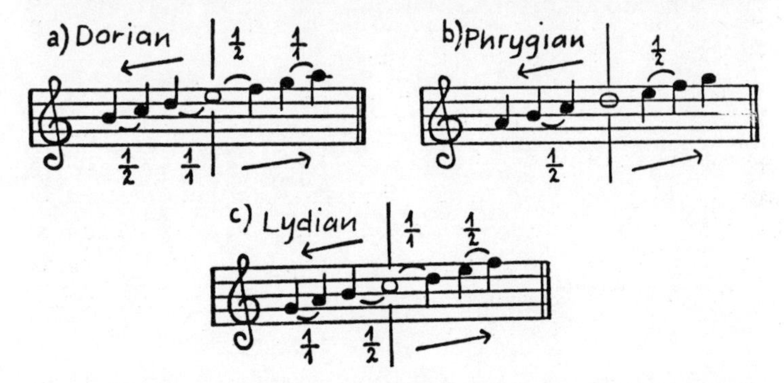

the principle of symmetry found in the pentatonic is only in the middle key, the Phrygian: the half and whole tones are in perfect balance. The other two structures, however, respond to each other in their polarities: the half tone E to F in the Dorian (a) upwards from the centre, corresponds to the whole tone E to D downwards. With the next step, F to G upwards and D to C downwards, a minor third above and a major third below are formed in relation to the centre. Finally we have G to A as a whole tone upwards and C to B as a half tone downwards, giving two perfect fourths, one on either hand. The third scale, the Lydian, is in its structure the exact opposite of the Dorian. It is understandable that this was needed to train a new awareness of difference between upper and lower, an awareness appropriate to the much more conscious ego.

For this new soul bearing connected with the finding of the ego, the semitone was an element of decisive importance. This, the pentatonic for the most part did not have. In listening to a diatonic semitone, not produced chromatically by raising or lowering a note, but by transition from one sphere to the next, an unmistakable reference back to the note of origin is always there. For example in

(a) C to D as well as C to B flat, as whole tones from C, make an opening movement, leading in an outward direction.

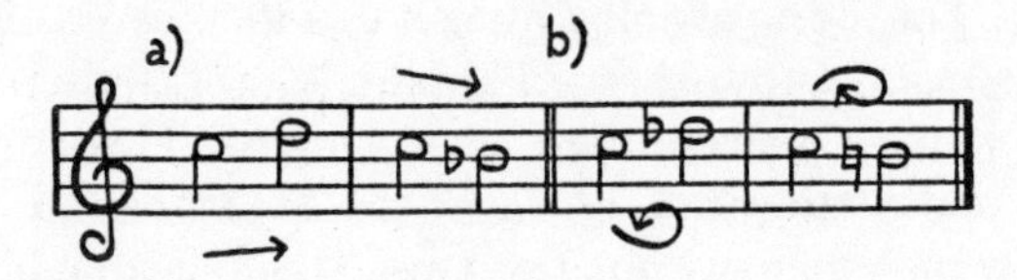

On the other hand, the semitones C to D flat and C to B (b) give the connection with the C in an inward direction, and really need a repetition of this note as confirmation.

This element of a laying hold of the self, requiring repetition, was determinative in the structure of the Greek scales: the position of the semitone gave this specific imprint. In it the young human ego was educated towards balancing between a forward step moving towards an assured goal, and a self-mastery, conscious and restrained. The Greek was trained to approach the ideal of the measure of all forms of life proclaiming the quality of wisdom. In such a manner he experienced in each tetrachord, whether up or down from the centre, alternating concentration (semitone) and release (whole tone). Goethe would have said: contraction and expansion, systole and diastole — the process of breathing. In this process of breathing the Greek learnt to hold firmly to his own centre. In such a merging of polarities, he could understand the words of Heraclitus: 'Connections: completion and incompletion, harmony and disharmony, concord and discord, out of all things one, out of one thing all.' Was this not the unprecedented, new and mysterious challenge — the will towards the self rising resplendent in mankind?

From this basic 'heliocentric' form of the seven there develops another — the octave form of the scale, with its entirely new meaning.

The fitting of both tetrachords into the space of an octave, from E to E , brings a new challenge to the soul. The carrying through of two successions of notes moving in the same direction brings a greater tension into the inner musical power of formation. This octave form of the scale of E — the note of the sun according to that time — takes its course in man's periphery of being, to the mastery and inner fulfilment of which the soul can only gradually be educated — two great waves descending from E to B and from A to E establishing man upon earth. One could speak here of a more geocentric bearing. The semitone in both cases at the end of the tetrachord — from C to B and from F to E — like a drawing of the breath in self-realization, leads to the acquiring of new forces.

For the first time in musical and spiritual evolution man is called upon to reach for the octave. Beside the semitone it becomes the most essential interval, towards which each musical event henceforth aspires. The concept of the octave *per se* arises, into which the scales are fitted. At that time this interval by no means had the significance it attained later. But its position within the total structure and the fact that man had started to expand towards the eighth step, indicated that through this higher 'unison with the note of origin' a new impulse in music was arising, the first murmur of a higher ego within the earth-ego anticipated with longing. Man stepping forward and wonderfully poised — that was the marvel of Greek sculpture. Here a corresponding musical marvel will come to pass: the birth of the octave itself as an expression of man striding in freedom through the spaces of heaven and earth.

It is not surprising that throughout the centuries after the event of Golgotha this Pythagorean system should be determinative in the music awakening in the West. Without entering here into such things as the many transformations, changes of name, alterations and transpositions through which these scales passed in the course of time, we can mention one remarkable fact. The original Dorian 'Sun mode' of the Greek, moving downward from E with the quite distinct tetrachordal structure of two whole tones and a half tone, gradually gave way to the Greek Phrygian, moving from D to D. In the Middle Ages, however, this was called 'Dorian'. In the case of the pentatonic as well as in the great change to the seven-note system it can be seen that in the evolution of mankind the transformation of an existent stage of consciousness to a new one always gave the true impetus to a corresponding transformation of musical forms and systems. One has to ask: What changed for the human soul through the Event of Palestine in the course of evolution? How can such a transformation as the change of the basic system from E to D be justified?

The difference was the new and shattering consciousness that from then on every single person was able to find the divine element in his own soul. In knowledge and freedom everyone could become 'bearer of the Divine' in the highest sense. Thereby a new brotherhood of the spirit embraced all mankind. In an earlier age people felt drawn together by a world of the gods working outside; now the individual awoke to his I through his inner soul-connection with the Christ Event; that is, through the working of this higher being in himself he could feel at rest and sustained by it. In the Greek epoch the young newly-awakened I found the way to the deepest core of its own being. From that time on it could learn to fulfil in a self-creative way the mystery of its divine kinship. In accordance with the divine prototype, it became possible for a human being to grasp and purify the forces of his soul with responsibility and self-surrender. The trinity of will, feeling and thinking was deeply connected with his notion of the Divine Trinity of the Son united with the Father and with the healing Spirit of the Universe. Powerful stirrings of the soul and forces of renewal were there, making it possible to grasp and transform the soul completely. From this time on, the whole course of life was prompted by a spiritualizing of the emotions towards an 'Imitatio Christi', hidden within the bosom of the Church and guided by it. It was not only the awakening and striving for individual strength and balance between polarities, as in the Greek epoch, but over and above this a new security: the vital sense of an all-embracing love illuminating everything. This became the attitude of all who knew they were united in Christ.

The musical corollary to this has to be a tonal structure which bears within it something like a reminiscence of earlier forms, symmetrical and balanced. The symmetry was the picture of a divine primordial unity, enclosed within itself and controlling everything. The scale that showed this symmetry perfectly was the Greek Phrygian from D to D, known as the Dorian in the church modes. In both tetrachords the semitone stood in the centre. In his *Republic* Plato recommends this scale:

> for a man who is occupied in a peaceful, not a violent occupation, without compulsion; who either persuades and beseeches someone to do a thing — by imploring a god or by advising a human being — or else lends his ear to one who beseeches and instructs or tries to convince; who sees his wishes fulfilled and does not behave in an arrogant way, but behaves prudently and with moderation in all these circumstances, and is satisfied with whatever comes to pass.

In another place he speaks of it as 'the mode of the philosopher', that is, the mode that befits a man whose soul strives towards the recognition of divine-spiritual forces working on earth. And from such a characterization one may conclude that the first Dorian church mode, from D to D — afloat, yet resting within itself in perfect balance — could beautifully express the whole pre-Christian development of soul.

With the advent of classical tonality several centuries of change can be taken together. There was the burgeoning of medieval polyphony within the church, and the gradual experiencing of the scales upwards, instead of downwards.

The arising of music for several voices can be seen as a direct consequence of the Christ Event, a kind of challenge. The expression of a new community, a brotherhood in spirit, arose as polyphony under the guidance of priests. It was true to the new spiritual situation. It was also the expression of the divine in each and every individual, who set his own voice against one or more other voices. In this way the very nature of the Logos was able to sound. It was spoken of as the totality of all spheres in harmony. To embrace the I and the community simultaneously in such a way and to rejoice in gratitude and adoration with the sound of so many voices — this was not possible in pre-Christian times in the ancient southerly stream of culture. Every tradition tells of musical systems stemming from the macrocosm, but only now could an individual begin to speak microcosmically of his own music. It is his own soul that is blessed as the dwelling place of the Logos. This golden age of polyphony with its melodic coming and going, its rising and falling, its slurring and detaching of notes, moving together, after each other, or over against each other — this pointed to the image of a divine wisdom out of whose creative, cosmic thought a universe could arise at any given moment. It is a thought-filled consciousness that streams into the human being and unites with his feeling.

The other factor, however, — the reversal in the direction of the scales — pointed to a quite definite stage in the evolution of consciousness. This could have been practised esoterically in a preparatory way under the secret control of the Mystery Centres. In the development of soul forces initiates always anticipate the general course of evolution. But now, as a general need and as the expression in music of something new, this upward direction became ever more prevalent. In addition to all conscious yearnings and strivings towards the higher I, towards that ultimate divine principle to be embodied in man through man on earth, there was also a much more alert personal attitude that sought expression within earthly reality. The duality of man in his relationship to heaven and earth, swinging happily to and fro in the pentatonic, was still felt as a gift from heaven in the seven- and eight-note scales of the Greeks. Now established in a gradually maturing process, its keynote upon earth, the scale could develop upwards. Man followed the path of the Son of God Himself. But now it was the former Greek Lydian mode from C to C, called Hypolydian in the church modes, which appeared in its octave form, a form filled with inner consciousness of self.

Then in the eleventh century something else occurred: the hexachord — that is a six-note scale instead of the seven- or eight-note form — was developed by Guido d'Arezzo. Two hexachords, C to A upwards and E to G downwards, overlapped in the central notes C, D and E.

Basically it is a combination of the Greek seven-note Dorian scale originating from E with the Lydian originating from C. But it shows a new principle of construction, in which the third replaces the tetrachord (curved slurs).

For the first time this interval, which in its major or minor form determined the whole of classical music, came into evidence as a structural force. In its pronounced subjective character the hexachord can be seen as a sign that mankind is on the point of filling all things musical with inner power connected with the earth. It is entirely personal and determined by destiny. This concept is amazing in its novelty and, irrespective of how it was sung in particular cases, when it is studied as a totality it is profoundly interesting. It is constructed quite symmetrically, embracing the central note D, as if to refer back to the old pentatonic form centred round this note with the F above and the B below included.

The tetrachordal corner stones — F upwards from C and B downwards from E (slurs) — form a diminished fifth (brackets). With the resulting semitones from F to E and from B to C, a distinct leading-note quality can be found. The two hexachords are dovetailed to form a totality, and in them can be found not only elements that essentially belong to the past, either revealed or concealed, but also musical laws for the future.

This new principle of the diminished fifth linking the thirds together through semitones requires chromatic notes when it is extended. Not only does the beginning of each hexachord, unfolding within a major third, require this enclosing by a specific leading-note, whether above or below, but the thirds as such have to be connected by a semitone (b).

One sees in the ascending part the lowering of notes through flats and in the descending the raising of notes through sharps (a). Every third has the diminished fifth enclosing it (b): E to B flat for the hexachord beginning on F, A to E flat for that on B flat, and so on, but downwards F sharp to C, C sharp to G and so on. In the transition from the tenth to the eleventh century one encounters a chromatic principle with the beginnings of transposition as in the later cycles of fourths and fifths.

The augmented and diminished intervals which were the result of a continuous linking through semitones must have been a challenge for the choirboys in the time of Guido d'Arezzo and his successors. Even today these altered sounds with their tensions are not easy for the unschooled to listen to or sing. They require a quite intensive conscious listening, an alert listening which is not to be taken for granted but has to be developed. The characterization of the tritone as the 'devil in music' during the Middle Ages — and often even in modern times — may well have originated in a deep and heartfelt sigh from the tormented singers of that time. Otherwise it is hardly understandable that in the restricted framework of the church the 'devil' should have been for centuries something for instruction and training.

As a matter of historical development: What actually emerged spiritually through this interesting appearance of Guido d'Arezzo and his hexachordal system? Tradition states that he had studied for a long time as a Benedictine monk in a monastery of St Maurice in Paris. We may rest assured that he had come into contact with all that the Arab invasion had brought to Europe in the way of musical culture through Spain and France. Paris itself was the stronghold of this spiritual life. The inner connection with the black St Maurice, the patron saint of the monastery, allows one to assume that through this representative of oriental wisdom the Arab system of music was introduced to Guido, elaborated to its full extent, and intermingled with all that had remained of Ancient Persian and Phoenician culture.

Within the framework of this chapter it is not possible to examine this Arab system. But it is interesting to note that it consisted of a structure of thirds connected by means of semitones, as was the case later with Guido. The number three governs the system in other respects also. The whole tones were divided into three, and the notes resulting from this were not derivations in chromatic form but were independent of each other. In this way seventeen notes arose within the octave as the semitone was not subdivided. Through Persian scholarship another system in the form of a tree was introduced. By connecting up the major thirds, the whole chromatic cycle of twelve could be presented on the basis of four augmented triads.

Such traditions of musical history, particularly those referred to in the musical history of Ambrose, show unmistakably one of the sources of Guido's system, modified by him in keeping with the pentatonic and the Gregorian system to comply with the requirements of the church. It is also indicated that — through the new element of thirds, of the chromatic with its sharps and flats, and the principle of diminished and augmented intervals — the way can now be paved for a new state of soul. These chromatic and altered elements have already been interpreted as a means of rousing a strong consciousness through attentive listening. In their subtle colourings and possibilities the finely elaborated musical systems of the oriental and Arab cultures bore the mark of a penetrating intellectuality. They came into conflict with the Aristotelian and Scholastic spiritual teaching arising at that time through the soul-force of thinking. But, in the incipient acceptance of the chromatic, one certainly sees in enharmonic variations something like a dissecting principle, a progressive dividing of interval-relationships, a tendency towards abstract dismembering. The difficulty already mentioned in singing accurately with the whole tones and semitones and with unaccustomed augmented intervals required the fully conscious response of a concentrated will-process in listening and performing. Music could no longer be directed by devotion alone. A new inner musical faculty was needed and had to be cultivated as the germ of a future soul-force. From this time on the chromatic and enharmonic progressions of Greek traditions, coming from the East and originally rejected by the church, streamed imperceptibly into Western music. The transposition of the hexachord moving both upwards and downwards introduced new tonal values. The relationship to the seven basic notes was retained, in contrast to the Arab system, giving rise to derivations. All this found a kind of conclusion in tempering, which had been known since the fifteenth century.

One should not end this short survey of the progress of the classical tonal system up to the beginning of our scientific era without glancing at a third musical stream which, in contrast to the Greek, stemmed from the North and later, from the tenth century onward, from the British Isles. One need only think of the difference in poetry between Greek prosody and Northern alliteration in order to understand that out of these contrasts new elements would work into music from the North. Prosody, already discussed in the chapter concerning the basic elements of rhythm, was shown to be built on the relationship of the heartbeat to the breath. Through it man felt himself borne horizontally, with long and short syllables, musically experienced, swinging to and fro. There is no heaviness in them. The balancing measure ruled in the interplay between reflection and activity:

Sing to me, Muse, of the deeds of the much-travelled man.

— . . — . . — . . — . . —

In the North, on the other hand, alliteration held sway.

Heaviness and lightness alternate, gradually leading to a grouping of beats. Man is not as if carried by breath in the horizontal, but upright in the vertical between above and below; weight and the power of standing erect become the most essential principles of form. This emphasis on alliteration with its strong accentuation stresses the words which bear the meaning:

> 'The man goes away from his weapons
> no foot on the field.'

So the formal element lays hold of the content in order to merge with it into a complete unity. It is understandable that in the proportions of these forms the soul was addressed and moulded right into its very depths. Such a unity of content and form can be acceptable only to that part of man which bears within it the same laws of completeness — that is the ego, the I. In this centre lies the power and the mission of grasping and binding together in full consciousness earth and heaven, stone and star. This was the social task through centuries of bard and minnesinger, of trouvère and troubadour, by whom many Northern peoples were inspired, and to whose songs and sagas the people as well as the sovereign powers listened. Everyone submitted to their advice and leadership as a matter of course.

What were the musical elements flowing into Western musical art as if by storm on this tide of spirituality, educating and transforming the people? Celts and Northerners brought a new polyphonic music — harmony, but this in the sense of the triad as the foundation of every melody; and as a further development came the division into bars. This movement also started from the natural series, that is with the single note and its overtones.

Here also the pentatonic lived. But for these people the most essential thing, upon which their music hinged, was the harmony resounding in the note. The first, the third and the fifth tone, the fourth tone sounding with the fifth and sixth — this was the world to which they surrendered, and in which they found themselves. Thirds and sixths as well as fifths and fourths were the sounding vessel into which melodies could be poured. This Northern musical culture was primarily one of singing and string playing. It flourished not only among the bards but belonged to the whole people. In every house the harp resounded, 'from morning till evening'; singing was encouraged from earliest childhood on. The musician was subjected to strict training in which the expression of cosmic laws held sway.

Everyone seemed endowed with a gift for harmony, just as we find it nowadays amongst Slavonic peoples. No wonder that the major or minor triad became the basis on which the whole concept of tonality right into the twentieth century rested. All intervals and chords were referred back to the keynote, which was felt to be the heart and centre. Just as in speech, 'weight' in the qualitative sense prevailed in this vertically conceived system. Harmonic differentiations, heavier or lighter in soul, began to control musical structure. By the fifteenth century all this coming from England and the Low Countries brought a tremendous change and something absolutely new into church music. The introduction of two new modes, Ionian as C major and Aeolian as A minor, came from this source. They laid the basis for the further development of Western music. So the harmonic heart-element from the North joined with the more thought-like element from the South and the more will-like chromatic element from the East. And it was only the union of these three spiritual streams which enabled European music to become the true expression of the I.

A brief additional remark may be of interest here. In his book *The Occult in Music* Fritz Stege mentions the scientifically proven fact that water resounds in C major, with an F as lower fifth! Is it not possible that in these northern lands — in the water-filled atmosphere with its rushing and rippling streams and the surging of its seas — nature found expression in this key of human music? Did the Northener, living so closely with the elements, perhaps find the sound of his homeland mainly in C major? The F being heard with it as a note of the earth's depths?

With the growth of secular music the diversity of church modes was by degrees relegated to the church. A system of scales arose in which C major and A minor were transposed to every chromatic and enharmonic degree. By the time of Bach, at the beginning of the eighteenth century, this development culminated in the abstract equal tempering of twelve notes within the octave, for which the semitone was taken as the basic relationship. Important as this was for the progress of polyphony, it contributed considerably in the course of time to the end that the feeling for variation in mood and colour of the major and minor keys was by degrees lost. The circle of fifths, into which the twelve single notes were fitted, would rarely be experienced again in its cosmic connection with the great zodiacal picture of the heavens; and, through the elimination of all the subtle differences in the intervals of the church modes, the connection was also lost with the planetary system and its manifold life-forces.

In the meantime, in the wonderful confluence of the three spiritual streams, the West experienced the re-echoing of its own soul-development of thinking, feeling and will. Upon this new musical foundation, prepared through centuries, a magnificent, unforeseen Golden Age arose, especially in Middle Europe, which was borne by an abundance of the most highly gifted personalities. Music determined the destiny and very being of the European; it was the expression of his inner life in constant interchange between external and internal existence, surging in the triune powers of soul, awakening ever more in the evolving consciousness of nature but decreasing ever more in cosmic and spiritual consciousness. In their work, based upon an intuitive, unconscious and ever creative certainty, it was the great mission of towering men of genius such as Bach, Mozart, Beethoven and Bruckner to preserve for mankind an echo of the divine universe. They based everything upon the unassailable foundation of heptaphonic diatonic tonality, in which they felt the self-evident and naturally bestowed expression of their inner world, revealing the subtlest motions of soul.

But, at first unnoticed and then ever more plainly, a great transformation began. Ever since the beginning of the twentieth century mankind has been in the midst of difficult arguments about tonality and atonality. It is extremely interesting to trace the way in which the above-mentioned connections of the soul-forces with the basic elements of music reveal the tendency of a change. Melody changes the seven- into the twelve-note system, and during this process is itself moulded through a continual change of rhythmic forms. Rhythm becomes harmonic through a synchronization of various arrangements of time and measure, while harmony expands into polytonality. What is more, the musical note as such, created by man — his creative material — fights for its life against electronics, and the noises which begin to overwhelm him with alarming but fascinating force.

It does not lie within the scope of this introduction to follow up this new development. The main task of Part Four in this work is to enable the magnificent human and cosmic background of musical keys to be experienced in full clarity before the heart loses its connection with this world. Step by step, through qualitative listening and by virtue of inner living experience, hitherto unsuspected possibilities may be discovered whose artistic worth has yet to be proved. A gateway to the future may also open up, stemming from tonality. Without wishing to undermine sympathy with a living transformation in any one direction or another, it is hoped these indications may contribute towards a further development of the phenomenon 'key' connecting up organically with what is coming to meet it. This can happen in the course of working with the phenomena, in which, as with Goethe in Weimar, 'pleasure, participation and reflection' may be stimulated anew and fired within the listening soul by following up the course of historical development. These reflections can provide a background, from the depths of which even the simplest study — apparently long since overcome — can be illumined anew as living experience in every soul. Then something like an inner musical rule, or measure, can arise that casts light on the path leading into the future, turning tentative seeking into clear vision.

Chapter Two

THE STRUCTURE OF THE MAJOR KEYS

In the heptaphonic diatonic system a major key can be defined by the succession of the seven fundamental notes — C, D, E, F, G, A, B — with the addition of the octave C. This succession of notes can be referred to as a prototype in so far as it has been the basis of the major/minor system for centuries. The particular relationship between C and the succeeding notes determines the structure of the major key, and corresponds to the state of modern consciousness — from the keynote the scale moves upwards. The diatonic series of seven notes, not taking into account any chromatic modification, may be regarded as the starting-point for studying the structure of a key.

On first hearing, this succession of notes gives the impression of a series of ascending steps, in which each note is higher than the preceding one. The following structure is revealed in the scale from note to note: from C to F, a sequence of two whole tones, C to D and D to E, and a semitone from E to F. Then three whole tones from F to B and a semitone from B to the octave C. This structure can be described as consisting of $2^1/_2$ plus $3^1/_2$, in which $3^1/_2$ constitutes the latter part of the scale.

Experience in qualitative listening reveals a strong dynamic form with dramatic contrasts, articulation, changes of direction and so on. In making an experience such as this one's own, one perceives from C to F an increasing inner intensification leading to a standstill — one might almost say to a centre. A sphere is reached from which there can only come a strong movement outwards, a change of direction. This occurs in the transition from F to G, which affects the listening soul like a breakthrough to the light. The scale then moves through an increasingly spiritual cosmic space culminating in B — a painful, dissonant struggling towards the light — which is rounded off and finds fulfilment in the octave C. All this has been discussed on various occasions in connection with the single notes and intervals.

Qualitative dynamic hearing reveals a division of the scale into three parts: the first part of four steps C, D, E to F contracting; the second part of three steps G, A, B, straining towards the light; and the third — a semitone from the seventh to the octave — rounds off what has been and gives the basis for a new beginning; it is at one and the same time an end and a beginning. The actual moments of change, from the fourth to the fifth stage and from the seventh to the octave, from contraction to expansion and then to the rounding off in the octave, gives the scale its basic character. This can be illustrated in the following way:

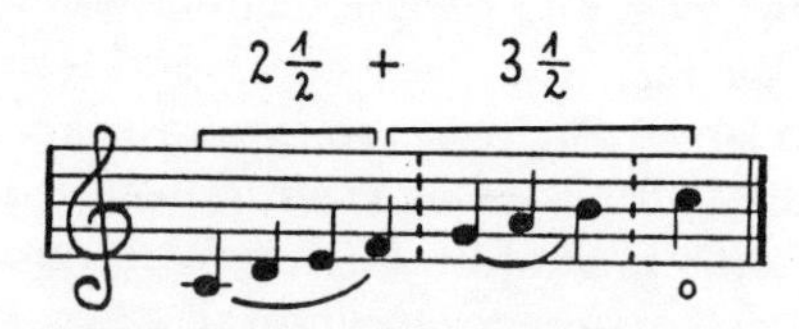

The trend in the notes forming the threshold, F and B, moves between light and heaviness. We can also see how very different — how very much more determinative — the octave has become, in comparison with the former tetrachordal structure.

Two streams can now be traced in an organic way, in which at any given moment a tendency to lightness or to heaviness is increasingly manifest. If the F presents the densest moment as threshold to G —the breakthrough to light — then the strong contrast between these two notes may be experienced as tension, which finds its musical expression in the raising of F to F sharp. The new series arising in this way, C-D-E and F sharp, moves the original semitone between E and F a whole tone up from F sharp to G. The structure of the first part, $2\frac{1}{2}$, is changed to an end structure of $3\frac{1}{2}$. That means that G emerges as octave of the new key.

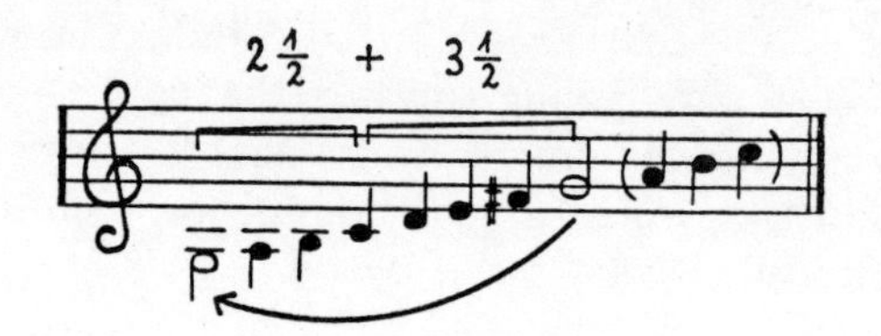

The keynote would then be found an octave lower. This proves to be the source of a stream of scales in major, which is defined by an ever-increasing intensification of the striving towards the light. The first four notes in the new scale always indicate a contraction, and each time it is the fifth which becomes the octave of the new key whose keynote is always an octave lower.

A corresponding counter-event arises when the rounded formative tendency of the octave C comes to meet the intensity of light and the tension in B. This turns towards the depths and darkens to B flat. The semitone from B to C moves down a whole tone from A to B flat. The $3^1/_2$ steps, F to C at the end of the first scale, are reduced by a whole tone to the starting formula of $2^1/_2$: F to B flat. The new key begins with F as keynote and is

completed upwards to the octave in the same kind of way as G major downwards.

From here the sharp and flat keys unroll in an organic way, in a repeated raising of the fourth step or lowering of the seventh. The fourth step is converted into the seventh and the seventh becomes the fourth. In the flow of sharp keys the new octave is always on the fifth and swings down into the new keynote. In the opposite flow of flat keys the fifth downwards becomes the keynote and the octave above is the starting note of the next flat scale.

What may be surprising at first is that the pattern of the sharp keys unfurls from high notes to low, but that of the flat keys from low notes to high. This has already been seen in the chromatically extended hexachord system of Guido d'Arezzo described in the previous chapter. The development seems to be the opposite of the usual one. There, for instance, the sharp flow begins low down and each succeeding fifth upwards is the beginning of a new key. In working with these two kinds of development it is important to distinguish between the two aspects of essence and of effect. Light, as a continually dematerializing spiritual principle, is at home in the higher regions. If one wishes to give expression to this it is justifiable, with the light increasing, to feel the unfurling of the sharp keys as beginning in the depths and intensifying towards the heights.

But the effect, the activity of the light, seeks the depths and unfolds there in the region of ever denser existence. The more the notes sink into darkness, the more the fullness and power of light breaks through. The power of illumination is revealed in the movement downwards — the light shining into the darkness — and it is expressed in the structure from above downwards (page 254).

Something similar may be said of the flat keys. The essence of weight lives in the depths, so that a stream guided from the heights to the depths is a process of progressive darkening.

But the effect can only unfold out of the opposite region. In a qualitative sense each flat bears within it something of loving inclination towards the depths and it is evident that this pure will can be grasped and gathered together most strongly in the lofty realm of the spirit (page 254).

However one may regard this arrangement of the keys the determining role of the fifth is obvious. In the actual linking together and overlapping, upwards as well as downwards, the beginning of a new key always falls on the upper or lower fifth. It is a structural factor of continually increasing significance, and further preoccupation with this important interval is called for. In qualitative listening the fifth produces in the soul the sensation of standing on a threshold between two worlds, which gives it the character of being suspended on the one hand and of being established within itself on the other. Listening from C to G upwards, a spiritual light-filled sphere opens up, in which one feels supported anew in cosmic space and formed, as it were, by the spirit. This was evident in the course of the original scale and in its intervals. As C to F downwards, however, the fifth brings a lovely relationship to the stability of earth. In both directions there is a forming principle in which the being of man, self-comprehending, self-knowing and self-creating is revealed. But connected with this experience of a formative life-principle is the demarcation and imprint of different centres of force. In the construction of the two series of scales, each fifth opens up a new portal for the influx of determining forces, which find their resonant vessel in the differing and ever changing constellations of keys.

The range of sound in general use at the present time embraces seven octaves. Within this span, rising by fifths from one field of force to the next, there are twelve steps until, with the note B sharp, in the tempered system one reaches the sphere of C again.

A similar series of fifths descending through the seven octaves embraces the same fields of force, but this time as flats, so

that when the structure of the keys is perceived as movement, the opposite relationships of the fifths give various enharmonic crossing-points, the reality of which must be given full recognition. We have already shown in Chapter Four of Part Three — 'Interval Forms in the Twelve-note Circle' — how important this whole question of the enharmonic is for a healthy evolution of music. It will not be enlarged upon here but another fact should be mentioned in relation to the twelve centres of force.

In concentrating on the C with which we started, a quite definite feeling arises for the power that lives in it. This is not connected with any one of its octaves but embraces the C through all its eight places in our tonal system.

In precisely the same way the enharmonic differentiations such as B sharp or D double flat, would rise as columns in an eightfold way in the same sphere. With the entry of a higher or lower fifth one has always to imagine a new column of sound ringing out and crossing over to the next field of force. This is a truly magnificent picture!

The two aspects previously mentioned — essence and effect — are both of equal value in the unfolding of the keys through the twelve centres. Every new key reveals a quite specific 'Stimmung', something that emanates a soul-creating and forming-force peculiar to this centre.

The twelvefold nature of these notes connects up easily enough with the laws of the zodiac. Until the Middle Ages knowledge was preserved of the 'heavenly homeland', of the harmony of the spheres, which holds sway in man as microcosm and finds its resounding image in his musical creation. Scotus Erigena (810-877) writes:

> The beauty of the whole created All is founded with wondrous harmony on similarity and dissimilarity, and is fitted together out of various types and many kinds of form through various arrangements of content, and the joining of these together forms an indefinable unity.

The traditional threefold division of music into *musica mundana, musica humana* and *musica instrumentalis*, expresses the indissoluble connection between man and cosmos. In our scientific and technological age we are unable, for the most part, to establish a living connection with such things.

Nevertheless one can still say that it is in keeping with a profound universal reality to refer to the zodiacal circle of twelve, which can be connected musically with the twelve fields of force mentioned above. From the qualitative experience of the fifth alone it would be justifiable to regard this picture of the twelve as a kind of threshold, the inner experience of which begins to foreshadow an approach to a region beyond the earthly, to the transcendental. In connection with such a relationship to the threshold, if one truly wishes to master it, a spiritualization, an etherization of life will be required. The temporal element of the seven unfurling from keynote to keynote — that is, from fifth to fifth to form each new key — is constantly filled with the form-giving forces of the twelve, at rest within itself. This continual interpenetration of time and space as the determining factors of earthly existence has its counterpart in music in the continual maintenance of both principles — of the diatonic seven and, from the standpoint of the essential nature of keys, of the circle of twelve. Other relationships would arise out of an atonal aspect but this is not under discussion here.

Attention should be paid to the following facts with regard to Plate 1. Each of the twelve centres is to be thought of as including all registers of the tonal system. The circle of the sharp keys, evolving upwards from fifth to fifth, begins with middle C and unfurls through seven sharp keys in seven fifths over four octaves. The notes are not only thought of as pitch but as an entire tonal sphere; they signify the keynote, the basis of the major scale that develops out of it. The same applies in a downward direction in connection with the flat keys. Starting from the C above middle C in the column corresponding to this sphere, seven keys evolve downwards to the lowest C flat below. C sharp major above and C flat major below would be the extreme forms of the major scale, in which all seven notes are audible in either a light-filled or a darkened form.

In Plate 2 there are the three places where five, six and seven accidentals overlap enharmonically and these are also indicated one over the other. A continuation of the pattern would lead to a return to the starting-point, and from there on to double sharps and double flats, where the tonal sphere of C is reached as B sharp or D double flat. From here in both directions, in two more fifths, the tonal realm of D is reached as C double sharp, as well as that of B flat as C double flat. C-C sharp-C double sharp and C-C flat-C double flat, joined up with one another produce a pentagram.

This is an ancient symbol for man standing within the universe. One reads in it certain streams of life-ether, whose movements run from the head down to the right foot, up into the left arm and horizontally over to the right arm and from there down to the left foot and finally up to the head again. This picture of man the microcosm, born within the macrocosm, finds wonderful expression in the *Occult Philosophy* of Agrippa von Nettesheim:

> Man, as the most beautiful and most complete work of God, as His very image, and as a world in miniature, has a more perfect and harmonious bodily structure than that of other created beings, and contains within himself all number, measure, weight, movement, elements — in short all things that belong to his perfecting — and in him, as the sublime master-work, all things attain to a perfection that the other complex bodies do not possess.

What was deep in the consciousness of leading spirits centuries ago found renewed confirmation in Rudolf Steiner's indications that in the elements of music the laws of the I are revealed.

Chapter Three
KEYS AS A WHOLE

The rather sketchy presentation of keys in the first chapter of this part can be enlarged upon in the following way. The key as a whole may be regarded as an enclosed organism of seven or eight intervals in the sounding column of its keynote. The question now arises: Where does the particular difference, say, between C major, D major and F major lie? People often think that such a distinction is either slight or non-existent. But is there not a basic element which could determine a qualitative difference? It is natural to think of the relevant keynote and to assume its character to be the only determining factor. But when one goes beyond C major this turns out to be dubious. In connection with C major it might still be valid: both the note C and the key of C major have a character of composure addressing the upright force in man in earnestness and serenity. In connection with the intervals this quality is found most plainly in the prime, the unison. But D major, for instance, shows a discrepancy between keynote and key. The single note D is experienced as questioning, moving and gentle, while the key which proceeds from it reveals, in complete contrast, a strong and impelling activity striving towards a goal. The supposition that the character of a key is determined by the keynote alone turns out to be incorrect. Further tests show that this is always so.

The fact, however, that with C major the coincidence occurs, provokes the question as to whether perhaps the significance of the note C extends to other keys. For centuries it has been the keynote of the diatonic system and the bearing which it evokes can be regarded as universally valid, even fundamentally necessary, in all things musical. It was this bearing that was characterized as being self-enclosed, rousing the forces of uprightness in man, earnestly and serenely established within the I. The bearing of C becomes universally applicable to all music and one is compelled to observe more closely the function which devolves upon it in every instance, as here in the course of a key.

Since the notes in the various keys are in changing interval-relations to one another, one may ask whether the interval formed between the keynote and the note C could perhaps be the factor determining the nature of a key. Thorough training in qualitative listening answers this question with a decisive: 'Yes!'. One may well speak of a determining interval in a key. The diagram makes the situation clear for the sharp keys.

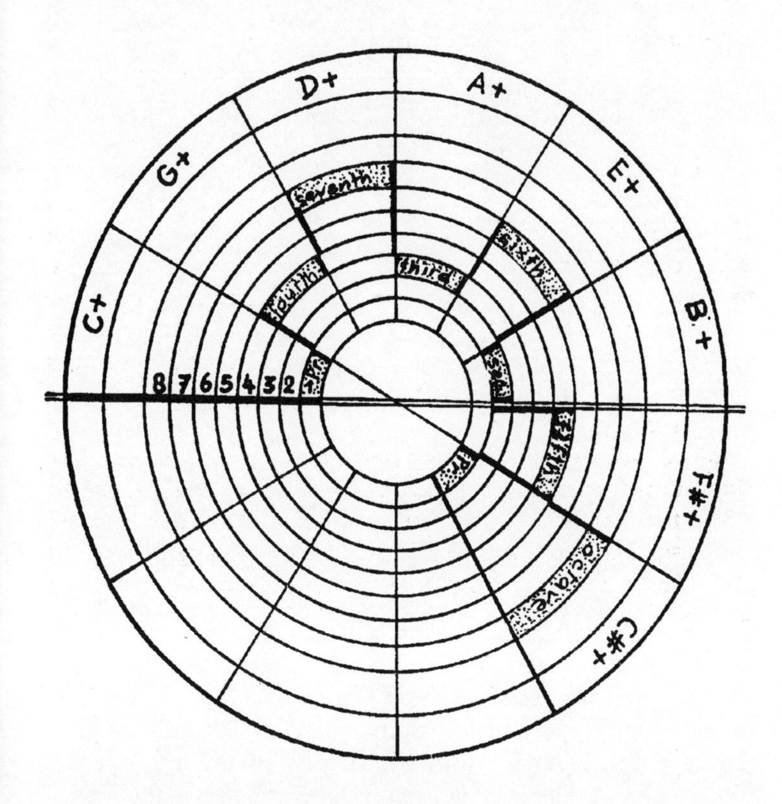

Eight circles in the centre give seven spaces for the intervals, which are arranged from the centre outwards, from keynote to octave (see numbers). Starting with C major one can see that with this firm foundation a certain character is revealed. The essential nature of the note C corresponds with its function as interval within the key. In connection with the key of G major the C takes over the function of the fourth. In the original scale this has already been described as an experience of strong inner concentration, which also holds the power to break through into the light. Something like the mystery of 'dying', through which a new 'arising' sounds as a promise, lies hidden in this fourth, revealing the very core of man's being and his true earthly destiny. In moving on to D major a strong light-filled striving towards a goal occurs, taking its character from the tension of the seventh, D to C sharp. From here on C appears in its light-filled form as C sharp. The wonderful inwardness and warmth of A major speaks of the function of the third, A to C sharp. It is in this interval that all inwardness, all heartfelt tenderness and all the subtleties of human feeling are beautifully brought to expression. In E major this intimate quality, this warmth of soul, becomes even more filled with light. A freer swinging element, determined by the quality of the sixth, lifts one's feeling out of the all too personal. And in B major the character of a calm objective clarity develops from note to note, determined by the second. F sharp major, determined by the fifth with its six light-filled stages, bears the character of a threshold, elevated and suspended as already mentioned and, as if given contour by the fingertips, something of starlight seems to be conjured into it. C sharp major, under the influence of the octave, brings to perfection this nature of the light and the forming of transparency. It emphasizes the keynote, but filled with spirit-light and raised to a higher level.

An account of a process such as this should not merely be read. It should be regarded as a stimulus to practise in accordance with qualitative hearing. A phenomenon such as a keynote, the note C, a fifth, a key, should be a summons through quiet individual listening to make it one's own and not only to accept what has been said through reading. In the first chapter on the 'Transformation of Hearing' attention was drawn to the three prerequisites — an awe-filled stillness, selfless dedication and discerning watchfulness.

In the course of such a transformation and development three further requirements arise. The most important factor is that of aurally working through all the basic elements of music by listening, without any reference to artistic application, but purely as phenomena. Without carrying something of oneself into them, without allowing oneself to be captivated by them in what they express in works of art, they proclaim as direct facts of practical experience their intrinsic nature, which is even today the nature of their divine archetypal being.

They need ever more and more to be practised in their own individual form. A circle of keys such as has just been explained will prove its value when, for example, the scale of C major is practised not only in a mere technical manner, without inner participation, but when, in working on it, the soul-bearing of prime and keynote is achieved. It is a bearing which only the sounding world of C major brings to life for player and listener alike. All work is then raised into the sphere of artistic experience. And it can be verified ever again that a world of sound revealed in this way acquires a forming and healing power that is spiritually creative and penetrates right into the physical.

Then there arises the necessity of forgetting. The moment the step is taken from the study of phenomena to the forming of a work of art, whether in creation or reproduction, it is important to voluntarily expunge from consciousness all individual practice and experience — even understanding. This is not easy, but it is indispensable in order to bring about that empty consciousness which is so often spoken of and so seldom attained. The very instant in the performance of a work of art — not while practising — one thinks: 'C major — ah! such and such...' intellectual rigidity excludes the possibility of spontaneous experience, of fresh inspiration. One can accept with confidence that the continual study of phenomena will gradually produce a transformation, an inner quickening, so that afterwards it is possible to surrender with every fibre of one's being, without premeditation, to direct experience and re-creation.

We can now turn our attention to a sphere which has so far attracted little attention but which is nonetheless indispensable for understanding what ensues. It is listening from the octave downwards. Keynote and octave do indeed constitute the corner-stones of every major scale. The keynote establishes the point of departure. It is the resounding exponent of the lower ego in man and finds its fulfilment in the octave as representative of the spiritually-orientated higher ego. From the keynote everything develops upwards and each interval is related back to it. The listener is absorbed by the nature of the interval being formed — a fourth upwards is experienced as a fourth and not otherwise. The gesture of the interval and the experience coincide. This is so much a matter of course that one may wonder why it is emphasized here.

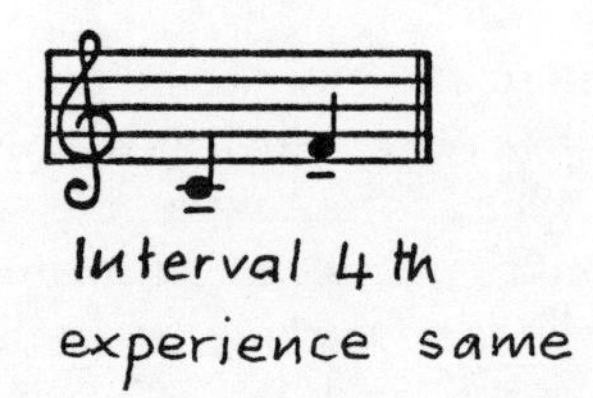

But from the octave downwards a significant and remarkable distinction appears. A fourth downwards by no means produces the experience of a fourth; the movement of this interval is not experienced as being significant.

In it a feeling arises similar to that of the fifth. One does not actually do this but it comes to meet one inwardly; it is encountered. In making a fourth downwards, a creative, complementary, counter-event arises inwardly — the feeling of a fifth — taking its course unconsciously. An interval such as this, the complementary interval, completes the octave down to the keynote. If in connection with the keynote, in keeping with its orientation towards the earth, one could speak of a coincidence of structure and experience in the interval, then the nature of the octave is revealed with its bearing towards the spirit in the descending interval, and expresses totality by completion to the keynote below.

By experiencing and observing these things an extensive musical complex of question and answer comes to light. We find we are in the midst of the major/minor problem, to the contrast of which the polar direction of experience points. And most important of all we find we are also at the threshold of polarity and complementary experience, of external activity and the spiritual counter-event arising from it. This sphere has already been discussed in the fourth chapter of the 'Transformation of Hearing', so that brief indications may suffice here. Glancing at the major/minor problem, which appears in this unexpected contrast in feeling between the ascending and descending interval, it is not sufficient to characterize the two archetypal facts as Goethe finds necessary in the aphorisms of his *Theory of Musical Sound*.

Realization of that contrast as the basis of all music cannot be expressed as 'masculine and feminine', or 'active and passive'. This seems accurate in itself but one finds that these principles are often interchanged or interpenetrate each other.

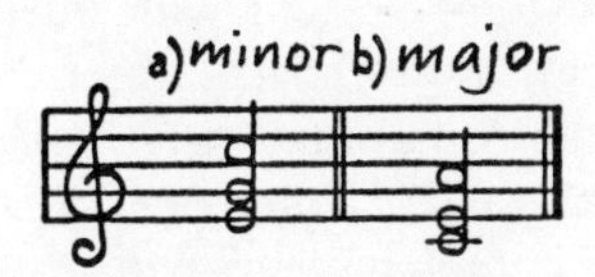

For example, a chord of the sixth in major (a) has a decidedly minor character, while conversely a similar chord in minor (b) gives the impression of being major. It is more comprehensive to link up with the living breath of contraction and expansion, with the basic principles of involution and evolution, densification and spiritualization or — in accord with the human ego-being — with incarnation and excarnation.

The major principle in all its manifestations is experienced as a force working from within outwards. It expands outwards from a centre creating a circumference, a periphery. It is revealed most plainly in the rising major intervals peculiar to the major scale. Starting from the keynote the soul opens out through its strong connection with the extreme upper note. The sphere of origin lies within the earthly, in the lower ego, with the tendency to make ever greater steps towards the spiritual and free itself from the lower realm in a centrifugal movement.

The intervals descending from the octave, on the contrary, work centripetally from without inwards, that is, out of the minor principle. The externally audible step, made in its own proper direction from above downwards, inaudibly evokes an inner spiritual, opposite interval. The soul is thrown back upon itself and experiences not the external actuality, but an opposite deed enkindled by it. These two events, however, fill the whole space of the octave from above downwards.

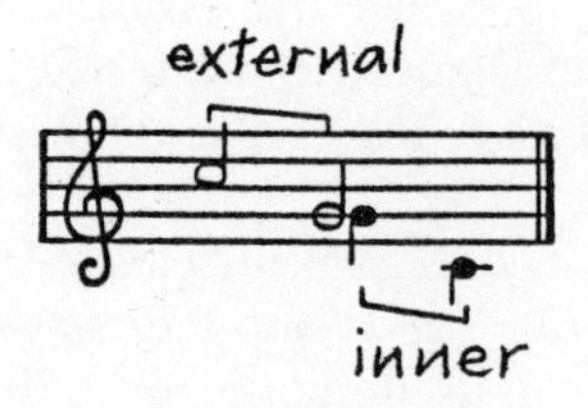

They bind man more intensively to himself, connecting him more deeply, through their descent, with creative regions in the depths of his own being. And whilst in experiencing the completion of the octave the spiritual organ of the higher ego is reflected, the soul creates in this duality a direct experience of the totality of its very being. The complementary nature of man is revealed.

It is now possible to find the determining intervals for the flat keys. The unfolding of the flat keys started from the octave and we too must start there, for in the sphere of the major scales the scales with the flat key-signatures represent the minor principle.

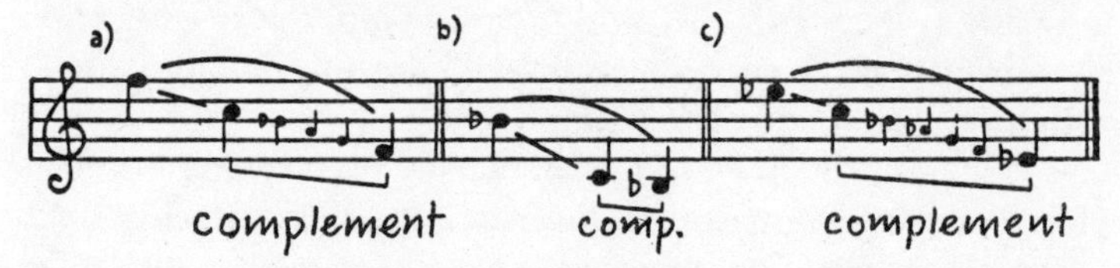

The interval to be sought will originate from the octave. For example, in F major (a) it will be the fourth downwards, in B flat major (b) the minor seventh, in E flat major (c) the minor third, and so on. In the last two keys of the series, G flat major and C flat major, the C appears in its darkened form as C flat. In seeking the determining intervals, it looks as if it is the same as for the sharp keys, beginning with a fourth and continuing in intervals of a fourth. But since the fourth F to C downwards produces the sensation of a fifth, this complementary interval evoked inwardly is the one that determines the character of the key.

In actual studies, as well as in performance, it is interesting to compare the mood of the fifth complementing the descending fourth from the octave with a fifth actually sounding upward from the keynote, as for instance in F sharp major. The entire picture of the circle of keys is given in Plate 3 in which, for the sharp

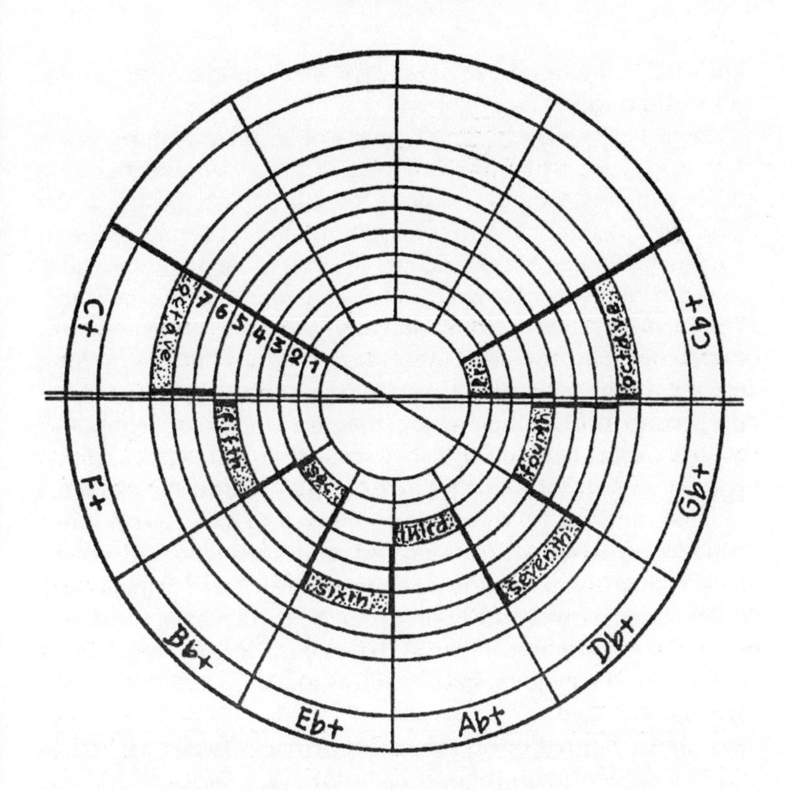

scales, the determining interval is given, but the complementary interval is given for the flat scales.

This basic law of man's complementary musical experience, goes through the whole circle of keys and this co-existence of an outer and an inner occurrence in polar opposition to one another — the outer one given, the inner one created — may be understood in various ways. The relevant geometrical plates may serve to present these laws in the simplest way and to allow, in practice and quiet meditation, that harmony and universal greatness to unfold in the soul which rises above all trivial personal pleasure or displeasure. Kepler speaks of these unpretentious, geometrical forms as the 'archetype of the beauty of the All'. And, in so far as one gradually succeeds in allowing them to sound through meditative reflection in their objective transparent purity, they will develop into a language of truth which has the power to open the gateway directly to higher knowledge. In the course of time it will be found that we cannot do without them.

Plate 4 shows these simultaneous polar relationships. From C major, from which the evolving of the sharp and flat keys begins, the first step to G major shows the fourth, G to C, as the determining interval. The corresponding inner form is given in F major with the complementary interval of the inaudible fifth. In regarding the whole circle of keys together these form a new, far-reaching totality. In the diagram, they are connected with each other. The next step, into D major, brings the determining interval of the seventh, corresponding on the opposite side to the second, both belonging together in a kind of superimposed octave. From stage to stage there is a working together of two corresponding points in the circle of keys, of contrasting spheres of sharp and flat. With regard to the key-signature, this inner connection is shown through the same number of sharps or flats: G major and F major, a key-signature of one, D major and B flat major of two, and so on up to the culmination of six and six in the enharmonic F sharp/G flat major. Here the intervals of G major and F major also coincide as fourth and fifth, but they are interchanged.

Progressing in this way through the circle of twelve a wonderful feeling of equilibrium arises in the soul. Outer and inner, audible and inaudible, hold the balance, anchored and borne by the feeling of a superimposed octave at one stage after another. The axis around which this structure is formed runs from the sphere of C to the opposite sphere of F sharp/G flat, and the experience it produces is fully harmonious and founded within itself.

Another relationship, which has already been indicated for study, is illustrated in Plate 5. Here, both externally formed intervals, whether above or below, are connected: the ascending fourth from the keynote in G major with the descending fourth from the octave in G flat major, the ascending seventh in D major with the descending seventh in D flat major, and so on. What immediately attracts attention, in contrast to the fourth chart, is the unenclosed, almost open aspect which maintains its unity only through the triangle C-C sharp-C flat.

Even the pentagram (page 259) can be found in C-C sharp-C double sharp and C-C flat-C double flat.

With this we conclude what has to be said here concerning the 'Key as a Whole', in the hope that it will stimulate further study. Each key taken as a whole, as a self-enclosed organism, coincides with a field of force in the circle of the twelve. But in so far as music is a temporal event we must still consider a key not only spatially but as an event in time, without losing the connection with the form-giving nature of the twelve. An attempt will be made in the next chapter to find a comprehensive answer to this question.

Chapter Four

THE TEMPORAL ASPECT OF THE MAJOR KEYS

In the first chapter attention was drawn to the dynamics of the seven basic notes of the scale — C, D, E, F, G, A, B and the octave C. This basic scale was shown to be divided into three parts and this grouping was applicable to all the other major keys. The first part consisted of four steps leading into a contraction — C, D, E to F; the second, of three stages G, A, B expanding towards the light; and the third was the enclosing octave C, the rounding off of what had been and the basis for a new start, representing at one and the same time an end and a beginning.

The course of a major scale reveals three outstanding moments. The active, purposeful nature of major is determined by a totality, and is formed by a development proceeding from a firmly established keynote and moving upwards towards the light, through every kind of transformation to the octave. In considering the major principle it was stated that, starting from the keynote, the soul opens out and has a strong relationship to the upper boundary-note. Keynote and octave are two moments of special significance. But qualitative listening reveals that the peculiar character of major, that is, the striving towards the light in the octave, does not show up straightaway. The first four notes, to F, show a tendency towards condensation and incline towards the depths. Only after the great change to G does the essential major character break through. It is only from the fifth onwards that one can experience something of the major event, which cannot be turned aside from its cosmic direction until it reaches the octave. Keynote setting the tone, fifth as culmination, octave as fulfilment — these are the three outstanding moments of every major scale.

The development of a scale experienced qualitatively in this way cannot be seen only in one centre of force or one sphere of sound. Just as from month to month in the course of the year there is a continually changing process, so also in the temporal aspect of the major scales a scale unfolds through several centres of force during its development. The diagram shows this for C major.

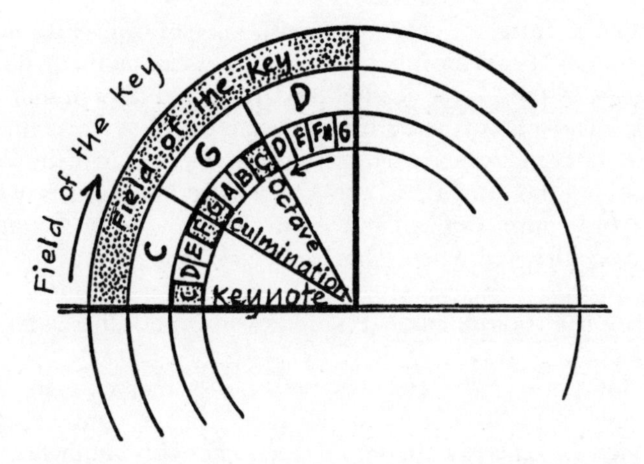

In the C field of force, the notes C, D, E, F are written in. Moving onwards, from the note G the next field of force is crossed and, tending towards the D field of force, the octave is reached. From all that has been stated about this wide and perfect interval, it is clear that the octave must be considered as working over out of the field of D (see arrow), and as bringing from there the enclosing force, so that one learns to feel it as a third more highly developed moment of the scale working out of a higher sphere. Three forces of three tonal-spheres—C, G, D—participate in the making of C major. The grouping together of these three may be called the field of the key.

Attention is drawn first and foremost, in a classification such as this, to the fact that in the circle of keys each place acquires a threefold significance. Plate 6 illustrates this between B flat major and D major. The more one becomes engrossed in the dynamic form of the scale through qualitative listening, the more forcibly is the true forming-force of the note of culmination revealed. With the breakthrough to the light it introduces an inner compulsion towards the octave. And this force impelling towards a higher spiritual sphere 'gives birth' as it were to a new keynote, the beginning of an even more light-filled series of sounds. However, this moment of culmination as revealer of the light bore within it the force towards the octave impulse of the previous scale. On the one hand the whole picture may be experienced as a spiral circling upwards without resistance. But, on the other hand, if the sharp and flat scales are conceived as two streams moving in opposite directions, then the culmination in tion in the centre, the octave of the previous scale, gives the new keynote, and bears the full import of the present moment, filled as it is with the I — an 'earlier' and a 'later' interpenetrate in 'today'. The spirit of the German language expresses this central event —incredibly rich in tension — of an orientation of the soul at one and the same time both forwards and backwards, with one word: 'einst' (future) and 'einst' (former). In this connection it is well to remember what has been said about the fifth: 'In both directions there is a forming principle in which the being of man, self-comprehending, self-knowing and self-creating is revealed.'

It follows that the essential nature of a major key is not determined exclusively by the keynote. On the contrary, the major character is evident only in the moment of culmination in the fifth. In the temporal aspect of the scale this central field will be considered the principal and determinative one, and the keys will be arranged accordingly. From the present point of view, supported by qualitative listening, C major finds its place in the note of culmination — that is, in a region of sound above that of its keynote. This centre is connected with two neighbouring regions, below with the sphere of the keynote, and above with the sphere of the octave. But, in so far as these neighbouring regions are also the culminating points of F major (green) and G major (orange), the whole realm of the key extends not only over three but over five tonal spheres. And a justifiable and still more comprehensive relationship with the dominant of this dominant extends the realm of the keys over seven centres of force. Plate 6 illustrates this.

It is possible to go even more deeply into a drawing such as this. A twelvefold circle connects the human soul quite naturally with the year's course and its festivals. Entering into this as an experience to which everyone has access, it can be seen that the outer cosmic-terrestrial event is supplemented by a certain contrast in the inner mood of soul. For example, towards Easter nature starts thriving, blossoming and burgeoning. From early morning the birds sing for joy, every day the sun grows warmer and the air is filled with delicate fragrance. Inwardly, however, in the spiritual realm the soul seeks an understanding of the mystery of death, of Good Friday and the Resurrection. In autumn on the other hand when leaves fall, when nature prepares for death, there starts to live in the human soul an inner life rich in thought. Only attention to these reciprocal conditions during the course of the year leads to a full experience of the season. What is naturally given in the cosmically determined external world is complemented by the spiritual soul-forces in man himself. It is the answer of the I to events in the universe.

It will therefore be understood that to the sevenfold concept of the key must belong a sevenfold spiritual counterpart so as to embrace the totality of the temporal aspect. As at each moment, in every place, in every situation in life, man has within him and reveals as microcosm the entire macrocosm, so is it also with each individual key: it is also in itself only a part, and yet it holds the sum of the whole circle. Plate 7 shows, opposite to the actually sounding C major, an inwardly answering F sharp major. To the subdominant there is also an answer on the opposite side: a B major answers F major; and with the dominant a C sharp major answers G major. In each case a keynote, a culmination and an octave answer out of the opposite region. Taken as a whole the arrangement gives the picture of a cross with an axis at right angles to the perpendicular of C major/F sharp major. In both these places, where overlapping occurs, there is a dovetailing in the realm of experience from without and from within. The upper and lower dominants of C major and F sharp major are also complementary to each other. From this form of a cross for a single key the germ of a law may be found which gives meaning to the later comprehensive picture of all the keys together.

Overlapping becomes even more apparent in another connection which may be shown in the temporal aspect of keys. If the sharp keys are drawn from C towards the right, up to the sevenfold raising of the notes in C sharp major, and the flat keys drawn to the left, down to the sevenfold lowering of the notes in C flat major (see Plate 8) then it is seen that both streams overlap in three places: C sharp major with D flat major, F sharp major with G flat major, and B major with C flat major. In the red and blue circles the diagram shows only the scales. C major is coloured purple because, with no key-signature, it is orientated to the sharps on one hand and the flats on the other, as are also the enharmonically connected scales of B/C flat, F sharp/G flat, and C sharp/D flat.

It will never be possible to do full justice to the enharmonic, which comes so fully into evidence here, by seeking to describe it as 'change', or 'transformation'. If within the tempered system a note like F sharp is set in the same place as G flat it may perhaps have a quantitative meaning and justification, but it effaces the essential musical reality. This demands a clear differentiation between two distinct realms of sound: the raised F and the lowered G. Each has its own individual character and works in its own way. They meet as polar opposites. If the one is experienced in the active sharp stream in the major, borne by the will and manifesting the light, the other finds fulfilment through a more self-surrendering element, laying hold of the depths through the flats. As the sharp stream moves outwards, from left to right, so does the flat stream moves inwards, from right to left, as is shown in Plate 8. The drawing gives a graphic representation of the enharmonic event. The note F (inner shaded circle) extends

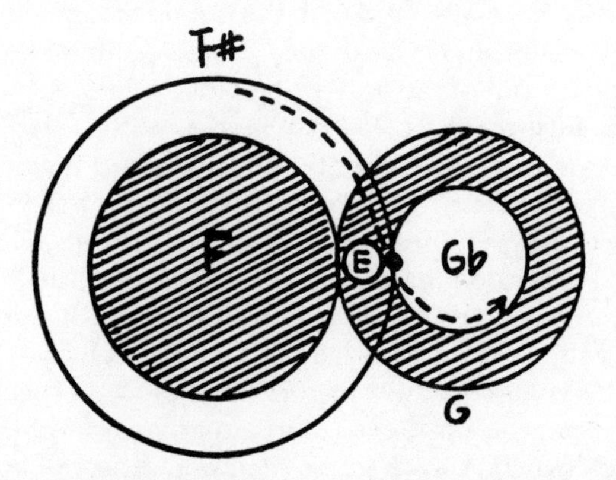

outwards to the circumference as F sharp, whereas G, moving centripetally, reaches the inner space of G flat. If an enharmonic 'transformation' occurs, the very nature of F extending to F sharp acquires something of the G-nature in G flat, thus passing through a qualitative transformation. This is caused by a change of direction. The entire dynamic is reversed from outside inwards (E denotes enharmonic). This change of direction is the determining factor in the enharmonic, a realm of modulation which has not yet been fully revealed. (With this one should compare what has been said in the chapter about the complementary series in the first part of the book).

There is still the question of complementaries — that of Plate

4, which was related to Chapter Three, 'The Keys as a Whole', and that of Plate 8 relating to the temporal aspect. How do they differ and how can they be united in a complementary way? The difference lies in the fact that in the first aspect the key is fitted into one sphere of sound as an organism complete in itself, but that then, for the purpose of completing the totality of the twelve, it is necessary to go from key to key in a process of time, which has to be connected with the complementary stages in the counter-pole of the starting-point. Starting with a small spatial picture of the single key progress in time is necessary in order to round off the whole circle of keys. No key in itself can embrace all twelve. The course of our study has brought us from space into time.

In the second case (Plate 8) the scale as it moves through time is fitted into the circle of fifths. This produces a threefold aspect of keys and, in considering the dominant factor on either hand as well as the spiritual complementary fulfilment, the circle of twelve is embraced by every single key. In contrast to the first this structure leads from time into space. We shall follow up this second aspect in subsequent chapters. It allows for the time element in the keys, as well as for the principle of space in its all-embracing totality.

It may seem as if this is somewhat theoretical and contrived. Each single phenomenon needs to be experienced qualitatively, referring continually to the guidance of the ear. These first four chapters may be taken together as a kind of introduction. They give a preliminary framework from which further thoughts may develop, leading deeply into the relationship of Man, Music and Cosmos.

Chapter Five

THE PRINCIPAL KEYS

In former times it was acknowledged that each individual key, even as a transposition of C major and with the same structure, revealed its own strongly marked character and mood. The fact that these moods, or attitudes of soul are closely connected with the twelve of the zodiac is little thought of today.

Attention has been drawn to the fact that all ancient cultures, guided by their priests and initiates, took from the firmament the musical laws which seemed to them essential at their particular stage of evolution. To their clairvoyant vision the universe was alive with divine creative beings. Embedded within a 'Theo-Sophia', world-harmony was to them a living reality. An earthly language of music experienced as part of a cult was the true expression of this unity of man and universe. In this way cosmic forces were drawn down to earth and it was known that the life of the human soul was regulated by the Divine. The statements of Scotus Erigena and Agrippa von Nettesheim, quoted in the second chapter, show the way in which knowledge of these things was preserved up to the Middle Ages.

Nowadays, however, the opposite holds good. It is no longer a vanished wisdom of vanished macrocosmic gods, but rather the wisdom of microcosmic man that is our earthly task. It is no longer appropriate to read the laws of music from the heavens, but rather to win back the laws of the heavens through music. This is only possible if, in the Goethean sense, each single phenomenon is allowed to speak within the human soul and one learns to hear and understand its language. This pure musical 'material', unobscured in any arbitrary way, provides a last gateway through which direct access to cosmic spirituality can be found.

This also holds good for knowledge of the nature of man himself. The path of knowledge through musical phenomena, as it continually activates and intensifies the soul forces, leads ever more deeply into experiencing the connections of music with the forces of thinking, feeling, will and equilibrium, as has already been shown in the third part of this work on the intervals; and in connection with thinking, feeling, will and equilibrium — it is not the way they live in the individual in a personal and arbitrary way, conditioned and burdened by destiny, but in the form which everyone bears within himself quite objectively as the prerequisite of his existence as man. And as long as man is considered a microcosm it must be said that the prototypes of these soul-forces — world-thinking, world-feeling, world-will and the great divine equilibrium — are prepared macrocosmically.

If in this sense we consider the keys in detail, then Plates 7 and 8 offer the most suitable starting-point. C major as a totality in the circle of keys leads to the form of a cross (Plate 7); attention has already been drawn to the probable significance of this. There is a wise saying of Plato's that in the cross the world-soul is fixed to the earth. The spiritual soul-being and the earthly form of the cross are inseparably connected, conditioned and determined by one another like life and death. But in spite of the fact that this saying of Plato's foreshadows the approach of the Mystery of Golgotha, the picture of standing within the cross has from time immemorial been one of the most profound symbols for the nature of man and for his earthly task in the trinity of his body, soul and spirit being.

In Plate 8, if the stream of sharps is followed round to the right, the cardinal points are C major, A major and F sharp major; and if the stream of flats is followed round to the left it is those of C major, E flat major and G flat major. One may ask whether and in what way these keys can be experienced as particular representatives of the soul-forces of thinking, feeling, will and equilibrium. The note C is recognized as our basic keynote and a study of this key will show that it gives an impression of resting securely within itself but with emphasis on the will. Note follows note in almost objective sobriety. It does not ask to be approached in a weak or easy-going way, but with a conscious and energetic bearing. The listener feels strengthened in his self-consciousness, securely established, braced at every step towards uprightness and united with the firmament through his raised head.

He realizes in himself the dignity of man, suited and pledged to creative moral activity in the heights and in the depths.

A major has a different quality. If this key were played with the same will-force as C major every sensitive listener would feel dissatisfied.

A gentleness is required and something akin to velvety warmth. The feeling appeals not to the will but directly to the heart. And it is this strong inwardness, which warms or even fires one, that makes this key important in music, for ultimately all music is a matter of pure heart-force. The whole nature of the sun is reflected in this central organ and the forces of the sun come to their purest and most intimate expression in A major.

F sharp major on the other hand diffuses a transparent atmosphere of clear consciousness. Instead of requiring a gentle linking together of the single steps, this key wills to be heard as if outlined in a delicate light design.

The soul follows the light-diffusing play of the six sharp notes, among which only B in the centre retains its original form, like a transparent guiding line of clear thought. Not the aspect of will, nor that of feeling, but thinking as a soul-force is here given unmistakable expression.

After moving through this semicircle in the light region of the sharps, we must try to grasp the other side, the flat keys, from C to E flat and G flat major. It is not without justification that E flat is considered one of the noblest of keys.

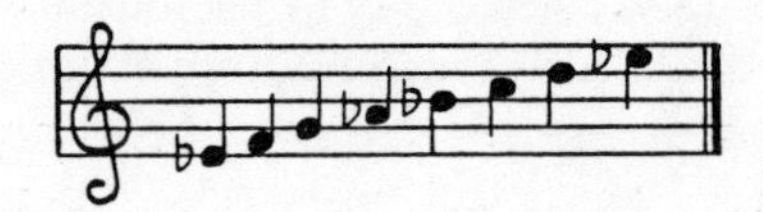

Essentially it reveals something like a summing up of the other three soul-forces, bringing them into a wonderful state of equilibrium. The will-force of C major has assumed a tranquil dignity and inwardness, the gentle feeling has received warmth and strength raising it beyond the personal, and the conscious element in thinking rounds off each note without falling into the danger of frivolity. This reveals man in the balance of his soul forces.

The next step leads to G flat major.

It is just here, however, that a new complex of questions arises through the enharmonic, F sharp/G flat. By listening and comparing these two scales one will begin to experience without difficulty that the flat key is not at all like the lightly outlined sparkling and playful F sharp major. It seems much more serious, delves more deeply. The very nature of thinking drives one forward to an objective connection with this enharmonic duality. A clear distinction can be made between the flashing light-bringing forces of intellect and a more meditative attitude, which reveals a relationship to the sphere of higher discernment, to wisdom. Here thoughts are not only conceptual, they are lived, in that one surrenders fully to the content of the thinking. An idea such as this is connected with: 'It is so'. G flat major can also be taken to correspond musically to this, for six flats reveal a state of loving internalization. The creative, ascending complementary interval is the feeling of the fourth, which points to the deep centre of essential being.

In contemplating Plate 9, we can recall the findings about the nature and activity of the four main keys, for from this the complete picture of man can rise resplendent. The axis C to F sharp/G flat is borne and illumined by the forces of will and thinking. C major spoke of self-consciousness resting within itself, the power of becoming upright, an assured establishing of existence in the depths and a uniting with the firmament through the raised head. The upright posture in standing and walking, and the capacity to think, are the two most essential features which distinguish man from all other living beings on earth. And where one or the other is not fully developed in a healthy way there is always an experience of impaired humanity. These two opposite forces of one vital and one conscious pole must not fall apart, must not exclude each other. The second axis from A to E flat, by making a cross with the first, shows from which sources and towards which forms of perfection this being of man, based upon harmony, is nurtured and upheld: feeling and equilibrium hold the balance.

There is still something to be said about the interval of the counter-poles. C to F sharp upwards is an augmented fourth, downwards a diminished fifth, the so-called tritone. There has been mention of this, especially in Part Three, Chapter Four. There is something contrary in this relationship which should be called to mind.

As an individual note as well as a key, C represents in the pole of will that tranquil almost stationary element which gives an immediate feeling of keynote. This decisive relationship of the soul to the earth needs as its counter-pole a spiritual element straining towards the light, which is represented in the pole of thinking through F sharp. In this domain it is worth following up the changes to which an interval will lead.

In the constellation of the augmented fourth (a) F sharp tends towards the repose of a new keynote or octave — it inclines towards G; while the secure foundation of the C loosens to B. The change leads to an expansion of the interval. On the other hand, from the diminished fifth (b) the resolution leads to the intimacy of a third in closed position with the same tonality, G major. In both cases it is a change to the next tonal sphere of the sharp stream, from C to G.

The constellation of the augmented fourth, or the diminished fifth between C and G flat, reveals the same law. Here, however, the change leads back into the sphere of the flat-stream, that is from G flat to D flat.

The tritone, whether as an interval between two spheres, or representing keys opposite to one another, impels a change from place to place in the circle of twelve; it leads over to the formation

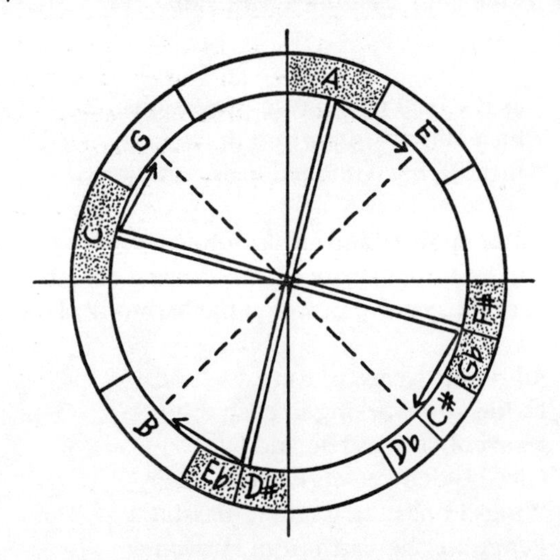

of a new axis (dotted lines) and consequently to a new constellation of tritones. This change is brought about through the axes in the circle from key to key. The diagram shows the change from A/D sharp to E, and from A/E flat to B flat.

What matters is the element of movement in the enharmonic. The fact that in the atonal twelve-note system this is not recognized, or follows other rules, will be discussed in the appropriate place.

By going more deeply into the laws of music there can arise in every listening soul a striving towards knowledge, a great, devout wonder; for behind all these pictures, notes and words — apparently theoretical and often seemingly unmusical — something grips the soul, as it does with Faust in his study, when he calls out:

> Was it a God who wrote these signs,
> Which still my inner tumult,
> Which fill my wretched heart with joy...

And behind the spiritual and musical events captured geometrically in their simplest form in Plate 10, one can assuredly begin to sense something of the creative power in the harmony of the spheres:

> All things weave to form a whole,
> Living and working in each other.
> Heavenly forces rise and fall,
> Give golden vessels each to other.
> Wings imparting fragrant blessing
> Penetrate the Earth from Heaven,
> In harmony All rings through All.

And where Faust, still full of despair, is compelled to utter:

> What a drama! But alas, only a drama!

we should now learn in gratitude, by listening to these musical phenomena, to trace their living reality within the soul.

In summing up, Plate 10 conveys the following: Plate 9 showed a square, with the culminating points of the main keys connected with one another. Two further squares are formed by connecting up the spheres of the keynotes and the spheres of the octaves. Seen from a more religious standpoint, as Prof. H. Beckh does in his book *Das Wesen der Tonarten (The Nature of the Keys)*, these can be expressed in the form of three crosses revealing an intimate connection with the mystery of the Divine Trinity. Each keynote gives the musical experience of a foundation resounding in earthly realms. In this finding of the foundation is revealed the Father-ground of all existence. Each octave sphere, on the other hand, proclaims a higher divine part of the human soul. From this creative part of his eternal being, the Son-principle, man forms his own destiny. Through it he can assist in revealing the spiritualization of matter. But where, in the struggle between lower and higher ego, between earthly death and the freedom of spiritual life, this redemption of earth can shine, where this dramatic struggle takes its course — there the healing power of the Spirit prevails. Plate 11 points to this Divine Trinity.

Four times the indivisible triune goes through the circle of twelve, pulsating through the wheel of Time with mighty wings, weaving through the structure of Space with the divine breath of life.

Chapter Six

THE SINGLE KEYS

The previous chapter showed how the human soul-forces of thinking, feeling, will and equilibrium could be arranged in the circle of twelve alongside the four principal keys — C major, A major, F sharp/G flat major and E flat major. It was found that the opposing forces of will and thinking were held in balance by the axis between feeling and equilibrium.

It may occur to those readers who have a close connection with Rudolf Steiner's well-established art of eurythmy that he pointed to a similar classification of the four soul-forces in the twelve gestures of the zodiac. (See Lecture Ten from the book *Eurythmy as Visible Speech*, under the heading 'Forms arising out of the Being of Man'). It is natural to assume that these can be transferred to musical relationships. In this connection it should be stressed emphatically that studies in listening have been pursued for decades, privately as well as in courses, quite independently of statements in connection with eurythmy which were seldom known to participants. Ever and again the same results emerge out of the same context and this may well be regarded as evidence of objectivity. In the consciousness of this awareness similar descriptions may be used for states of soul connected with the keys, even if the building up of the musical structure takes a different course.

We shall now look at the twelve keys individually. It is important to start in the right place. In considering the principal keys it seemed most expedient to start from the axis, C to F sharp/G flat. In the polarity between will and consciousness, the upright picture of earthly man is represented. But, in keeping with the nature of music, it was also shown that the other axis, at right angles to it, of feeling and equilibrium — A major/E flat major — is of equal significance. In this axis the soul is intimately connected with the regulating power of the harmony of the spheres, which in the Middle Ages was still referred to and experienced as the conversation of the spiritual hierarchies, as the direct expression of the Logos. Fundamentally, though perhaps often still unconsciously, it is this heart-force of the world which those who truly love and pursue music proclaim. The structure of the keys will best be followed up if, starting from the pole of will in C major, we pay attention to the inner state of soul, revealed on the one hand in the transition to A major, the pole of feeling, and on the other to E flat major, the pole of equilibrium. The opposite aspect, from F sharp/G flat to A and E flat major, will then be considered.

There is always an impression of strength when working with C major. The listener feels he is ready for action. It reaches the centre of his will-nature — hence the great composure. Every action, however, in so far as it does not arise from the sphere of instinct but out of freedom, out of creative moral knowledge, is a quite distinct word of the I. In this power of the word in the most comprehensive sense, man recognizes he is the responsible bearer of a divine quality of being, for his deeds as creative expressions of life transform the earth, in a progressive or destructive sense. They are determined by an outer as well as by an inner standpoint, to which he refers everything. The prime, the relationship of the keynote to itself, is the determining interval. And this founding within the I and establishing within the earthly gives to the whole life of soul a certain self-assurance imparted by the very nature of the ego. But we must first of all free ourselves from the weariness and apparent emptiness into which C major has sunk. If we do not let ourselves be disturbed by this 'shell', we shall be rewarded by the ever stronger experience of an unfathomable and mysterious kernel. Readiness for action, in the sense of the creative power of the word, will take hold of the soul.

Every action has as its prerequisite the faculties necessary to carry it out, and the disposition and training of these is decisive. On the other hand each action will call forth new faculties. If after C major one listens attentively to G major, and plays it, an agility greater by far and more unburdened is revealed in this key. Its contours bring to life an inner joy in movement as such. As the child plays for the joy of playing — so a similar joy appears here in playing for the sake of playing — a state which every music student knows well. In this is manifest a hidden or even a conscious will towards technical control for the sake of freedom and ease in creative playing. The inner driving force is the freeing, the dematerialization of the physical with its restraints, and the striving towards a more etheric penetration and control of the possibilities of expression. The interval of the fourth in this key is determinative, and the inner connection is evident: its clear outline is necessary as the preliminary stage towards, and transition into, the spiritual.

It is a fact of practical experience that technical faculties are developed most quickly in the key of G major, just as all children, with their joy in movement, sing most happily in this key. This step may be referred to in the keys in the region of will as that from *Deed* to *Capability*.

From this move out of C major into the first sharp key a fifth higher the pendulum swings to that on the flat side a fifth lower, to F major. One can hear immediately that a new, clear and intimate, much more serious character sounds within this key —

the region of flats begins. But what does that mean? From now on the determining interval is heard from the octave downwards and finds expression in the feeling for the complementary interval. Everything which up to the moment of the *Deed* was the result of activity upwards from the keynote, now turns to the question: 'What has been wrought?' It is not only determined by the earthly ego but the higher ego makes its judgement. The deeds of man surround him. Ever and again they come towards him. He must learn to regard them inwardly and to bear their consequences. They have freed themselves from him as facts of life, significant for his destiny. The strong, more inward expression of F major speaks of these things. Amongst other things this key is called the key of Spring. That seems a contradiction, but deeper observation shows that Spring brings the Easter Festival and the death that of necessity precedes it. Otherwise there could be no joy in a new beginning. This contemplation in spirit, called forth again and again through established facts of life, is a kind of threshold. It is linked up with the experience of the fifth which appears as complementary interval. Roused by the octave, man bears within himself a picture of what he has released through his deeds; and the objective contemplation of these facts gives him new strength impelling him towards further development. This stage, reached from C, is designated as *Fact*.

The next step on the sharp side as an inner impelling force is a striving towards the higher ego. Musically this is the function of the seventh which, as the determining interval D to C sharp, rules the new key, D major.

The will towards light-filled, clearer goals, aiming towards the octave, needs to be developed and gives this key its truly aspiring tone. But a new stream of warmth can be felt when listening attentively. It reveals the transition from the sphere of will into the sphere of feeling. And the word repeatedly given to the state of soul prevailing here is *Incentive*.

It is clear that the next swing of the pendulum into the direction of the flats must lead from the external activity of *Incentive* into a quiet inwardness. This is all the more so because, at this juncture with the two flats, the connection with the field of equilibrium is found. B flat major proclaims this.

The inwardness which arises here with the descending minor seventh gives this key a feeling of something like a calm stepping, whereby the steps are experienced as inner rather than outer. In a musical sense 'logic' envelops the soul in a wonderful way, as is sometimes experienced when the wisdom-filled guidance of destiny becomes clear and moves one to thankful devotion. Each experience of the second, which sounds here as complementary interval, reveals this from note to note — a capacity for changing and transforming from stage to stage. Through this a new relationship to the course of destiny becomes possible. The actions of man's hands and the imprint of his feet upon the earth become new and are filled with responsibility when, in B flat major, they come to expression in a moving way. This stage is felt within the great and all-embracing word, *Destiny*.

A major, with the light of three sharps, has already been referred to as the key of the heart, the sun-force.

The inwardness belonging to it is borne by the determining interval of the major third, A to C sharp, which is the expression of a quite personal warmth laying hold of and moving the soul. Such a stream of light, of warmth, even of love, is always experienced when man is in direct contact with his higher being. Every Bruckner symphony, for example, or Bach's *Art of the Fugue*, or the last Beethoven Quartet — they all lead to this threshold of the region beyond the earth. Not that such a work must always be written in A major. But the deep emotion and joy, enthusiasm, perhaps quite calm and not loudly expressed, proclaims the stirring of that sphere of the heart which is revealed clearly in A major. This never occurs without a feeling of being summoned towards the new and, fired with enthusiasm, towards the 'better', which inspires man as the soft or loud word of his higher ego — it awakens his heart to knowledge of the presence of the Holy Spirit. In a beautiful sense the power of dedication can become the gift of such inspiration, streaming out from the key of *Feeling*.

In this way we complete the first part of the keys moving from C major to *Feeling* in A major, which forms the axis with *Equilibrium* in E flat major. It is something which can be experienced by anyone who listens selflessly. Plate 12 gives a picture of it, and it is clear that the individual stages work together organically. Every key runs from the keynote upwards in a left to right direction. On the whole, however, the sequence goes around the middle C in a continuous swing of the pendulum between sharps and flats, shown by the red arrows. A similar course will be considered from the consciousness pole of

Thinking to *Equilibrium*, rounding off the circle of the twelve major keys. It may have become evident that artistic work and performance, directed from these exalted points of view, can reach that much sought after objectivity without in any way forfeiting the purely human element. These soul-gestures heard musically are, as Rudolf Steiner described them in his lectures on eurythmy, 'Forms arising out of the Being of Man'.

The next keys to be considered begin in the pole of *Thinking*, with F sharp major.

The fifth rules as determining interval and C major corresponds to this key in the pole of will, *Deed*. When such a light-filled ability to create contours with translucent outline arises in the soul, then this forming in spirit can well be spoken of as a creative deed. Just as the deeds of man imprint his nature on the surrounding world and just as his action becomes determinative for him and his surroundings, so does each pure thought acquire significance for him and for others. In keeping with this, F sharp major mediates security and delight, not least through the determining interval of the rising fifth.

This pole of consciousness, however, is the centre of the enharmonic. We must point out again that the dual nature of thinking is to be taken into account and that there must be practice in distinguishing between the experience of F sharp major and that of G flat major. In the first key, the character of scintillating light comes more into prominence, while in the second it is more an element of meditative dedication.

The security imparted by the key of F sharp leads over to the next step. If one plays C sharp major and D flat major, then in both cases the spiritual force is consolidated into a marked character of firm resolution.

This is wonderful, for do man's thoughts not determine his resolutions? C sharp major brings this to experience so strongly that involuntarily one is reminded of the pole of will—*Deed*. That which in F sharp still sounds loose, light and contoured, here becomes more forceful, not as weight, but as a sensation of all-embracing significance. The octave as determining interval makes its presence felt. D flat, on the other hand, requires a deepening darkness in its performance which, from the complementary interval of the major seventh, receives a wonderfully sustained tension.

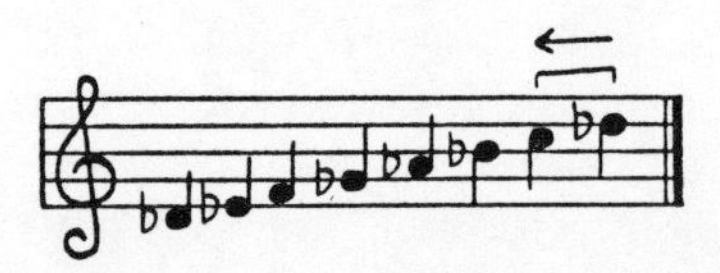

In both cases a quiet force streams through the soul, unerring and resolute, capable of moving towards a goal and never losing sight of it. These keys cannot be better characterized than by the word *Resolution*, prepared by the spirit and carried through by it.

Following the swing of the pendulum from sphere to sphere, the next keys are B, or C flat major, both still within the pole of thinking.

In B as well as in C flat major, which is rarely used, a wave of inner warmth still streams, making one conscious of the nearness of the field of feeling. The determining interval in B major is the major second. It has already been met once in B flat major as the interval complementary to the minor seventh. Here it prevails audibly between the keynote B and C sharp, and calls up within the soul a state of balance, as everyone striving for knowledge well knows in his continual linking up, separating off, changing and transforming of concepts.

In C flat major, warmth comes still more into evidence.

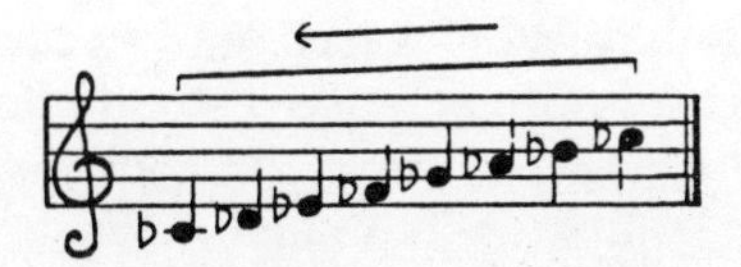

Above all it is a central force profound and fully established within itself, in which the balancing out of the sharp key finds its complement, like the hypomochlion of the scales. The word *Balance* is right for this sphere.

A flat major is the next place in the swing of the pendulum, and the forces of equilibrium make an impact upon the listener.

It is no wonder, particularly when one remembers what has been stated in connection with C flat major, that there resounds here something like a dipping down into a mystic condition of soul. It is not by chance that on the one hand A flat major is referred to as the gentle, sacred key of Christmas, of adoration woven out of mystery. And it is not without foundation that it expresses the motif of the Last Supper in Richard Wagner's *Parsifal*. This most intimate region of the soul is, however, not only tender and without problems. Whatever happens demands at this point a free and unbiased bearing and a moral *Coming-to-Terms*. From note to note it bears the mark of an earnest inner struggle; and it is this which one finds foreshadowed in A flat major. The major third formed as complementary interval leads the listener, gropingly as it were, to every veiled mystery, and it is the velvety depth of this key which seems to promise the dawning of a new light as the next step.

It can be clearly experienced that in E major there is illumination, touching the soul with distantly soaring pinions.

Its determining interval is the major sixth, which always brings an impulse towards expansion. A feeling of freedom arises like a breath of relief, clear and light, as if one stood before a wide sunlit landscape. The relationship between I and universe, illumined by a knowledge still strongly united through the heart with feeling, is connected with the warmth of the sun and leaves behind a happy impression of undefiled purity. This is most often expressed as *Contemplation*.

In listening to the next step, E flat major, one may well ask what this key has yet to bring.

Is a further intensification possible? The sixth is the complementary interval. Compared with the previous path of development the ultimate gradually lights up in the soul: the fulfilment of destiny as a breakthrough into light-filled purity, the awakening of I and Universe — Sun-forces of the heart from the region of A major — none of this can be fully realized as long as man remains preoccupied with his own life, however mature the outlook, as long as he bears, or rather forbears, only himself. The soul must rise to a higher sphere of experience beyond the personal. In this sense the equilibrium of E flat major touches upon something like a new expansion of being, borne by innermost self-comprehension. Outer and inner as Universe and I counter-balance each other. It is manifest in words such as 'man the microcosm': only he who embodies cosmic-spiritual world-consciousness can stand in a state of equilibrium between two worlds. Where this is possible, the affairs of life are determined from an exalted standpoint. And it is the major sixth which, as inner complementary interval, ensures for E flat major this future standing of full humanity.

It is worth taking note of the difference between this expanse and the one in E major. In adopting this mood in the two following forms it is not necessary to play the intermediate notes;

the sixth allows the difference of direction between inwards and outwards to become apparent. This key with three flats betokens a step in development which makes it clear that this sphere of equilibrium finds its expression in the zodiac in the picture of the bearer of God, Christophorus; that is, it has found the expression of the redeemed angel-being in man. In keeping with what has already been stated, Plate 13 shows the way from the pole of *Thinking* to E flat major, on the axis with *Feeling*.

From a certain point of view it would be understandable if statements such as these were regarded as an idle pastime. The objection: 'You fancy you hear such things', is also understandable, as long as there is no unbiased attempt to undertake a qualitative method of study. And it is regrettably clear in practice that most people, even though thoroughly trained in a certain way, are no longer able to bring to this an open mind. Goethe's remark: 'All that perishes is but semblance' is for modern man far-fetched, as he no longer knows what the single note or key is the semblance of. For the world which Goethe indicated, in which the true prototype and the archetypal events of all music were to be sought, is a goal to be achieved; that is, a direct spiritual experience not readily accessible today. For all that, what may yet be possible to everyone of goodwill is quiet, selfless, qualitative listening in the discovery of basic phenomena. Where this happens these phenomena start to speak. Nothing else needs to be done. Only listen, and act in the light of what they have to say. This opens a gateway to the spiritual world; music becomes at one and the same time self-knowledge and world-knowledge. Every relevant geometrical picture, every stroke in it, acquires a deep and real symbolic significance, the unsealing of which can unite man once more with the source of his higher being.

Chapter Seven

THE RELATED MINORS

In seeking the transition to the realm of minor scales it is essential to refer back to the first chapter of Part Four, which dealt with the structure of the major scales. It is a structure of whole tones and semitones, $2^1/_2$ plus $3^1/_2$. Can a similar objective starting point be found for the minor scales?

The reciprocal relationship of the partial series and its counter-series revealed the fundamental law of counter-events betwixt outer and inner, audible and inaudible. There is no need to ponder on how a complementary series would become audible under other conditions—temporal, spatial, or scientific. In the light of the foregoing explanations we may assume its reality.

We can also see this complementary law as the basis of the polarity of major/minor. This means that the structure is exactly the same, but descending: $2^1/_2$ plus $3^1/_2$, giving the following succession of notes.

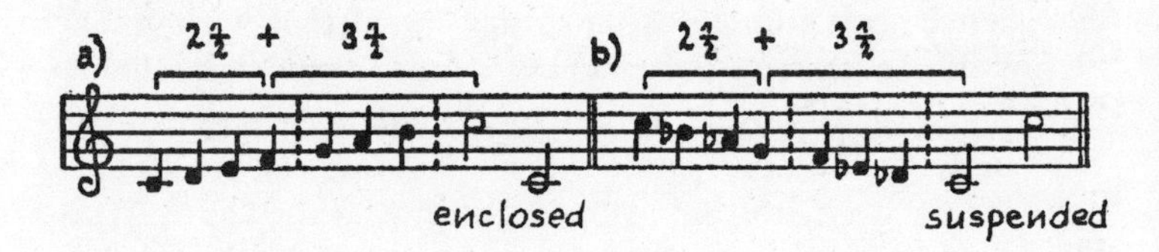

It can be called the reflected scale. In listening, a distinct difference can be heard between the ascending major and this descending reflected scale. It clearly bears a minor character. The octave in the major scale needs the keynote connected with it. The whole structure is unquestionably complete within itself, rounded off (a). But it is different with the reflection. If, in keeping with the major form, the octave upwards is added, then a feeling of suspension arises in the listener, not a feeling of conclusion. The true experience of the keynote is missing. Without relating this series of notes to a familiar system of keys — say A flat major, F minor or Phrygian, as often happens in consequence of superficial associations — an attempt should be made to find the real keynote. It will be found in F in the centre, corresponding in a sense with the major: there the upper fifth came to the fore as dominant and culmination; here the fifth downwards bears the character of keynote, through which a culmination in the minor is revealed. Only now can one speak of an archetypal minor form. In the partial series and its complementary series C major and F minor belong together. We should also call to mind the fact referred to in the first chapter, that all water sounds in C major with F as undertone. Apart from the opposite direction of the two scales, there is a contrast that seems like an inversion in the position of the keynotes. The following sketches attempt to portray it:

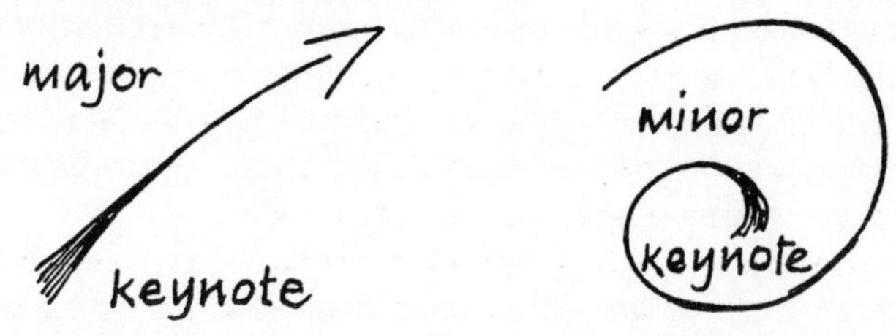

The tendency towards a straight line upwards from the keynote in major; the tendency to curve inwards to the keynote in minor. The major is clearly an expansion, reaching out from below into the distance. The minor, on the other hand, contracts from periphery to centre.

We find that just as in the major there are three outstanding moments in the course of the scale, so here also there are three such moments. In listening one can observe that neither the first note nor the last points to a foundation such as might be anticipated in the descending movement through the octave. In both these poles everything remains in suspense. Neither of them is satisfactory in itself; both move towards the centre. We cannot speak here of keynote, culmination and octave, as in the major. In the minor the octave at the beginning has to be regarded as note of origin. The key is formed by it and seeks the centre or, more correctly, the keynote. It finds it in F and for this reason one can properly speak of a central keynote. From here the movement goes towards a new dominant, which lays hold of the centre for a second time. The threefoldness of the essential moments is indicated by the spheres of the note of origin, keynote and dominant. The drawing shows the tendencies are in complete contrast.

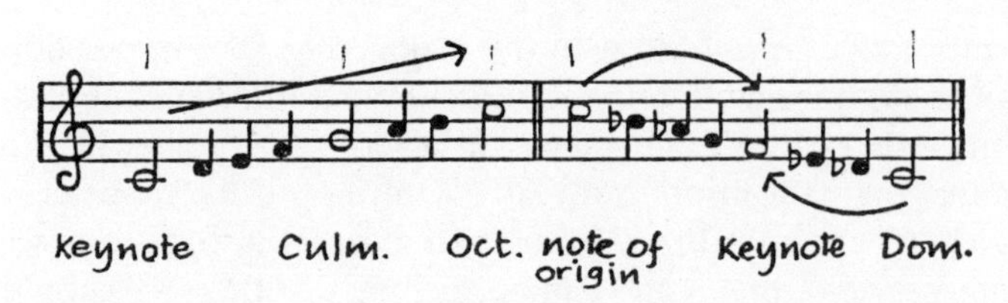

In the major the culmination in the upper fifth leads into the periphery of octave and keynote; the dominant in the centre is enclosed by its octave. In the minor, on the other hand, all tendencies lead to the centre, the culmination being in the lower fifth; the dominant encloses the centre from above and below. By incorporating these into the circle, it can be seen how six

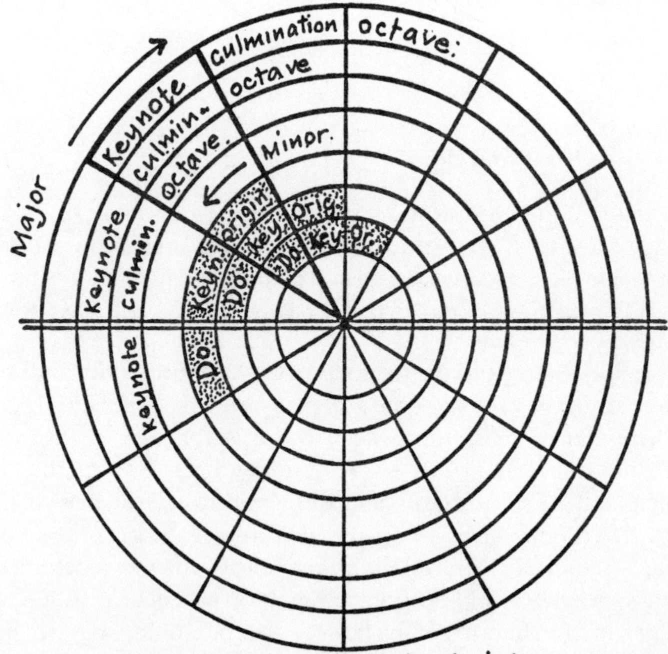

Keyn.=keynote. Orig.=note of origin.

Do=dominant. Culm.=culmination.

different functions fall into each field of force. In the major, keynote, culmination and octave of three keys fall together. In addition to these three functions, we have three more in the minor: the note of origin, corresponding to the octave in major; the keynote, corresponding to the culmination note, and the sphere of the dominant corresponding to the keynote in major.

In discussing the archetypal form of the minor as such, we should also consider the related minors of each major key. It has been customary to consider only one, the relative minor. The relationships and laws of will, feeling, thinking and equilibrium were found in the entirety of the soul-nature, and it is permissible now to seek out a path which will do justice to this. For this purpose the threefoldness of the human soul can be extended into the threefold organization of body, soul and spirit. In connection with the dynamic form of the basic scale which was presented initially (page 252), one can say: every keynote mediates a physical principle, every third an element of soul, and every fifth a breakthrough into the spiritual sphere, a principle of spirit. From this, one must infer that these three steps are important for the answer to the question about related minors.

Beginning with the reflected scale we have F minor formed by descending from the keynote C. With the minor construction of $2\frac{1}{2}$ plus $3\frac{1}{2}$ steps descending, we can also start from the third of the scale E and form the minor scale with A as the keynote — and descending from the fifth note G we reach C minor.

So for C major we arrive at the following three related minors: F minor formed from the keynote C, A minor from the third E, and C minor from the fifth G. The result is that in addition to the reflection from the keynote, that is, F minor, we have the reflection from the third, A minor, which has the same key-signature as C major, and the reflection from the fifth, C minor, which has the same keynote. The inner connections between the major key and its related minors are clear. There is a reflected scale, a key with the same key-signature, (relative minor), and a key with the same keynote (tonic minor). Each major key has these three related minors.

It is still possible to ask whether these three related minor scales really call up within the soul, through qualitative listening, an experience which is more physical, more of soul, or more of spirit, as might be expected from their originating out of the first, third and fifth notes of the major scale. One starts to become aware of this by comparing the related triads with the tonic triad of C major. A preliminary exercise can be made as follows:

C major-F minor-C major (a), C major-A minor-C major (b), or C major-C minor-C major (c). Without any doubt one can experience that the first (a) represents a beautiful, strongly polarized element, like two pillars which, by complementing each other, create a physical basis. The second, on the other hand, makes a gentler impression, laying stress on feeling. The third illumines a quiet inwardness, no longer externally determined but determined only through the contrasting thirds, as if pointing to the mystery of the spiritual part within man.

A second exercise in listening could be to analyze the triads: the major rising from the keynote and the minor descending from the note of origin. While C major to F minor until recently called to mind the plagal cadence and a certain mystic tendency, it has now taken on much more the character of a strong inner activity, of a great supporting foundation from the depths. The C loses a part of its essence as keynote and becomes a centre, orientated in two directions. In the second example, C major to A minor, one feels involved in an up and down movement, in feelings of certainty and doubt, in an outer and inner being, in a weaving within the soul of a personal kind. The character of what we have called the note of origin becomes prominent with the E in the minor form. The lower A has not so much the sound of a keynote, but moves in a fluid and almost questioning way. The most remarkable effect, however, is observed in the third example, in the interplay of the two keys with the same keynote, C major and C minor. By constant repetition and attentive listening the impression is given of an interchange of mode. C minor becomes more and more major in character, more full of force. Eventually it seems that one is listening not to E flat but to D sharp. C major, however, takes on the character of gentle relaxation like a smooth resolution on to a concord. In this spiritual relationship it is not so much the outer event as such that matters — major as major, and minor as minor — but an inner, spiritual counter-event. Major takes on the character of minor, and minor the character of major. This interchange becomes apparent through attentive listening. It is not the first time that this phenomenon has been revealed to the listener. In the 'Theory of Intervals' we saw this occurring in the tenth and it is one of the most convincing examples of the complementary events we have constantly emphasized.

As the third stage of the exercise we can include listening to the scales that belong together. It can be confirmed that F minor still tenaciously preserves a pronounced minor character, while C minor in its relationship to C major has a more active colour.

One sees how rich and varied the realm of the related minors becomes when applied to the whole threefold being of man and not, through a similarity of key-signatures, merely to a part of his being. Nevertheless this matter cannot be left without finding that fourth factor corresponding to the soul-condition of equilibrium. For this purpose, however, it is necessary to work out a systematic arrangement of the minor keys in the circle of twelve. This will be done in the following chapter.

Chapter Eight

THE ARRANGEMENT OF MINOR KEYS

It is readily understandable that we must start arranging the minor keys from those same three centres of force which constitute the field of will for C major. In the last chapter attention was drawn to the reflected scale. It was developed downwards from C as the archetype of minor and the three outstanding moments in it were the note of origin, the keynote and dominant. The reflections from the first, third and fifth notes of the major triad gave the related minors: the reflected minor from the keynote, the minor with the same key-signature reflected from the third, and the minor with the same keynote reflected from the fifth. In order to find the minor key corresponding to the soul-condition of equilibrium we must start again with C major.

This fundamental key, whose culmination —*Deed*— lies in the central field of force in the domain of will, began with its keynote in the field of *Fact* and reached out into the region of *Capability*. We can follow up the sober, matter-of-fact beginning of this key which, from the culmination onwards, becomes filled with an active power of will and finally attains to the sphere of creative freedom. A comparison with other keys makes it quite clear that this soul-process belongs particularly to C major. In its field of force keynote, culmination and octave embrace the spheres of C, G and D with the soul-conditions of *Fact*, *Deed* and *Capability*.

With the minor, if we are to fill in this field of keys we must start from the sphere of the note D, of *Capability*, and allow the minor scale to take its course from there. It goes through the same fields of force as the scale of C major but downwards. The result is G minor.

In the same kind of way as from C upwards one can now, through repeated listening and practice, experience downwards the opposite soul-process in G minor. This gives the point of departure for arranging the minor keys in the circle of twelve and also gives the fourth minor key related to C major. This can all be confirmed later with further examples.

We now have to ask the question: How can the unfurling of the minor keys be developed in an organic way? One might think that, in keeping with the fifth upwards in the major, C, G, D and A major, there would be a fifth downwards in the minor, G, C, F and B flat minor. In this connection the following figure gives

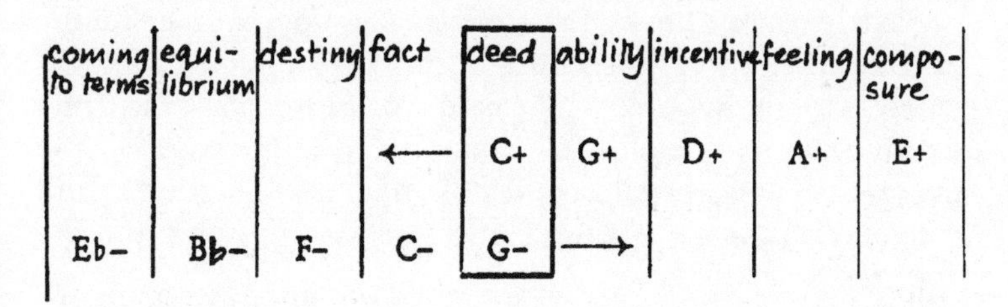

major and minor with the respective soul-bearing. But does C minor really reveal *Fact*, or E flat minor a *Coming-to-Terms*? In this rather intellectual arrangement a basic fact is disregarded; namely, the difference between the major and minor principles. We have already indicated in major the tendency towards a straight line and in minor the curving towards a centre (page 295). We distinguished between an attitude of soul streaming out into the spaces of the environment, and one much more centred within its own inner being. Further investigation into the structure of keys must be made from this point of view.

The tendency towards a straight line in major is easily found in the succession of fifths both up and down, the fifth at any given stage giving the impulse for the new key. But it does not correspond with the nature of minor if one tries to follow up the key-structure in the same way. It has to be determined by the tendency to curve, to move to the centre of the circle. But how?

We must bring to mind again the course of the reflected scale, in this case G minor. From the note of origin D the scale moves downwards but it does not pass by the keynote merely in order to go straight on; it swings up a fourth from the lower dominant D in order to grasp the keynote G in the centre.

A circular tendency out of the periphery moves towards the centre. The keynote does not lie in the periphery as in major, but in the centre of the form, and is determined from below by the fourth upwards. There is a counter-movement of a complementary kind: from the dominant note below with a centripetal movement upwards, and from the note of origin a fourth downwards to A (dotted lines). This reveals a new note of origin for the next key, D minor. Proceeding in this way, a circle of fourths emerges for the minor keys, the nature of the interval concurring with the minor principle in the same way as the fifth does with the major. Keynotes as well as notes of origin move in fourths and concur with the soul-bearings in the circle of twelve and the appropriate major key.

coming to terms	equi-librium	destiny	fact	deed	ability	incen-tive	feeling	compo-sure
Ab+	Eb+	Bb+	F+	C+	G+	D+	A+	E+
B-	E-	A-	D-	G-	C-	F-	Bb-	Eb-

However surprising this musical concordance of major and minor is at first glance, it is fully confirmed by qualitative listening. After all, can their tendencies to movement and form not be heard? The related key formed in this way can be considered related in the sense of balancing out, or as being related in the same field of force. The whole circle is presented in Plate 14.

Having worked through this somewhat complicated region there seems to be a kind of summons to review the related scales in connection with the soul-bearings. It must be remembered that the related keys were formed in a threefold way from the major: by reflection from the keynote, from the third and from the fifth of the tonic chord. With the reflection we find a complete contrast, not only due to the opposite movement; it can also be confirmed inwardly. For example, each will to action and especially every *Deed* as such, goes into the outer world (C major); *Incentive*, on the other hand, works within (F minor). A similar comparison would hold good with B flat major, *Destiny* (outer) and E flat minor *Contemplation* (inner); or between A flat major, *Coming-to-terms* and C sharp minor, *Thinking*. In Plate 14, the reflected minors are indicated by dotted lines.

It is different with the related keys in connection with soul-quality, those with the same key-signature. If the relationships through reflection may be indicated by two arrows which move in opposite directions, here there is something more like an interlacing, an interweaving, which entwines and gives mutual support. C major, *Deed*, is inextricably entwined with A minor, *Destiny*; A-major, *Feeling*, with the spiritual *Resolution* of F sharp minor, and D flat major with B flat minor and so on. It might grow out of the picture of the gyrating circle of the 'Tai-Ki' of the Ancient Chinese which has already been given (page 233 [b]). In the legend there are two birds, Yang and Yin, symbolizing the masculine and feminine principles. In Plate 14 the related keys with the same key-signature are connected by black lines.

The third, most spiritual relationship, that of the related keys with the same keynote, was one of interpenetration, of a reciprocal transformation, of an interchange of forces. The Seal of Solomon — two interpenetrating triangles forming a hexagon — provides a picture of this. The knowledge-seeking, 'pondering' element of B major is filled with the forces of the inner, moral *Coming-to-Terms* of B minor. The *Incentive* of D major turns outwards and is merged with the demand for an inner view of the *Facts* in D minor, and so on. These related keys are marked in Plate 14 in red. The more deeply one learns to know these differences in the individual keys through meditation, the further will the doors be opened into a new realm of musical expression. For it is only to an inner language of the heart that they begin to state their revealed mysteries.

When one gradually becomes acquainted with this realm the

question arises concerning the note A which, with its key A minor, provides for the minor a starting point similar to that which the note C and the key of C provide for the major.

From time immemorial all descending scales have been called 'heavenly' in contrast to the ascending 'earthly' ones. And if today, in accordance with what Rudolf Steiner says, one learns to regard music as the revelation of the laws of the I, then one can see in A minor that stream arising which flows into the innermost kernel of man's being as that of a higher World-I. In connection with this the working together of the partials and the complementary series has already been mentioned in the first part of this book. In A minor the seven notes are unchanged by sharps and flats just as in the case of C major. The basic structure of $2^1/_2$ plus $3^1/_2$ descends from E as the note of origin and curves into the central note A. The whole major/minor system is built up on these two basic notes, C and A — C representing the sphere of the human I; and A, the note of the Sun-sphere, a cosmic centre of life revealing the heartbeat of the universe.

Plate 15 shows these two basic keys of C major and A minor in the circle of twelve. Both scales overlap, connect up and interlace in F major and D minor in the field of *Fact*. These two keys having the same key-signature in the same field of force shows this to be a crossing point to which every further event on either hand is referred. C major begins in the field of *Fact* and culminates in the realm of *Deed* in the creative power of the word. A minor, streaming in the opposite direction, originates in the realm of *Fact*, and finds its centre and keynote in the field of *Destiny*. The interweaving is clear: each *Deed* (C major) is subject to *Destiny*, just as the particular *Destiny* of the individual bears within it the possibility of *Deed* (A minor). Both keys have something of the character of an objectively given *Fact* of life, within which one is placed. They both issue from the same field of force.

Something else still needs to be considered in connection with the nature of the minor. A glance shows that sharps and flats are placed differently, even opposite to the way in which they are placed in the major. Usually a sharp is regarded as a more active element: in the major cycle it controls increasingly the upper half of the circle, the 'light half'. The flat represents a more loving inclination towards the depths, towards gravity; it controls the lower darker part of the circle. It is understandable that the sharp keys in major, striving outwards towards the light, conform most nearly to the true major character. But now there is an indication that in the domain of minor all flat keys have a character more active — one might say, more rousing than that of the sharp keys. A flat in the minor emphasizes the centripetal inward direction, reveals the minor impulse through its own intrinsic nature. The grasping of the centre can be experienced as an intense activity, in contrast to which the sharps bring to expression a state of soul that is calmer and more receptive. Corresponding fully with the upper, more active lighter part of the circle, one finds the minor flat keys there: G major and C minor, D major and F minor, and so on. And in keeping with the events of the lower part of the circle we find the minor sharp keys: E flat major and E minor, A flat major and B minor, and so on. In this sense, keys like C sharp minor or F sharp minor have a contemplative character, which is concordant with the character of their special spheres, while F minor and C minor have an agitated and almost disturbing character. Plate 16 shows these complementary conditions in a wonderfully harmonious way, particularly when the picture is taken as a whole in association with the major. The two axes start from *Deed* and *Destiny* — C major and A minor. The dotted lines connect the same key-signatures, the black lines the number of sharps or flats in major or minor.

For many people it may be far from easy to adapt to these differentiations and to the often entirely new inner connection and complementary relationship of keys with one another. If we can free ourselves from custom we shall find that these rules speak directly out of the phenomena. A great part of the value and meaning of these exercises lies in their objective detachment from an anchorage in feeling — probably justified through centuries — of certain kinds of experience that have in general been valid.

We have yet to consider the determining or complementary intervals of the minor keys, for do they not indicate the bearing of the key? We shall deal with this briefly. The determining interval in the realm of major was found in the relationship of the keynote to the note C. One might easily think that in the realm of minor the note A would assume this changing function. This law stemmed from the importance of the keynote or its octave, depending on whether it was the sharp keys unfolding from the keynote upwards or the flat keys from the octave downwards. For the minor keys the unfurling downwards from the note of origin or upwards from the dominant is the appropriate procedure. In major the starting point was the note C. In minor the corresponding starting note is D, as dominant to G minor. This takes over the same function as the C in the realm of major. Just as there the function of the note C is sought between keynote and octave, so here the relationship of D is sought between the note of origin and the dominant sphere below. It is not A, as might be assumed, but the first note of origin D that takes over the changing function in the succession of minor keys.

The flat keys are determined by the complementary interval between the note of origin and the note D. In G minor this means note of origin and octave, which in essence corresponds to sure and comprehensive stepping from note to note. F minor, from the note of origin C downwards, has the complementary interval of a minor second, a stirring and almost dramatic pressing on towards the lower dominant sphere, corresponding to the field of *Incentive*. E flat minor, on the other hand, starting from B flat in the field of *Contemplation*, has an intimate minor third arising in the soul as complement to the sixth. In the sharp keys the determining interval from the dominant upwards to D becomes the controlling one.

As has already been shown for the domain of the major keys, so Plate 17 shows for the circle of minor keys the changing function of the first note of origin D. There are three distinct colours: blue for the flat keys, red for the sharp keys and purple for the starting point, A minor, and its enharmonic counter-region. In order to show the harmony between major and minor in the world of keys, grey shading shows the determining and complementary intervals in the major keys. It should be noted that the keys in the third chapter (page 261 and page 267) were registered in the place of the keynote and *not* in the point of culmination, and therefore they differ from the present arrangement by a fifth. This was because the arrangement from the temporal aspect had not yet been given, and it was only possible after this to lead to the culmination as the central point.

If during the course of study we gradually work our way

through the contrasting major and minor keys in each situation — A minor and B flat major, D minor and F major, B flat minor and A major, B minor and A flat major and so on — another example of harmonious relationship will be found between the determining and the complementary interval. Taken together these always form an octave: F major has the fifth as complementary interval, D minor the fourth; A flat major a major third as complementary interval, B minor a minor sixth, and so on.

We must draw attention to an essential difference in the structure of the two kinds of keys; in the minor we have a circle of fourths, not of fifths. A double circle formed out of the totality of keys speaks distinctly of the differences found even in the dynamic of the various intervals. It is worth freeing oneself from many a customary method of perception and standardization. Just as in astronomy one speaks of different directions of movement and intensities, or distinguishes between the daily and the yearly movements of the sun's cycle, or of the retrograde movement of the vernal equinox, so here also there are two circles in motion which are not at all of a similar nature. The one bears the centrifugal impulse of the circle of the fifths in major, the other the centripetal impulse of the circle of the fourths in minor. Those guided by the fifth unite with the periphery, while the others connect with the centre through the nature of the fourth.

Seek in the surrounding world
and thou findest thyself as man.
Seek in thine own inner being
and thou findest the world.

These words given by Rudolf Steiner point to a contrast we find also in the world of music. The separate moods in major speak more personally, while the minor allows a universal consciousness to arise in the heart. In studying Plate 18, imagine that there is a fold along the central perpendicular, through which the two sides of the circle can lie one against the other. The picture would then clearly depict the relationships mentioned here.

Chapter Nine

CONSTELLATIONS OF KEYS

Through this study we have become involved in the question of the relationship of keys to the twelvefold zodiac. This magnificent realm is of great importance for the deepening of spiritual knowledge and can only be indicated within the framework of this book. Since we are striving to trace the laws of the ego, a few words may be added to what has already been said about microcosmic man. He was seen in ancient times as being in connection with these heavenly forces, especially with regard to his form.

At the end of the second chapter of this part — Part Four — we indicated the extent to which the Middle Ages recognized man in all his dimensions and proportions as a copy of the harmony of the spheres. 'Musica humana' was the expression of this knowledge. The beautiful words of Agrippa von Nettesheim quoted from his mystery teaching (see end of Chapter Two, Part Four) bore eloquent witness to this. And in the fifteenth century a Platonic view of music was given by Marsilius Ficinus, quoted by Dr H. Pfrogner in his book *Music:*

> Through the sense of hearing, however, the soul absorbs wondrous harmonies and rhythms, and through these images it is reminded of and stirred by divine music and is able to contemplate it in a deep spiritual sense. The commentators on Plato differentiate between two kinds of divine music; according to them one exists in the eternal spirit of God, but the other exists in the order and movements of the heavens, and this is the music with which the heavenly bodies and heavenly spheres bring forth a wondrous harmony. In both kinds of music our soul participated before being enclosed within the body... Through them it is brought to a deep, inner, silent memory of the harmony which it once enjoyed...

According to such a picture as this of world and man, certain constellations of a universal and musical kind poured down their forces through every constellation of the zodiac. These twelve heavenly spheres are portals for the incoming cosmic forming forces which work upon man, each in its own appointed way. It was known that in a pre-natal condition of a purely spiritual kind man was given to the creative activity of these universal forces. Permeated by and interwoven with the cosmic rhythms of these twelve creative heavenly forces, the human form is adapted to that wisdom-filled unity of which Plate 19 provides some indication.

For a full understanding of Plate 19 one should call to mind the fact that this totality exists between head and feet, and also the other way round. Two streams can be followed: on the one hand the major stream from the place of *Fact*, in which F major and D minor concur and which reaches its conclusion in *Destiny*. This stream fashions man from above downwards, from forehead to feet. The minor stream on the other hand unrolls from *Destiny* to *Fact*. It begins at the feet and rises to the brow.

Through the *Ram* streams the force of becoming upright. Man stands vertically between heaven and earth. Depending on his vocation he grasps the possibility of combining both regions through the power of his head. From the *Bull*, the larynx is formed, that is to say, man can become the bearer of creative and healing word-forces. The *Twins* work between right and left in the symmetry of the body and in the mystery of diagonals. Through *Crab*, *Lion*, and *Virgin* stream the forces which form the organs of breathing, heart and solar plexus. The solar plexus enables man to develop delicate, ethereal forces of supersensible sight, through which a particularly intimate insight can be developed into events in heavenly space. In the form of Makarie in *Wilhelm Meister* Goethe depicts such a soul, full of virginal mystery in the purest sense. The *Scales* lays hold of the small of the back while man, with his hips and a kind of organ of balance in the pelvis, is incorporated into the earth's gravity. Man's reproductive nature is created out of *Scorpion*, while *Archer*, *Goat*, *Waterman* and *Fishes* are portals for world-forces working on the limbs. Thigh and upper arm, knee and elbow, lower leg and lower arm, and finally feet and hands, are laid hold on by these four heavenly regions. Following the minor stream we would follow up the structure of the human being from feet and hands in the place of *Destiny* in the *Fishes*, and would end with becoming upright in the power of the *Ram*.

At this juncture we must forgo any attempt to enter more

deeply into these twelve regions of the heavens. Yet the inner connection of their form-giving aspect with the soul-aspect of the keys is for the most part so clear that the reader might be deprived of the best part of his work if these facts were presented through dogmatically fixed ideas. A major/B flat minor — *Feeling* and heart in the *Lion* — belong together; hands, feet and *Destiny* in A minor/B flat major belong to the *Fishes*. With the spiritual power of *Resolution* in D flat or C sharp major/F sharp minor, the soul-force which is resolved and ready to move towards a goal brings us to the *Archer*, flowing directly into the freedom of movement in thigh and upper arm. The mystical A flat major/B minor is reflected as a spiritual *Coming-to-Terms* in every flexible movement of the joints, in the bending and stretching of knees and elbows whether upwards or downwards, forwards or backwards, whether tense or relaxed. But the fact that *Equilibrium* — E flat major/ E minor — strikes down physically into the lower leg and lower arm is experienced by everyone who watches a tightrope walker, or attempts to walk along a narrow plank himself. Progressing from sphere to sphere in a study left to the reader, not only will the truth and grandeur of these facts be confirmed but, in a truly objective way, invigorating sources of inspiration, arising out of the nature of the subject, will begin to flow into artistic creation. They open the way to an objective, cosmically orientated music teaching and music therapy.

In the chapter about the four main keys it was pointed out that the musical representatives of the three soul-forces of thinking, feeling and will, and then also of equilibrium, were found in C major, A major, F sharp/G flat major and E flat major. In the minor keys this is given in G minor, B flat minor, C sharp minor and E minor. Later we shall come back to this and scrutinize these things in detail. Of foremost interest here is whether and in what way these four spheres may be distinguished in the structure of the human form.

In the sphere of will *Deed* is significant with the formation of the larynx as the organ of the word in the *Bull*. It is clear that this alludes to the sphere of divine origin proclaimed at the beginning of St John's Gospel, which Goethe in his *Faust* translates as: 'The Spirit helps me! Suddenly I see my way, and write: In the beginning was the Deed.'

The faculty of speech, which ennobles only man among all

living creatures, gives direct evidence of his being a child of God. If the world is recognized as the living and creative Word of God, if speaking is synonymous with becoming manifest in the earthly, then the reflection of this creative activity may be seen in the human power of the word. From this standpoint, the experience and responsibility for the word extends to every original expression man is able to give as witness of his creative impulse. The larynx is the specific organ in this connection, man's own particular divine inheritance and vocation. The *Bull* is the starry space revealing these mysteries.

The connection between the powers of *Feeling* encaptured musically in A major/B flat minor and the forming of the central organ of the heart are revealed in the *Lion*. The power of the Sun that determines and gives warmth to life is concentrated here in the circulation of the blood and the beat of heart. This is the cosmic region where the sacred forces of love and sacrifice unite with man, calling on him and giving him for that purpose the right faculties in spirit and soul as well as in body. In old pictures in which the tamed lion lies at the feet of the saint, and when the legends of the Middle Ages depict Count Hermann of Thuringia in the thirteenth century as a 'lion-tamer', or speak of 'Henry the Lion'; when in his *Märchen* Goethe lets the child lead the dreaded lion peacefully and fearlessly — then an exalted, kingly humanity is indicated, which in a courageous inner struggle has overcome the consuming fire of instincts and passions and has learnt to purify and control the forces of the heart.

The constellation of the *Scorpion* is connected on the one hand with the organs of reproduction and on the other with *Thinking*, as an attribute of the soul. As such, it is the symbol of death: the Scorpion crawling in the dust with the death-dealing sting is the reality of the intellect bound to the earth and for the most part leading to arid abstraction. But also in this region lies the actuality of the devastating disease-ridden dangers of sexuality. In the far distant past the forces described here were those of the Sun-eagle, which set man's thinking free for living flight into heavenly heights. It was also the time when matters relating to sex were regulated and safeguarded as sacred by priests for the well-being of humanity. Here lies mankind's great future task — to release the spirit from its excessive fall into matter: to transform the *Scorpion* back again into the *Eagle*.

The fourth sign, of *Equilibrium* in the *Waterman*, embraces the lower legs and lower arms and is often represented as the bearer of water, as angel, or as Christophorus. Cosmic man was regarded from time immemorial as bearer of the higher divine ego, which bestows on earth and mankind the water of life. In the lofty flight of the eagle we pointed out the path to a spirituality which overcomes death, and the one who strides through the waves represents a humanity for whom firm ground beneath the feet does not disappear and is no longer the sphere of death. The ability to move in the higher realm of living and flowing ethereal forces is the true basis of existence. It is well to remember what was said in considering the key of E flat major (page 292) about cosmic world-consciousness. Its forces of equilibrium in the Waterman allow heaven and earth to rejoice together as in olden times. The four corners of the zodiac are still apparent today, as they have been from time immemorial. Think of the sphinx — the *Bull*, the *Lion*, the *Eagle* and the *Waterman* — the great fourfold beast, whose primal forces reveal man in his entire being as the image of God. It cannot be sufficiently emphasized that it is in music, the art of the ego centre, if studied in the light of the spirit, that this prototype continues to exercise its powers in all its greatness, going beyond the personal and embracing the universal. Plate 19 gives the twelve signs of the Zodiac with the attitudes of soul as well as the form of man and the relevant major and minor keys as they unfold around the square of the 'fourfold beast'.

Against this background the constellations that a key occupies with its related keys in the circle of twelve acquire much greater significance. Plate 20 shows C major with the four minor scales belonging to it: F minor, the reflected minor; A minor the relative minor with the same key-signature; C minor, the tonic minor with the same keynote; and G minor related in the field of force. It can be called the related key in the zodiac, that is to say, it assumes the same place in the zodiac as the major key from which it stems. The minor scales form the inner prerequisites for the major key from which they are derived. A glance at the constellations confirms this. No *Deed* will be implemented by a being with *Will*, if it is not impelled by inner *Incentive* — F minor in the *Crab* — or better said, if it is not suffused with the breath of spirit, of true inspiration, and stimulated by it. Here we see the connection of the *Crab* with the chest and the breathing process. But the *Twins* carry the *Deed* as *Capability* between the duality of right and left, between active and passive existence, between giving and receiving (C minor). Neither can there be a *Deed* unless it is linked with *Destiny* and leaves its mark on life. It is the work of the hands as well as the stepping of the feet (A minor). But the related zodiac key (G minor) shows the controlling balance between an inner and an outer aspect, upon which the *Deed* is based. In listening to the four related keys one is amazed to find how much is revealed of these individual features and how much G minor, in contrast to the others, gives the impression of an objectivity both calm and firm.

This constellation broadens out when one includes the two dominant spheres of G major and F major, which produce the picture of the twelve related keys in the whole field of *Will*, as Plate 21 shows. To the four minor keys of C major we must still add: for G major C minor as reflection, E minor as relative minor with the same key-signature, G minor as tonic minor with the same keynote, and C minor as related in the zodiac. For F major there is B flat minor (reflection), D minor (key-signature), F minor (keynote), and once more D minor (zodiac). In both dominants a minor key is included twice. In G major, C minor is not only related in the zodiac but is also the reflected key (red semi-circle). In F major, D minor is related in the zodiac but also has the same key-signature (red semi-circle).

The same laws and the same subtle distinctions of mood apply in the opposite field of *Thinking*. (Plate 22). Between the spheres of *Will* and *Thinking* related keys come into evidence in *Lion* and *Waterman*. It is noticeable that there is no apparent interpenetration of keys but that something more like an antithesis is brought to expression.

This occurs on the axis of *Feeling* and *Equilibrium*, *Lion* and *Waterman*. The force of *Feeling* in the soul is the connecting centre just as the heart, connected with the *Lion*, maintains life, quickening and controlling it with the power of the Sun. If, with the aid of Plate 23, we seek out the connections which in the related minors are thrown like bridges across the soul's path (blue and purple), then these relationships are seen as moving to the opposite side or the adjacent sides in the zodiac. Plate 24 shows this in greater detail. A penetrating search shows that an 'exalted kingly humanity', which was spoken of in connection with *Feeling* in the *Lion*, is inconceivable without an inner relationship with the forces of uprightness in the *Ram*, standing between the upper and the lower with the true power of the ego; with the forces of the *Fishes* in the experience and forming of *Destiny*; and with a clear and resolute spiritual force from the *Archer*. Two of these positions form the arms of an equilateral triangle — D minor and F sharp minor in *Ram* and *Archer* — while the connection between A major and A minor points like a pendulum, to the place of *Destiny* in the *Fishes*. E flat major as the key of *Equilibrium*, representative of a higher cosmic humanity, is connected in the arm of the triangle with right and left in the *Twins* (C minor) and with a real balancing out in the *Scales* (A flat minor). But the central pendulum of the Angel in man appears in E major in the *Virgin*, the place of the solar plexus, of the ethereal power of vision and of intimate insight into the realm of the stars.

In Plate 23, first taking each point singly and then allowing it to work on the soul as a whole, a devout wonder can be enkindled, even something of the mood of prayer, which is the beginning of all knowledge. And by entering into the grandeur of these cosmic relationships it may be possible to bring to life the foreshadowing of a deep 'resounding stillness', through whose breathtaking silence the reality of the harmony of the spheres may be bestowed upon us.

Plate 25 summarizes the places that are touched upon by the 48 related minors of the twelve major keys: the fields of *Will* and *Thinking* (red and yellow) stand in polar opposition to each other, those of *Feeling* and *Equilibrium* (blue and purple) intertwine and bring life to the whole. The fourfold beast portraying man in the spirit unites the four soul-forces, which have formed the basis of our work.

These observations on the nature of keys and the way they work should not be concluded without glancing at the opposite sphere: the fact that from every minor key there are four related majors. From the note of origin of G minor we get the scale of D major as a reflection upwards, just as in major the reflection goes downwards from the keynote. Then upwards from the third, B flat major with the same key-signature, the relative major; and upwards from the fifth, G major as the key with the same keynote. The fourth related key would be C major, related in the zodiac. In the relationship of these keys to their place of origin, G minor, it is possible to hear the same kind of moods as in the opposite sphere, of major (page 298). Here also the reflection brings to the note of origin the experience of a strengthening of the foundation; here also the related key with the same key-signature, the relative major reflected from the third, sounds gently as if sinking into the domain of feeling. The related key with the same keynote stresses this sinking down and takes away from G major its peculiar clarity in its alternation with G minor. This can be followed up in all keys.

In a wonderful way the picture of the constellations shows up a similarity between the two keys in one and the same place in the zodiac. G minor is united with D major in the *Crab*, with B flat major in the *Fishes*, and with G major in the *Twins* — that is, with the same places as C major and its related minors F, A, and C minor. This can be found in every key and shows how each of the twelve places in soul and zodiac has its own essential complementary zones — a law not to be broken. We can speak in the fullest sense of the 'constellations' of each key, whether major or minor.

The practical person may ask: What do I do with all this information? Is it not abstract and trivial?' To which we reply: Things remain abstract and lifeless if one only reads about them and does not listen to and work with them. All that is given by way of example must be personally tested. Much material, many questions and many different aspects remain untouched. These indications can serve as a practical guide for years to come. This book could even become a friend and counsellor. Every qualitative study proceeding in a selfless and objective way with each phenomenon, allowing only this to speak in the soul, transforms the human being by working through the senses in a moral way. It forms new organs in man. Goethe's words to Zelter give an answer to the above question:

> Man must be capable of raising himself to the highest level of discernment in order to establish contact with the

> Godhead revealed in the archetypal phenomena, physical as well as ethical, behind which it is maintained and which proceed from it. But the Godhead is active in the living, not in the dead; it lives in the process of growth and transformation, but not in what is finished and rigid.

The Divine which works in the process of growth will be invoked when man traces within his soul the living power of the phenomena. In such an inner dialogue creative forces lead to conscious experience and living knowledge, and in his closeness to them man is brought into contact with the power of the Divine Word and transformed by it. He will then approach all things musical in a new way and everything he does and towards which he aspires will gradually be irradiated by this divine proximity. A breath from beyond the earth will bring new and essential inspiration more than ever before. Is this not 'practical' in the deepest sense?

Chapter Ten

THE COSMIC BACKGROUND IN THE WORK OF JOHANN SEBASTIAN BACH

Any study on the nature of keys almost inevitably calls to mind Bach's *48 Preludes and Fugues*. It is known that he studied the work of Werkmeister with great interest and welcomed with joy the reduction of the components of musical sound to twelve notes within the octave, tuned in equal temperament. We may accept the fact, on the grounds of historical tradition, that in many respects Bach was much too deeply connected with the mysticism of Tauler for this arrangement of twelve notes not to reveal to him the gateway to realms beyond the earthly. It was through his genuine and deeply religious world-outlook that he was able to find in Werkmeister a kindred spirit. In his work, *Die Zwölfordnung der Tone* Dr. H. Pfrogner makes the following interesting statements, which refer to authentic sources in the writings of Werkmeister:

> ...not without reason does Werkmeister gradually show an inclination towards a strange mysticism which somehow causes him to speak of the tuning of his keyboard as a kind of spiritual tempering of the 'musical Harmonia', as a reflection of the macrocosmic 'circulation in and upon the terrestrial globe and also in man as microcosmos'; or, in the tempered 'lowering of all fifths a twelfth of a comma' to refer to a certain theologian who wrote of this process 'in a strange treatise, since it proclaims and quotes several mysteries of the Holy Scriptures, where he not only deduces and extracts all musical consonances from Solomon's Temple, but also quotes a mathematical description of the casting of the molten sea carried by twelve oxen that there may be contained therein true musical tempering as GOD Himself ordained it.'

In the light of this quotation it is reasonable to ask how far J. S. Bach has reproduced macrocosmic relationships in his works in the various keys. Albert Schweitzer, Bach's great biographer, also feels this 'manifestation of that primordial power revealed in the endlessly revolving universe'. In this chapter it may be permissible to go into this question, investigating the themes and development of a number of preludes and fugues from the 48, and also a two-part *Invention*, against a cosmic background. It is clear that within the framework of this book it will only be a matter of aphoristic indications. They will not only serve as indications but rather as a stimulus towards deeper understanding of this wealth of material.

To begin with the four cardinal points, the 'image of man', will be of greatest interest. ***The Prelude in C major with its Fugue in Part I*** is known not least by Gounod's sugary-sentimental treatment of it, so it is all the more necessary to try and reinstate it in its true spirituality. This has already been discussed in the last chapter of Part Three but it can be considered again here. The key occupies the field of *Will* in the circle of twelve. It has its keynote in the power of becoming upright in the *Ram*, its culmination in the power of the Word in the *Bull*, and its octave in the symmetry-producing forces of the *Twins*. In the first place one is amazed at its delicate heavenly character. With the creative archetypal spheres in mind, a 'word' signifies the loving sacrifice of an individual being, a streaming forth of the self, whose spiritual goal it is to fit the self harmoniously into the life and work of the whole world. All this is indicated in the form of this prelude, seemingly so unpretentious. A simple foundation in the bass not only gives the keynote of C major, but the word as Deed inclines towards the depths while cosmic sounds stream upwards in broken harmonies rising like sacrificial incense.

The whole prelude swings between upper and lower in this octave-like movement. This musical event spreads and culminates before it closes with eight bars on a dominant pedal G, while after the ascent of the upper voice a middle voice follows like a last inner echo of what has gone before. The foundation in the bass, emphasizing so fittingly the force of incarnation and the ability to become upright in the *Ram*, then prepares the way for

the theme of the fugue which, with its austere fourths, brings the cosmic prelude into the earthly domain. The Fugue, the 'fitting together', stands under the law of continual condensation, drawing the entries together in ever closer stretti.

It is not so much the relationship of keynote to octave that is emphasized, but rather the fourths and fifths which lead into the third.

A complement to this is given in the *Prelude and Fugue in G minor in Part II*. An active, will-like character is conveyed by the terse rhythm throughout the piece.

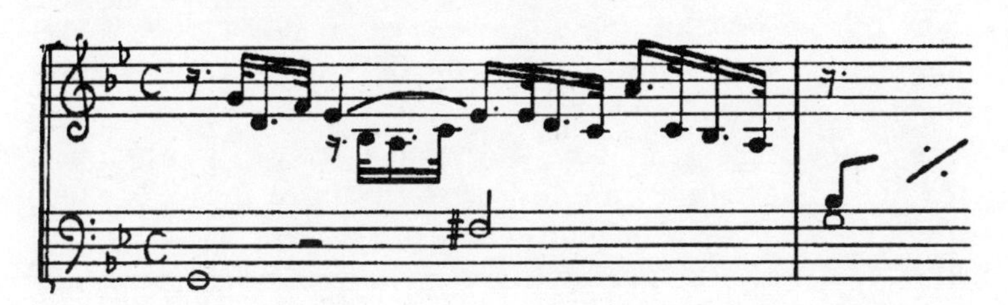

One can feel the impact of an action which is like the stroke of a hammer. The theme of the Fugue takes up this element of will.

It is intensified by the rests before the quavers and particularly in the sevenfold repetition of the C. The theme is concentrated in the upper part of the minor scale between the note of origin and keynote, and the swing to the E flat only serves to intensify the downward direction of the minor. That the two other works in C major (Part II) and G minor (Part I) are apparently quite different from these in their basic mood is due only to a superficial observation. Through careful investigation it is possible to discover in them also their cosmic anchorage in the field of *Will,* if perhaps from a rather different aspect.

It is illuminating to move from here to the field of *Thinking* and the *C sharp minor Prelude and Fugue in Part I.* It has already been pointed out that in minor the sharp brings to expression a receptive frame of mind, a being endowed with the gift of light. Through listening in this way the C sharp minor is found to bear an obvious meditative character, inwardly open and harkening.

Developing from the dominant quietly to the keynote, the subject then unfolds upwards to the octave, ending in a calm way on the note of origin. The octave in the middle is very impressive, embracing as it does the distant spaces of heavenly light. The subject is then continued in an even greater 'deepening'. The complete melody, moving in a peacefully swinging 6/4 time, is like light streaming down from above, in face of which the soul opens up from time to time in a gesture of longing. The three places of the key — *Archer* as note of origin, *Scorpion-Eagle* as keynote and *Scales* as dominant — find remarkable expression. The Fugue shows a principle similar to the one connecting the Prelude and Fugue in C major:

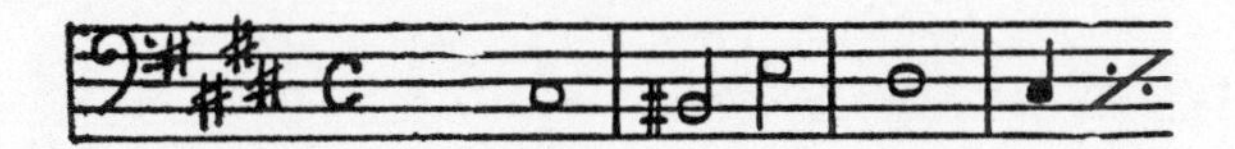

The prelude runs its course in the upper and even soaring sphere of the dominant, while the fugue concentrates its subject on the keynote. Every truly meditative event connects man with his creative ego centre. The interval of the fourth and the repetition of a note belong to the basic musical elements bringing this self-comprehension clearly to expression. In the magnificent structure of this five-part fugue, from bar 49 onwards a second subject sounds with a fourth (a) and remains inseparably united with the first.

It is introduced by a descending sequence of quavers (b), the first note in each motif repeated three times and the whole moving through a fifth. The quaver figures for the most part fill the space of a fourth. In this way it is possible to draw a little closer to the reality of a supersensible world-order with which a devout spirit like Bach was still connected.

For the axis *Feeling/Equilibrium*, that is, *Lion/Waterman*, three examples may be given: the *Prelude in A major* and the *Prelude and Fugues in B flat minor and E minor in Part One*. In A major, we recall the key of an 'exalted, kingly humanity', of the purified heart-forces of the *Lion*, warmed through by the Sun and bound up with it, full of life, love and light, expressed through the third. Of this, a finer example than the little A major prelude can hardly be found.

It is conceived in the harmony of three interweaving voices. The swing from a third-motif to the sixth, which turns into a suspension of the fifth, is followed by a sequence of thirds, both up and down; an exultantly swinging movement is held by fifths. One might even think of the bliss of angels soaring up and down. And it is only some chromatic steps in the bass that anchor the whole to the earthly. A short modulation to F sharp minor in the twelfth bar swings over to the possibility of a spiritually determined force of resolution and the setting of a goal, then it returns once more to A major and comes to a close.

A very different mood breathes through the *Prelude in B flat minor*! We have already discussed the fact that for the minor keys in flats, in the same way as in the major, the complementary interval must be found to the interval made by the note of origin and the note D. From F that would be D flat, the minor sixth.

And the whole piece stands within this mood. The soul struggles towards a dramatic climax through passions and sufferings to the purification of the heart.

And it bears the inner sound of the desire-to-surpass-the-self until, after the powerful breathless tension leading up to the chord of the diminished seventh three bars before the end, we find the wonderful release into B flat major: the key of *Destiny* in the field of *Equilibrium*. The bracketed accents in the above extract show the dissonances which accompany this moving path of joys and sorrows. Throughout there is the deepest expression of *Feeling* whether experienced cosmically or in the realm of personal inner life. After this wonderfully reconciling close to the Prelude the clarity and force in the structure of the Fugue reveals the inner grasping of 'kingly humanity'. The subject is in two parts:

from the keynote in the middle to the dominant below in the first bar, then a ninth striking into the upper octave, and a descent and ascent in perfect balance, each within the range of a fourth. So forcefully is the state of soul presented, that all further developments, still in keeping with *Feeling*, are borne more and more by progressions of thirds and sixths, piled up in harmony in ever closer stretti. It also closes with a chord of B flat major so that, royal and proud and in complete control, it fits freely into the cosmically determined path of *Destiny*.

As a final example of this axis of *Feeling/Equilibrium* we take the *Prelude and Fugue in E minor*. Without being able to enter into further details, we can point out the semiquavers constantly running through the base as a gentle caressing rippling movement, to which in the upper part a melodic voice resounds in a free figure: *Waterman* — Christophorus stepping through the waves, bearing the Christ child on his shoulders.

But then, in transition to the sphere of the note of origin, to A minor in the *Fishes*, more violent storms begin. It is the domain of *Destiny*! The waters change more and more, mounting to a presto until eight bars from the end the dominant is reached, and through the waves a succession of strong minims rings through and preserves the balance. The Fugue brings a subject which, as if playing out of the octave of the keynote, allows notes to fall down chromatically like rain. It is the only two-part Fugue in both parts of the *48 Preludes and Fugues*.

And it could be said that it is on account of the two voices that the feeling of *Equilibrium* between upper and lower, between right and left, controls and beautifully fills the soul with its ethereal transparency.

It is not possible to consider all the *48 Preludes and Fugues* in this detailed way. This would be the subject for a voluminous work. But in order to link together the circle of keys apart from the four cardinal points, it may be prudent to consider briefly the spiritual structure of some of the themes in order to shed more light on the connection between Bach's world of musical ideas and the harmonies of the spheres. Here again it is best to start with the axis of *Will* and *Thinking* and to seek out the transition on either hand to the fields of *Feeling* and *Equilibrium*.

The *Prelude in G major in Part II*, for example, demonstrates that effortless technical ability which is required by the *Twins*, *Capability*.

Listener and performer alike are enchanted by the joy in movement as such, without difficulty. This is invariably the mood of G major, as it is also in the ensuing Fugue and in the *Prelude and Fugue in Part I*.

The same pronounced character of movement is also shown in the C minor pieces in both parts, only in a much more

inward way. The *Prelude in Part I* brings into play *Incentive* from the *Crab* as formative sphere, as well as *Deed* in the *Bull*, the sphere of the dominant, and every two bars it brims over with a new creative impulse without leaving any impression of fragmentation.

The subject of the *Fugue in Part II* is a fine example of *F major* in the *Ram*, the power of becoming upright. It aims three times for the octave, by way of the fifth and then of the sixth, (see accents in example) and then back again from the higher ego

towards the depths. This gives an inner tautness followed by relaxation. The 6/16 time-signature points to the importance of each single step, while the rests allow for a drawing of breath in readiness for a new and higher ascent.

The two keys that frame the counterpole of *Thinking* are B major tending towards *Feeling*, with G sharp minor, and tending towards *Equilibrium*, C sharp major and F sharp minor. *B major* standing in the Scales has the second as determining interval. It is this that is wonderfully imprinted in the *Prelude of Part I*. Fully awake in looking and stepping forward, each crotchet step incorporated rightly upon the earth—this gives the mood of soul in this part of the zodiac.

G sharp minor as relative minor and related through the zodiac in the *Scales* is given convincingly in *Part II* — swinging in two parts, balancing between upper and lower, with the bass

in the semiquaver figure showing a resemblance to the figuration in the G major of the *Twin*. The fact that through the *Waterman* both these places are connected to form an equilateral triangle gives a slight indication of an inner relationship.

C sharp major with its culmination in the *Archer* needs to swing in freedom between keynote and octave, sure of its goal. It is marvellous to experience this in the *Prelude in Part I*.

Up to the syncopated octave in the seventh bar (accent), of which full use is made thematically in the course of the piece, everything breathes that alert comprehensive power of spiritual decision, illumined sevenfold. The playful interchange moves between above and below, under and over, until in the final arpeggios swing through the air and free it of every earthly constriction. In truth, only a spiritually gifted composer completely at home in this sphere can cast such a stroke of genius.

The neighbouring sign to the *Scales*, the *Goat* or *Goat-Fish*, with the soul-bearing of *Coming-to-Terms* has already been discussed in connection with A flat major. Concerning the minor, it is certainly not by accident that Bach wrote his Mass in B minor. This key bears the mark of quiet humble devotion in which folded hands are raised and knees are bent. Something of this lives in the subject of the *B minor Fugue in Part I* which is given here.

A struggle from step to step pervades the whole event. After a higher step the soul inclines again to a lower one. Nevertheless everything is carried by an inner equilibrium, although in almost every bar a new constellation of voices requires a new adjustment in the harmonies. Everything is steeped in a mood of intimacy — B minor at its most beautiful.

For the other neighbouring place to the *Waterman*, *A minor* in the place of *Destiny* in the *Fishes*, the *Prelude in Part II* may be of value.

It is not without interest that in it, as in the B minor, there are suspensions above and below, showing an inner relationship with the maintenance of *Equilibrium*. Only there it was like an overlapping of stages, while here the change of direction really gives the feeling of stepping out, or better, a pendulum-movement with tension upwards and relaxation downwards, kept in balance by the chromatic steps in the bass. This condition of being harnessed between sharp and flat, rising and falling, lightness and weight, produces a sure feeling of guidance, which stands over against the inner dramatic element controlling it, almost as if in contemplation.

Lastly, we move to the two neighbouring places to *Feeling* in the *Lion*: *D major* in the *Crab*, and *E flat minor* in the *Virgin*, both in *Part I*. In D major the Fugue subject, following an agitated hurrying Prelude, comes as a terse theme which, despite its brevity, or perhaps because of it, contains compression and

energy which can hardly be surpassed. The crotchet rest before the entry is like a drawing of breath, which gathers itself up in the demisemiquavers and swings boldly out into the sixth, so as to collect itself in the dotted quavers and semiquavers. Once more it is a threefold arrangement, from the keynote in the *Twins* as *Capability*, to the culmination as *Incentive* in the *Crab*, which is wonderfully combined with the courageous warmth of the *Lion*. D major is often called a 'Michaelic' key. Something of this Sun-spirit with flaming sword striving against the forces of the deep is captured in this fugue, shining out in triumph.

To conclude the round of the zodiac of keys, let us listen to the *Prelude in E flat minor in Part I*, associated with the feeling of *Contemplation* in the *Virgin*.

It should be realized that here the solar plexus is formed as tender seed for a clairvoyance which opens the eyes of the soul to the life of the stars. Bach bids everything arbitrary, everything of will to be silent. The heart of the universe beats harmoniously with a regular pulse and a voice sounds out from the heights, gently and impressively proclaiming the will of God. Man is united with the source of his being. His soul, pure and virginal, can feel something of *re*-ligion, a reuniting in the truest sense, which breathes only security and peace. In this connection we can quote the beautiful words of Albert Schweitzer in his biography of Bach:

> Nowhere so well as in the *48 Preludes and Fugues* does one understand that Bach was sensible of his art as a religion.

To this Schweitzer adds:

> He who has once experienced this wonderful reassurance understands the enigmatic spirit revealed through the mysterious language of music and is indebted to it as one is indebted to the great masters, to whom it is given to reconcile man with life and to bring him peace.

Could a better thank-offering be made than that of trying, through listening, to unseal this 'mysterious language of music'?

This deep anchorage in the harmonies of the world-order, won of his mysticism, gave J. S. Bach that sense of responsibility which we admire in the amazing spiritual form of his work. There is not the smallest detail, often seemingly unimportant, which does not obey a superimposed 'logic' in the purely musical sense — 'logic' that reveals its true source in the 'Logos'. The question that so often arises as to whether this logic has been created consciously or not is rather an idle one. The religious relationship of his whole being to a spiritual world present in his soul may well be assumed with Bach. It gave to him the possibility of becoming, in his moments of creation, the mouthpiece for the 'Logos' of the world.

In this connection, to conclude the chapter, we shall turn to the *Two-part Invention in B flat major*. The *Inventions* were also written in definite keys. Bach himself attached considerable significance to them as teaching pieces. As title of the main autograph, he wrote:

> Precise indications, by means of which is shown — particularly to lovers of the 'Clavier' but also to those desirous of instruction — a clear method, not only of learning to play in two voices but also, with progress, of learning to handle three parts correctly and well; the while not only receiving good Inventions but also performing them well and, most important, achieving a cantabile style in playing and acquiring through it a healthy foretaste for composition. Composed by Joh. Seb. Bach, Kapellmeister at the Court of Anhalt-Cöthen. Anno Domini 1723.

Bach was well aware that his pupil was to be influenced, in the sense of the Middle Ages, and educated through the spiritual background of the work. There were strong unconscious reactions to the cosmic influences which developed these capabilities in individual creation as well as in playing. The *Invention in B flat* can be followed through in connection with the cosmic background of its keys.

B flat major unfolds from the *Waterman* by way of the *Fishes* towards the *Ram*. In the musical sense it moves from *Equilibrium*, through culmination in *Destiny*, to the power of becoming upright in the I. Following up how *Destiny* unfolds for every person according to his divine archetype, we find his individuality in the trinity of body, soul and spirit embedded in the harmony of the universe. For this trinity, macrocosmically as well as microcosmically, the triad is the archetypal musical expression. Bach spells out this *Invention* thematically in this sense: a breathing up and down movement in simple sequences of clear harmony, which even in the first bars is established in the threefoldness of the cadence (a).

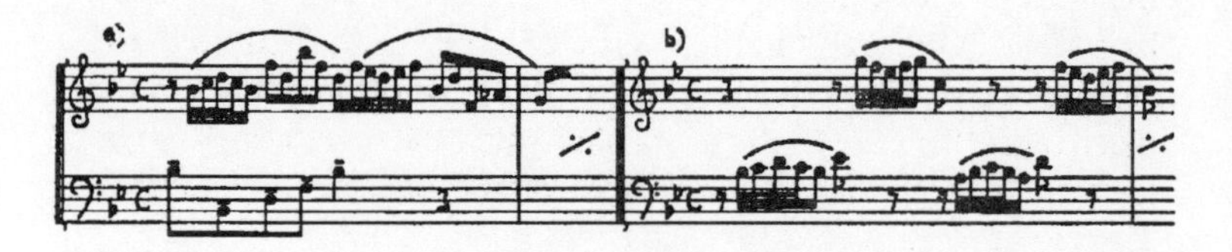

The next thing one experiences, after being born into earthly life, is a growing awareness of the environment. The little demisemiquaver motifs, like a preliminary question and answer, play together in the second bar and give expression to this (b). The next three bars bring an individual consciousness: the force of becoming upright in the I, imprinted in the earthly depths as the F major subject in the bass. The human being, awakened in this way to the feeling of self, now experiences the beginning of a path of destiny as his consciousness lights up in the changing relationships, situations and demands which he meets. Three bars of modulation make it possible to read in the zodiac what is to be developed in man as knowledge and strength — G minor in the *Bull* as power of the healing word in *Will* and *Deed*, E flat major in the *Waterman* as goal, to grow to maturity as the Christ-bearer, and C minor in the *Twins* as controller of the faculties of giving and receiving. From now on man looks upward, grasping his higher ego through the octaves.

Beyond the personal, cosmically united, these rise ever higher in canon, their entries at a fourth. Then figures in thirds flow down in the opening and closing of motifs, until they reach the keynote in the bass. The last bars, from 16 to 19, bring the subject in canon again in B flat major. In perfect 'Imitatio' both voices follow each other through the cadence form, harmoniously pursuing the prescribed course of destiny in earthly depths. The closing bar emphasizes this ultimate affirmation of maturity through an octave unison at rest within itself. In wonderful architectural symmetry, this soul-picture takes its course in three parts: eight bars — three bars — eight bars, and in the twentieth bar it is summed up in the closing octave. The axis of symmetry in the whole event lies in the place of the keynote in the cross of the physical (Chapter Four), in the *Ram*, which is determinative for a right incarnation upon earth. The picture of the analysis is given in Plate 26.

It is still possible even today to imagine that the spiritual and cosmic reality of such a work must deeply influence player and listener alike. In an age not yet so materialistic, so divorced from the spirit as we are living through today, man could receive and experience such influences differently. One may truly believe of J. S. Bach, that a soul so permeated by spiritual law was granted 'a healthy foretaste for composition' which was still wrapped in a veil of mystery and borne and nourished by a feeling of strong moral responsibility. The clear, transparent and apparently simple logic of this B flat major should convey a presentiment of the light-filled wisdom bestowed on all who have ears to hear the expression of moving correctly through the course of destiny.

The deep relationship with the laws of the universe that Bach incorporated into his music is indicated in the brief examples given in this chapter. They have been chosen deliberately from works which are accessible and well-known to every music lover. They might even have been the same that the organist in Berka played to Goethe in his church. The undying words of the poetic genius about the musical genius are quoted to close this chapter as further witness to a world which lies at the basis of all creation. Bach sought to attain it, in that he obeyed to the end the words of his spiritual guide, Tauler: 'Be mindful of the fundaments...' Goethe wrote to Zelter in June 1827:

> I said to myself: it is as if eternal harmony held converse with itself, as perchance it may have done in God's bosom shortly before the creation of the universe. So did it stir within my inner being, and it was to me as if I neither possessed nor needed ears, least of all eyes, or any of the other senses.

Chapter Eleven

RICHARD WAGNER

Bach's musical creations, anchored as they are in the cosmos, are indeed something absolutely unique. So far they have not been superseded. It is none the less worth considering another musical personality whose work also had these cosmic connections, albeit in another kind of way and in another musical and artistic sphere. It is Richard Wagner, who was much disputed in his time. With Bach one can become aware of a 'Pythagorean' spirit being revealed in supersensible musical mathematics and architecture, in a symmetry of numbers handled in a masterly way; but in the works of Richard Wagner a deep connection, ordained by destiny, is apparent with the Nordic-Germanic world and with the Grail-Stream. Earlier mysteries rise up within him like unconscious memories. An old initiation, macrocosmic experience of a most magnificent kind, holds sway in the unconscious depths of his soul and grows within him to powerful musical intuitions. So it is understandable that we hear in his works music of a macrocosmic character, far beyond what is personal, and that the texts of his works had to be created out of the realm of myth, of saga. In Wagner's letters on *The Music of the Future*, we read:

> Saga, of whatever time or nation, has the advantage of taking only the purely human content of its time and nation, and of giving this content in an appropriate form, precise in meaning and therefore easy to understand... In the world of saga the spirit is transplanted into a dreamlike state through which it soon reaches full clairvoyance. It then becomes aware of a new relationship to world-phenomena of which it could not become aware with the eyes of normal waking consciousness...

After these brief indications it may be permissible to give some examples. A few words from the letter already quoted on *The Music of the Future* can serve as a preface to these reflections. He writes as a poet might speak to the writer of a symphony:

> Spread out thy melody boldly, so that it flows through the whole work like an uninterrupted stream; in it speak what I conceal, for only thou canst say it, and in silence shall I say all, because I lead thee by the hand. In truth the greatness of the poet lies in what he conceals; being silent himself he lets the inexpressible speak to us. But it is the musician who brings that which is concealed to expression in the clarity of musical sound...

The choice of theme and especially the leitmotif, to which the clear sounding of 'that which is concealed' is entrusted, is actually a miracle of cosmically heard mysteries in soul and spirit. There is no question of any kind of 'tonal symbolism'. An artist's soul is revealed as being at home in the supersensible, bringing to life with unfailing intuition realities of the spirit-world in and through its mythical figures; and this in connection with the intervals, through which what is inexpressible is able to resound in individual motifs as well as in the use of keys. It is on this that the strong spontaneous effect of Wagner's music is based and impressed indelibly on every unprejudiced soul.

Who, for instance, can resist the mystic enchantment of the opening sounds in the overture to *Lohengrin*, the Grail-motif in A major, which — soaring in light-filled heights — proclaims in thirds the tidings of the love of the Swan-knight sent by God? Who is not impressed by the robust motif of the *Flying Dutchman*, with the intervals of fourth, fifth and octave — central to the I — striving towards the upright and reaching shore? The chromaticism of the first bars in the overture to *Tristan*, full of yearning and sounding in A minor, the dramatic key of Destiny; or the unforgettable theme of the sacrament in *Parsifal*, woven of mystic secrets in the sphere of A flat major — are these not characterizations which, in their very 'rightness', express through music that universal-human element towards which we aspire?

But it is not only the themes that can be followed up in this way from work to work. The more Richard Wagner grew into the musical and poetic mission of his 'comprehensive artistic work', the more he was able to let the situation in soul and spirit sound in his leitmotifs through the modulations. In this he is unique: the motif does not pass through metamorphosis outwardly, but a change of key from time to time becomes transparent for the drama of destiny, the 'inexpressible' transitions in soul. For example, the Siegfried motif in the opera of this name sounds seventeen times, each time in a different constellation of keys. Three forms of this leitmotif can be given here. Firstly, from the third act of the *Valkyrie*, where Brünnhilde proclaims Siegfried to his mother, Sieglinde, as the fruit of her womb; secondly from the first act of *Siegfried*, where he beholds his own picture in the clear brook; and thirdly in the overture to the *Twilight of the Gods*, where Siegfried pledges his faith to Brünnhilde with Alberich's ring.

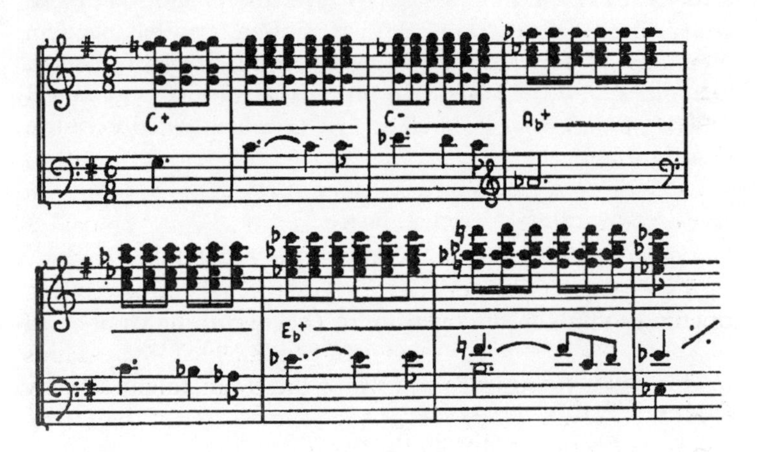

The first words begin in C major (see Plate 27a) with Brünnhilde proclaiming:

> The sublimest hero of the world
> dost thou, O woman, shelter
> within thy protecting womb.

Then the music leads through C minor and A flat major to E flat major. This is a wonderful picture of the future hero in outline: as hero of the *Deed* (C major — *Will* in the *Bull*) of the striving towards creative *Capability* (C minor in the *Twins*), and as bearer of an initiation (A flat major in the *Goat-Fish*), which allows him to win through to *Equilibrium*, to cosmic world-consciousness through the higher ego (E flat major in the *Waterman*). The beginning and ending of this path foreseen by the gods can be outlined in the square of the Spirit. The axis of this event is drawn from the *Bull*. Two poles of the cosmic picture of humanity are touched upon: the point of departure in the creative *Will* towards the Word, and the goal in the higher eternal being of the Angel.

This preview of the spiritual form of the hero drawing near to incarnation stands in the first act of Siegfried in contrast to another form of motif. It is the scene where Siegfried questions the dwarf Mime about his origin. He is pressing for knowledge of himself. In the weaving life of nature and of other beings he does not find himself. He knows himself to be of another kind, feels himself called to a higher sphere, and cannot recognize himself as the descendant of a small dwarf who has become repugnant to him. Rather is it his concern to free himself from this sphere of life which is determined by an ordinary egotistical thinking that fancies itself clever. He sees his reflection in the clear brook:

> Now came I to a clear brook:
> there did I espy the trees and animals in reflection;
> sun and clouds
> as they are,
> so do they appear in the glistening reflection.
> *Then saw I there*
> *also mine own image*
> quite different from thee
> I thought myself to be:
> Does a shining fish resemble a toad?
> Never was fish spawned by toad!

Siegfried awakens to the knowledge of his connection until now with the lower intellect and takes the first step towards overcoming it. A ferment of storm and stress fills him. He seeks deeds that will raise him to the freedom of his own humanity; deeds which in his agitation he feels foreshadowed within him. Wagner brings this to expression by guiding the motif in a triumphant youthful manner from G major, the *Twins* — the place of creative forces — to G minor, *Deed* in the *Bull*. While the eternal being of the ego lights up in the soul as the goal of existence, the theme lingers for two bars in E flat

major, the higher equilibrium of *Waterman*, in order then, recognizing the path of *Destiny* — B flat major in the *Fishes* — to flash over to the radiantly powerful D major, *Incentive* in the *Crab* (Plate 27b). With this D major as the true culmination of inner development, the soul-picture is established in the square of the spirit, and also in the square of the physical. The higher meaning of earthly existence is recognized and raised to the *spiritus agens*. The two axes in the *Bull* and the *Ram* also mark this situation.

A third metamorphosis of the Siegfried motif is found in the prelude to *Twilight of the Gods*, in the scene between Siegfried and Brünnhilde. Even in the chart of keys (Plate 27c) one can see that the whole musical stress following on the *Destiny* situation is now in the field of *Thinking*. The awakening of Brünnhilde is for the individuality of the hero the great achievement of his life. The flaming path of purification, which he trod without fear, was to give him purity to overcome his sense-existence. In that he found Brünnhilde he could free his own undying soul, could unite with her spiritually, giving as pledge the ring he took from Fafner.

> In exchange for thy runes
> do I pass thee this ring.
> It encloses what I have done
> in action, in virtue.
> I struck dead a savage dragon
> which had long guarded it fiercely.
> Now do thou control its power,
> as a dedicated pledge of my faith.

The whole way of initiation which Siegfried has tragically taken only in part, and which he would have had to fulfil if he were to raise himself to this mystic union with the divine part of his soul, is recorded in the succession of keys for the words, 'It encloses what I have done in action, in virtue'.

Beginning in A flat major, the sphere of initiation in the *Goat-Fish*, there follows an enharmonic transition to G sharp minor. This key, bestowing the balancing forces of knowledge, leads over to pure vision in the E major of the *Virgin*. Through its purifying forces the sexual nature of the *Scorpion* (C sharp minor) can be overcome and *Thinking* receives the power of the *Eagle*. This leads to the insepar-able spiritual unity of the two life-principles, masculine and feminine. The words in the closing part of the prelude seem to be pulsating with supreme happiness, even if only imperfectly attained. The motif flows into the key of D sharp major with its nine sharps in the Angel, the *Waterman*. Part of the text of this concluding scene may be given here. It is raised far above the sphere of the merely human.

S. No longer do I look upon myself as Siegfried,
I am only Brünnhilde's arm.
B. Oh, if Brünnhilde were thy soul!
S. Through her, courage is enkindled within me.
B. So wert thou Siegfried and Brünnhilde.
S. Where I am, both are harboured.

And the sanctity of this unity resounds in joy:

B. Parted — who will sever it?
Severed — it will never be parted!
S. Hail to thee, Brünnhilde,
resplendent star!
Hail to thee, radiant love!
B. Hail to thee, Siegfried,
conquering light!
Hail, radiant life!

The perfect, cosmically uplifted humanity revealed in this mystic picture finds in the keys its fullest expression, in that this third metamorphosis fits into all three rectangles: from the axis of the spiritual and of the physical of the first two settings we come, through the climax in E major in the *Virgin*, to the third axis of the soul, drawn from the *Twins* to the *Archer*. Wagner draws in the music the picture of that which actually ought to have happened. Siegfried's tragedy consists in the fact that despite this lofty experience he is not sufficiently purified to succeed in his passage back to earth, but fails.

To finish this chapter let us take two examples from Wagner's *Parsifal*. This last and most mature work offers throughly spiritualized fruits in relation to the cosmic background of modulation and sequence. Some of it seems to have been raised to an ultimate straightforward simplicity. The first example, the passage to the Grail Castle in the first act (Plate 28a), brings a succession of keys in the Bell- and Grail-motifs in periods of four and more bars. It rises in minor thirds: E major, G major, B flat major and D flat major. This course — the way to the centre of the Christ-mystery in the Grail — falls into the square of the soul, the cross of the Son, and has its axis in *Twins/Archer*.

In connection with the words of Gurnemanz the stages of this path acquire a deeper significance, and their mysterious and hidden sense only becomes transparent through the keys. In the music there rings out clearly what is concealed in the words. To Parsifal's enquiry:

Who is the Grail?

Gurnemanz answers:

That cannot be told —

and goes on speaking in riddles.

No path leads to it through the land...

There is a path, not to be found in the physical, but which is revealed to the higher senses, to spiritual vision: E major in the *Virgin*.

G. And no one could tread it but he whom it would accompany...

Moreover it is a path which is not ready-made and cannot be surveyed, but can only be taken step by step through inner guidance. New self-creative capabilities have to be developed in order to attain to the Grail: G major in the *Twins*! In progressing from here to B flat major, the key of *Destiny* in the *Fishes*, Parsifal begins to have a premonition that in this sphere, inwardly grasped and seen in retrospect, each small step is able to open up infinite soul-space:

P. I hardly tread, yet I seem to have gone far.

And now, in greater intensification to D flat major, the *Archer*, we hear the profound statement of his companion:

G. Thou seest, my son, that here Time turns into Space.

Consciousness of destiny, presented in such a way, conjures memory pictures into the soul and experiences of what has gone before. What happened in the course of time on earth is seen in its totality in living space. Only here is man able to keep in mind goals and decisions of spiritual worth. A new picture of the world arises, in which man knows himself to be divinely ordained. Parsifal is still not sufficiently awake to assimilate all this consciously; yet he stands before the inner eye of Gurnemanz as a chosen one on whom the answer to the question concerning the mystery of the Grail is not lost. In this passage through the circle of keys, simple as it may seem, everything is revealed musically which unites the soul of the old sage with that of the aspiring young man on their common path of destiny.

Much more concisely, but all the more forcibly, does Wagner form the last of the examples given here: the regaining of the spear at the end of Act II (Plate 28b). Only this indicates the enormous power with which decisions are made. In this act Parsifal shows himself to be the one summoned to redeem the Grail and to become King of the Grail. Wagner lets the beginning of the motif of the Grail-castle sound three times, always changing from major to minor and going back to major again.

Briefly and magnificently the Grail-hero is depicted here: full of Michaelic incentive and strength— D major; inwardly coming to terms with the universe and destroying the practices of black magic — B minor; maturing for the control of creative forces, that know themselves guided by the higher ego in the soul — G major and E minor; prepared for action — C major; determined by destiny and deciding the future — A minor; creating the fact through which mankind gains health for the consciously responsible ego-force uniting heaven and earth — F major. The whole is fitted together in the cross of the physical, of the Father. The way opens for the transubstantiation of the earth through the spiritualization of matter.

This example concludes the analysis of keys. There could be many more but this would go beyond the framework of this book. Whoever participates with open heart in the way described, first of all in the structure of the major and minor keys; then, with quickened soul, proceeds to the background of cosmic world-forces — not only will he acquire a new connection with the works of the great masters, but he will also be able to make his own contribution. Through earnest striving and seeking, a path may be prepared that connects music again with its origin in the spheres.

It may seem to some readers that these reflections go too far into the underlying laws of the human being. But any true theory of music can do no other than read from the objective actualities of music the laws of the microcosm. The human soul-organism, in whose subconscious depths musical experience lives, is created by the cosmos through the harmony of the spheres. The more the future succeeds in disclosing these connections between world, music and man, and bringing them into a form of experience suitable for our time, the more will all things musical be raised again to a universal human and social factor. Then for the art of music the earnest words of Goethe could become reality:

> We know of no world but in relation to man; we wish for no art that is not a likeness of this relationship.

Chapter Twelve

CONCLUSION

It is well known that everyone has a preference for certain keys while other keys do not interest them at all. This preference also changes during the course of life. The indications given here about the keys in their relationship to man have been given in general, but in considering them much can be gathered about the state of soul of a particular person at a given moment, especially if that person is of a deeply musical and artistic nature.

From this point of view it may be expected that a survey of the keys in the nine symphonies of Anton Bruckner could raise the curtain on the mystery of the inner development of such a creative personality. A survey such as this may be undertaken with Beethoven or any other of the great masters, and comparisons could lead to interesting insight. We can approach the works of Anton Bruckner in this way. In his well-known book, *Anton Bruckner*, Erich Schwebsch stresses that one should become conscious of the fact,

> that basically speaking the keys represent space in soul and spirit and, depending on the key, experiences can differ. They determine in a way the constellation of a theme in a symphony, 'the law by which it enters in', and assert their will, just as the constellations of the zodiac determine the rhythm of twelve months in the year, each with its special nature and its special effect upon the human soul...

Schwebsch also tries to follow up a 'soul-biography' of Anton Bruckner through his works, but without going into zodiacal connections. It is this which we shall briefly illustrate here. Plate 29 may help to elucidate this cosmic soul-process.

The first two symphonies both begin in *C minor*. Twice Bruckner sets out to gain mastery in creative activity. But in the first work we find a wild effervescent joy in creative play as such, while the second goes a step further on the path towards attaining more conscious capabilities. The first symphony was written by 'It' sounding through him; the second was written more out of himself.

This now prompts the question of the purpose of life. Individual existence stands before the soul as fact and challenge. It is a matter of coming to terms with one's self, poised between the world of the earthly and that of the spirit. One fruit of such an instance of destiny is Bach's *Art of Fugue*, sounding out of a profound D minor, his individual name set on it as a seal. Such fruits of life become conscious in Beethoven's last symphony, the Ninth in D minor. In a similar though still youthful struggle and challenge tc the self, Bruckner is able to reach the sphere of D minor: it turns into the third symphony.

The confirmation of this finding of the I is the attainment of the E flat sphere in the next symphony, the fourth. The relationship to the origins of the wisdom-filled world-will sounds through here, just as in Richard Wagner's overture to the *Rheingold* in E flat major. One feels Bruckner's growing maturity in cosmic world-consciousness. The God Whom he, as a Christophorus, begins to bear in his innermost being is met by a mighty 'Tat tvam asi = That art thou' sounding out of the environment. Man in the equilibrium of his soul-forces experiences himself as an important member of the world-order.

It corresponds fully with this stage of inner development that Bruckner has to incorporate himself with his fifth symphony into the space of *Destiny*, of B flat major. The 'angel-consciousness' of E flat major is such that it must always be acquired anew, step by step. The difficulty, the solitude and the responsibility of an overwhelming artistic destiny, but also the uplifting grace it brings, must be made to sound. It must prepare the way to a conquest of the personal and show the way to an all-embracing power of love — to the *Lion*.

In his sixth work Bruckner reaches this Sun-sphere of A major. And if earlier on it could be said that all true music has its source in this A major region, it is not surprising that at this point Bruckner wins through to a high level of pure musical inspiration. But even here he makes a kind of preliminary trial for the next stage. Erich Schwebsch also draws attention to this:

> Through the twelve spaces in the world of musical sound which, as zodiacal spaces, form the whole heaven of sound for our present-day music, Bruckner lets the phases of the main theme ring through all twelve keys.

This seeing and hearing of the musical whole, as if taken in advance from the *Virgin*, would have been referred to in the Middle Ages as the experience of the 'Logos'. For present-day humanity, taking its bearings from Christianity, the zodiacal *Lion* is considered to be the warmth and sun region of *Feeling* and of 'kingly humanity', the sign of the Christ.

Something of the warmth of the A major sphere and particularly the new experience of a totality in the round of the zodiac is fully revealed in the next work, the seventh symphony in E major. A work of resounding light, after the previous sun-warmth, has to be developed. On this path to the heights, which leads the spiritual nature of Bruckner towards perfection, dimensions are attained which sound in a divine, star-like way to the by now clairaudient ear of the maturing master. A supra-terrestrial resonance in the harmony of the spheres raises the music thus inspired to the luminous sound-world of the universe. Once again pure *Virgin* forces of the soul bear within them the seed of the next creative sphere. This ability to live in the realm of the stars implies being at rest within a centre of being which, patiently controlled through strength, allows the polarities of existence to play into one another.

And so we come to the sphere of the *Twins*, of creative play in a higher sense, which Bruckner approaches for the third time, now as master: once more a C minor rings out in the eighth symphony. To have become 'master' — is that not the absolute maturity where all one knows inwardly, all 'taking' in spirit, knows it is capable of 'giving' in equal measure to the earth? It is the complete control of the unity of content and form in which one's every faculty works without question and without difficulty.

The D minor of the uncompleted ninth work can only be a kind of crowning 'finale'. It is the same profound mystery that Bach approaches in his *Art of Fugue* in the same key. This place in the zodiac is also touched upon twice. The first time it was the beginning of a process of development towards the I — the why and the how, the facts of earthly existence seeking for expression with their pressing demands; but here it is the other end, the end of a life which, as if taking leave, seeks once more the cosmic sphere of the proper 'power of becoming upright'. Bach answered the soul's great question: 'How did I stand upon earth?' with his own name, B-A-C-H*, as the last subject for his monumental quadruple fugue, whose audible fulfilment was never given. Bruckner too was quietly called away while working on his last great 'Word'; he was no longer able to make the last movement of this symphony audible on earth. The great 'finale' of his life and work was experienced by him inaudibly. He was called to life in the sphere of all-pervading cosmic music, whose quiet, modest and yet powerful messenger he had always been. The height he reached through his music was not fully completed any more than it was with J. S. Bach. The threshold to the spirit remained open, awaiting the appointed successor who would start a future cycle of development.

But which places in the zodiac did *not* become audible in Bruckner? Which heavenly regions were silent, impelling him out of the inaudible? This is also of importance, for it is the spiritual counterpart that makes the twelve a whole.

One sees the impulse towards the creative word, to *Deed,* working out of the *Bull*; one sees *Incentive* streaming from the *Crab*; but the forces of the *Scales*, the *Eagle*, the *Archer*, the whole field of *Thinking*, remained as if in undisturbed purity in the spiritual world, guiding its messenger directly from there. Neither does the sphere of the *Goat-Fish* sound, because this profoundly mystic region of *Coming-to-Terms* entirely fills him, controls him in spirit. In these four last-mentioned spheres, where the region of *Thinking* goes over into the region of *Equilibrium*, lie the essential evolutionary tasks for present-day humanity and for the future: the transformation of *Thinking* from the *Scorpion* to the *Eagle*; the transformation of the sexual; the conscious passage through the sphere of death for the sake of a 'Parsifal' path of initiation, which found its deepest expression in Wagner's motif of the sacrament in A flat major. Anton Bruckner trod this path in the unconscious, united as artist with the world of divine origin, but not as yet with clear waking consciousness. It was precisely this state of soul which protected him from any sort of deviation or experiment. It led him unerringly, pointing out the path to one who knew himself to be a child of God and created as such!

* Note: In the German language B is the English B flat, H the English B.

The final words in a book in which the reader has been taken on a long journey have nothing sad about them, so long as they are able to open up a way into the future.

This fourth part 'The Nature and Activity of the Keys', is related to an archetype against which the human being can be experienced objectively. It is built into him like the sevenfoldness of the intervals, the threefoldness of the cadence form, the major/minor principle. It has been indicated that this archetype of man, his spirit and soul structure, is born out of the twelve cosmic archetypes in the zodiac. They appear visibly in space in the twelve well known pictures of the fixed stars.

Over against the cosmic sphere of the archetypes stands the region of the earthly image. This insight can be fully disclosed by deeper observation, and was given in the following words in the 17th century by Johannes Kepler, the great discoverer of the planetary laws — out of an experience and knowledge of the beings working in the harmony of the spheres.

> A true picture of the zodiac and of the whole firmament is imprinted by God into the soul of the earth.

In this connection, Hermann Beckh writes in his important book, *Cosmic Rhythm in the Gospel of St John*:

> ...we would have to distinguish an earthly zodiac of twelve signs, and an actual star-zodiac, a zodiac of the constellations, as two distinct revelations of one and the same spirit — therefore also the wholly justifiable similarity of the names. In the case of the one, the earth-zodiac of the signs, we are actually only in the periphery of the earth, in the 'aura' of the earth, in that sphere in which the year...runs its course. Only in the zodiac of the constellations are we in the star world. The spiritual element in the zodiac common to both is revealed in the earthly, just as in the starry world.

During a so-called Platonic Great World-year, comprising 25,920 earth-years, it is well known that the vernal equinox of the sun, as a result of the retrograde revolution of the earth's axis, runs through the whole visible region of the twelve zodiacal constellations, until, after 12 times 2,160 years, it returns to the point from which it began. The position and relationship of the original cosmic spheres and of the earthly region consequently move apart continuously and gradually. The point of time in which 'the heavens were open' the last time, that is to say, when the constellations and the zodiacal signs coincided, was at the beginning of our age, in the Greek cultural epoch, when the event of Golgotha brought about a change in the whole evolution of earth and humanity. At that time the vernal equinox stood in the *Ram* — sign and constellation coincided. Man finally became upright, his thinking ego orientated towards the spiritual. In each period man can gauge where and how in the prevailing cultural epoch his relationship to his archetypal form lies. For man's cosmically determined development has advanced since the transformation of the earth by Christ. One understands this in the light of the above statement concerning the vernal point of the sun, which at the present time is no longer in the *Ram* but in the *Fishes*, and which in the future will go over into the *Waterman*, determining a new culture.

The result of this, considered musically, is that the aspect of the keys for today has moved a sign in the minor direction. This means that C major in its cosmic sphere is anchored in the domain of *Fact*, of the *Ram*, and has its culmination in the field of *Will* in the *Bull* and its octave in the field of *Capability*, in the *Twins*. However, for the region of the earthly images, in which man has to work during his earthly existence, this basic scale of C major, by constant progress, starts today from the field of *Destiny* in the *Fishes*, has its culmination in the *Ram*, and its octave in the *Bull*. It is evident that, in keeping with the minor tendency, all other keys go back a place in the zodiac. This aspect is shown in Plate 30, though only for the four main keys — C major, A major, F sharp/G flat major and E flat major. From this one sees how the soul of present-day man has changed since the time of the *Ram*, in the same way as the intervals of a sevenfold structure have to be transformed into a twelvefold structure. But what is the bearing of man at present for his earthly activity?

C major, the key of *Will*, is seen in the place of *Destiny* in the *Fishes*. More than ever before the need is expressed, not only to enjoy to the full an impulse towards creative activity — following an inner 'must' in pursuit of self satisfaction — but also to bring this impulse into union with the demands of destiny, clearly and consciously. In this deeper sense the experience of destiny is centred in the laws of repeated earth-lives. Rudolf Steiner has made this knowledge accessible to Western consciousness through Anthroposophy, the Science of the Spirit. The culmination point of C major moves into the field of *Fact*, whence reincarnations are controlled. From here all activity that does justice to the demands of the present time is brought to fulfilment in the sphere of *Deed*. The objectivity so strongly characteristic of C major is released from its sobriety and raised to a higher sphere.

In the same way, A major finds its culmination in the *Incentive* of the *Crab*. This is the new stage in the region of *Feeling*; for the soul-force of warm devotion previously determined by the *Lion* is no longer the same. This is clear in everyday life. When feelings are not consciously willed and called forth, especially such positive feelings as love, reverence, gratitude and so on, they are often simply not there. They have to be taught. From youth onwards we are controlled by a critical, so-called objectivity. The anchoring of A major with its keynote in the *Twins* evokes *Capability* in *Feeling*, and is connected with the field of *Will*, culminating where this impulse becomes a continuous driving power of the heart. *Feeling* — so purified, so acquired — will then rightly stand as octave in the *Lion*. The gentleness which characterized A major will acquire something like an inner fiery kernel, raising everything romantic or sentimental to something inspired by the cosmos.

Thinking finds its new foundation in the *Virgin*. Today a cosmic orientation breaks through on every hand and gradually teaches us to cross the threshold to the supersensible. F sharp major and especially G flat major find a new culmination in the *Scales*. No longer is the sparkling, glittering and agile element the essence of this soul-force, but rather an endeavour to reach a calm, impersonal objective balancing-out of things, one with another. With this deepening, however, the possibility is revealed of pressing forward to a pure thinking transformed by the *Scorpion* in the octave. The sixfold illumination through six sharps in F sharp major is the Word of a striving for light which, in time, might gradually lend to this key a greater inner tension.

But E flat major in its connection with the Angel in man will be increasingly concerned with spiritual decision; it will be a question of an initiation indicated by the culmination of this key in the

Goat-Fish, in the place of *Coming-to-Terms*. This key will also acquire a more mysterious character, which will much more strongly emphasize becoming the bearer of God, rather than the ideal of achieving perfection. The sphere of *Equilibrium* in the *Waterman*, the true Christophorus being, is not attained until the octave, and closes the circle of keys in the place of *Destiny*, of the *Fishes*.

It is left to the reader, through listening and reflection, to make the intermediate stages of this new structure, and also the minor keys belonging to it, his own. In the aspect of the *Fishes* the background of the present time is revealed in the whole deeply instructive content of its truth. Both things are given: according to Goethe, the awe-filled contact with the Godhead, disclosed in the pure primal phenomena at work in the development of man; and, according to Rudolf Steiner, the nature of music as that art in which 'the laws of the I are revealed'.

In this sense every musical occurrence places man right in the centre of his own proper earthly mission, which is to contribute towards the spiritualization of matter. The axis in Plate 30 is that of the Father, of the physical. The axis of the time of the *Fishes*, however, in which the beginning of the circle of keys is C major, is that of the Son (dotted lines).

The classical age of the major/minor system was irradiated by the evening glow of the *Ram*. With full justification and conviction every study could, and indeed must, set out from there. But today it is worth adjusting to the path that runs its course under the influence of the next place in the zodiac. For future generations may the blessings it holds in reserve become so much their own that with the healing and transforming power of music they may be champions of a new Christ-bearing humanity.

PLATES

In the German edition the plates were printed in colour. In this edition a code has been used to indicate the original colours.

..... red --- blue -.-.- purple

\\\ yellow 33 green (plate 6 only)

PLATE I

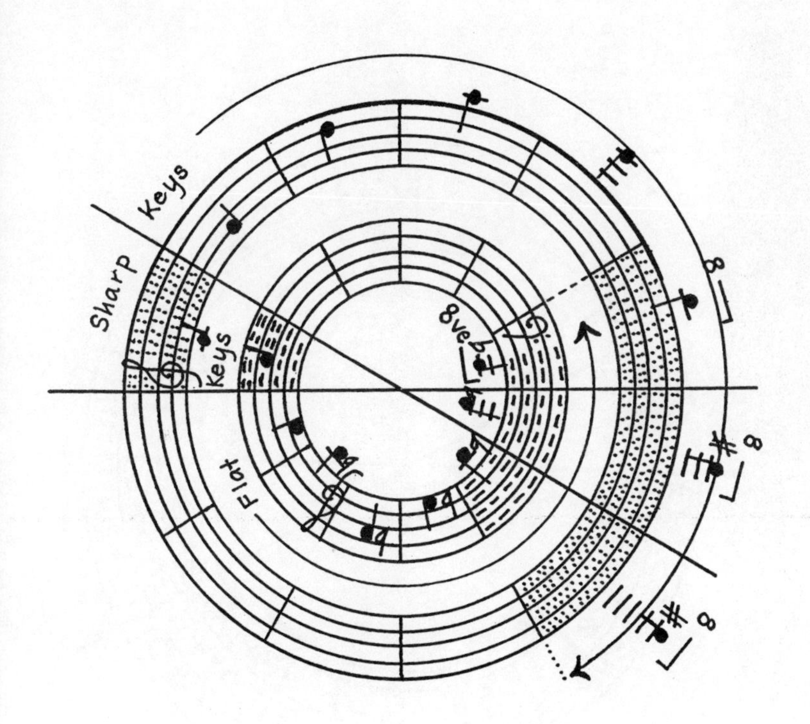

The Circle of Fifths

PLATE 2

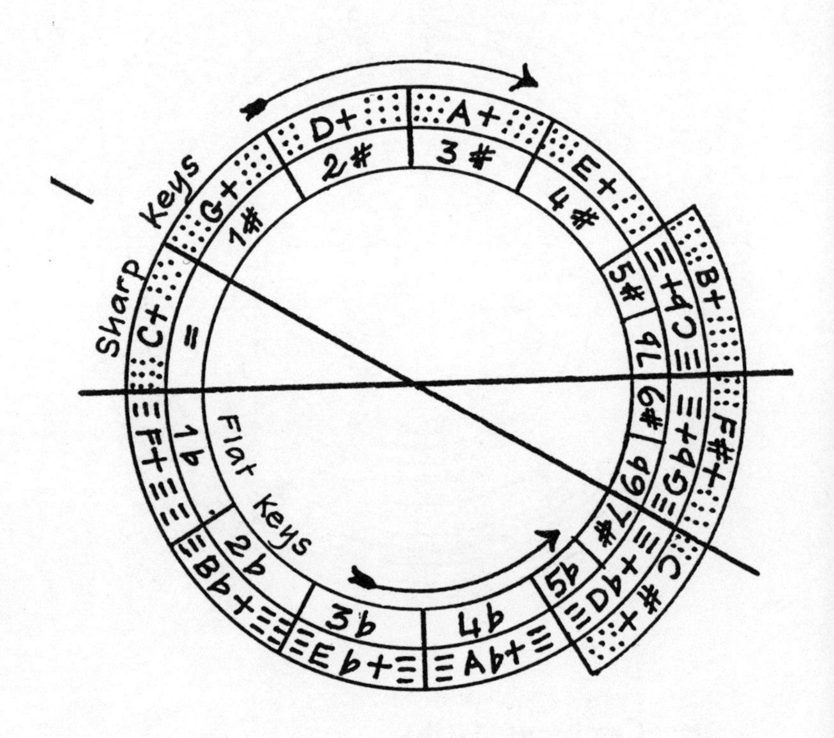

The Circle of Major Keys

PLATE 3

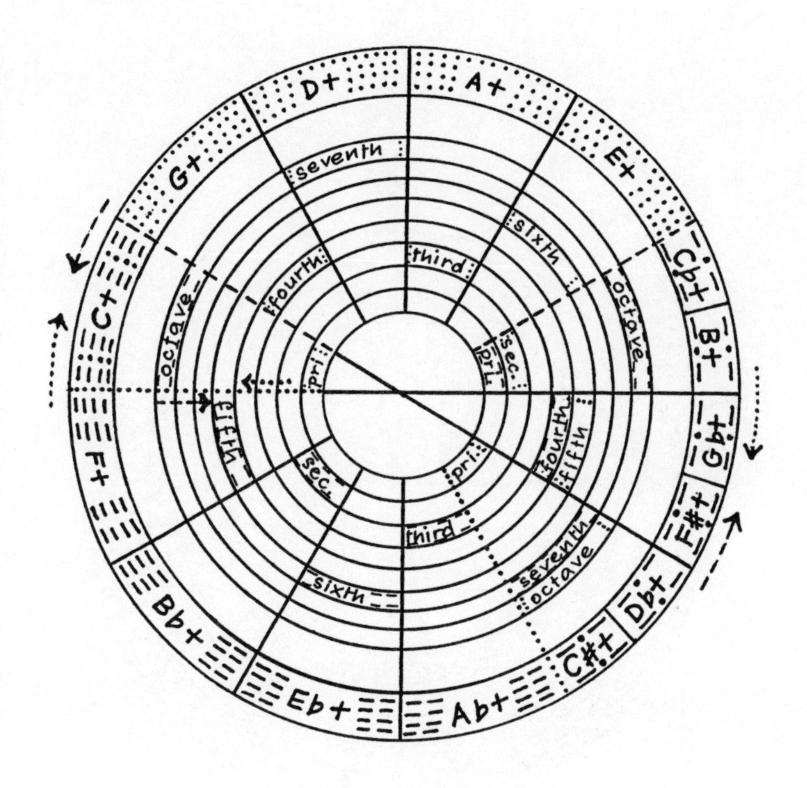

The Whole Circle of Keys

- interval and experience the same

b - interval and experience complementary

pri.=prime sec.=second

PLATE 4

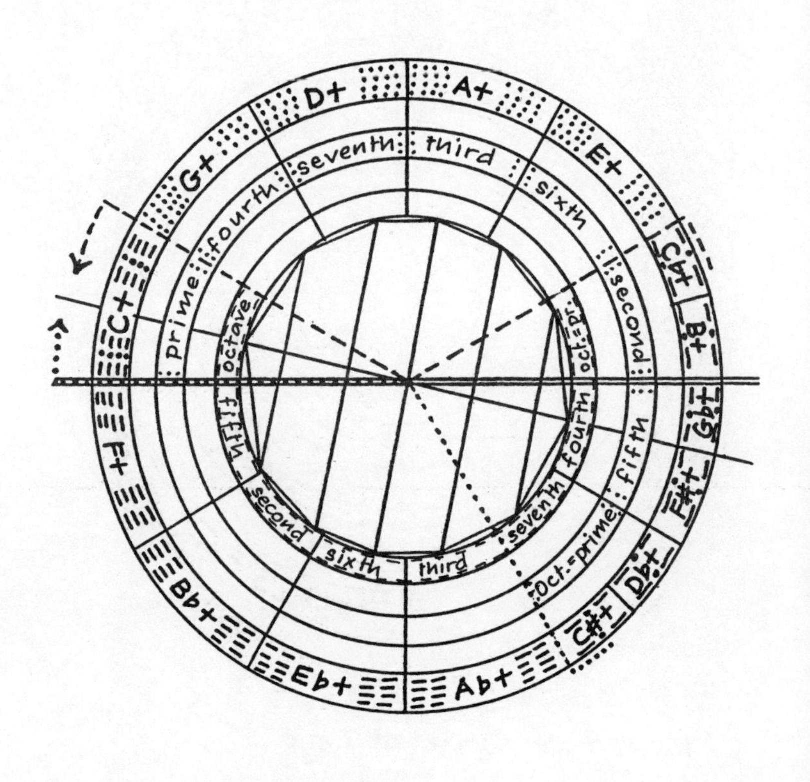

Complementary Relationships I

PLATE 5

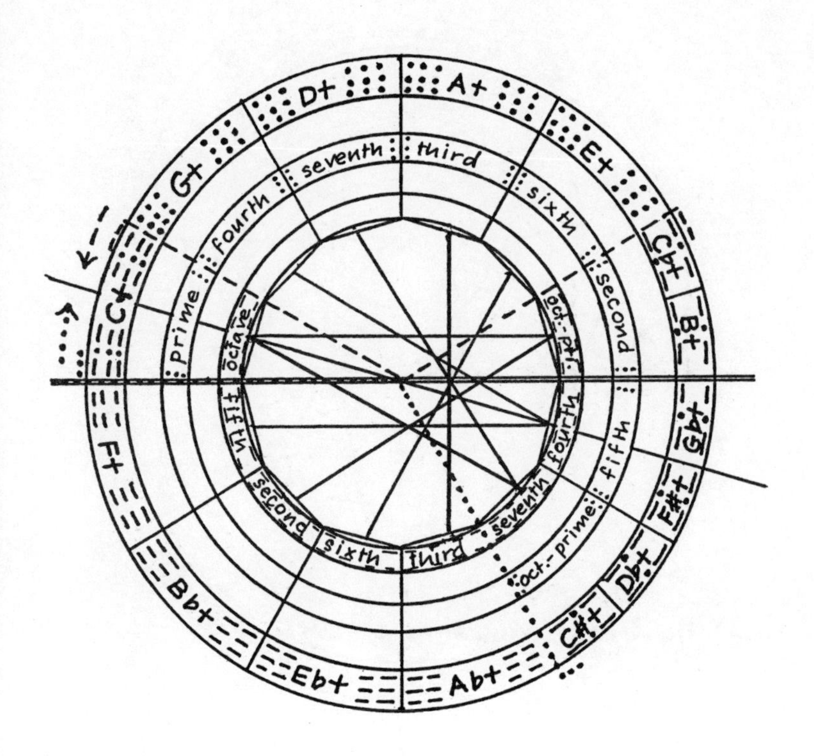

Complementary Relationships II

PLATE 6

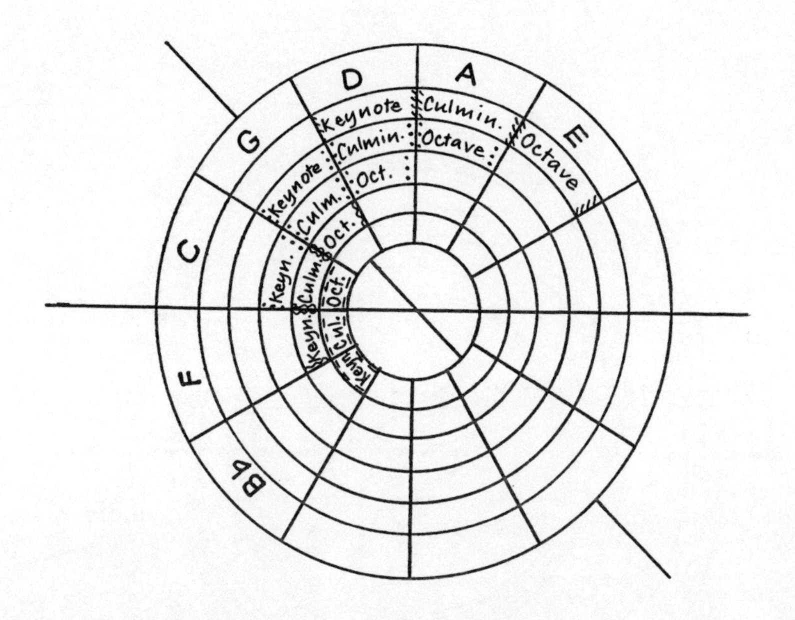

The Threefold Function of Each Note

PLATE 7

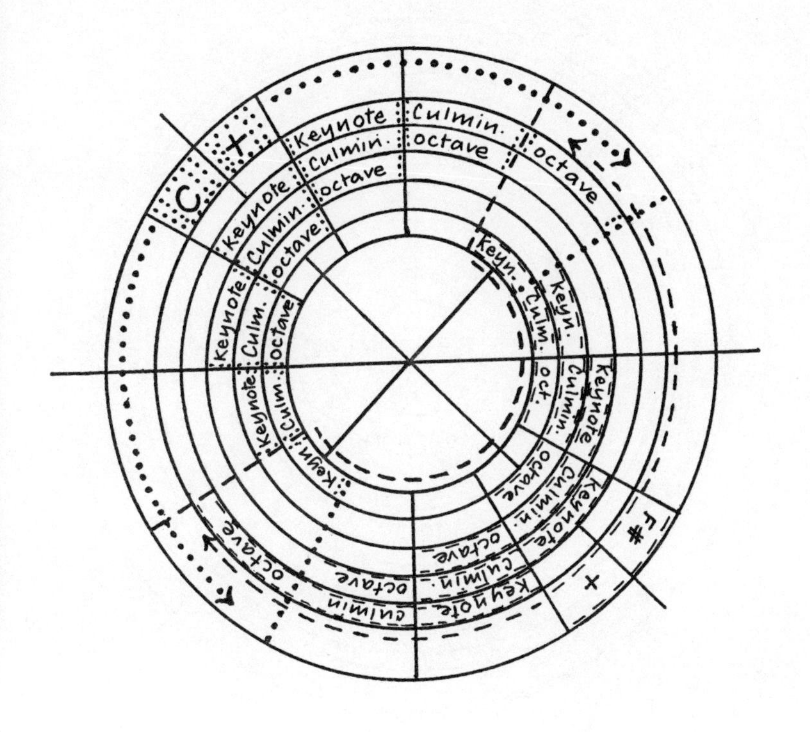

The Totality. C Major with Dominants and its Spiritual Counter-Region

PLATE 8

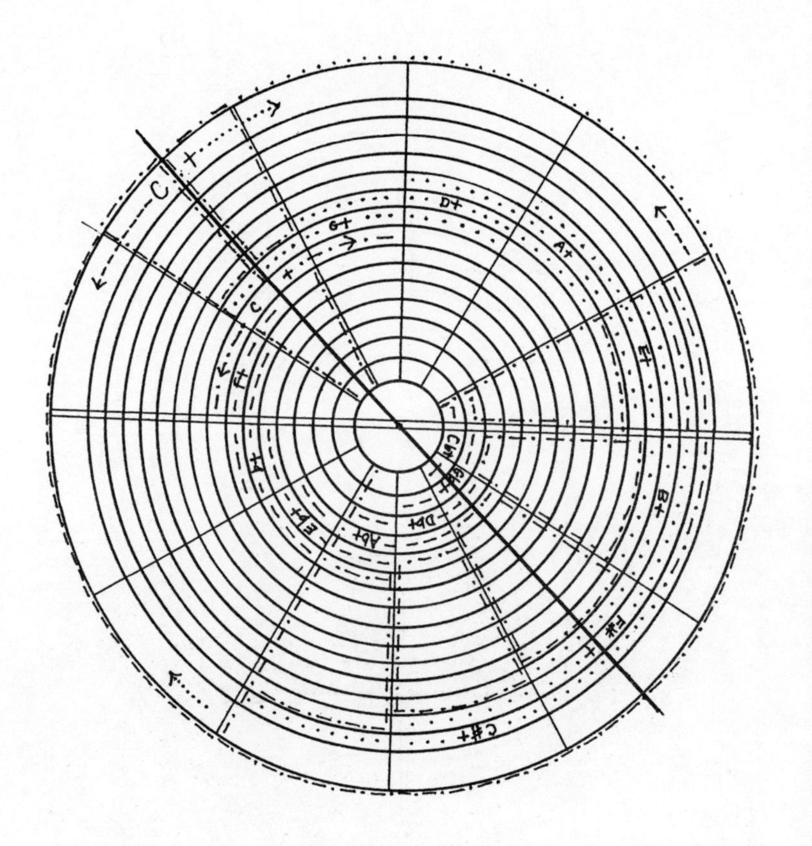

The Spiral of Keys

The areas enclosed thus [dashed trapezoid symbol] were coloured purple in the German edition

PLATE 9

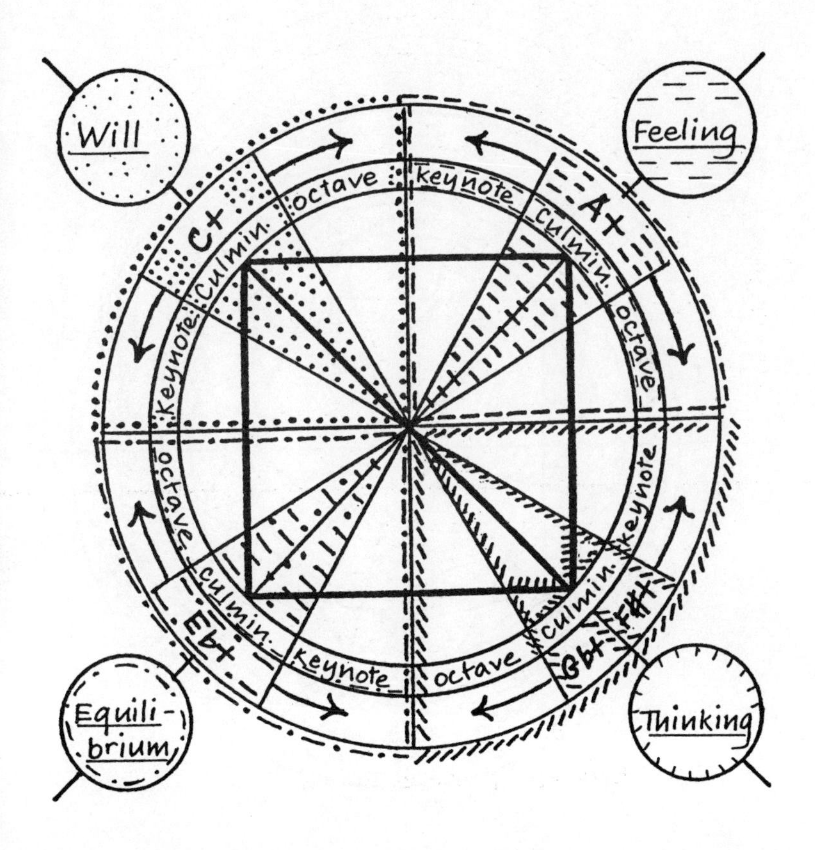

The Main keys (the soul-forces)

PLATE 10

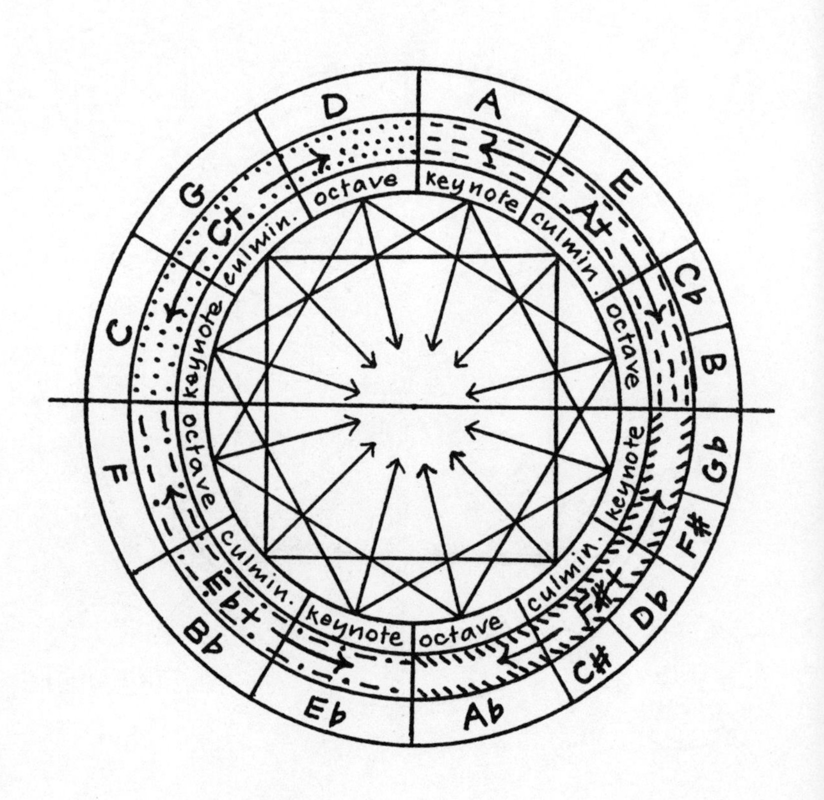

The Three Squares

PLATE II

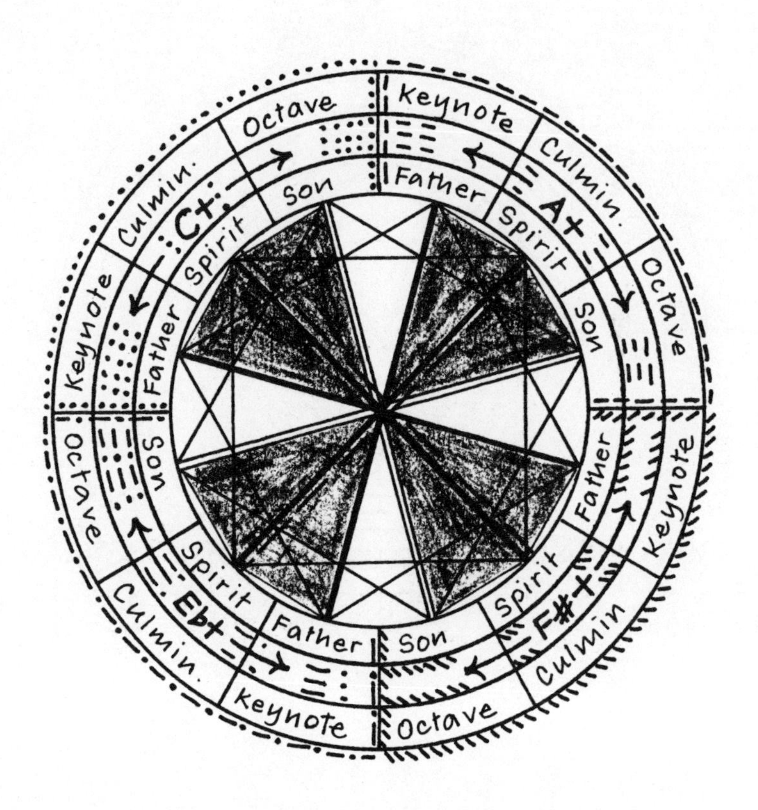

The Three Crosses

— Father = = Spirit ═ Son

PLATE 12

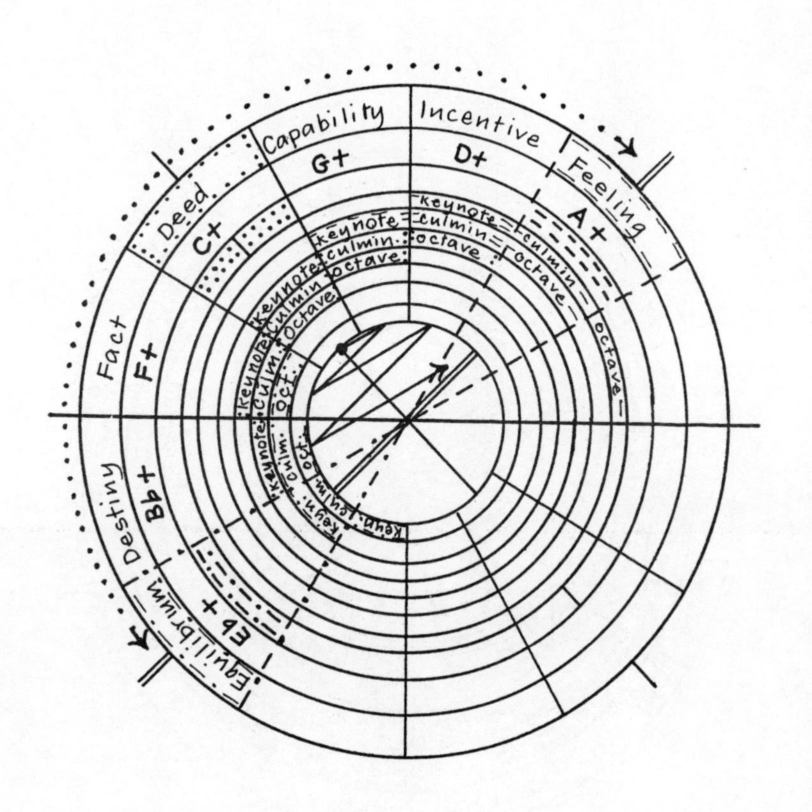

The Soul-Bearings (Part 1)

PLATE 13

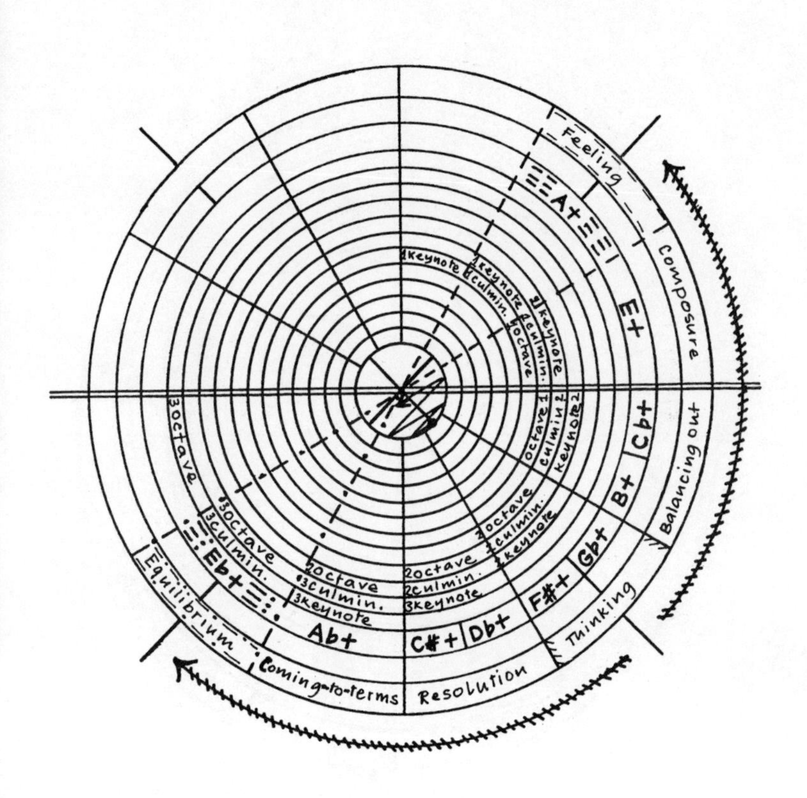

Soul-Bearings (Part 2)

Key to inner circles

1 = blue
2 = yellow
3 = purple

PLATE 14

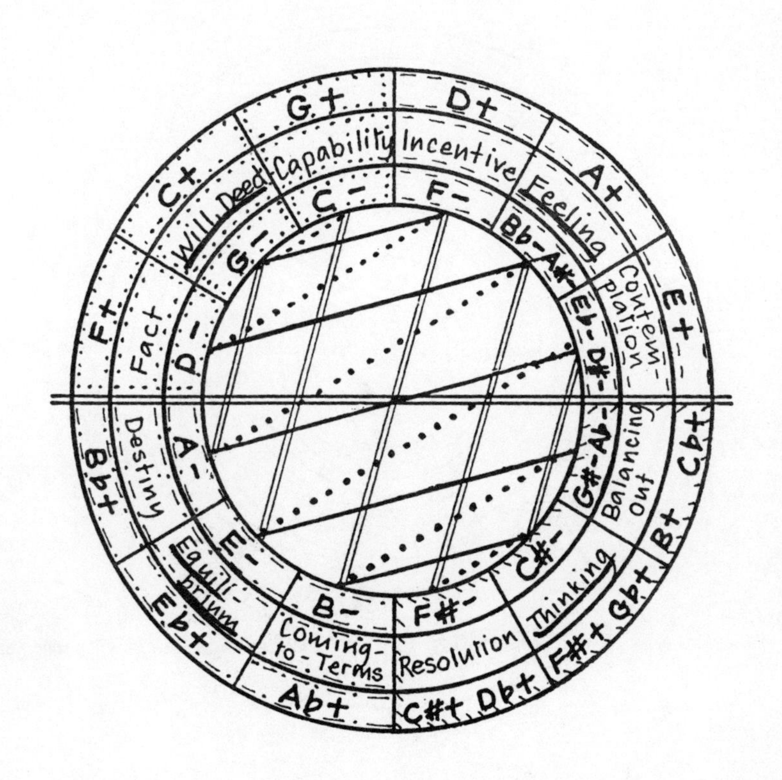

Corresponding and Related Keys

— Reflection

═ Key-signature

····· keynote

PLATE 15

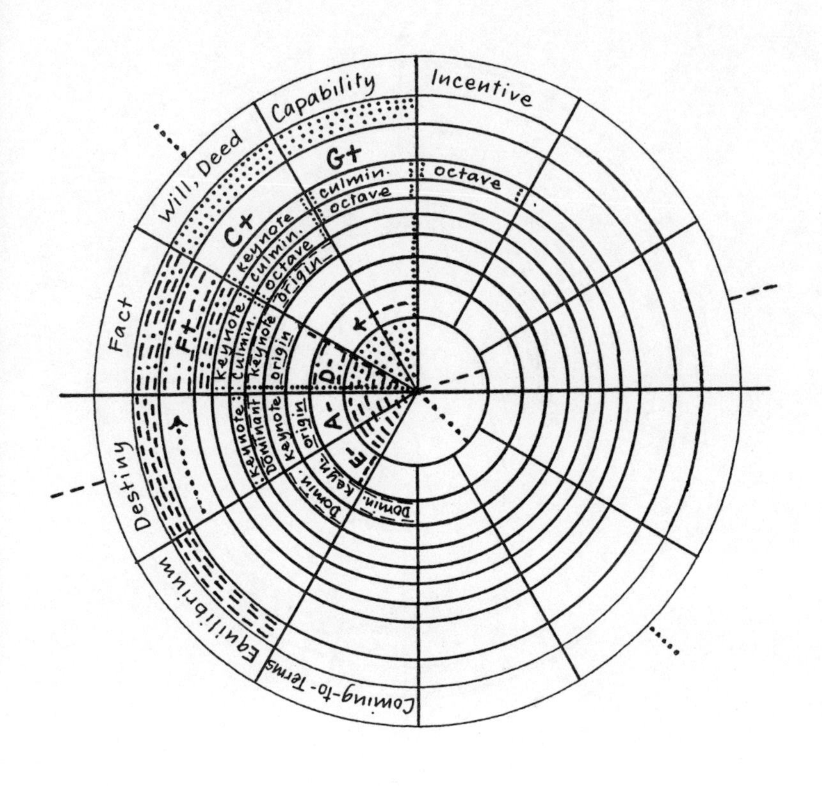

C Major – A Minor

(connected in F major and D minor)

PLATE 16

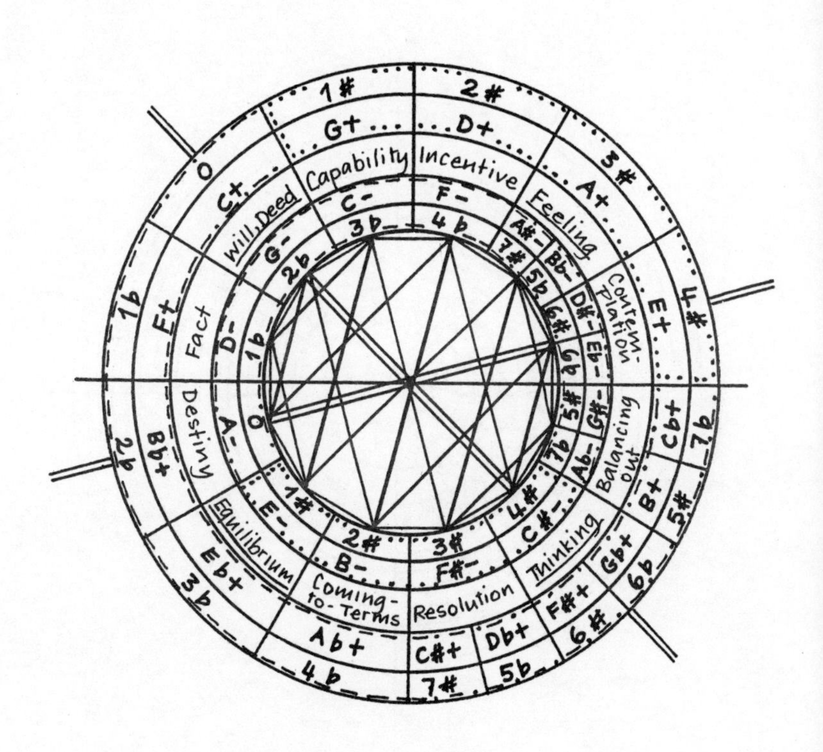

Complementary Sharps and Flats

..... #
--- b
-.-. C+, A- enharmonic

PLATE 17

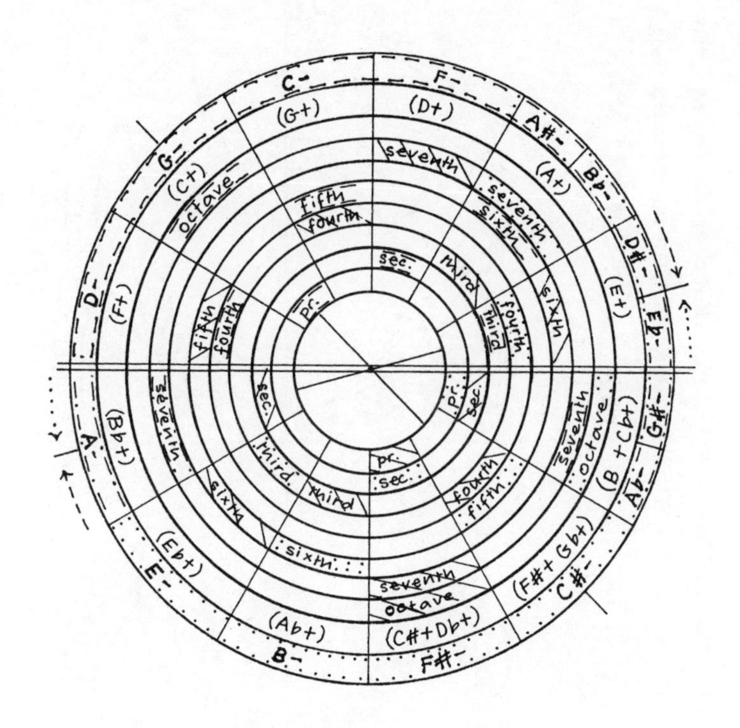

The Changing Function of Note D in Minor
Determining and Complementary Intervals

-·-A- Enharmonic ····# Determination upwards

\\\ Major Keys ---b Complementary downwards

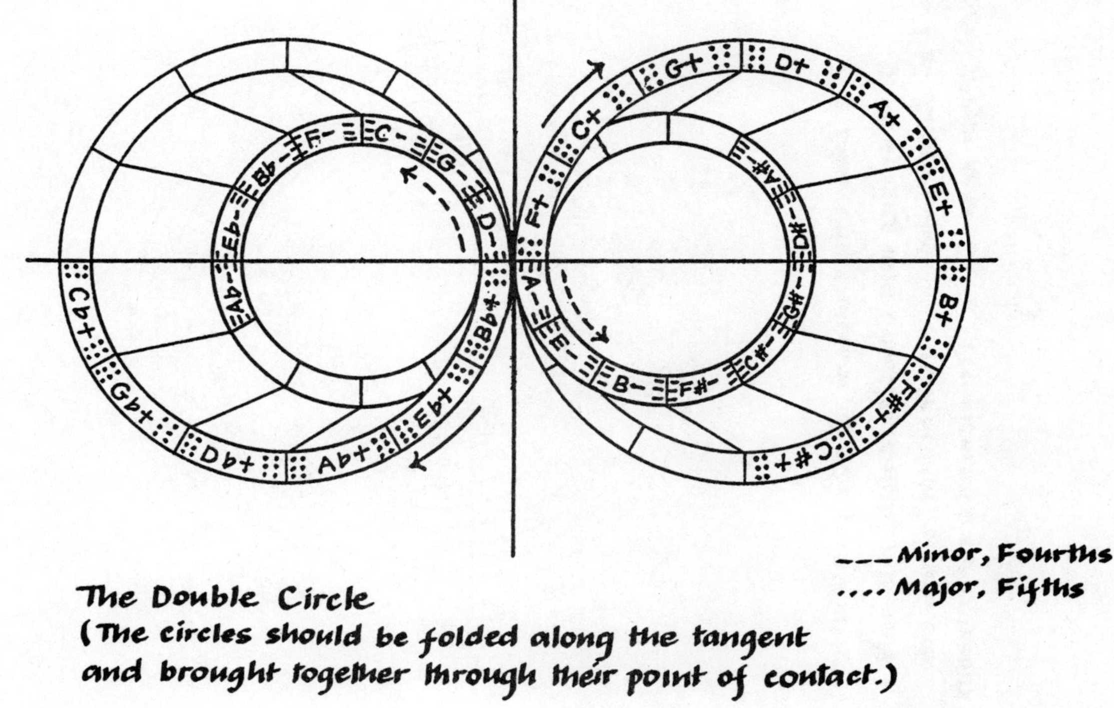

The Double Circle
(The circles should be folded along the tangent and brought together through their point of contact.)

PLATE 19

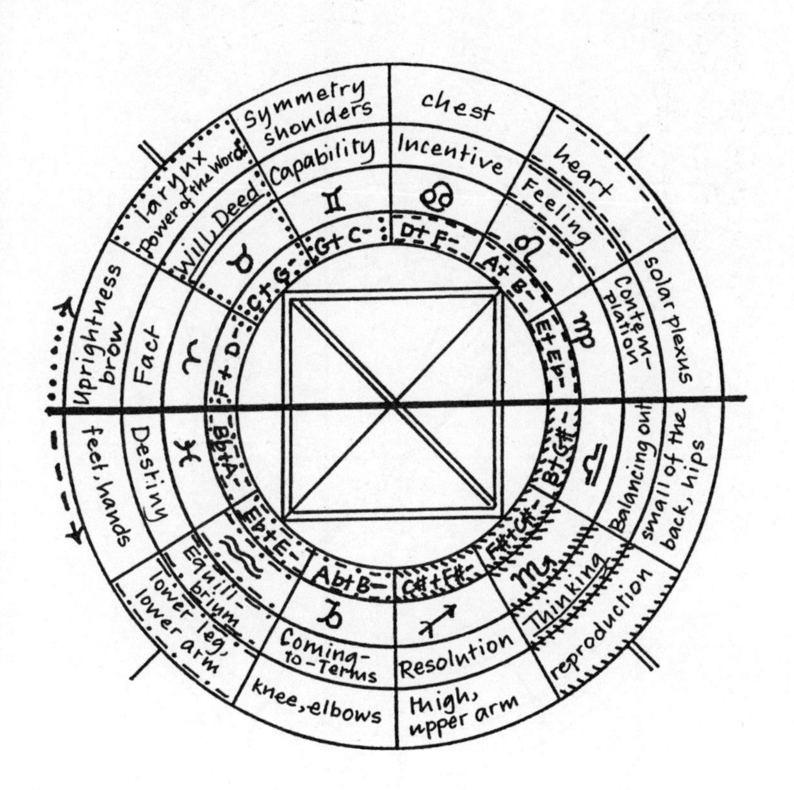

The Zodiac with its four cardinal points

♈	Ram	♌	Lion	♐	Archer
♉	Bull	♍	Virgin	♑	Goat
♊	Twins	♎	Scales	♒	Waterman
♋	Crab	♏	Scorpion	♓	Fishes

PLATE 20

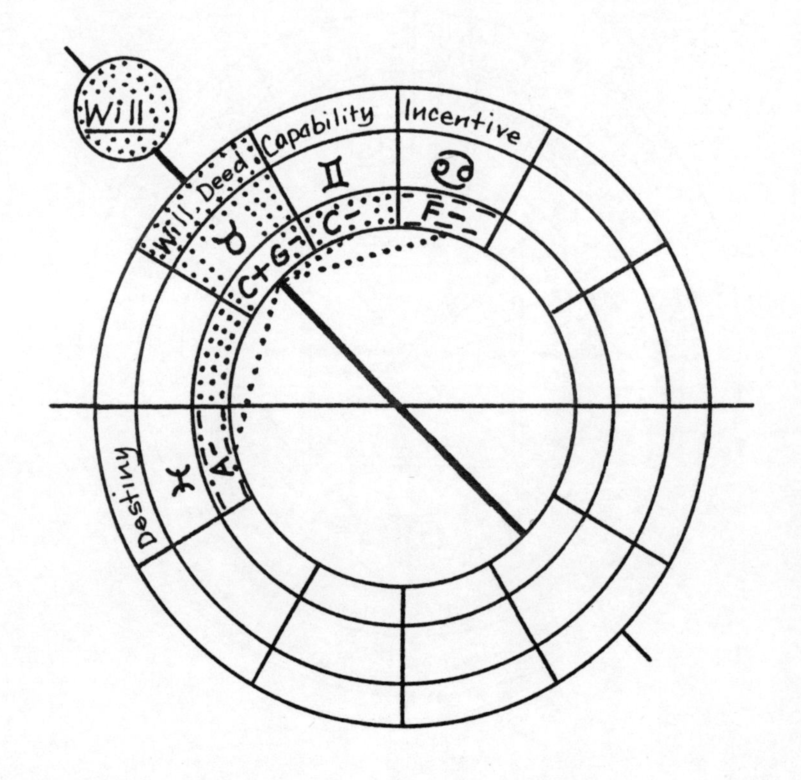

Constellation of C Major with its four related minors

PLATE 21

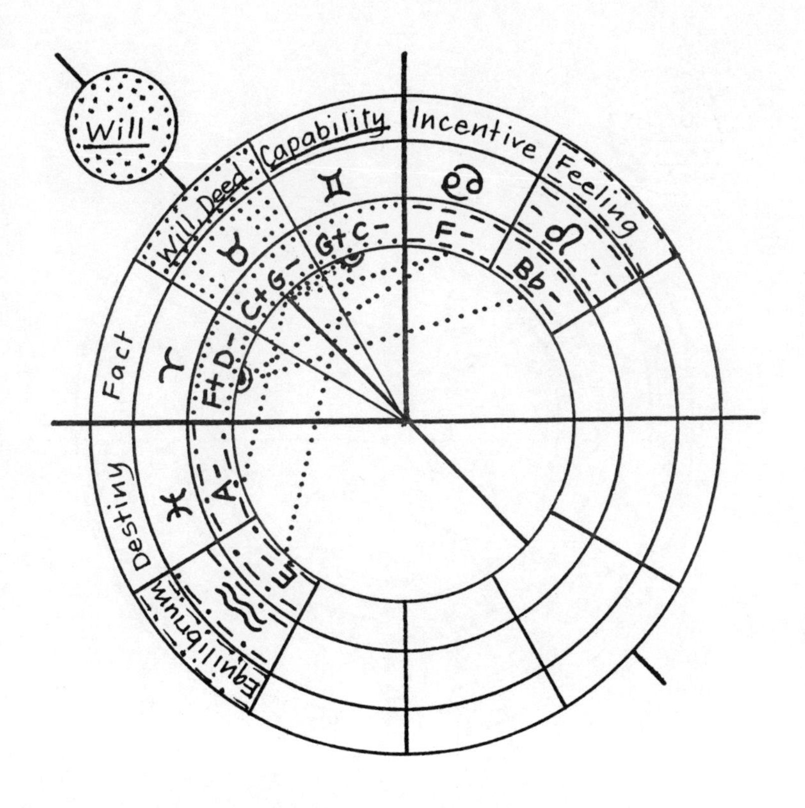

The Field of Will

(12 related minors)

PLATE 22

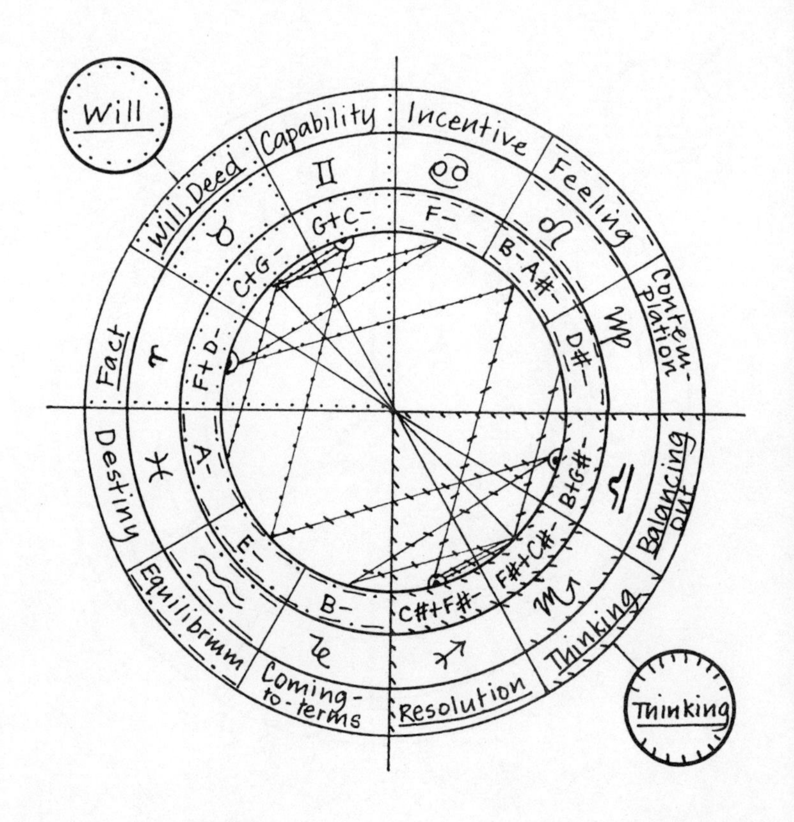

The Fields of Will and Thinking

24 related minors

PLATE 23

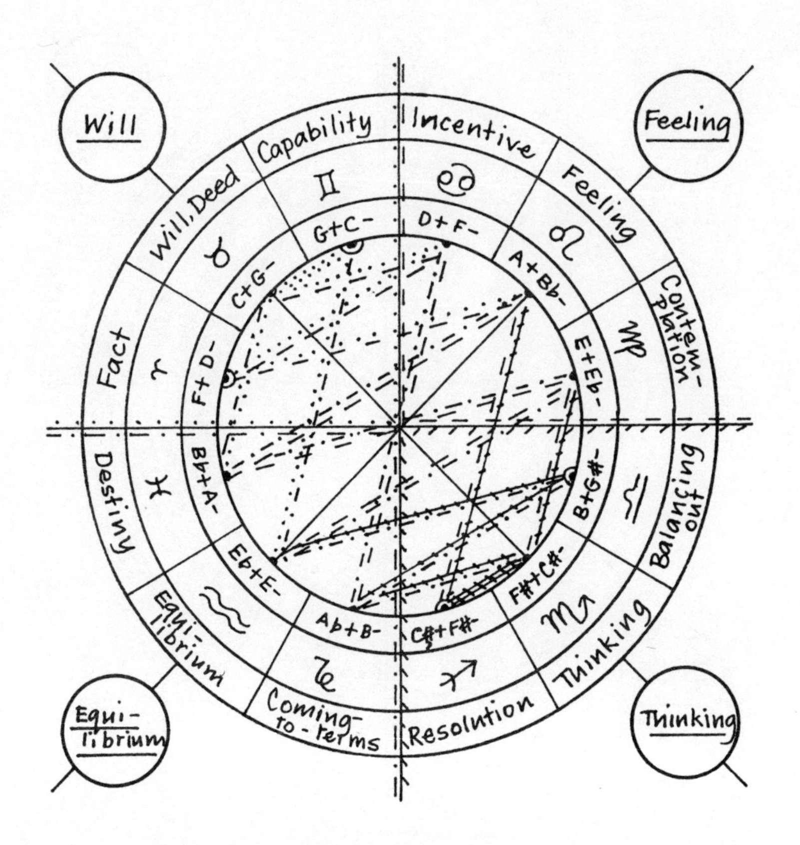

The Soul Picture

(48 related minors)

PLATE 24

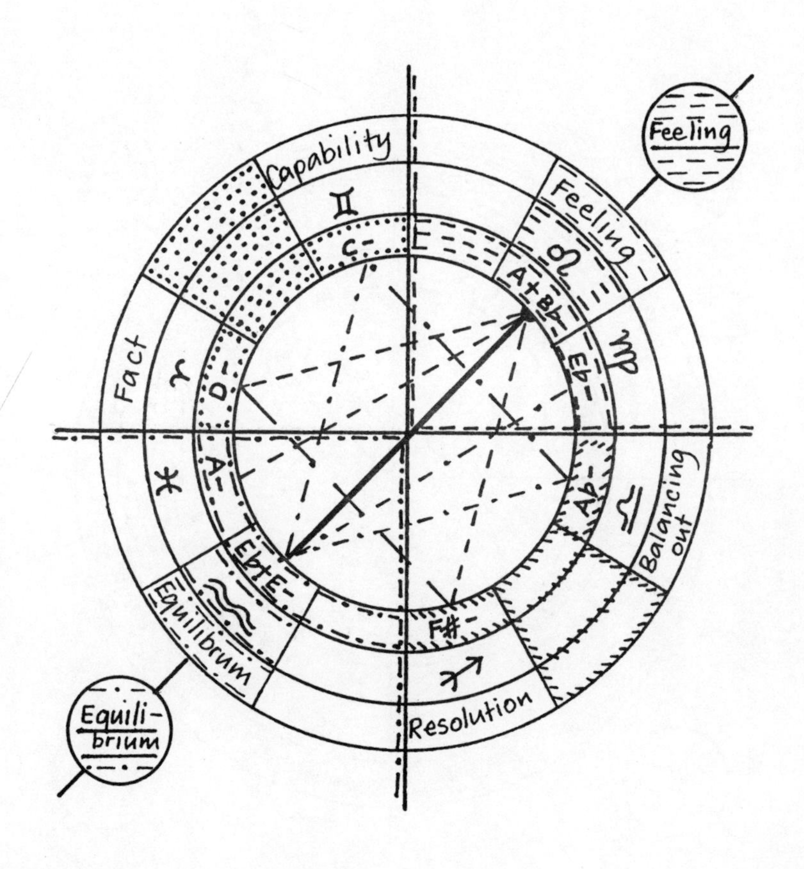

A Major and E flat Major
Feeling and Equilibrium

PLATE 25

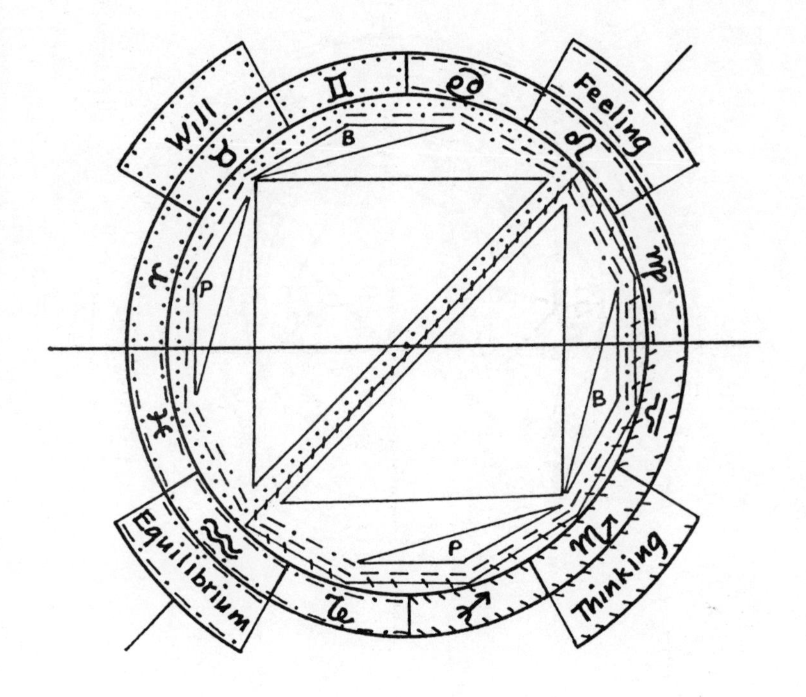

Related Keys

B=blue P=purple

PLATE 26

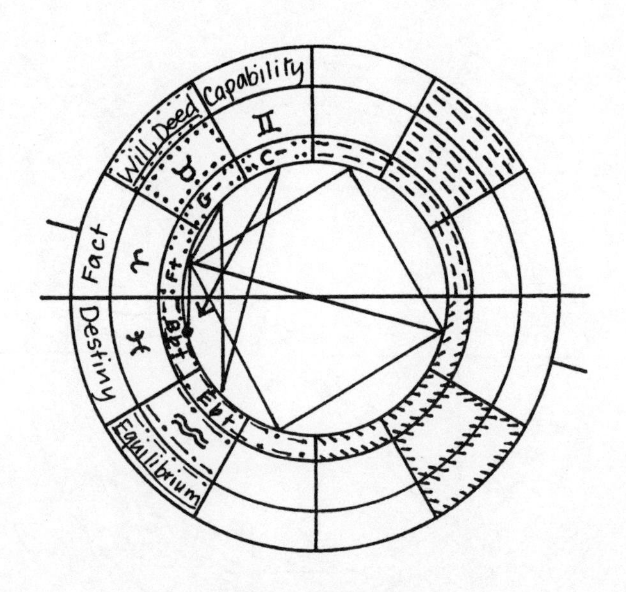

J. S. Bach. 2 part Invention in B flat major

PLATE 27

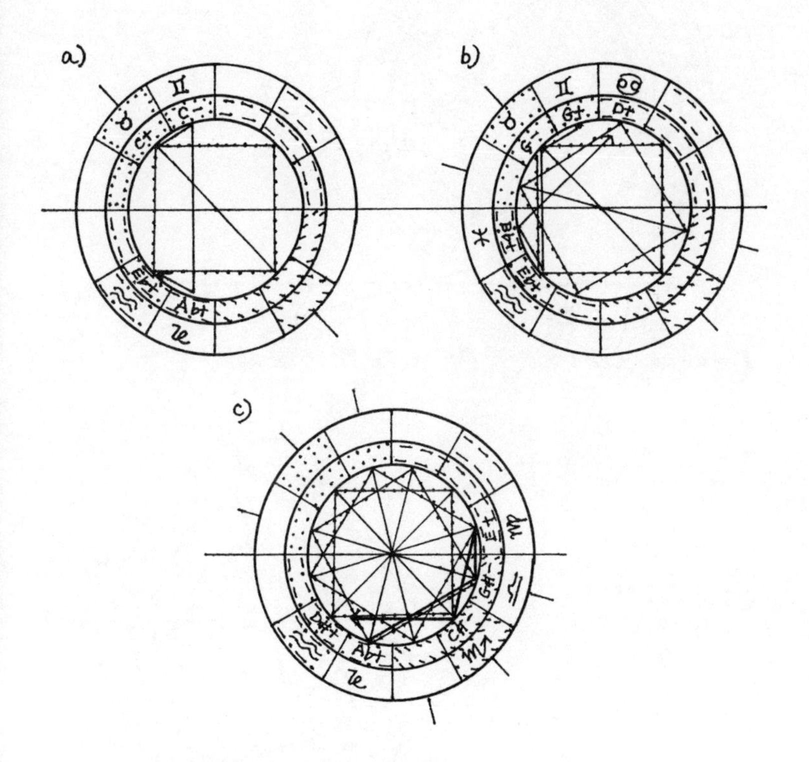

Richard Wagner: The Siegfried Motif

a) in Valkyrie b) in Siegfried c) in Twilight of the Gods

PLATE 28

Parsifal, Act 1: The Path to the Grail

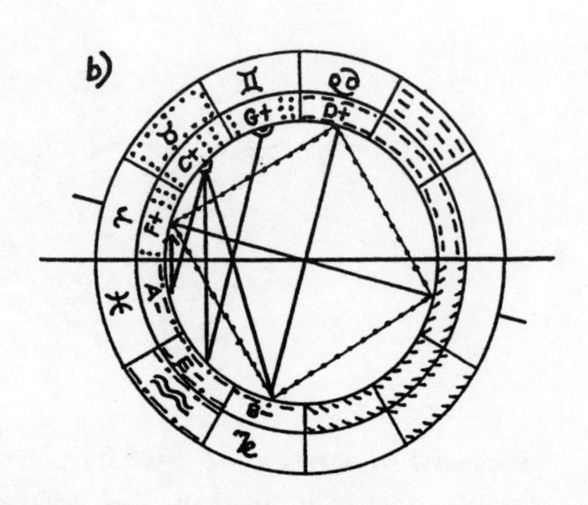

Parsifal, Act 2: Recovery of the Spear

PLATE 29

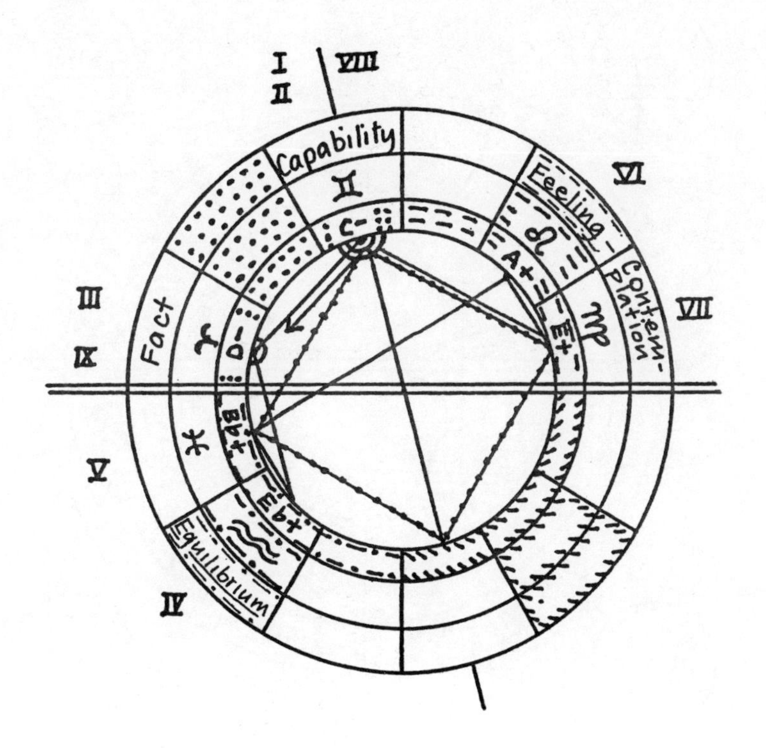

Anton Bruckner, Successive Symphonies

PLATE 30

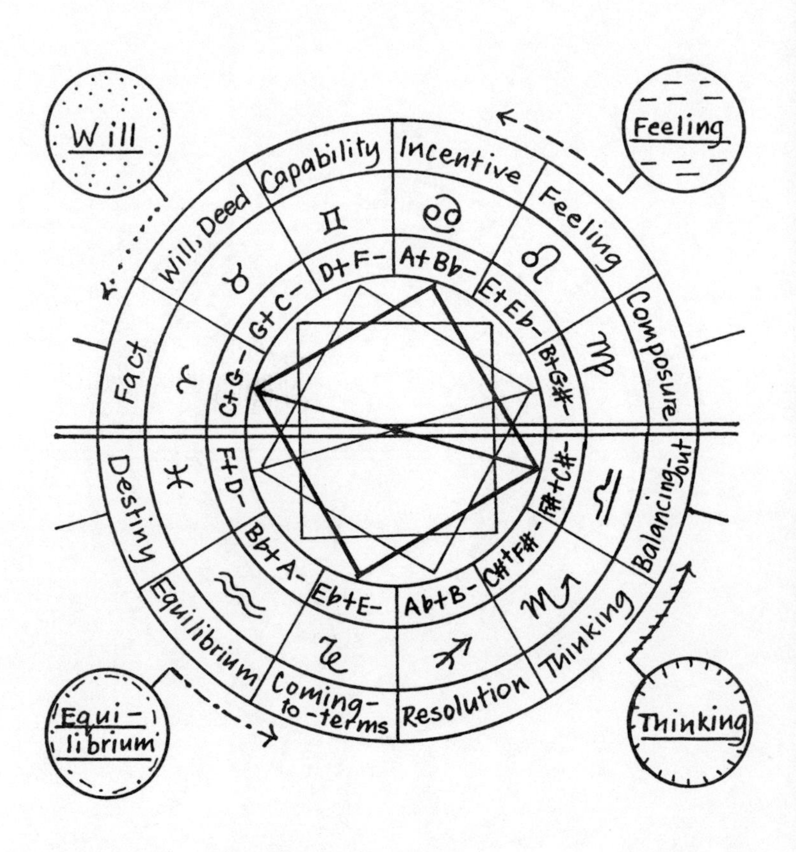

Keys in the Age of the Fishes